Stefan Zweig and World Literature

Studies in German Literature, Linguistics, and Culture

Stefan Zweig and World Literature

Twenty-First-Century Perspectives

Edited by
Birger Vanwesenbeeck
and Mark H. Gelber

CAMDEN HOUSE
Rochester, New York

Copyright © 2015 by the Editors and Contributors

All Rights Reserved. Except as permitted under current legislation, no part of this work may be photocopied, stored in a retrieval system, published, performed in public, adapted, broadcast, transmitted, recorded, or reproduced in any form or by any means, without the prior permission of the copyright owner.

First published 2015 by Camden House
Reprinted in paperback 2017

Camden House is an imprint of Boydell & Brewer Inc.
668 Mt. Hope Avenue, Rochester, NY 14620, USA
www.camden-house.com
and of Boydell & Brewer Limited
PO Box 9, Woodbridge, Suffolk IP12 3DF, UK
www.boydellandbrewer.com

Paperback ISBN-13: 978-1-64014-007-3 | ISBN-10: 1-64014-007-7
Hardcover ISBN-13: 978-1-57113-924-5 | ISBN-10: 1-57113-924-9

Library of Congress Cataloging-in-Publication Data

Stefan Zweig and World Literature: Twenty-First-Century Perspectives / Edited by Birger Vanwesenbeeck and Mark H. Gelber.
   pages cm.—(Studies in German Literature, Linguistics, and Culture)
Summary: The twenty-first century has seen a renewed surge of cultural and critical interest in the works of the Austrian-Jewish author Stefan Zweig (1881–1942), who was among the most-read and -acclaimed authors worldwide in the 1920s and 1930s but after 1945 fell into critical disfavor and relative obscurity. The resurgence in interest in Zweig and his works is attested to by, among other things, new English translations and editions of his works; a Brazilian motion picture and a best-selling French novel about his final days; and a renewed debate surrounding the literary quality of his work in the London Review of Books. This global return to Zweig calls for a critical reassessment of his legacy and works, which the current collection of essays provides by approaching them from a global perspective as opposed to the narrow European focus through which they have been traditionally approached. Together, the introduction and twelve essays engage the totality of Zweig's published and unpublished works from his drama and his fiction to his letters and his biographies, and from his literary and art criticism to his autobiography.
   Includes bibliographical references and index.
   ISBN 978-1-57113-924-5 (hardcover : alk. paper)—
   ISBN 1-57113-924-9 (hardcover : alk. paper)
   1. Zweig, Stefan, 1881–1942—Criticism and interpretation.
   I. Vanwesenbeeck, Birger, editor. II. Gelber, Mark H., 1951– editor.

PT2653.W42Z81734 2015
838'.91209—dc23   2014045889

This publication is printed on acid-free paper.
Printed in the United States of America.

Harry Zohn (1923–2001)

in memoriam

Contents

List of Illustrations ix

Acknowledgments xi

Introduction 1
Birger Vanwesenbeeck and Mark H. Gelber

Part I. Reception

1: A Stefan Zweig Revival? 15
Birger Vanwesenbeeck

Part II. Drama and Fiction

2: Stefan Zweig's Drama *Jeremias* in Context 35
John Warren

3: "That Voice in the Darkness!": Technologies of the Tropical Talking Cure in Stefan Zweig's *Der Amokläufer* and *Verwirrung der Gefühle* 56
Geoffrey Winthrop-Young

4: Narrating Alterity: Stefan Zweig, Emmanuel Levinas, and the Trauma of Redemption 74
Robert Weldon Whalen

Part III. Criticism and Essays

5: Stefan Zweig and the Concept of World Literature 93
Mark H. Gelber

6: Landscape, "Heimat," and Artistic Production: Stefan Zweig's Introduction to *E. M. Lilien: Sein Werk* 108
Richard V. Benson

7: Stefan Zweig's Non-fictional Prose in Exile: Mastery of the
European Genre of "Kunstprosa" 122
Klaus Weissenberger

Part IV. Politics and Exile

8: True to Himself: Stefan Zweig's Visit to Argentina in
September 1936 155
Robert Kelz

9: Exile and Liminality in "A Land of the Future": Charlotte
and Stefan Zweig in Brazil, August 1941–March 1942 173
Darién J. Davis

10: Stefan Zweig's Concept of Brazil in the Context of
German-Jewish Emigration 191
Marlen Eckl

11: Stefan Zweig: Life in Cities of Exile 213
Klemens Renoldner

12: The Writer's Political Obligations in Exile:
The Case of Stefan Zweig 224
Jeffrey B. Berlin

Notes on the Contributors 257

Index 259

Illustrations

I.1.	"Navigare necesse est"	xii
1.1.	Freud Eulogy	14
2.1.	Certificate of Identity	34
5.1.	Letter from James Joyce	92
8.1.	Title page of *Schachnovelle* typescript	154

Acknowledgments

THE EDITORS ARE GRATEFUL for the support of Virginia Horvath, president of the State University of New York at Fredonia; John Kijinski, dean of the College of Liberal Arts and Sciences at the State University of New York at Fredonia; and the English Department's Mary Louise White Fund. We also would like to thank the personnel of Reed Library, in particular Gerda Morrissey, curator of the Zweig Collection; Jeremy Linden, former head of Special Collections and co-chair of Fredonia's 2009 Zweig Symposium; and Randolph Gadikian, director of Reed Library. We would like to thank the Abrahams-Curiel Department of Foreign Literatures and Linguistics at Ben-Gurion University in Beer Sheva for financial support. Also, we are particularly grateful to Alana Sobelman of Ben Gurion University for technical editorial help in preparing this volume, and to Matthew Perloff for compiling the index. We would also like to thank Jim Walker, editorial director at Camden House, for his assistance in publishing the volume. Finally, Birger Vanwesenbeeck would like to thank Doğa Vanwesenbeeck, who, with never wavering enthusiasm, assisted his father during numerous copying stints at the Fredonia Zweig Collection.

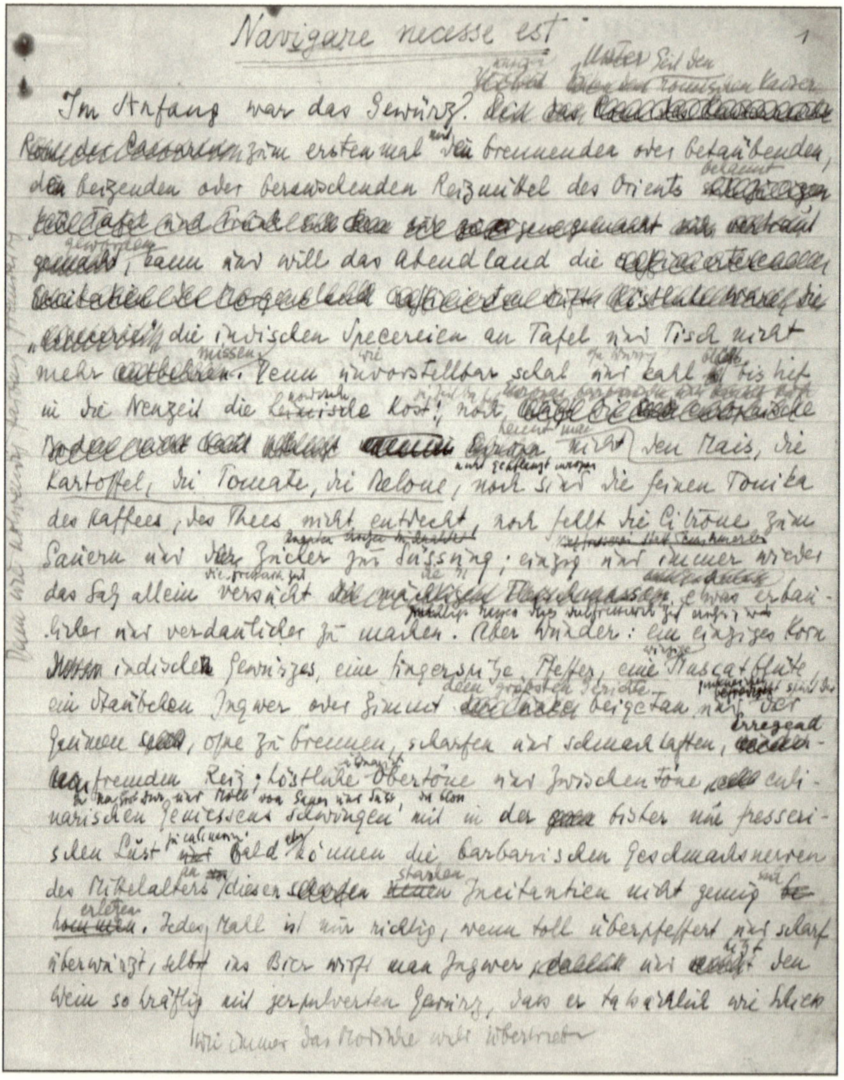

Navigare necesse est

Im Anfang war das Gewürz.

Fig. I.1. "Navigare necesse est" (It is necessary to take to the waters).
Courtesy of the Stefan Zweig Collection at Reed Library,
State University of New York at Fredonia.

Introduction

Birger Vanwesenbeeck and Mark H. Gelber

QUO USQUE TANDEM ABUTERE, *Stefan Zweig, patientia nostra*? How much longer, Stefan Zweig, will you be testing our patience? This well-known opening question from Cicero's *In Catilinam* orations (63 BCE), addressed not to Stefan Zweig, but to the Roman senator Catiline, may serve as a model for the exasperation and indignation that the name Stefan Zweig continues to inspire in certain literary and intellectual circles.[1] Mockingly referred to in his lifetime as "Erwerbszweig" (commercial branch) and famously attacked by Hannah Arendt for his apparent refusal to articulate political opinions in public,[2] Zweig has, perhaps more than any other modern writer, suffered from a steady barrage of attacks on his work and person, even as readers worldwide and in large numbers have continued to read his works. Time and again in such diatribes Zweig has been evoked as a kind of bad seed, as a literary populist whose "plotting," like the more malicious scheming of the Roman senator Catiline, makes his continued presence within the "Republic of Letters" intolerable to those "senators," that is, those critics committed to serious literary value.

Michael Hofmann's highly publicized attack on Zweig in the January 28, 2010, issue of the *London Review of Books* is perhaps the most prominent recent example of a literary polemic against him.[3] As does Cicero in his orations against Catiline, Hofmann accuses Zweig of mendacity and deception: "Stefan Zweig just tastes fake. He's the Pepsi of Austrian writing." Noting that there is something "'not quite right' about this popular-again popularizer," Hofmann launches into a series of ever-more specific, demonstratively determined epithets: "*this* un-Austrian Austrian and un-Jewish Jew"; "*this* cosmopolitan loner and blue-riband refugee."[4] Like the anaphoric structure of Cicero's opening questions, these formulations draw their rhetorical strength from a sudden shift in tone and form. In Cicero, this shift moves from the senatorial "we" that structures his rhetorical questions to the all-inclusive apostrophe of the age itself that immediately follows it: *O tempora, o mores* (O times, o traditions). If the continued presence of Catiline in the Senate is evoked by Cicero initially as damaging the credibility of Rome's republican institutions, by the end it appears to reflect badly on the age as a whole.

Hofmann follows a similar rhetorical trajectory in his essay, except that he reverses direction. Moving from the more general to the more specific, he opens with a catalogue of what *others* have remarked about Zweig. For example, he cites Romain Rolland's surprise at the thought of a writer who doesn't like cats, as well as the visceral, negative reactions to his work in "catty Vienna." In closing, Hofmann comes to the "revelation" that things are, after all, personal. Zweig, so runs Hofmann's concluding epithet, is "this person whose books I briefly thought I wouldn't mind reading, before, while setting down the umpteenth of them amid groans (it was the novella *Confusion*), adding the stipulation to myself: yes, but only if they'd been written by someone else." After a lifetime spent trying to stop worrying and love the bombast of Zweig's prose, Hofmann declares that he cannot and will not do so any longer.

Notwithstanding its rhetorical prowess, Hofmann's essay cannot hide the fact that there is something formulaic and mechanical about his diatribe against Zweig. In fact, Hofmann sounds less like Cicero than that other great Roman orator, Cato the Elder who famously concluded every speech before the Roman Senate with the stock formula, "*Ceterum censeo Carthaginem delendam esse*" (And, by the way, I am convinced that Carthage should be destroyed.)[5] Meant to remind a younger generation that no contemporary political issue could ever be so pressing as to outweigh the ongoing geopolitical threat of Rome's arch-enemy across the Mediterranean, Cato's stock phrase presents itself as an aside ("*ceterum*") even as its strategic positioning at the end of a speech gives it certain rhetorical weight over the actual speech itself. Both in this willed deflation of the topic at hand and in the explicit reliance on his seniority, Cato serves as an obvious model for Hofmann's argumentation. By presenting an ad hominem attack on Zweig disguised as an objective book review of a new English translation of his popular late autobiography, *Die Welt von Gestern* (translated, as Hofmann notes, "by the excellent Anthea Bell"), Hofmann addresses readers from the vantage of an older authority who faults a younger generation of readers for "plotting" a "Zweig revival." "Older" here means old-world, continental European, for, according to Hofmann, it is the relative absence of comparable intellectual traditions across the seas that accounts for the misconception that Zweig's works have literary value. In Hofmann's words:

> Stefan Zweig was a purveyor of *Trivialliteratur* and, save in commercial terms, an utterly negligible figure. From the distance of Britain or America now one erroneously supposes something more like the opposite to be the case: that here is someone who is among the best his country and language and period have to offer, and who comes with the good opinion and endorsement of his peers. Partly it's the distinction—far more rigidly observed in Germany than in

the English-speaking world—between serious and popular (*e* and *u* in German parlance, *Ernst* and *Unterhaltung*) but there is more to it than that.

The question of Zweig's continuing popularity is here reduced, rather unconvincingly, to the Anglophone reader's supposed inability to distinguish between high (serious) and low (trivial) literature, as well as to the "nice paper and pretty formats" in which Zweig's works have recently been reissued in English translation by the London-based Pushkin Press.[6] Indeed, this characterization is particularly unpersuasive when major international filmmakers from Wes Andersen to Xu Jinglei,[7] and established essayists like George Prochnik and Will Stone rank among those who have recently turned to Zweig.[8]

World Literature

In calling for the need to consider Zweig within a narrow European context, Hofmann follows a strategy that has long been characteristic of both Zweig enthusiasts and opponents alike. For the former group, Zweig is usually viewed as "der grosse Europäer,"[9] who advocated for solidarity and peace among European nations; he is the cultural mediator whose "Villa Europa" on the Kapuzinerberg overlooking Salzburg served as a preferred meeting place for continental writers and artists during the 1920s; he is the "remembering European" (as he fashioned himself in the subtitle of *Die Welt von Gestern*) who desperately sought to preserve the cultural memory of a continent torn to pieces by two world wars. For the latter group, by contrast, Zweig is a writer of popular stories who lacked the artistic edge of his European contemporaries (Hofmann cites Joseph Roth as a counterexample). He had an overly simplified understanding of European Jewry. He overstated the Italian ancestry of his mother's family in order to present himself as the genealogical product of North and South.[10]

Although no one can doubt the level of Zweig's identification with Europe, with its languages and its mores, both his life trajectory and his literary interests give evidence of a scope that extends well beyond Europe. His fictions include stories set in Vienna and Geneva as well as in Dutch-controlled Indonesia and aboard an Argentina-bound steamer; his literary-biographical interests extend from Balzac and Verhaeren to Walt Whitman and Mary Baker Eddy; his travel writings focus on Belgium as well as Brazil. The Latin title of the opening chapter of Zweig's biography of the world explorer Magellan, "*Navigare necesse est*" (it is necessary to sail),[11] could furthermore be read in this regard as an artistic prerogative on the part of the author. One must take to the waters—that is, venture outside of Europe—in order to write. This is also the underlying credo grouping together the twelve essays in this volume. The first book-length scholarly work on Zweig to appear in the United States in over a quarter-century, *Stefan Zweig and World Literature* aims to offer a global perspective on his career and writings. Recognizing the need for a global framework within which to consider the Austrian-Jewish author, the essays collected here—some of which are revised and expanded versions of papers first read at the international conference "Stefan Zweig's Transatlantic Connections," held at the State University of New York at Fredonia in 2009—approach his works through the lens of world literature. This term, one that Zweig held dear, has recently advanced to the forefront of contemporary literary criticism. Focusing on the totality of Zweig's literary output, including his fiction and letters along with his essays, dramas, literary criticism, biographies, translations, and memoir, *Stefan Zweig and World Literature* explores the author's relevance and significance at the beginning of the twenty-first century.

"Weltliteratur, wie Goethe sie vorausnahm, schwebte [Zweig] als höchster Besitz vor" ("world literature," in Goethe's sense of the term, meant everything to Zweig), wrote the Austrian author Felix Braun, a longtime acquaintance and contemporary of Stefan Zweig, in his 1949 autobiography.[12] As a translator of Romain Rolland and Émile Verhaeren, Zweig contributed significantly to the circulation of these francophone authors' works in Germany and Austria. As initiator and editor of Insel Verlag's "Bibliotheca Mundi" series—which produced handsome editions of world masterpieces in their original languages, including French, English, Hungarian, and Hebrew—he also actively contributed to the spread and distribution of world literature within Europe. Zweig wrote introductions for numerous editions of authors whose works were translated into German or into French. In addition, he regularly spoke at PEN conventions worldwide—from New York City to Buenos Aires—and expressed his satisfaction with the reception of his books beyond his native Austria and the boundaries of the European continent.

Although Zweig's interest and place in world literature have never been a secret, it is only recently, with a new wave of global adaptations of his works and a renewed influx of theoretical analyses of the concept of world literature, that the relevance of this concept for Zweig's writings has become at once obvious and acute.[13] In light of the technological advances fueling the processes of globalization, world literature has increasingly come to be viewed within a global framework.

Thus, aesthetic and political values which may have been generated in specific languages and cultures are now being tested in vastly different cultural settings from their original contexts as texts circulate and are received throughout the world. There has been a distinct tendency to contextualize debates about the limitations of globalization and the tenacity of national traditions outside of the European cultural sphere. Already during his lifetime, Stefan Zweig was recognized as an excellent example of a writer whose works were eminently transportable, capable of appealing and gaining in valence as they crossed national borders in translation far from the European continent. Furthermore, many of Zweig's writings have retained their worldwide appeal, especially in Brazil, Argentina, China, the Far East, and elsewhere, just as new interest in his works has been registered in Central European and in Anglo-American cultures. The concept of world literature that is emerging in the early twenty-first century may prove capable of reformulating the criteria for determining literary value, while attributing primacy to writers like Zweig, whose global reach and importance are being augmented by contemporary digital and film culture. Zweig scholarship will no doubt be challenged to explain and analyze this new phenomenon.

The Essays

In the opening paragraph of *Mute Poetry, Speaking Pictures*, Renaissance scholar Leonard Barkan reminisces about a high school assignment that would turn out to be significant for his later academic interests in the relationship between art and literature:

> Shortly before I turned sixteen, I took part in a high school film project. Each member of the group was required to write and direct a movie in the course of the summer, and we all served as each others' crew. My fellow-cineastes devoted laborious thought to the choice of a subject, only to end up with the sorts of themes—rock-and-roll, science fiction, the pangs of young love—that doubtless could have provided rather predictable maps of our various adolescent preoccupations. I, however, seized on some rather arcane material, and without a moment's hesitation. In German class, I had just been assigned a Stefan Zweig story called "Die unsichtbare Sammlung," and I decided it was perfect for a movie.[14]

The seemingly incongruous inclusion of Zweig's name at the beginning of a Renaissance scholar's inquiry into the relationship between word and image is of interest for two reasons. First, it provides further evidence of the now ubiquitous ways in which Zweig's works have become central to some of the leading areas of inquiry of contemporary literary criticism, including world literature, exile studies, trauma,[15] and—in Barkan's case—the long-standing question of *ekphrasis*, or how to paint with words. Set during the economic depression of the Weimar Republic, "Die unsichtbare Sammlung" ("The Invisible Collection," 1925) tells the story of a family forced to sell off their father's prized artworks to make ends meet. The father, now blind, does not know that the lithographs he still lovingly takes from their portfolios have since been replaced by blank sheets of paper. Presented in this fashion, the text poses the question of *ekphrasis* on two levels: in being asked by family members to play along, the story's nested narrator finds himself faced with the same task as the painter-poet trying to recreate a visually absent artwork in words. Yet the integration of word and image on which the trope of *ekphrasis* hinges also begets highly specific historical significance within Zweig's story, for it is in enumerating and extolling the haunting qualities of the blank canvas that "Die unsichtbare Sammlung" establishes its affinity with the art and literature of modernism:

> Mir lief es kalt über den Rücken, als der Ahnungslose ein vollkommen leeres Blatt so begeistert rühmte, und es war gespenstisch mitanzusehen, wie er mit dem Fingernagel bis zum Millimeter genau auf alle die nur in seiner Phantasie noch vorhandenen unsichtbare Sammlerzeichnen hindeutete.[16]
>
> [I shuddered as the unsuspecting enthusiast extolled the blank sheet of paper; my flesh crept when he placed a fingernail on the exact spot where the alleged imprints had been made by long-dead collectors.][17]

Like the black and white squares of Kazimir Malevich's art; like the staged nothingness of Ionesco's and Beckett's dramas; or—like their musical equivalent—John Cage's composition "*4'33*," Zweig's story elevates emptiness to the level of an aesthetic category in an attempt to safeguard the work of art from an ever more encroaching commercial culture. Tellingly, "Die unsichtbare Sammlung" opens with a Berlin art dealer's exasperation over the new class of "neuen reichen" (*M* 408; nouveaux-riches) who are buying up artworks as if they were "Ware" (*M* 408; wares); its closing sentence, obviously meant as a commentary on the blind collector and (apocryphally) attributed to Goethe, is that "Sammler sind glückliche Menschen" (*M* 425; collectors are happy people).

This modernist paradox is partly what drove the young Barkan to "Die unsichtbare Sammlung." As he explains, "I got hooked on 'The Invisible Collection' because I believed that the most cinematic thing of all (which is usually taken to mean the most *visual* thing of all) would be the recurring shot of an empty page."[18] If *ekphrasis* challenges the verbal imagination by trying to make words into something they are not—visual objects—then the lyrical evocation of the absent visual work of art transfers that artistic challenge onto the cinematographer's craft, as Barkan so astutely diagnoses. Such, we might say, is also the cinematic appeal of a novella like *Brief einer Unbekannten* ("Letter from an Unknown Woman," 1922), which was adapted for the screen twice. It confronts any film director with the task of how to depict a protagonist who, in Zweig's story, only exists through writing—that is, as absence. Part of Zweig's continued appeal for filmmakers—from the young amateur Barkan to Max Ophüls and, more recently, to Wes Andersen—thus lies in the cinematic challenge posed by his stories' evocation of visual absence.

But there is more to Barkan's seemingly incongruous reference to Zweig than this. His anecdote also indicates that, contrary to a persisting myth, Zweig's works sustained a substantial reading audience throughout the second half of the twentieth century. Can one really speak then—as does Hofmann—of a "Zweig revival" when his works remained a permanent presence in high school curricula, both within Europe and across the Atlantic? How does the recent surge of scholarly engagement with Zweig alter the postwar legacy of his works? These questions are at the heart of the "Reception" section that opens this volume. Birger Vanwesenbeeck's essay questions whether it is appropriate to speak of a Zweig "revival," while at the same time he explores the reasons behind this renewed scholarly and artistic interest in Zweig (and the persistent need felt by some scholars to disavow his literary value). As Vanwesenbeeck makes clear, answering these questions requires a reconsideration of Zweig's complicated and strained relationship to modernism.

The second section of the volume, "Drama and Fiction," groups together three essays that analyze the two genres for which Zweig was perhaps most well known during his lifetime. John Warren's contribution takes a fresh look at Zweig's Biblical play *Jeremias* (*Jeremiah*, 1917) by placing it within the larger context of expressionist anti-war drama. His essay suggests that the fate of the Jews in this play is to be understood as an allegory for Zweig's war-besieged European contemporaries. Arguing against critics who have long dismissed the play as pacifist and as bearing no references to the First World War, Warren shows how much this play owes to the particular Austrian experience of that war. Geoffrey Winthrop-Young's analysis of Zweig's complicated relationship to literary modernism draws parallels between the evocation of state-of-the-art technology in a colonial context in Zweig's novella *Der Amokläufer* ("Amok," 1922) and in other modernist works such as Joseph Conrad's *Heart of Darkness* and Franz Kafka's "In der Strafkolonie" ("In the Penal Colony," 1919). Like these texts, Zweig's novella registers an awareness of the impact of technology and new media on human consciousness.

Robert Weldon Whalen similarly explores the ethical-political thrust of Zweig's stories—a decidedly neglected area in Zweig scholarship. His essay draws parallels between the representation of the Other in such novellas as *Geschichte eines Untergangs* ("Twilight," 1910) and *Die Mondscheingasse* ("Moonbeam Alley," 1914), and in the philosophical writings of Emmanuel Levinas.

The third section of the volume groups together three essays, each of which analyzes parts of the considerable body of work that Zweig left behind as a translator, biographer, and literary critic. According to Mark H. Gelber, it is in his role as "cultural mediator" that we must relocate Zweig's main contribution to world literature. Drawing on the works of David Damrosch, and focusing on Zweig's relatively little-discussed criticism of two towering figures of English literature—Byron and Dickens—Gelber shows that, even though Zweig's own literary works may no longer feature as prominently in the pantheon of world literature as they once did, his literary criticism greatly contributed to the way foreign-language authors were received in Central Europe and how they may indeed still be perceived today.

Richard V. Benson's contribution to this volume takes a closer look at Zweig's 1903 introduction to the Jewish-Galician visual artist E. M. Lilien and critically analyzes the notion of "Heimat" as theorized in Zweig's essay. Like Benson, Klaus Weissenberger focuses on the question of homeland and exile and its relationship to Zweig's nonfiction. These writings, Weissenberger argues, should be understood as belonging to the genre of "Kunstprosa." Relying on recent scholarship on the theory of "Kunstprosa" (and distinguishing the term from what in the Anglophone world is now often called "creative nonfiction"), Weissenberger's essay shows the far-ranging relevance of this generic term for understanding Zweig's non-fictional output, ranging from his historical miniatures *Sternstunden der Menschheit* (1927) to his biographies of Erasmus and Montaigne and his autobiography, *Die Welt von Gestern* (*The World of Yesterday*, 1942).[19]

The final section of this volume, "Politics and Exile," explores the political dimensions of Zweig's person and works, a topic that has long been the Achilles heel of Zweig studies. Robert Kelz's essay seeks to counter the view of Zweig as an apolitical writer, as he was portrayed by the Argentine media during his visit to the country in 1936. Focusing on the recording of a class lecture that Zweig co-presented with the German writer Emil Ludwig to Jewish immigrant pupils of the Pestalozzi Schule in Buenos Aires, Kelz shows that this previously unpublished lecture was not only far more political than the articles Zweig published in the Argentine press during his visit, but that it also left a lasting imprint on the pupils, as documented by personal interviews Kelz conducted in Argentina. It remains to be seen whether the findings and arguments of Berlin and Kelz will help pave the way to a new political image of Zweig altogether.

Like his travels to Argentina, Zweig's visit to Brazil and what he wrote about the country merits critical consideration. Marlen Eckl's essay in this volume offers a new analysis of the total corpus of Zweig's Brazilian writings, including his diaries and his book, *Brasilien: Ein Land der Zukunft* (*Brazil: A Land of the Future*, 1941), by comparing Zweig's writings with the work of other German immigrant writers living in the country at the time. Eckl argues that Zweig's mythographic vision of Brazil can only be properly understood in comparison with that of other Brazilian émigré writers. Darién J. Davis's essay extends this discussion of Zweig's experience of Brazil through an analysis of the letters Stefan and his second wife Lotte Zweig sent from their exile in Brazil in the months and weeks before they committed suicide in 1942. Klemens Renoldner's essay also focuses on Zweig's exile experience by comparing his various impressions of such places as Bath, Petrópolis, and New York City. Relying on hitherto unavailable archival materials, Jeffrey B. Berlin contests the tenacious perception of Zweig as an ivory-tower author aloof from politics. Through a close analysis of Zweig's political essays and speeches from the 1930s and early 1940s, Berlin formulates a correction to this long-held misconception.

This volume may be seen as complementary to several other collections of essays or projects concerning Stefan Zweig that have recently appeared or are being edited and published more or less concurrently. Some of these activities have been initiated by Klemens Renoldner, director of the Stefan Zweig Centre in Salzburg, which was Zweig's place of residence until 1934. A volume on Zweig and the world of the European theater appeared in the Zweig Center's series in 2013,[20] and Salzburg is host to a visible and active International Stefan Zweig Society, whose president is Hildemar Holl. Two other conference volumes about Zweig are currently in production: the first on Zweig and Great Britain, following the major international conference held at the University of London in 2012; the second a collection of lectures presented at a major international Stefan Zweig conference organized in Beijing in 2012. Arturo Lacarti and Klemens Renoldner are preparing an ambitious Stefan Zweig handbook of some eight hundred pages, to be published by De Gruyter in Berlin: *Stefan Zweig: Leben—Werk—Wirkung*. A critical edition of Zweig's late masterpiece, *Schachnovelle* (Chess Novella; *The Royal Game*, 1942) and a new anthology of Zweig's writings have recently appeared.[21] In addition, at least two new scholarly studies, one by Rüdiger Görner and one by Mark H. Gelber,[22] attest to a new momentum in Zweig scholarship, which may indeed signal a more intensive encounter with Stefan Zweig and his writings in the first part of the twenty-first century.

Notes

[1] Quintus Tullius Cicero, *First Catilinarian Oration*, trans. Karl Frerichs (Wauconda: Bolchazy-Carducci, 2006), 3.

[2] Hannah Arendt, "Portrait of a Period," *Menorah Journal* 31 (1943): 307–14.

[3] Michael Hofmann, "Vermicular Dither," *London Review of Books*, January 28, 2010, http://www.lrb.co.uk/v32/n02/michael-hofmann/vermicular-dither.

[4] Italics added.

[5] It should also be noted that the late Zweig strongly identified with Cicero, as evidenced by his essay on Cicero (written in 1940) that is included in later editions of his *Sternstunden der Menschheit: Vierzehn Historische Miniaturen* (Frankfurt am Main: Fischer, 2009), 250–75. Zweig's empathetic evocation of the sixty-year-old orator forced into exile from his beloved Rome during the political turbulence following the murder of Julius Caesar had obvious autobiographical appeal for the then (almost) sixty-year-old author similarly forced into exile by political turbulence on his home soil.

[6] The recent Pushkin editions Hofmann is referring to include a deluxe edition of his short stories, *The Collected Stories of Stefan Zweig*, and of the novella *Angst*, published as *Fear*, both translated by Anthea Bell (London: Pushkin Press, 2013), as well as a new translation of *Die Welt von Gestern*, published as *The World of Yesterday*, also translated by Anthea Bell (London: Pushkin Press, 2010).

[7] *The Grand Budapest Hotel*, directed by Wes Andersen (Los Angeles: Fox Searchlight Pictures, 2014); *Letter from an Unknown Woman*, directed by Xu Jinglei (Beijing: Asian Union Film & Media, 2004).

[8] George Prochnik, *The Impossible Exile: Stefan Zweig at the End of the World* (New York: The Other Press, 2014). Will Stone provided a new translation of selected travel writings, published as *Stefan Zweig, Journeys* (London: Hesperus Press, 2010). Both Prochnik and Stone also wrote rebuttals to Hofmanns's essay: George Prochnik, "Stefan Zweig's *World of Yesterday*," *The Quarterly Conversation 21* (2010); Will Stone, "About Stefan Zweig and Michael Hofmann: A Riposte," http://willstonepoet.wordpress.com/.

[9] Hanns Arens, *Der Grosse Europäer: Stefan Zweig* (Munich: Kindler, 1983).

[10] Michael Stanislawski, *Autobiographical Jews: Essays in Jewish Self-Fashioning* (Seattle: University of Washington Press, 2004), 112.

[11] Stefan Zweig, *Magellan: Der Mann und seine Tat* (Frankfurt am Main: Fischer, 2009), 1.

[12] Felix Braun, "Das Licht der Welt," in *Stefan Zweig—Triumph und Tragik: Aufsätze, Tagebuchnotizen, Briefe*, ed. Ulrich Weinzierl (Frankfurt am Main: Fischer, 1992), 13 (translation ours).

[13] Some of these recent theories of world literature include: Pascale Casanova, *La République Mondiale des Lettres* (Paris: Seuil, 1999); David Damrosch, *What Is World Literature?* (Princeton: Princeton University Press, 2003); and Emily Apter, *Against World Literature: On the Politics of Untranslatability* (London: Verso, 2013). For an overview, see Theo D'Haen, César Domínguez, and Mads Rosendahl Thomsen, eds., *World Literature: A Reader* (New York: Routledge, 2012).

[14] Leonard Barkan, *Mute Poetry, Speaking Pictures* (Princeton: Princeton University Press, 2013), 1.

[15] The topics of trauma and exile are explored in this volume by Robert Whalen, Jeffrey Berlin, and Marlen Eckl.

[16] Stefan Zweig, "Die unsichtbare Sammlung," *Meisternovellen* (Frankfurt am Main: Fischer, 2012), 420 (hereafter cited in text as *M*).

[17] Stefan Zweig, "The Invisible Collection," trans. Paul Eden and Cedar Eden, in *Selected Stories* (London: Pushkin Press, 2009), 148.

[18] Barkan, *Mute Poetry, Speaking Pictures*, 3.

[19] Stefan Zweig, *Sternstunden der Menschheit* (Leipzig: Insel, 1927). This work has been translated into English a number of times and with different titles: *The Tide of Fortune: Twelve Historical Miniatures*, trans. Eden and Ceder Paul (New York: Viking, 1940); *Decisive Moments in History*, trans. Lowell A. Bangerter (Riverside, CA: 1998); *Shooting Stars*, trans. Anthea Bell (London: Pushkin Press, 2013).

[20] Klemens Renoldner and Birgit Peter, eds., *Zweigs Theater: Der Dramatiker Stefan Zweig im Kontext Europäischer Kultur- und Theatergeschichte* (Würzburg: Königshausen & Neumann, 2013).

[21] Stefan Zweig, *"Ich habe das Bedürfnis nach Freunden": Erzählungen, Essays und unbekannte Texte*, ed. Klemens Renoldner (Vienna: Styria Premium, 2013).

[22] Rüdiger Görner, *Stefan Zweig: Formen einer Sprachkunst* (Vienna: Sonderzahl, 2012); Mark H. Gelber, *Stefan Zweig, Judentum und Zionismus* (Innsbruck: Studienverlag, 2014).

Part I. Reception

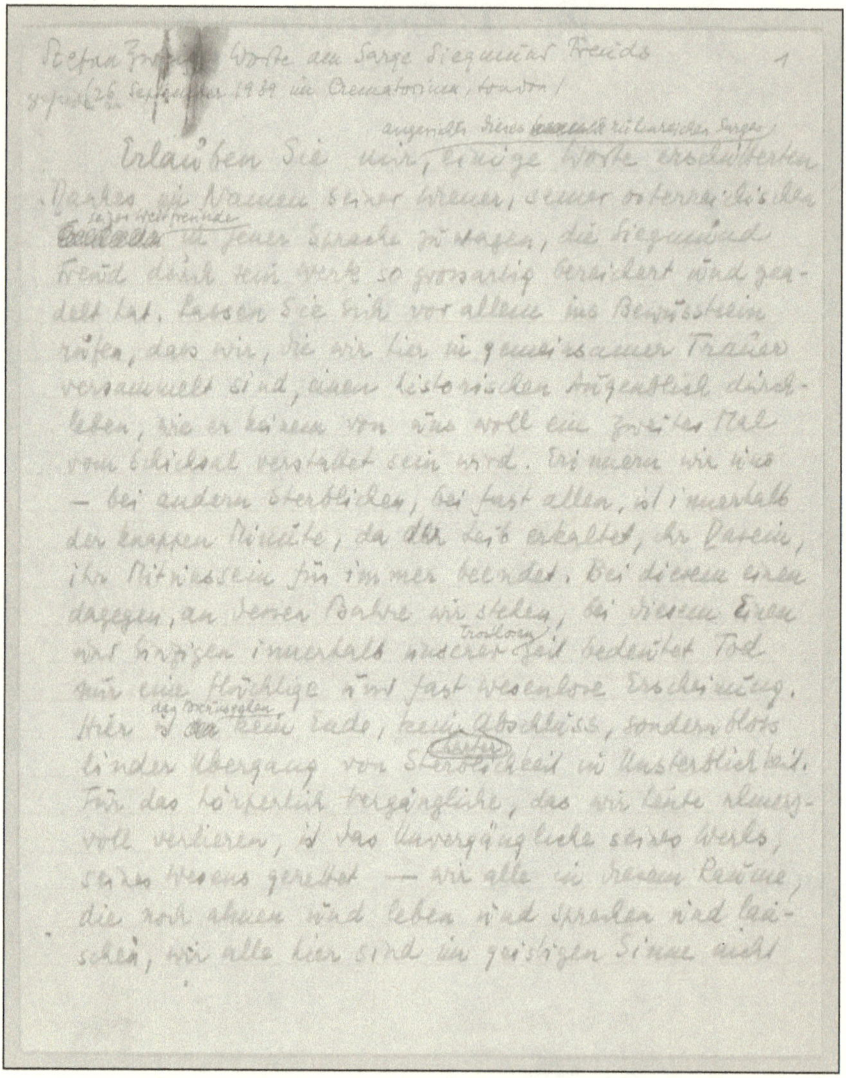

Stefan Zweig: Worte am Sarge Sigmund Freuds 1
gesprochen 26 September 1939 im Crematorium, London

Erlauben Sie mir, angesichts dieses ruhmreichen Sarges einige Worte erschütterten Dankes im Namen seiner Wiener, seiner österreichischen, seiner Weltfreunde in jener Sprache zu sagen, die Sigmund Freud durch sein Werk so grossartig bereichert und geadelt hat. Lassen Sie sich vor allem ins Bewusstsein rufen, dass wir, die wir hier in gemeinsamer Trauer versammelt sind, einen historischen Augenblick durchleben, wie er keinem von uns wohl ein zweites Mal vom Schicksal verstattet sein wird. Erinnern wir uns – bei andern Sterblichen, bei fast allen, ist innerhalb der knappen Minute, da der Leib erkaltet, ihr Dasein, ihr Mitunssein für immer beendet. Bei diesem einen dagegen, an dessen Bahre wir stehen, bei diesem Einen und Einzigen innerhalb unserer trostlosen Zeit bedeutet Tod nur eine flüchtige und fast wesenlose Erscheinung. Hier ist der Hinübergang kein Ende, kein Abschluss, sondern bloss linder Übergang von Sterblichkeit zu Unsterblichkeit. Für das körperlich Vergängliche, das wir heute schmerzvoll verlieren, ist das Unvergängliche seines Werks, seines Wesens gerettet — wir alle in diesem Raume, die noch atmen und leben und sprechen und lauschen, wir alle hier sind im geistigen Sinne nicht

Fig. 1.1. Freud Eulogy. Courtesy of the Stefan Zweig Collection at Reed Library, State University of New York at Fredonia.

1: A Stefan Zweig Revival?

Birger Vanwesenbeeck

THE FIRST DECADE of the twenty-first century has witnessed a resurgence of cultural and critical interest in the works of Stefan Zweig (1881–1942). With the appearance of new English translations, along with two recent biographies, several motion pictures, and a bestselling French novel about his final days, renewed debate within the English-speaking world regarding the literary value of his work has been vigorous, and this calls for a critical reassessment of his legacy and works.[1] Known in his time as perhaps the most translated serious author in the world and as a generous advisor cum networking agent for aspiring writers, including the young James Joyce, Zweig fell into near oblivion during the second half of the twentieth century. His writings and persona were often deemed too straightforward and sentimental for a modernism that championed impersonality and difficulty, and too Eurocentric for the era of decolonization that was the second half of the century. Thus dismissed on aesthetic as well as on political grounds, Zweig's works long seemed destined to survive primarily though their various film adaptations, such as Max Ophüls's successful 1948 Hollywood movie *Letter from an Unknown Woman*.[2]

How is it possible to account for the sudden reemergence of Zweig's works—of his fiction as well as his non-fiction—at the beginning of the present century, more than a half-century after his name and fame tumbled as quickly as they had risen? How can one explain the once-again global appeal of a figure so seemingly and forbiddingly rooted in the culture of old Europe? "It's good to have him back," Salman Rushdie wrote approvingly on the back cover of a new English edition of the only full-length novel Zweig published during his lifetime, *Ungeduld des Herzens* (*Beware of Pity*, 1939).[3] In a recent *New Yorker* essay, Leo Carey similarly expressed hope that the "current Zweig revival" might also lead to a new appreciation of his biographical essays, which Carey considers the author's best work.[4] Yet such appraisals have thus far done little to account for the curious nature of Zweig's comeback in itself. Neither is the term "revival" necessarily the most felicitous one for an author whose presence and influence never so much went away as it went unacknowledged. One example may serve to illustrate this point. Every year countless high school and college students in Europe and the United States are first introduced to psychoanalysis and to Freud's tripartite theory of mind via the famous iceberg metaphor. Like the iceberg, so their teachers tell them, most of our mind resides below the waterline, which is to say that we are unconscious of it. This metaphor, which nowhere appears in Freud's own writings, has long been attributed to his first biographer Ernest Jones, who mentions it in his three-volume biography of Freud, published between 1953 and 1957.[5] Yet this is to overlook a now little-known book by Zweig that appeared already a quarter-century earlier. In *Die Heilung durch den Geist* (Healing through the Spirit; *Mental Healers*, 1931), a now dated comparative study of Anton Mesmer, Mary Baker Eddy, and Sigmund Freud, Zweig wrote:

> Wer deshalb das unbewusste Wollen nicht bei allen Entschliessungen mit einrechnet, der sieht irrig, weil er damit den wesentlichsten Antrieb unserer inneren Spannungen aus der Berechnung lässt; so wie man die Stosskraft eines Eisbergs nicht nach dem Bruchteil einschätzen darf, der von ihm oberhalb der Wasserfläche zutage tritt (die eigentliche Wucht bleibt unter dem Spiegel verdeckt), so narrt sich selbst, wer vermeint unsere taghelle Gedanken, unsere wissenden Energieen bestimmten allein unser Fühlen und Tun.[6]

> He who fails to make due allowance for the unconscious element in all our decisions is making a great mistake, for he is ignoring the chief factor of our internal tensions. He is like the one who should estimate the size and the destructive possibilities of an iceberg only upon the ground of what is visible above the surface of the water, whereas nine-tenths of the colossus lie beneath the waves. That man deceives himself grossly who believes that our conscious thoughts, the energies of which we are fully aware, exclusively determine our feelings and doings.][7]

Although the metaphor is not fleshed out here with all the topographical specifics it is afforded in the contemporary college classroom—where the id, ego, and superego are assigned specific places—the passage nonetheless presents us with a good sense of Zweig's rhetorical skill at finding compelling images to explain abstract theories to a popular audience. (One other simile in the book compares the methodical apparatus of Freud's depth psychology to a "Taucherglocke" [diving bell] that penetrates below the waterline.)[8] In a letter to Zweig, Freud—a longtime admirer of Zweig's works—lauded his highly capable layman's familiarity with the discipline of psychoanalysis. Given that *Die Heilung durch den Geist* appeared at the peak of Zweig's global influence as a writer of both biographies and novellas, it is altogether possible that the iceberg metaphor stuck to psychoanalysis (or the layman's understanding of it) as a result of the popularity of Zweig's book.

Zweig's formulation of the iceberg metaphor does not establish a case for the possibly enduring relevance of what he wrote about Freud for contemporary psychoanalysis. In fact, it may be that it was not even Zweig who coined this metaphor. But this example illustrates well the pitfalls for any scholar who seeks to reopen the question of the ups and downs in Zweig's scholarly and popular reception over the past half-century. All too often the story of that reception history has been presented in caricatural terms as either a most undeserved fall from grace, on the one hand, or as a much overdue reckoning for a producer of literature in bulk, on the other. Monochromatic views of this nature obscure the nuances in that story, such as the often unacknowledged persistence of his influence in areas of inquiry as diverse as psychoanalysis and historiography. For example, in his biography of Marie Antoinette, he was among the first to adopt a psychobiographical approach to his subject matter.[9] One must also consider the fact that in some countries—France and Russia, for example—Zweig's books never went out of fashion in the first place, so one can hardly speak of a "revival" in these and other countries.

In a way, Zweig's presence and influence as a writer during the first three decades of the twentieth century were, like Freud's, so pervasive that many of his ideas and metaphors seeped into the culture at large without being recognized as his. In this regard, their fate may be productively compared to Freud's own notion of the uncanny—as something that was always there even though its presence may not always have been as readily acknowledged. In this context one might employ the well-known phrase Freud borrowed from Schelling: "[It] ought to have remained a secret and hidden but has come to light."[10] In an age where the process of reading finds itself embattled by the instant availability of other media, it is indeed hard to imagine a more striking polemic *against* the rediscovery of a writer than Michael Hofmann's 2010 attack on the "Zweig revival" in the *London Review of Books*.[11]

In order to understand better the deep-seated reasons for the persistently felt need by critics such as Hofmann to disavow Zweig's place within the annals of literature, it is useful to turn to an early critical probing of his popularity by one of Zweig's own contemporaries. In the essay, "Wie erklären sich grosse Bucherfolge? Stefan Zweigs Novellen" (How Can the Great Success of Some Books Be Explained? The Novellas of Stefan Zweig), originally published in the *Literaturblatt der Frankfurter Zeitung* in March 1931, Friedrich Burschell identified two characteristics in Zweig's novellas of the 1920s—the era when his success as an author and translated writer was at its height—that help account for their widespread appeal.[12] There is in Zweig's stories, so Burschell argued, a relative ahistoricism that keeps the temporal setting of their characters' emotional dilemmas and internal struggles purposively vague and unspecific, thus facilitating a universalist interpretation that resonates with readers across cultures and languages. At the same time, most of these stories are, explicitly or implicitly, set "in der Welt des gebildeten und gesicherten Bürgertums" (FB 55; in the world of the cultured and secure bourgeoisie) of the immediate pre-First World War era, a period that, particularly during the 1920s, evoked feelings of nostalgia and loss. In the opening chapter of *Die Welt von Gestern* (*The World of Yesterday*, 1942) Zweig describes this era as "das goldene Zeitalter der Sicherheit" (the golden age of security):

> Wenn ich versuche, für die Zeit vor dem Ersten Weltkriege, in der ich aufgewachsen bin, eine handliche Formel zu finden, so hoffe ich am prägnantesten zu sein, wenn ich sage, es war das goldene Zeitalter der Sicherheit. Alles in unserer fast tausendjährigen österreichischen Monarschie schien auf Dauer gegründet und der Staat selbst der oberste Garant dieser Beständigkeit.[13]

> [When I attempt to find a simple formula for the period in which I grew up, prior to the First World War, I hope that I convey its fullness by calling it the Golden Age of Security. Everything in our almost thousand-year-old Austrian monarchy seemed based on permanency, and the State itself as the chief guarantor of this stability.][14]

It is to this curious dialectic of suggested timelessness on the one hand and pre–First World War nostalgia on the other that, according to Burschell, Zweig's stories owe at once their popular appeal and their "tragic" quality: "Die Welt des gesicherten Bürgertums wird hier als etwas Unveränderliches angenommen, sie wird als Kunstmittel benutzt, um die Leidenschaften und Gefühle besonders tragisch werden zu lassen." (FB 55; The world of the secure bourgeoisie is here presumed to be immune to change. This premise is employed as a technique to give the passions and feelings [of his characters] a particularly tragic appearance.) Politics, which Zweig, following Napoleon, considered to be the modern "Fatum," acts in these stories as the blind and relentless force against which his characters, like a modern Oedipus or Medea, carry out their doomed and fated struggle.[15]

Yet, unlike the tragic perfection of Sophocles or Euripides, for Burschell Zweig's stories are but an "epigonalen Beschwörung einer antiquierten Welt" (acolyte's conjuration of the ancient world); they offer but "einen Similiglanz der Volkommenheit" (FB 56; simulated splendor of perfection) since they lack the ancient tragedians' impartiality, and they avoid rather than confront conflicting ideologies. Instead of allowing his readers to traverse the emotional rollercoaster of pity and fear that Aristotle saw as tragedy's central function, Zweig's stories, according to Burschell, bring their middle-class readers only flattery and confirmation:

Anderseits wird durch die betonte Anteilnahme des Autors am Schicksal seiner sympathischen Helden [...] es dem Leser leicht gemacht, sich fortschrittlich und über herkömmliche Ideologien erhaben vorzukommen. Der gehobene Leser—denn nur um solche handelt es sich bei Stefan Zweig—fühlt sich geschmeichelt und vag bestätigt. (FB 56)

[On the other hand, because of the obvious sympathy that he has for the fate of his characters [...] Zweig makes it easy for his reader to feel progressive and elevated above conventional ideologies. The elevated reader—and that is the reader we are always talking about in Stefan Zweig—feels flattered and vaguely validated.]

This idea of elevating the reader—Burschell's second point—is conveyed by Zweig's notoriously florid style, which gives readers the illusion of floating up "im hohen und strengen Bereich der Dichtung zu schweben" (FB 57; into the high and strictly defined domain of poetry). In reality, however, readers are merely dealing with "der Suggestion eines kultivierten und geschickten Epigonen" (FB 55; the suggestiveness of a cultivated and skilled imitator). According to Burschell, Zweig's popularity is thus "symptomatic" for what he, alluding to the title of one of the author's more well-known novellas, calls a "Verwirrung der Gefühle" (FB 55; confusion of the emotions). The wide appeal of Zweig's novellas, according to this critical perspective, thus finds its origin in the mistaken views of a specific readership that is unable to distinguish literary quality from kitsch, and that wrongfully turns to literature as one would to a self-help guide, seeking flattery and validation rather than truth and aesthetic recognition.

World Literature

This demystification of Zweig's novellas as inauthentic, excessively ornate, and, ultimately, all too well-tailored to the worldly concerns of the middle-class audience that first gave the genre its *raison d'être*, is what saddled Zweig early on with the epithets of "Erwerbszweig" (commercial branch) and "Literaturindustrieller" (producer of literature in bulk) in Vienna. Subsequent variations of critical appraisal along the lines established by Burschell, now usefully compiled in a book by Ulrich Weinzierl,[16] resurfaced in many negative commentaries regarding Zweig from the height of his popularity during his lifetime to the 1981 centennial celebration of his birth and up to the present time, including Michael Hofmann's categorization of Zweig as "the Pepsi of Austrian writing," whose literary output "just tastes fake" (Hofmann).

Yet there is something entirely unconvincing about this charge against Zweig. Popular literature is usually defined by what it is not, namely literature that has a staying power beyond a single generation. Every new generation invariably finds its own popular writers. Hofmann's polemic thus does little to account for the current re-emergence of Zweig. Instead, it rather tediously takes the reader one more time through all those dismissive appraisals and anti-Zweig anecdotes already compiled in Weinzierl's book—which Hofmann nowhere references—without adding anything not already included in Burschell's 1931 essay. Still, the argument against the *Bildungsbürgertum* on which Burschell's Marxist analysis relies can no longer suffice to explain the contemporary appeal of Zweig in a late-capitalist society now more than a century removed from the pre-First World War era of security and economic prosperity. Although Burschell may have been correct in drawing attention to a certain universalist strain in Zweig's writings that goes a long way towards explaining his appeal, there is still too much emphasis on him as a European writer dealing with European themes of particular relevance to an interwar European audience. Burschell does not even address the question of the immense success of Zweig's novellas in translation as a possible index of the much broader scope of his international appeal.

From the opposite end of the temporal spectrum, Hofmann's approach reduces Zweig's contemporary appeal to an exclusively Anglo-Saxon fad,[17] thus misleadingly suggesting to his English-language readers that no one in Germany or Austria, where paperback reissues of his works have always been available, can still be found reading Zweig. Hofmann also fails to mention Zweig's considerable and ongoing popularity in non-Anglophone countries such as China, Brazil, and France. In her 2004 adaptation of Zweig's novella, *Brief einer Unbekannten* (*Letter from an Unknown Woman*, 1922),[18] Chinese filmmaker Jinglei Xu transports the Viennese setting of the original to 1930s Beijing.[19] Both the boldness and the stunning success—the film won the Best Director award at the 2004 San Sebastián International Film Festival—of this cultural-geographical transposition from old Europe to twentieth-century Beijing, attest to the appeal of Zweig's works to the non-European as well as to the European artistic imagination. Throughout the movie Xu cleverly balances her references to Zweig's story with allusions to Max Ophüls's aforementioned 1948 Hollywood adaptation of the novella while still staying true to the sociopolitical and historical particulars of 1930s Beijing. She thus creates a global narrative whose artistic genealogy spans three continents and as many languages.

In the English-language feature film *Lost Zweig* (2002), a largely fictional re-imagining of Zweig's final days, the Brazilian filmmaker Sylvio Back similarly offers a fresh and universally accessible approach to Zweig's suicide—on February 22, 1942, in Petropolis, Brazil—by emphasizing the private rather than the political nature of his final act. "My name is Stefan Zweig and this is the story of the strangest week of my life," says Back's eponymous protagonist.[20] The strangeness alluded to in the opening line of Back's movie is reinforced throughout the film by the broken accents of German actors speaking English, and it soon exerts an impact on the viewers who see themselves—much like in the case of Xu's movie—uncomfortably forced into the role of voyeurs peeking in on the fated end of the unholy week in which Zweig and his second wife Lotte committed suicide. In a way, Back's movie marks a belated attempt to regain some of the privacy and strangeness of Zweig's death, more than half a century after the snapshot of Zweig and his second wife Lotte (née Altmann) on their deathbed taken by the Brazilian police was insensitively distributed to the media.

Another recent attempt to re-establish Zweig's relevance for the world of today is the bestselling French novel by Laurent Seksik, *Les Derniers Jours de Stefan Zweig* (2010),[21] which subsequently appeared as a graphic novel produced by Guillaume Sorel (2012).[22] In the novel Zweig worries about the fate of a writer who, prohibited from publication in Nazi-controlled Austria and Germany, sees himself forced to publish exclusively in translation: "Could one be a writer if he [*sic*] weren't read in his own language?"[23] In the novel this reflection on language and exile takes on tragic dimensions. Seksik's Zweig is a worn-down figure who has long "entertained the slightly foolish notion that he would one day have learnt so many languages that his German vocabulary would simply dissolve into a melting pot of foreign words."[24] But, as it turns out, even the tarnished German language does not give up that easily. It is "tenacious" in its hold on Zweig, and the author continues to write his final works—*Die Welt von Gestern*, *Schachnovelle* (*The Royal Game*, 1942), and a biography of Montaigne—in German, the language of the Nazis.[25]

What connects Xu's, Back's, and Seksik's recent creative engagements with Zweig—and what distinguishes them from earlier adaptations and biographies of Zweig—is their explicit focus on translation and on the difficulty of articulating one's own experience within a global context. The Zweig that appears in these works is a writer who, because of his experience of exile and his multilingualism, often turns his attention to the fate of language within a global context. In trying to tell a fellow European the story of a recent traumatizing stint in Dutch-controlled Indonesia, the physician-protagonist of *Der Amokläufer* ("Amok," 1922) sees himself forced to rely on a term from the native Malay language: "Wissen Sie, was Amok ist?," he asks, "Es ist mehr as Trunkenheit . . . es ist Tollheit, eine Art Trunkenheit bei den Malaien . . . ein Anfall mörderischer, sinnloser Monomanie."[26] ("Do you know what 'amok' is? . . . it is more than drunkenness . . . it is a madness, a kind of human rabies . . . an onset of murderous senseless monomania.")[27] Only the use of a non-European, native term suffices to express here the physician's colonial experience. This example demonstrates an impasse in translation that draws attention to one of those foreign words or "quirks," as Wai-chee Dimock has recently called them, which are apparently resistant to or lost in translation.[28]

Dimock is one of several North American critics who over the past decade or so have given new relevance to the Goethean notion of world literature and to the imperative value of studying literature within a transnational context. Although Zweig is yet to be assigned a place within this renewed debate, the above-cited examples should clarify why he is an obvious candidate to consider within this framework. Translation, taken not just literally but in the broader etymological sense of "carrying over," is the master trope that structures almost all of Zweig's writings, from his translations of Verhaeren and Verlaine to his travel writings and his biographies, to his preference for the embedded narrative, where, as in *Der Amokläufer*, a framed narration invariably expresses the narrator's desire or need to carry over his traumatic experience to a third party. At the same time, the renewed appeal of Zweig to artists in contemporary China, France, and Brazil fulfills the two criteria by which, according to David Damrosch in *What Is World Literature?*, a work "enters into world literature" by being recognized *as* literature (in this case by peers) and by "circulating" beyond one's culture of origin.[29] According to Damrosch this process is subject to constant revision: "A given work can enter into world literature and then fall out of it again if it shifts beyond a threshold point along either axis, the literary or the worldly. Over the centuries, an unusually shifty work can come in and out of the sphere of world literature at several different times; and at any given point, a work may function as world literature for some readers but not others, and for some kinds of reading but not others."[30]

If the reference to canonical instability describes rather well Zweig's falling in and out of favor with readers and critics over the past century, then the idea of circulating "beyond its linguistic and cultural point of origin" is what makes world literature into a literature of exile,[31] always at a remove from its native ground. The latter is a condition that Zweig, both in his own works and his literary endeavors for others, embodies particularly well.

As it did for Goethe a century earlier, popular success came early and dramatically to Zweig, which helps explain why the relationship between commerce and art—between "Handel" and "Kunst" in the terms of Goethe's *Wilhelm Meister*—looms so large in his works.[32] Rackner, the Berlin art dealer and protagonist of Zweig's *Die unsichtbare Sammlung* ("The Invisible Collection," 1925),[33] is critical of the uneducated and avaricious war profiteers of the Weimar era who are buying up old masters without the expertise and knowledge of his pre-war customers. Yet he is equally skeptical about the possibility of art to persist or thrive in the absence of any monetary support. Indeed, when Rackner meets

Kronfeld, an old acquaintance of the auction house and a now blind art collector, he discovers that Kronfeld's prized collection has been sold from under him by his daughters in order to make ends meet during the difficult Weimar years. Even though the story concludes with the aphorism—attributed to Goethe—that "Sammler sind glückliche Menschen" (*M* 425; collectors are happy people) one cannot help but question the validity of this claim when all that its intended referent is contemplating is the blank and unread page. The dialectic between commerce and art explored here may be said to capture the same opposition at the heart of world literature in Damrosch's (neo-Goethean) sense: only when works of literature are circulated, read, or sold do they become world literature; however, when this circulatory or commercial aspect becomes an end in itself (as it does for Rackner's contemporary customers), then the artistic or literary value disappears.

Bearing in mind this particular discussion concerning Zweig and world literature, while reflecting on the criticism of those like Hofmann and Burschell, one must acknowledge the importance of this global, world-literary element in Zweig. The Zweig that is being rediscovered by artists and readers at the beginning of the twenty-first century is no longer the "remembering European" championed by his early biographers, and by Zweig himself in his own autobiography. Rather, he is now viewed more and more as a writer who, because of his engagement and interest in translation and intercultural exchange, has again become relevant at the beginning of the globalized twenty-first century. Both his life trajectory—from Austria to England and Brazil—and his writings bespeak an ethos that is at once more global and more actual than the old world epithet, the grand European, could imply.

The last lines of Zweig's suicide note, composed on February 22, 1942, in Petrópolis, Brazil, may serve as a case in point. Written thousands of miles away from his former Austrian home in Salzburg and "dedicated" to the people of Brazil, a country he had earlier referred to as "Ein Land der Zukunft" (a land of the future)[34] the note concludes with a valediction that is both future-oriented and evocative of a global context: "Ich grüsse alle meine Freunde! Mögen sie die Morgenröte noch sehen nach der langen Nacht! Ich, allzu Ungeduldiger, gehe ihnen voraus" (I salute all my friends! May it be granted them yet to see the dawn after the long night! I, all too impatient, go on before).[35]

Although the hypothetical and vague evocation of a new "dawn" following the Hitler era may offer insufficient solace when found in a suicide note, this concern with the future is nonetheless also mirrored in the meticulous care Zweig still took to make sure he finished his final novella, *Schachnovelle*, and to mail separate copies of it to his publishers in New York and in Argentina so that it might be published posthumously. The latter move may be dismissed as motivated by strictly careerist concerns regarding legacy, but even then there is something striking about the rhetoric of this last writing of Zweig. As an example of bidding farewell, the suicide note has more in common with the host country where Zweig finished correcting the work to which the note is frequently appended, his posthumously published memoir, *Die Welt von Gestern,* than with the Austrian literary tradition proper. It recalls, for instance, the ending of *Moby Dick* where, after depicting the self-willed demise of Ahab's crew, Melville concludes the novel with a one-page "epilogue" wherein he informs his reader that Ishmael "did survive the wreck" and thus lived to tell the tale.[36] Melville thus closes the work by suggesting, as do Zweig's final lines, the possibility of a regeneration following a seemingly absolute demise. One might hear an echo in Zweig's note of his beloved Walt Whitman, whose reference to "lasting lilacs" in his commemorative poem for his "Captain" Abraham Lincoln, suggests in a comparable manner the irrepressible dawn that follows the long night of his president's murder and the Civil War.[37]

The reference in the suicide note to what Zweig called his "geistige Heimat Europa" (spiritual home Europe) does not diminish the regenerative rhetoric of these American tropes; rather they signal the hybrid cultural legacy within which his writings should be located, or at least had come to reside in by his life's end. As one of the first European writers of stature to devote a book to the then still relatively unknown country of Brazil, Zweig acted as a cultural mediator between Europe and the Americas in the same way as Alexis de Tocqueville had done a century earlier in his book on the nascent democracy in the United States.[38] Indeed, the phrase "a land of the future," which Zweig coined in his Brazil book, remains a familiar expression in the economically thriving Brazil of today, much as de Tocqueville's insights regarding American democracy are still commonly cited by contemporary American politicians.

It is no coincidence that Zweig devoted one of his immensely popular historical miniatures, *Sternstunden der Menschheit* (first translated as *The Tide of Fortune,* 1927),[39] to the successful telegraphic transmission across the Atlantic between Ireland and Newfoundland in 1858.[40] The success of this transatlantic communication no doubt held particular symbolical appeal for an author whose own writings transmitted so well to the American reading public of his time that pirated versions of his books—published under the name "Stephen Branch"—circulated widely on the black market.[41] It is also noteworthy that many of Zweig's better-known novellas—*Der Amokläufer, Die unsichtbare Sammlung, Schachnovelle*—are set in locations that are actually between places: aboard an ocean liner or ship, for example, or on a train. This literary characteristic suggests a dimension of global space that Zweig embodied in life as well as in his works.

Zweig and Modernism

Acknowledgment of the global, world-literary element in Zweig has long been eclipsed by the image of the author as an old-world European unfit for exile. In part, this is an image created and perpetuated by other German expatriate writers who, from Thomas Mann to Hannah Arendt and continuing to Michael Hofmann, have sought to distinguish *their* experiences and understanding of exile and *their* sense of world-belonging from those of Zweig. The discussions of Zweig's suicide note are a case in point. In a letter dated February 24, 1942, written to his daughter Erika, one day after news of Zweig's suicide reached him in Pacific Palisades, Mann wrote:

> Ja, und der Zweig Stefan? Aus Gram kann er sich nicht getötet haben, auch nicht aus Not. Sein hinterlassener Brief ist ganz unzulänglich. Was heisst in seinem Fall *reconstruction of life*, die ihm zu schwer gefallen sei? Es muss wohl das liebe Geschlecht dahinterstecken, irgendein Skandal gedroht haben. Grosse Erschütterung kann man nicht empfinden, aber es ist doch wieder ein Untergang, der nach dem Triumph jener unwiderstehlichen Geschichtsmächte aussieht.[42]

> [And what about Zweig, Stefan? It cannot have been out of anger or need that he killed himself. The letter that he left behind is entirely insufficient. What, in his case, can it have been that made *reconstruction of life* seem so hard to him? The fair sex must have something to do with it, a scandal in the offing? One cannot experience great distress, but it is once again a defeat that looks like a triumph for the irresistible powers of history.][43]

Hofmann's discussion of the suicide note echoes both the content and tone of Mann's quotation:

> [Zweig] left a suicide note which, like most of what he wrote, is so smooth and mannerly and somehow machined—actually more like an Oscar acceptance speech than a suicide note—that one feels the irritable rise of boredom halfway through it, and the sense that *he doesn't mean it*, his heart isn't in it (not even in his suicide). (Hofmann)

Zweig's decision "to go with a whimper and not with a bang" (to evoke T. S. Eliot's phrase) is rejected, but not out of personal grief. For Mann, it causes "no great distress," and it leaves Hofmann but "irritated." Nevertheless, both deem it *politically* unacceptable. Whereas Mann sees the suicide note as "ganz unzulänglich" and as "ein Untergang" to the "Geschichtsmächte" of the day (that is, Hitler and Nazi Germany)

Hofmann takes issue with Zweig's moderation and what he calls the "manneredness" of the note. For him, it is symptomatic of Zweig's life-long inability to make a strong commitment, up until the time of his own death.

In a memorial for Zweig published a week after his passing in the New York–based German-Jewish expatriate newspaper, *Der Aufbau*, Mann further expanded on this critical view, now explicitly evoking the context of exile: "Der Tod Stefan Zweigs lässt eine schmerzliche Lücke in die Reihen der europäischen literarischen Emigration" (The death of Stefan Zweig leaves a painful hole in the ranks of the European literary emigration).[44] He concluded the piece with a direct and dismissive allusion to the final lines of Zweig's suicide note by stating that "desto kummervoller ist es, dass [Zweigs Humanität] selbst nicht robust genug war, die Finsternis zu überleben und den Tag zu sehen" (It is all the more sorrowful that Zweig's humanity was not vigorous enough to survive the darkness and to see the day).[45] The picture of Zweig that emerges here, notwithstanding how much Mann rhetorically strove to maintain a positive image of the author, is clear: in contrast with other, "more robust" exiles, Zweig is evoked as an expatriate weakling unable to carry out the "reconstruction of life" that exile demands. That Mann uses the original English for this last phrase is an attempt to attest to his own exemplary assimilation into the culture of his host country.[46]

Mann's and Hofmann's pieces are more than ad hominem attacks, however. As the explicit focus of both authors on the suicide note indicates, their criticism is also meant as a dismissal of Zweig's *writings*. Their implicit claim to be a *literary* representation of exile similarly needs to be delegitimized in order to vindicate "other" literatures of exile, which Mann exemplified in his works and of which Hofmann has long been one of the most outspoken champions, both as translator and as critic. The obvious reference in this context is to the literature of modernism; many of its most important works, including Joyce's *Ulysses* (1922), Mann's own *Doktor Faustus* (1947), and Rilke's *Duiniser Elegien* (1923), were either conceived in exile or written by figures who, because of ethnicity or language, were already marginalized within their own native environments. The "official" version of the relationship between exile and modernism as it emerges from these writers and as it has been theorized by critics runs as follows: although many modernist writers faced considerable emotional and financial hardship resulting from exile or exclusion, they were ultimately able to triumph over these challenges through the mastery of their language; and if they did self-destruct, then they did so only as part of a larger scheme of things. One might consider in this context the depressed narrator of Mann's *Doktor Faustus*, Serenus Zeitblom. This figure may recall Stefan Zweig by his first and last initials, or by his mediating role as narrator, or by his restraint, reinforced by his first name. But, in dealing with the Nazi domination of his country, he opts for an altogether different response than Zweig. Instead of taking the path to exile and suicide, Zeitblom robustly grooms himself to wish for the destruction of his own country by the Allied Forces. Interestingly, the act of writing is what allows him to triumph over this impossible predicament. As news of the advance of the Allied Forces reaches him in Bavaria, he remains devoted to writing the life story of his longtime friend, the exceptionally gifted composer Adrian Leverkühn, whose own self-sought destruction is transcended by the masterly music he left as his legacy.

By contrast, neither Zweig's suicide nor the lack of a notable experimental urge in his writings has ever been compatible with this modernist rhetoric of triumph, hence the continuous need, particularly felt by modernist-oriented writers and critics, to devalorize his writings. His reemergence at the beginning of the twenty-first century thus sheds new light on the "ideology" of modernism which, as Fredric Jameson has shown, was already established in the 1940s and 1950s. It makes sense that Stefan Zweig, the period's most widely known writer, had to be excluded from this ideological grouping in order for modernism to become synonymous with mastery (or triumph) and formal experimentation. As Vivian Liska argues in an essay that assesses Zweig's critics (among them, Thomas Mann): "the ambiguities and the inconsistencies of their critical statements in turn shed light on the limitations of the premises of late twentieth-century theory once they become theoretical dogmas and get divested of the contextual, contradiction-ridden 'life' breathing through these documents that were still contiguous to Zweig's own world."[47]

It is no coincidence, then, that the global rediscovery of Zweig in the first decade of the twenty-first century has been contemporaneous with a renewed scrutiny of the ideological underpinnings of modernism. Indeed, the two are largely complementary phenomena in that they both prompt a reevaluation of the question of what does and does not constitute serious literature. Some of that reevaluation may already be found at work in Zweig's own fictional writings of the high-modernist period inasmuch as their frequent exploration of the mechanisms of invisibility, secrecy, and misrecognition can easily be read as so many allegories for and reflections on the author's own exclusion from the serious literature of his time. Consider the opening of *Brief einer Unbekannten*, which tells the story of a woman's decade-long loyalty to a man who never recognized her despite repeated amorous encounters over the years. Here "der bekannte Romanschriftsteller R." (*M* 151; the well-known novelist R.) sorts through a pile of mail that has accumulated in his Viennese apartment during a three-day absence from the capital and is struck by one item in particular:

> Lässig sah er den Einlauf an, riss ein paar Kuverts auf, die ihn durch ihre Absender interessierten: ein Brief, der fremde Schriftzüge trug und zu umfangreich schien, schob er zunächst beiseite. (*M* 151)
>
> [Looking idly at what had been put before him, he opened a couple of envelopes that interested him owing to who had sent them. He put aside for the time being one letter which looked too bulky, addressed in unfamiliar handwriting.]⁴⁸

Its reading temporarily interrupted by the tea being brought in at this moment by a manservant, the bulky "letter from an unknown woman" referenced in the title is not read by R. until after some browsing in a newspaper and flipping through a few circulars:

> Inzwischen war der Tee aufgetragen worden, bequem lehnte er sich in den Fauteuil, durchblätterte noch einmal die Zeitung und einige Drucksachen; dann zündete er sich eine Zigarre an und griff nun nach dem zurückgelegten Briefe. Es waren etwa zwei Dutzend hastig beschriebene Seiten in fremder, unruhiger Frauenskript, ein Manuskript eher als ein Brief. (*M* 151)
>
> [Meanwhile tea had been brought. He leaned back comfortably in his armchair, glanced through the newspaper again, and some circulars; then he lit a cigar and picked up the letter he had put aside. There were about two dozen hastily written pages in an unfamiliar shaky, feminine hand, a manuscript rather than a letter.] (*RG* 182)

The rapid concatenation of different kinds of leisurely readings in this opening passage, together with the temporal deferral of his reading of the letter, is suggestive not only of R.'s worldliness (as conveyed by the tea, the cigar, and the manservant), nor simply of his poise (he is "lässig" and "bequem"); rather, it points furthermore to a certain hierarchy of different *kinds* of writing that moves downward from the seriousness of R.'s own occupation—the novel—to the more mundane examples of the newspaper and the circulars (*Drucksachen*, literally "printed things"), and finally, to that which is no longer worthy of being printed at all and is thus handwritten by default: the private letter. This hierarchy, the letter's remove from the serious writing of R., is further highlighted by the latter's perceived generic instability ("ein Manuscript eher als ein Brief"), its lack of restraint ("hastig beschrieben") and measure ("unruhig"), and, finally, by its gender, since it is characterized pejoratively it seems, as "Frauenschrift." That all of these stylistic epithets are attributed to its author before a single line of the woman's letter is actually read seems an important point because this emphasizes R.'s failure to recognize the unknown woman by extending that misrecognition even to her writing.

The greater allegorical significance of this failure to recognize writing is that, in a very direct and precise way, it thematizes modernism's own strategic misrecognition of mass culture as something deemed similarly hasty and incongruous from which it needed to distance itself. As Andreas Huyssen has argued, this mass culture was often associated with women, whereas "real authentic culture remains the prerogative of men."[49] Zweig's story thematizes the same point in its depiction of R.'s opposition to the woman. In this manner, *Brief einer Unbekannten*, published in the same *annus mirabilis* as *Ulysses* and *The Wasteland*, can be read as an allegory for modernism's own genealogy, how it needed to rid itself of the "Frauenschrift" of mass culture, including the effeminate or insufficiently robust sentimentalism of a writer like Zweig, in order to establish the modernist canon as one of masculinity, difficulty and form.

As a fictional exploration of the theme of unreciprocated love, *Brief einer Unbekannten* belongs in the company of Flaubert's *Education Sentimentale* (1869) and Gabriel García Márquez's *Love in the Time of Cholera* (1985). Yet it also has a raw quality about it that distinguishes it from the latter two. Reading Zweig's novella, one is never sure whether to be more haunted by the idea of a woman who for over a decade persists in her adoration of a man who fathered her child but never recognized her, or to be more haunted by the amnesia of a novelist apparently so caught up in his own art and fame that he does not realize he has slept with the same woman twice. Stylistically, the novella owes part of this haunting appeal to Zweig's adept use of the nested narrative format. Like the *kuchuk hanem* of Flaubert's Egyptian letters, the protagonist of *Brief einer Unbekannten* remains unnamed. Yet, unlike Flaubert's Egyptian courtesan, Zweig's unknown woman is allowed to speak in a voice of her own. The bulk of the novella consists, after all, of her letter being quoted verbatim to the reader at the same time it is being read by R. One of the rhetorical effects of this adopted narrative structure is that, with every anaphoric return of the letter's motif-phrase "Dir, der Du mich nie gekannt" (*M* 151 and passim; you who never recognized me, *RG* 182), readers are made to feel that that they, too, have somehow failed this woman, and that they, too, may be responsible for her untimely death. In fact, she is already speaking from beyond the grave by the time they read her letter.

In its use of the epistolary form to highlight a communicative impasse of sorts, Zweig's novella recalls two other famous letters of Austrian high modernism: Hugo von Hofmannsthal's *Lord Chandos Letter* (1902) and Franz Kafka's (unsent) *Letter to his Father* (1919). Here, too, a son and a writer of fiction, respectively, struggle and fail to speak up to a father, or, as in the case of Lord Chandos, struggle and fail to speak at all. If this struggle to communicate has generally been taken as a central feature of modernism as such, emblematized by such disparate advocates of silence as Samuel Beckett, Ludwig Wittgenstein, and John Cage, then *Brief einer*

Unbekannten may serve as a reminder that, historically speaking, this struggle has always been a lot less enabling when confronted by a woman. There is a striking parallel, for instance, in the deference felt by both Kafka and the unknown woman which makes it so that neither of them can bring themselves to actually accuse their respective addressees: "Ich klage dich nicht an" (*M* 178; "Never, never will I accuse you," *RG* 198) the unknown woman says repeatedly throughout the letter, just as Kafka, in the letter to his father, states: "I too believe you are entirely blameless in the matter of our estrangement."[50] Yet, in their reception by both the intended and non-intended addressees, the two letters could not have fared more differently. Whereas Kafka's non-fictional letter has in time come to be read as a modernist masterpiece in its own right, and thus as an example of the male writer's triumph over his struggle to communicate, the notable lack of secondary criticism on Zweig's novella indicates that, much like R.'s initial response to the letter, its literary value has remained largely unrecognized. In a paradoxical fashion that exemplifies only all too well Freud's notion of the uncanny as the "secretly familiar," *Brief einer Unbekannten* may thus be said to both document Zweig's contiguity to the modernists of his day as well as to thematize on an allegorical level his exclusion from their company.

Notes

[1] Many of these new editions of Zweig's works in English have been published by Pushkin Press in London. The two recent biographies are Oliver Matuschek, *Stefan Zweig: Drei Leben* (Frankfurt am Main: Fischer, 2006) and George Prochnik, *The Impossible Exile: Stefan Zweig at the End of the World* (New York: Other Press, 2014). The Brazilian motion picture is *Lost Zweig*, directed by Sylvio Back (Alphaville Barueri: Europa Filmes, 2002). The bestselling French novel is Laurent Seksik, *Les Derniers Jours de Stefan Zweig* (Paris: Flammarion, 2010).

[2] *Letter from an Unknown Woman*, directed by Max Ophüls, 1948 (London: Second Sight Films, 2006), DVD.

[3] Stefan Zweig, *Ungeduld des Herzens* (Berlin: Insel Verlag, 2013); *Beware of Pity*, trans. Phyllis and Trevor Blewitt (New York: New York Review of Books, 2006).

[4] Leo Carey, "The Escape Artist: The Death and Life of Stefan Zweig," *New Yorker*, August 27, 2012, 70–76.

[5] Ernest Jones, *The Life and Work of Sigmund Freud* (New York: Random Books, 1953), 1: 374.

[6] Stefan Zweig, *Die Heilung durch den Geist: Mesmer, Mary Baker-Eddy, Freud* (Frankfurt am Main: Fischer, 2007), 313.

[7] Stefan Zweig. *Mental Healers: Franz Anton Mesmer, Mary Baker Eddy, Sigmund Freud*. Trans. Eden and Cedar Paul (New York: Frederick Ungar, 1962), 292.

[8] Stefan Zweig. *Die Heilung durch den Geist*, 312.

[9] Stefan Zweig, *Marie Antoinette: Bildnis eines Mittleren Charakters* (Frankfurt am Main: Fischer, 2009).

10 Sigmund Freud, "The 'Uncanny,'" in *The Critical Tradition: Classic Texts and Contemporary Trends*, ed. David Richter, trans. James Strachey (Boston: Bedford, 2007), 517.

11 Michael Hofmann, "Vermicular Dither," *London Review of Books*, January 28, 2010, http://www.lrb.co.uk/v32/n02/michael-hofmann/vermicular-dither (hereafter cited in text as Hofmann).

12 Friedrich Burschell, "Wie erklären sich grosse Bucherfolge? Stefan Zweigs Novellen," in *Stefan Zweig—Triumph und Tragik: Aufsätze, Tagebuchnotizen, Briefe*, ed. Ulrich Weinzierl (Frankfurt am Main: Fischer, 1992), 54–58 (hereafter cited in text as FB. Translations of Burschell are mine).

13 Stefan Zweig, *Die Welt von Gestern* (Frankfurt am Main: Fischer, 1970), 15 (hereafter cited in text as *WvG*).

14 Stefan Zweig, *The World of Yesterday*, trans. Ben Huebsch (Lincoln: University of Nebraska Press, 1964), 1.

15 Stefan Zweig, *Romain Roland: Der Mann und das Werk* (Frankfurt am Main: Literarische Anstalt Rütten & Loening, 1921), 208.

16 Ulrich Weinzierl, ed., *Stefan Zweig—Triumph und Tragik: Aufsätze, Tagebuchnotizen, Briefe* (Frankfurt am Main: Fischer, 1992).

17 Hofmann's hypothesis of the Anglophone reader's inability to recognize Zweig for what he truly is is explored in greater detail in the introduction to this volume.

18 Stefan Zweig, "Brief einer Unbekannten," in *Meisternovellen* (Frankfurt: S. Fischer, 2012), 151–97.

19 *Letter from an Unknown Woman*, directed by Xu Jinglei, 2004 (Beijing: Asian Union Film & Media, 2004), DVD.

20 *Lost Zweig*, directed by Sylvio Back, 2002 (Alphaville Barueri: Europa Filmes, 2009), DVD.

21 Laurent Seksik, *Les Derniers Jours de Stefan Zweig* (Paris: Flammarion, 2010).

22 Guillaume Sorel and Laurent Seksik, *Les Derniers Jours de Stefan Zweig* (Tournai: Casterman, 2012).

23 Laurent Seksik, *The Last Days*, trans. André Naffis-Sahely (London: Pushkin Press, 2013), 18.

24 Ibid., 62.

25 Stefan Zweig, *Schachnovelle*, in *Meisternovellen* (Frankfurt am Main: Fischer, 2012), 426–91; Stefan Zweig, *Montaigne* (Frankfurt am Main: Fischer, 2001).

26 Stefan Zweig, *Der Amokläufer*, in *Meisternovellen* (Frankfurt am Main: Fischer, 2012), 117.

27 Stefan Zweig, "Amok," in *The Royal Game and Other Stories*, trans. Jill Sutcliffe (New York: Holmes & Meier, 2000), 62.

28 Wai-chee Dimock, *Through Other Continents: American Literature across Deep Time* (Princeton: Princeton University Press, 2006), 84 and passim.

29 David Damrosch, *What Is World Literature?* (Princeton: Princeton University Press, 2003), 6.

30 Ibid.

31 Ibid.

32 Johann Wolfgang von Goethe, *Wilhelm Meisters Lehrjahre*, in *Goethes Werke*, vol. 8 (Hamburg: Christian Wegner, 1959).

33 Stefan Zweig, *Die unsichtbare Sammlung*, in *Meisternovellen* (Frankfurt am Main: Fischer, 2012), 408–25 (hereafter cited in text as *M*).

34 Stefan Zweig, *Brasilien: Ein Land der Zukunft* (Frankfurt am Main: Insel, 1981).

35 The full, original German-language text of Zweig's suicide note is included in Stefan Zweig, *The World of Yesterday*, trans. B. W. Huebsch and Helmut Ripperger (Lincoln: University of Nebraska Press, 1964), 438.

36 Herman Melville, *Moby Dick* (New York: Penguin, 2003), 625.

37 Walt Whitman, "When Lilacs Last in the Dooryard Blooom'd," in *Leaves of Grass* (New York: Bantam, 2004), 274–82.

38 Alexis de Tocqueville, *Democracy in America*, trans. Gerald Bevan (New York: Penguin, 2003).

39 Stefan Zweig, *Sternstunden der Menschheit* (Leipzig: Insel, 1927). This work has been translated in English a number of times and with different titles: *The Tide of Fortune: Twelve Historical Miniatures*, trans. Eden and Ceder Paul (New York: Viking, 1940); *Decisive Moments in History*, trans. Lowell A. Bangerter (Riverside, CA: 1998); *Shooting Stars*, trans. Anthea Bell (London: Pushkin Press, 2013).

40 Stefan Zweig, *Sternstunden der Menschheit: Vierzehn Historische Miniaturen* (Frankfurt am Main: Fischer, 2009).

41 Harry Zohn, "The Burning Secret of Stephen Branch, or a Cautionary Tale about a Physician who Could not Heal Himself," in *The World of Yesterday's Humanist Today*, ed. Marion Sonnenfeld (New York: State University of New York Press, 1983), 302–13.

42 Thomas Mann, "Brief an Erika Mann," in Weinzierl, 138 (italics mine).

43 Ibid. (italics and translation mine).

44 Thomas Mann, "Gedenkworte für den 'Aufbau,'" in Weinzierl, 139 (translation mine).

45 Ibid.

46 The notion of Zweig as an "impossible exile" is also at the center of George Prochnik's new biography of Zweig. See in particular pages 10–12.

47 Vivian Liska, "A Spectral Mirror Image: Stefan Zweig and his Critics," in *Stefan Zweig Reconsidered*, ed. Mark H. Gelber (Tübingen: Niemeyer, 2007), 217.

48 Stefan Zweig, "Letter from an Unknown Woman," in *The Royal Game and Other Stories*, trans. Jill Sutcliffe (New York: Holmes & Meier, 2000), 182 (hereafter cited in text as *RG*).

49 Andreas Huyssen, *After the Great Divide: Modernism, Mass Culture, Postmodernism* (Bloomington: Indiana University Press, 1986), 47.

50 Franz Kafka, "Dearest Father," in *Dearest Father: Stories and Other Writings*, trans. and ed. Ernst Kaiser and Eithne Wilkins (New York: Schocken, 1954), 139.

Part II. Drama and Fiction

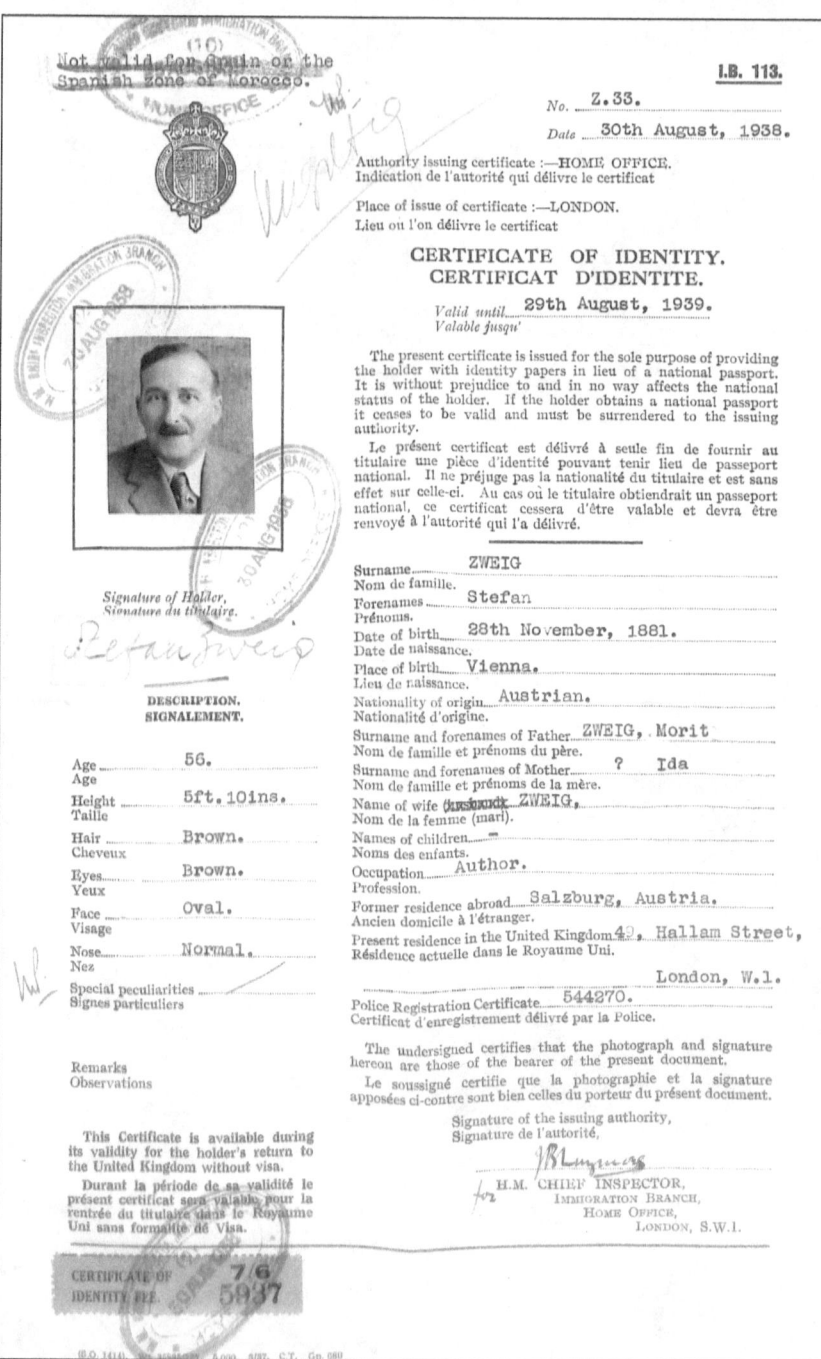

Fig. 2.1. Certificate of Identity. Courtesy of the Stefan Zweig Collection at Reed Library, State University of New York at Fredonia.

2: Stefan Zweig's Drama *Jeremias* in Context

John Warren

IT MAKES SENSE TO RECONSIDER STEFAN ZWEIG'S place as a dramatist in the history of interwar German drama because literary criticism, from Bernhard Diebold onward, has not dealt kindly with Zweig's drama.[1] Indeed, few critics writing of German drama between the wars mention him at all. There is only one book devoted to Zweig's drama, by the French critic Robert Dumont.[2] The article on Austrian drama in a recent compendium of essays on twentieth-century Austrian literature is symptomatic of the continued lack of interest in Zweig's drama elsewhere: it contains but two brief references to the drama *Jeremias* (*Jeremiah*, 1920) and no reference at all to any of his other plays.[3] However, like so many Austrian writers of his generation, Stefan Zweig was prepared to tackle every literary genre, and as a son of Vienna, which some have called a "theater city," it is not surprising that early in his literary career, in 1905–6, he, too, tried his hand at drama with *Tersites*, a play in verse about "the fate of the most ugly and most malignant of the Greeks before the walls of Troy."[4] But, as his autobiography makes clear, Zweig's attitude towards writing drama was conditioned by a series of tragic events surrounding three actors who were slated to act in his plays, but died before the plays could be performed.[5] Nevertheless, the complete edition of his dramas contains fourteen plays written between 1907 and 1935.[6] Five of these were translations: three of dramas by Émile Verhaeren and, more significantly in the context of this essay, an excellent translation of Romain Rolland's *Le temps viendra* (The Time will Come, 1902). The latter was a powerful anti-war drama set in the Boer War, first performed in Vienna in 1921 and later produced by Erwin Piscator in Berlin in 1923. These productions were followed by a free adaptation of Ben Jonson's comedy *Volpone*, based on a cursory reading of the play's outline in Taine's *Histoire de la littérature anglaise*. This was performed at the Burgtheater on November 6, 1926, with the great Viennese actor Raoul Aslan cast in the role of Mosca. It was described the following day by Raoul Auernheimer, theater critic for the *Neue Freie Presse*, as an improvement on the original English text, not a mere translation ("Nicht nur eine Erneuerung, sondern auch eine beträchtliche Verbesserung der englischen Urform").[7] Performed in Vienna in the style of *commedia dell'arte*, it was a comedy about money, with Zweig's witty poem "Das Geld, das Geld regiert die Welt" (Money, money rules the world) set to music and choreography. Translated into French by Jules Romains, it was a tremendous success in Paris in 1928, running for over 250 performances. It was staged around the world, including at the Theatre Guild in New York, where it starred Alfred Lunt. In addition, Zweig also translated Pirandello's drama *Non si sa come* (One does not know how, 1933) into German as *Man weiß nicht wie* (1934) at the author's request. There was also the excellent libretto for Richard Strauss's opera *Die schweigsame Frau* (The Silent Woman), based on a comedy by Ben Johnson, written in 1932 and premiered in Dresden in June 1935 amidst considerable controversy. This, of course, was after the National Socialists had taken power in Germany.[8] It was reviewed for the *Neue Freie Presse* on June 25 by Joseph Reitler from Dresden, who made the comparison with *Volpone*. Conducted by Karl Böhm, the reviewer sensed it was a "farewell opera." One other foray into the world of theater, not included in the volume of his dramas, was a collaboration with Austrian author Alexander Lernet-Holenia Zweig completed under the pseudonym Clemens Neydisser. This trivial comedy is what gave the young Austrian actress Paula Wessely her first stage success.[9]

Zweig's first play to be performed by Austria's national theater, the Burgtheater, was *Das Haus am Meer* (The House by the Sea, 1911), probably inspired by Tennyson's *Enoch Arden* and dealing with a family tragedy at a time when Germans were being press-ganged to serve in the English army in the American War of Independence. It was accepted by Alfred Berger, who died before the play was performed on October 26, 1912. This somewhat melodramatic and at times long-winded drama only received modest reviews. With his play *Das Lamm des Armen* (The Lamb of the Poor) first performed at the Burgtheater on April 12, 1930, Zweig joined the wave of German-speaking dramatists who, partly under the influence of Emil Ludwig's tremendously popular biography, tackled various aspects of Napoleon's life and career. The play, which Zweig called a tragi-comedy, is set first in Egypt in 1798, where Napoleon's roving eye has been caught by Pauline, nicknamed Bellilotte, the pretty wife of Lieutenant Fourès. To get rid of Fourès, Napoleon has him sent as courier back to France, but he is captured by the English, then released, and returns to reclaim his wife. It is hardly a serious drama on the Napoleon theme, such as the plays by Grabbe, Unruh, and even the Italian dictator Mussolini.[10] For the most part it received good notices and on March 15, 1930, it actually received one of those mass premieres so popular in Germany between the wars—with performances in Breslau, Hannover, Lübeck, and Prague. One suspects, however, that the good Viennese notices were as much due to the quality of the actors—Ewald Balser, Hilde Wagener, and Raoul Aslan as Napoleon[11]—and to the current vogue for what was termed "Die Flucht in die Geschichte" (the flight into history) as to any merits in the play. For although the plot was suitable for comedy, Zweig chose to emphasize more of the tragic elements.

But of all Zweig's theatrical works, it is *Jeremias* on which his legacy as a dramatist hinges, the play having been revived after the Second World War in Salzburg and Vienna, and, more recently (and with great success), in Oberammergau in 2007. Before we can come to an assessment of *Jeremias*, however, we must consider Zweig's reactions to the First World War. Zweig was thirty-two when the war broke out. He provides a description of the outbreak of war, and his reaction to the war, in two chapters of *Die Welt von Gestern*.[12] These chapters, and the articles he published in the *Neue Freie Presse* and *Das literarische Echo*, provide a more positive reminiscence of those fraught years than can be found in his wartime diaries and letters, which show the move from initial patriotic fervor to unhappiness and despair at the way events unfolded. Apart from feuilleton articles for the press, and the odd poem, the drama *Jeremias* was his only major work written during the war years.

But if reading what he wrote during the war does suggest a certain tendency to "run with the hare and hunt with the hounds," he is at least honest in admitting that his natural reaction was to avoid dangerous situations, and in suggesting that he may have been at fault for not being more heroic (*WvG* 262). His feelings towards the war are revealed in a variety of sources. Articles written at the outbreak of war as well as the accounts given by Zweig's biographer Donald Prater[13] and by Zweig's first wife, Friderike,[14] demonstrate the author's enthusiasm for the war. Others provide a harsher critique of Zweig's behavior during the war. C. E. Williams, in an essay on Zweig in his book, *The Broken Eagle*, provides a thorough account of Zweig's changing position during the war, commenting on the varying stands taken in his essays for the *Neue Freie Presse*—from initial enthusiasm and support for the Central Powers through to pacifism—and linking this to changing attitudes in Austrian government circles.[15] Edward Timms, in *Karl Kraus: Apocalyptic Satirist* (1986), writing in the spirit of the acerbic Karl Kraus, is less charitable in his treatment, stating that: "Zweig was a pacifist who lacked the courage of his own convictions. His private diaries reveal the dismal spectacle of a writer aghast at the horrors of war and yet active in collaborating in the writing of propaganda."[16] But one must point out, in Zweig's defense, that he only published one essay in the magazine *Donauland* that issued from the "Kriegsarchiv" (Austrian War Archive). Apart from the earliest feuilletons for the *Neue Freie Presse*, there is no evidence of any other prowar propaganda written by Zweig.

Zweig's life during the war falls into three parts: he initially responded to the war with enthusiasm; next, from the autumn of 1914 to 1917, Zweig, like many other Austrian writers, supported the war effort as a journalist and writer of propaganda for the Austrian War Archive. Finally, in November 1917, he obtained his release to Switzerland where he was able to meet pacifist friends—most notably Romain Rolland—with whom he had maintained close correspondence throughout the war. There, in Zurich, he saw the first performance of his pacifist drama *Jeremias*.[17]

Zweig's immediate reaction to the war was that of the majority of his contemporaries throughout Europe. In Belgium when war was finally declared, he traveled home, succumbed to the euphoria of the moment, and immediately went to the offices of the *Neue Freie Presse* for which he wrote the first of his feuilletons that would appear throughout the war years. "Ein Wort von Deutschland," published on August 6, 1914, was a document of unequivocal patriotism celebrating the comradeship of arms with Germany—an article resounding in its praise for Germany and the German role in Austrian life and culture. In it, he asserted: "Mit beiden Fäusten, nach rechts und links, muß Deutschland jetzt zuschlagen, der doppelten Umklammerung seiner Gegner sich zu entwinden" (Germany must strike out with both fists, right and left, in order to escape a double encirclement by its opponents).[18]

But his diaries and letters soon reveal a rapid revulsion against the war as men he knew were killed; as he read the statistics of battle losses; and we see him reacting to the flamboyant pro-war publications of Austrian colleagues such as Alfons Petzold, Hans Müller, and Hermann Bahr. As early as August 28, 1914, he was writing in his diary about events on the western front: "Das Blut friert einem in den Adern, all das auszudenken, was dort oben geschieht" (The blood freezes in one's veins when one thinks about all that is happening over there).[19] By September 2, 1914, Zweig is torn between horror at the bloodshed and the joy of victory on the eastern front. The hills of Lemberg must be red with blood, he wrote on September 2 (*T* 95), and a few days later, on September 11, he records reading in the *Berliner Tageblatt* that 70,000 men were lost at Lemberg (*T* 98) and writes that the Austrian military administration must be incompetent. By year's end (*T* 127), he is reading Goethe in conversation with Eckermann on the subject of war.[20] Zweig was so impressed by this that he wanted to pin the quote above his desk, "um mich nicht wankelmutig zu werden gegen meine eigenen Überzeugungen" (*T* 127; so that I don't waver in my own convictions). His diary entries and his letters continue to show a certain ambivalence as he welcomes victories, but on May 8, 1915, he is appalled at the sinking of the Lusitania: "Diese brutale Kriegführung ist jetzt einfach Wahnsinn" (*T* 164; This brutal waging of war is simply madness). And, a few days later, on May 15, he was greatly moved by an event on a tram when an elderly woman broke down into frightful sobbing as she saw a soldier who had lost a leg trying to seat himself: "Ich werde es nie vergessen" (*T* 171; I will never forget it), wrote Zweig. Strangely enough, he had already written a poem about a one-legged soldier for the Christmas edition of the *Neue Freie Presse* (December 25, 1914).

Letters can be less reliable than diary entries as evidence of personal feeling, as one often writes what one thinks the correspondent will want to hear. But reading from the wide range of what he wrote during the war years, we do obtain a fair idea of Zweig's standpoint.[21] His letters to Romain Rolland in Switzerland provide a commentary on his efforts to establish a group of international writers to oppose the war. Letters to other friends and literary colleagues describe his feelings towards the conflict, and, more importantly, how the play *Jeremias*, which he had begun writing in the spring of 1915, had become his escape from the pressures of the war. On September 25, 1916, Zweig wrote to Arthur Schnitzler about his "große Arbeit, die ich mit zusammengebissenen Zähnen vorwärtstreibe" (*Briefe* 116; major work that I am driving forwards with closely clenched teeth) suggesting that he should come to see him and read the early acts of *Jeremias* (*Briefe* 116).[22] We find him writing to Alfons Petzold in October 1914, taking him to task for his pro-war brochure "Krieg": "Mir ist alles verhaßt, was den Krieg feiert ... Wir haben nur eine Pflicht heute, die Gehässigkeit zu vermindern" (*Briefe* 26; I hate everything which glorifies war ... We have one duty today and that is to reduce the hatred). Later, in September 1917, he was to write a very firm letter to the ebullient Hermann Bahr, urging him to buy back his "Kriegssegen" (*Briefe* 151–52; blessings of war).[23]

On April 4, 1915, he published a lengthy article in the Sunday supplement of the *Neue Freie Presse* that further indicated his growing opposition to the war. The article, entitled "Warum nur Belgien, warum nicht auch Polen?" (Why only Belgium, why not Poland, too?),[24] was directed at the neutral states and outlined the horrific situation in war-torn Poland. If the Germans were to be blamed for violating Belgium's neutrality, so runs Zweig's argument, then there might be a case for condemning Russia for flooding into areas of (what today is) Poland. Seen in a negative light by some critics, this is to my mind an honest attempt to show the fuller extent of the horror caused by conflict. A few weeks later, an event that was crucial in changing his attitude to the war took place. This was Zweig's visit in July to war-ravaged Galicia, which helped further to confirm his disdain for the war. This, too, he wrote about in his autobiography (*WvG* 257–86). By then he had already decided to write the drama *Jeremias*, mentioned in a letter addressed to Julius Bab on July 19, 1915, upon his return from Galicia where, in addition to witnessing the results of unlimited warfare, he had also witnessed "viel jüdisches Elend" (*Briefe* 78; much Jewish misery). From now on many references to progress on the drama occur throughout his correspondence, one of the most revealing perhaps in a letter to Martin Buber on May 8, 1916 (*Briefe* 106–7). He tells Buber he is writing a major Jewish tragedy, one without a love interest and "ohne Theaterambitionen" (without ambitions for theatrical performance), but a drama that will show the tragedy of the Jewish people in the sense of "des ewigen Leidens, des ewigen Niedersturzes" (eternal suffering and eternal subjugation). Already we can see that what began as a specifically pacifist piece was now changing in concept to become the story of the Diaspora. On January 2, 1917, he wrote to Julius Bab that he had been working at something which he hoped would make his friends recognize that "his silence of several years was not weakness or laziness" (*Briefe* 127). Writing to Ami Kaemmerer on May 3, 1917, he comments on the political situation facing both Germany and Austria, and claims not to have taken part in the enthusiasm for the war so publicly displayed by Hugo von Hofmannsthal, Felix Salten, Hans Müller, and Richard Schaukal, writing, in a letter to Paul Zach dated September 7, 1915, that he has taken refuge in his writing: "Mein Ventil, um nicht zu ersticken in einer Welt, die einem das Wort verschloß" (*Briefe* 83; My escape from suffocating in a world where one was not allowed to publish). He was also able to report that the play was finished and had been sent to his publisher, the Insel Verlag in Germany. Much to his surprise the sales figures were so remarkable as to require a reprint. The figures he cites in his autobiography have been disputed and, writing at a distance of many years, he may be forgiven for thinking that his play was the first German-language anti-war drama to be performed (*WvG* 291–92).

A few months later, however, as Austrian attitudes towards the war changed, he was given permission to go to Switzerland, where he continued writing feuilletons for the *Neue Freie Presse* and met with his friend and political ally Romain Rolland and many others who had been campaigning against the war. In Zurich, as already mentioned, he saw the first performance of his play. Having received a contract with the *Neue Freie Presse* that enabled him to stay in Switzerland, it was from there, in the final year of the war, that he sent more positive articles back to the print media outlets in Vienna, many of which, such as the articles on Berta von Suttner [25] and on Henri Barbusse's novel *Le Feu*, have now been republished in the volume cited above, *Die schlaflose Welt*. Looking back on the writing of the play shortly before he died in 1942, Zweig tells us he saw himself as being in the tragic situation of the "defeatist" (*WvG* 252–54). Indeed, one of the feuilletons he sent back from Switzerland in July 1918 was a remarkable essay titled "Bekenntnis zum Defaitismus" (Admitting Defeatism), which ended with the exhortation: "Schreien wir unsere Kriegsfeindschaft mit diesem Wort in die Welt. Seien wir Flaumacher in der eisernen Zeit! Soyons défaitistes! Siamo disfattisti!" (Let us shout out into the world our hatred of war with these words. Let us be defeatists in this oppressive age!).[26]

Turning now to the play, we see that Zweig chose as his hero the symbolic figure of Jeremiah, the prophet whose warnings were given in vain.[27] Zweig claimed he was not setting out to write a specifically pacifist drama, but that he wanted to show that a man despised as weak and fearful at a time of uncontrolled feeling is generally the only one who, when defeat comes, can not only endure misery, but can rise above it. Reading both his autobiography and many of his letters we realize how much the writing of this play meant to him.[28] However, among the criticisms one might make of the work is the fact that having started with a pacifist message, the focus of the play changes, ending not in a direct attack on militarism but in the apotheosis of defeat. Stephen Beller has described it thus: "It is ultimately the Central European, emancipatory interpretation of Judaism, of the 'temple in your hearts,' which becomes the dominant theme. 'World-wandering is our abode, suffering our field and God our home [*Heimat*] in time.'"[29]

The play is loosely based on the book of Jeremiah, influenced by Joseph Ernest Renan's *L'histoire du people d'Israel*, and incorporates Renan's view of Jeremiah as a sort of pre-Christ figure. One could see the drama as a "godchild" of Richard Strauss's *Salome*, of Franz Werfel's prewar drama *Die Troerinnen* (which, as it happens, was performed in Vienna in 1916 although there is no record that Zweig attended a performance), and of Zweig's own first drama, *Tersites*. However, as we shall see, it also has much in common with the anti-war drama of German Expressionism.

The nine scenes unfold as follows: in scene 1, "Die Erweckung des Profeten" (The Awakening of the Prophet), Jeremias experiences a terrible vision of Jerusalem's forthcoming fate. In a long and painful confrontation between Jeremias and his mother, the mother threatens Jeremias with a curse if he proclaims God's word. Scene 2, "Die Warnung" (The Warning) shows—and this is derived from Zweig's own experience—the frenzy marking the outbreak of war, in this case a people wanting to unite with Egypt in alliance against Nebuchadnezzar. While the prophet Hananja proclaims a Holy War, it is Jeremias who presents a vision of a peaceful state, comparing it with his vision of war. Scene 3, "Das Gerücht" (The Rumor) reflects the part played by rumor, something Zweig witnessed in wartime Vienna, as we find mentioned repeatedly in his diaries. We also see the constant use of the patriotic slogan "Ewig währet Jerusalem" (Jerusalem will endure forever), matched in Austria and Vienna over many years, and during the war, by the cry "Österreich über alles wenn es nur will"/ *Austria erit in orbe ultima* (Austria will triumph if only it has the will).[30] Scene 4, "Das Wachen auf dem Walle" (Guard Duty on the Ramparts) brings a discussion about the rights and wrongs of war between two soldiers, while scene 5, "Die Prüfung des Profeten" (The Testing of the Prophet), returns to the domestic note of the first scene: Jeremias reaching his lowest point following the death of his mother. He is accused of murdering her and condemned to be thrown into the moat that serves as a refuse disposal for the city. Scene 6, "Stimmen um Mitternacht" (Voices at Midnight), introduces the weak

King of Jerusalem, Zedekia, who, faced with Nebuchadnezzar's demands for complete capitulation, is torn apart by a combination of pride and naked fear. Scene 7, "Die letzte Not" (The Final Deprivation), provides a reflection of the actual situation in Vienna, with Jeremias commenting on the fickleness of the mob (as Zweig did in his diaries), now driven to their lowest ebb by food shortages and attacking Jeremias in their desperation. Scene 8, "Die Umkehr" (The Reversal), portrays the day after the fall of Jerusalem, and like Job, Jeremiah turns against his God. We see a cellar full of refugees (recalling Zweig's experience in Galicia): the Chaldeans have occupied the city. Now Jeremias will try to rebuild the "temple" in the hearts of the people by giving a new and more positive meaning to the slogan "Ewig währet Jerusalem." It is with this scene that Zweig begins the move from anti-war drama to his commentary on the fate of the Jews. Finally, in scene 9, "Der ewige Weg" (The Eternal Road), we see the mob as leaderless: they have lost their rulers, with Zedekia blinded and his sons murdered. The message from Jeremias is a cruel one, pointing out that the Jews have not been chosen for a peaceful existence, but for exile. As they leave Jerusalem to embark into the Diaspora, their victors, noting their proud bearing, realize that "Man kann Menschen töten, aber nicht den Gott, der in ihnen lebt" (*Dramen* 508; One can kill men but not the God that dwells within them).

The vitality and vigor of the confrontational scenes between the Prophet and the crowds and between Jeremias and the Hananja (the people's prophet), allied to the biblical stage settings, would seem to have destined the play for a production by Max Reinhardt with a stage-set by Alfred Roller. Also dramatically impressive is the rise and fall of tension as Jeremias is spurned, then cast out, and finally given audience. However, as a play to be performed, it is far too long, and a more experienced dramatist, however troubled his soul, would not have allowed it to grow to such length—216 pages in the 1918 edition. But it is relatively easy to cut, and at the first performance in Zurich in February 1918, as we learn from Zweig's diary, three of the nine "Bilder" were deleted: "Das Gerücht" (scene 3), "Die Prüfung des Propheten" (scene 5) and "Die letzte Not" (scene 7). When performed in Vienna at the Deutsches Volkstheater in 1919, it was cut even more drastically by the director Alfred Bernau, losing four of its nine scenes.[31]

There are other faults in the play, some of which were noted by contemporary critics. Alfred Polgar, exercising that ironic wit of which he was a master, wrote a negative review of the Viennese production for the *Weltbühne*, showing little sympathy for the anti-war rhetoric and suggesting that the prophet's passion was never dramatic but only rhetorical.[32] He also noted that the two most striking moments in the play—the reversals of attitude towards Jeremias by Baruch and by the king Zedekia—were too sudden and in no way motivated. The German theater critic

Bernhard Diebold, while recognizing many of the play's strengths—the crowd scenes, the contrasted opponents, the use of day and night—noted the lack of a clear forward drive from anguish through to fulfillment, and found the play shared a similar quality of monotony with Werfel's *Die Troerinnen*.[33] Viennese critics of the 1919 performance were more positive, and as we shall see, both Raoul Auernheimer of the *Neue Freie Presse* and Otto König of the *Arbeiter Zeitung* noted the play's relevance for Vienna's recent history.

Looking at the play as an anti-war drama, we find, unsurprisingly perhaps, that the major pacifist elements appear in the earlier scenes featuring strong statements by the prophet Jeremias attacking war with fiery rhetoric: in scene 1, "schon steiget des Krieges rot Gestirn aus der Nacht" (*Dramen* 369; already war's blood-red star is rising out of the night); in scene 2, "Groß in Büchern aber ein Würger ist er in Wahrheit und ein Schänder des Lebens" (*Dramen* 377; It may be great in books, but in reality it strangles and violates life), and "ein bös und bissig Tier ist der Krieg, er frißt das Fleisch von den Starken und saugt das Mark von den Mächtigen, die Städte zermalmt er in seinen Kinnladen, und mit den Hufen zerstampft er das Land" (*Dramen* 383; War is an evil and vicious animal, eating the flesh of the strong and extracting the marrow from the mighty, towns he crushes in his jaws and he crushes the land under his hooves). This language is every bit as evocative as that of Georg Heym's famous pre-war poem "Der Krieg" (War, 1912)[34] and, used here in the confrontation between Jeremias and Hananja, is as dramatically compelling as the language used in a similar disputation between the pleader for peace, Eustache de Saint Pierre, and the French knight, Duguesclin, in Georg Kaiser's *Die Bürger von Calais* (The Citizens of Calais, 1916).

Jeremias follows this by stressing the importance of "life": "Abtut Gottes Namen vom Kriege, denn nicht Gott führet Krieg, sondern Menschen! Heilig ist kein Krieg, heilig ist kein Tod, heilig ist nur das Leben!" (*Dramen* 384; Remove God's name from war, for it is not God who wages war but mankind! No war is holy, nor is death, only life is holy!). In scene 4, two soldiers on guard duty discuss the rights and wrongs of war. This provides at a simple level an effective analysis of pro-and anti-war positions (*Dramen* 403–6). The scene, which is reminiscent of a similar discussion in Romain Rolland's *Le temps viendra* and of the Socratic discussion between the first and fifth sailors in Reinhold Goering's *Seeschlacht* (Naval Encounter, 1917), is an effective way dramatically of positing the arguments for and against war.[35]

One of the soldiers asks: why do men go to war? He receives the answer that that's the way it has always been. He next asks why God wants war and is told that the people want it for his sake. Then, logically, comes the question as to who the people are, to which no answer is given. More pertinently, the next question asks how it is that war and death come from a God who gave us "life" for the sake of life? To which the answer comes: "Ich tu mein geheiß, schärf mir den Speer und nicht meine Zunge" (*Dramen* 404; I do my duty and sharpen my spear not my tongue). We get no further, then, than Gerhart Hauptmann's reply who, when asked to condemn the sacking of Louvain, is reported to have replied succinctly: "Krieg ist Krieg" (War is war).[36] The enemy is described as being cruel as cats and perfidious as snakes, and when the doubter suggests they must be surely be men like us with wives and children at home just like us, he is told quite simply: "Sie sind unsere Feinde und wir müßen sie hassen" (*Dramen* 405; They are our enemies and we must hate them.)[37] The final question is: "Aber Gott hat gesagt und es stehet geschrieben: 'Du sollst nicht töten'" (*Dramen* 405; But God has said and it is written down, Thou shalt not kill.) As answer, the questioner is told that it is a question of "Aug um Auge, Zahn um Zahn" (an eye for an eye, a tooth for a tooth). The message comes down to the old mantra: "Ours is not to reason why. Ours is but to do and die." One can compare this scene of Zweig's with the pivotal scene in Goering's play,[38] and also with the discussion in act 2 of Rolland's play where there is a more positive outcome in that one soldier lays down his arms, refuses to fight further, and is of course shot as a mutineer (*Die Zeit wird kommen*, *Dramen* 541–47). Zweig's play then widens his attacks on those who accept war: women who seem happy to lose their sons, those who prefer honor over sacrifice, and those commanders happily prepared to throw away thousands of lives. As in scene 6, "Wie ihr doch redet vom Sterben! Wie leicht werft ihr das Wort! Siebenzigtausend tötet euer Trotz, bedenket es ihr Eilfertigen." (*Dramen* 444; How lightly you speak of dying. How easily you toss out the word! Seventy thousand killed by your defiance. Just think of that, you zealots.)

But as we have seen, Zweig was writing this play for himself, not as a stage production, and this may account for the shifting of perspective away from its pacifist beginnings. Many of his letters show an increased interest in the fate of the Jews, such as that to Abraham Schwadron on June 9, 1917 (*Briefe* 145), telling him he has finished *Jeremias* and wondering what the possible Jewish reception of the play might be. Martin Buber, he writes, who has just seen the final section, is clearly against Zweig's feeling that the Jews should strive for an "eternal Jerusalem" as their spiritual home. Buber favored the return to Palestine. "Für mich," writes Zweig, "ist es die Größe des Judentums übernational zu sein" (*Briefe* 145; For me the greatness of the Jews is to be above nationality.) Certainly, in retrospect he was to refer to the play as presenting the glorification of defeat rather than as being a straightforward pacifist, anti-war drama.

Formally, the play has been seen by some critics as a work that could be linked to the German Expressionists, several of whose plays, listed below, raised a banner against the war. It is perhaps of interest to note that

Zweig, writing in the *Literarische Echo* as early as 1909, had discussed the new German literary movement with some sympathy as well as criticism. This essay was then used in his book on Émile Verhaeren in 1913 and at the same time used as an introductory essay in Paul Zech's short-lived journal *Das neue Pathos* of the same year. Zweig draws attention to two dangers in the Expressionists' use of pathos in their poetry: first, to the use of empty gestures not arising from inner conviction; and second, to the misuse of language:

> Die Banalisierung der Worte *plus sonores que solides* ist die andere. Hier aber in diesem neuen Pathos ist dazu noch eine neue, die der Überhitzung des Gefühls, die der Übermäßigung, ungesunden Exaltation, die dann notwendig einer Abspannung weichen muß. Man kann nicht konstant fiebern in Erregung, nicht ununterbrochen begeistert sein. Und in diesen Gedichten ist der Wille zur unaufhörlichen Ekstase.[39]

> [The cheapening of words *plus sonores que solides* is the other. But here in this new pathos is yet another, that of the overheating of feeling, an unhealthy exaltation, which then of necessity has to weaken to an anti-climax. One cannot constantly be in a fever of excitement, be constantly inspired. In these poems one finds the desire for never ending ecstasy.]

That Jeremias and others in the play frequently break out into "Ekstase" doesn't need to be mentioned here, but the use of a wildly rhetorical language, and at key points in the drama, the change into a more heightened form of language, free rhythms, and a choric mode of speech[40] does take us into the language of the Expressionist dramatists as, for example, where the sailors in their gun turret at the end of Goering's *Seeschlacht* chant their feelings. We must admit that in Expressionist drama a superfluity of language sometimes threatens to stifle the visionary element, as is the case in Zweig's *Jeremias*. The "Schrei," the "scream"—that existential outburst of "Angst" which comes from man's tormented and puzzled soul—is another feature; *Seeschlacht* starts with such a scream and one certainly seems to be hovering over Zweig's play. Another common element of Expressionist drama can be seen in the use of symbolic characters, often completely impersonal (i.e., He, She, Mother, Father, Son), but here it is the figure of the prophet. Expressionist dramatists were fond, too, of what is known as "Stationendrama," whereby a succession of episodes or "stations" replaces a continuously developing action. This has been seen as an analogy to the depiction of the Stations of the Cross and in several Expressionist plays the "cross" itself is featured. The symbolic hero, sometimes hailed as "der neue Mensch" (the "new man"), is often seen as a Christ-like figure, as is Jeremias. We see the mob wanting to crucify him and he stands with his arms stretched out in the form of a cross. Here we see similarities with the endings of both Kaiser's *Die Bürger von Calais* and Fritz von Unruh's *Ein Geschlecht* (A Family). Throughout Expressionism we find figures whose self-imposed task is to take upon themselves the suffering of the world; such men as Eustache de Saint Pierre and Jeremias. He is ready and willing to suffer, wishing only to be the sacrifice of atonement in bringing peace to Jerusalem and its inhabitants.

But *Jeremias* has more than such elements in common with these plays, to which we may add Romain Rolland's early work of 1902, *Le temps viendra*, which Zweig translated in 1918/19 as *Die Zeit wird kommen*, and which, as mentioned above, was performed in Vienna (1921) and subsequently by Piscator in Berlin. Zweig claimed that his *Jeremias* was the first pacifist drama and it certainly was in Austria; however, Zweig's German contemporaries were also producing anti-war dramas, all of which seemed to be written at about the same time, and managed, if only briefly, to evade censorship and reach the German stage. Writing anti-war drama during a war in a country with strict censorship was not easy, but that several German dramatists managed it—albeit for very limited runs—can be seen from the following list:

- René Schickele, *Hans im Schnakenloch* (Hans of Schnakenloch, 1916), Frankfurt am Main, 1916, then Berlin, 1917.
- Georg Kaiser, *Die Bürger von Calais* (The Citizens of Calais, 1916), Frankfurt am Main 1917, then Vienna, 1917.
- Walter Hasenclever, *Antigone* (Antigone, 1917), Leipzig, 1917.
- Reinhard Goering, *Seeschlacht* (Naval Encounter, 1917), Dresden, 1918, then Berlin, 1918.
- Stefan Zweig, *Jeremias* (Jeremiah, 1917), Zurich, 1918, then Nuremberg, 1918.
- Fritz von Unruh, *Ein Geschlecht* (A Family, 1917), Frankfurt am Main, 1918, Berlin, 1918. [41]

Of these dramas, only Kaiser's *Die Bürger von Calais* was performed in Vienna during the war, but, as critic Alfred Polgar has pointed out, the most problematic sections of the text were excised for that production. To avoid direct confrontation with military censorship, deception was necessary. Hasenclever turned to Greek myth, Kaiser to the Hundred Years' War between France and England, Unruh to "abstract" Expressionism (showing in symbolic form the effect total war could have on a family), and Zweig to the Old Testament. There were, however, two plays given more realistic settings: Schickele's *Hans im Schnakenloch* was set at the outbreak of war in Alsace, giving a picture of Prussian militarism with the local policeman being called "der Teufel" (the devil) by the anti-Prussian element. Although Schickele claimed that his play had nothing to do with the war, the last act presented in graphic detail the results brought about by war—a burning barn, corpses onstage, and troops advancing. This was permitted for the limited performance in Frankfurt, but the German Embassy in Vienna managed to intervene to prevent the Vienna production from taking place, and soon after that the ban was extended to Germany.[42] Reinhard Goering started his play with a "Schrei" (the expressionist scream), and set it in the gun turret of a German battleship at the Battle of Jutland, where, despite the disputation, no one mutinies and we witness a horrific and dehumanized final scene, with the sailors now in gas masks. The Berlin correspondent for the *Neue Freie Presse*, Paul Goldmann, noted in his March 1918 review that Goering solved the problem posed in the discussion about the rights and wrongs of war, not through thought, but by the disembodied voice of command, and that the play's message was "duty," a message he saw as a truly German one: "Die Lösung die das Drama gibt, lautet die Pflicht [. . .] ein echt Deutscher!"[43]

It is clear that pacifist drama would share many key concepts. There is no mention in his diaries or his letters that Zweig had any idea of what his fellow dramatists were writing, but comparing key elements of these dramas will show how his play was firmly set in the body of German pacifist drama. I have already mentioned the questioning of obedience and duty, and we note that the discussions in the plays by Zweig and Rolland are at a more natural level than the more Socratic discussion between Goering's "God seeker" and his "believer in humanity." These ideas appear in different forms in other dramas, as for example in Hasenclever's *Antigone*, where the heroine's refusal to obey Creon represents the voice of humanity rising up against authoritarianism and tyranny. In the first act of Kaiser's *Die Bürger von Calais*, we see the clash of two philosophies: peaceful economic activity versus duty and honor. In the play's first act, Eustache de Saint Pierre, who represents the peaceful town of Calais, firmly rejects the course of militaristic duty as outlined by the character of the French officer Duguesclin in the play. Kaiser reinforces the hollowness of the military ethic when Duguesclin, hearing of the defeat of the French king's army, immediately offers himself and his sword to the English forces.[44] In symbolic mode, too, in Unruh's *Das Geschlecht*, we see the very basis of duty and obedience as an obligation on the citizen crumble away as the play moves toward a new dawn and a new world and the officer's red cloak is left to be bleached white by the rising sun.[45] Alongside the concept of duty ("Pflicht"), a number of additional key concepts must be discredited: for example, "Ehre," and "Vaterland" (honor and fatherland). In scene 6 of *Jeremias* there is much debate as to whether they should accept Nebuchadnezzar's brutal conditions. When Jeremias faces King Zedekia he tells him: "Besser als Ehre ist Friede, besser Leiden denn Sterben" (*Dramen* 452; Peace is better than honor, to suffer better than to die). Hasenclever's Antigone turns on the crowd in act 2, scene 4, and scornfully points out that the true meaning of the words "Krieg, Feind, Ehre" (war, enemy, and honor) results in plundered homes and desecrated temples.[46] Another example comes from the last scene of Goering's *Seeschlacht* as we hear the voices of the dying sailors: "Vaterland, Vaterland, o lieb Vaterland./ Wir sind Schweine,/ Die auf den Metzger warten./ Wir sind Kälber, die abgestochen werden." (Fatherland, dear fatherland. We are swine waiting for the butcher. We are calves waiting to be slaughtered.)[47]

Among the many features these plays have in common is the use of the vision. We have noted that Zweig's play opens with Jeremias's vision of oncoming disaster, while in the second scene ("The Warning") he presents visions both of the peaceful state and of war. Hasenclever's Antigone, too, has a vision of a new brotherhood of mankind which will be born out of the horrors of war, and in the same play Tiresias, like Jeremias, conjures up a visionary representation of the results of war (act 3, scene 6,)[48] Eustache de Saint Pierre's vision in Kaiser's play (act 1) is of a peaceful and prosperous Calais set against the destruction brought about by war. The central vision of these wartime Expressionist dramatists however is that of the regeneration of mankind, symbolised in the person of "der neue Mensch" (the new Man) who becomes a central figure in German Expressionist drama and in this context is represented by the self-sacrificial deaths of Antigone and Eustache de Saint Pierre.

The hero figures speak for themselves, but what of the rulers and the masses they wish to influence? *Jeremias* and *Antigone* both reveal the "ruler," Zedekia and Kreon, as willfully ruthless and, in the case of Kreon, brutal. Both these rulers were seen by contemporary critics as having strong similarities with the respective emperors of Austria and Germany. Goering's *Seeschlacht*, however, suggests that guilt is not the prerogative of the ruler alone: the sailors, now speaking in chorus and responding to the orders of the anonymous voice over the loudspeaker admit that, although they did not choose the way, they did what they were told and are equally guilty.[49] As for the treatment of the masses, it is probably Zweig, influenced as his diaries show by his own observations of the Viennese reactions to victory and defeat, who exploits them with greatest impact on stage. We see from his diary entries that Zweig witnessed the shifting moods of the Viennese in the streets, as for example, at the news of the fall to the Austrians of Lemberg in June 1915. Jeremias must face up to the crowd, its fluctuations, rumors and inconsistencies: (scene 3, 396). Zweig knew, too, how Viennese morale changed as hunger and deprivation began to bite in Vienna by 1917. The prophet points out the fickleness of the mob, now driven to their lowest ebb by lack of food: "Die jetzt Friede schreien, hörte ich toben nach dem Kriege [. . .] Doppelzüngig ist deine Seele, und jeder Wind wendet deine Meinung" (*Dramen* 465; Those who are now crying for peace I heard raging for war [. . .] two-faced is your soul and every wind changes your opinions). Zweig is particularly strong on the way hatred can be aroused in a mob situation, and he wrote to Ernst Hardt on October 21, 1915, that the Old Testament was a world of hatred (*Briefe* 91). Hasenclever, in his *Antigone*, orchestrates the mob with greater subtlety, but its fickleness and latent menace are clearly revealed in their desire to strip and stone Antigone.[50]

How far, we may ask, do these plays provide a resonance with the then-contemporary situation in Austria and Germany? Quite apart from the pacifist message, some of these works possessed a quite particular and easily recognizable parallel to contemporary events and personalities. Schickele's realistic play, set in Alsace on the frontier, revealed the divided loyalties of the inhabitants of that much fought over province. Kreon uses words and phrases beloved of Wilhelm 11 (act 1, scene 3),[51] while King Zedekia could be taken either as a general comment on the "ruler," but also more particularly as a direct comment on the young Emperor Karl. Raoul Auernheimer, in his very positive feuilleton "Das Trauerspiel des Pessimisten" (A Pessimist's Tragedy) published in the *Neue Freie Presse*, October 10, 1919, makes the connection with Karl, while others have seen a reflection of the old Emperor Franz Josef, one of whose titles was "King of Jerusalem," and Zweig uses the words of both Franz Joseph and Wilhelm concerning the war, "Ich habe es nicht gewollt" (I did not want it). Finally, the enthusiasm of the Viennese masses for the Habsburgs and for Vienna that is captured with so much irony by Kraus in what may be the greatest of anti-war dramas written after the war, *Die letzten Tage der Menschheit*, was splendidly displayed by Zweig in his portrayal of the mob with its constant cry of "Ewig währet Jerusalem." Looked at more closely, the parallels between the Jerusalem of Zweig's drama and Vienna in 1917 seem to be precisely plotted; the question of the Treaty with Egypt and relations with that country parallel the relationship that existed between Vienna (Austria) and Berlin (Prussia). The question of "doves and hawks" (the "hawks" allied to a fanatical faith) providing two sets of advisers had their parallels in Vienna, while, on a personal as well as a general note, the treatment of the pacifist as "Sprachrohr gegen den Krieg" (a mouthpiece against the war) was extensively covered by Zweig. In this play the charges leveled against the anti-war protester Jeremias are clearly outlined: cowardice, madness, being in the pay of the enemy, being defeatist, and undermining morale. One further practical impact of the war on Vienna is also featured at the end of the play—desperation caused by hunger resulting from acute food shortages.

Is there any commonality, one asks, in the endings of these pacifist dramas? For their conclusions often seem ambivalent and puzzling, insufficiently clear, in works that supposedly take a direct stand against war. Romain Rolland's much earlier play *Le temps viendra* (1902) ended on a hopeful, if rather simplistic, note: "Die Zeit wird kommen, da alle Menschen um Wahrheit wissen werden, da sie Pflugscharen schmieden werden aus den Schwertern, und Sicheln aus den Lanzen und der Löwe weiden wird neben dem Lamme. Die Zeit wird kommen." (*Dramen* 558; The time will come when mankind will know the truth, as they forge ploughshares from swords and sickles out of lances. And the lion will feed alongside the lamb. That time will come.)

Alfred Polgar ended his review for *Die Weltbühne* with the cynical but sadly realistic comment that either the lion's claws would have fallen out or the lamb would have grown some ("Möglich. Aber da werden dem Löwen die Krallen ausgefallen oder dem Lamm welche gewachsen sein.").[52] These plays written during the war, however, provide no such optimistic conclusion. In *Antigone*, after Kreon (like Kaiser Wilhelm) has abdicated, the "mob" accepts that a supernatural force has triumphed and sinks to the ground in prayer, but it is not clear whether this is from fear or from the desire to renounce war and welcome the new brotherhood of man. The sailors of *Seeschlacht* accept their lot as "lambs to the slaughter," albeit as an oblique comment on the concept of "dying for the 'Vaterland.'" It was easier to obey and fire their guns than to mutiny. The message in *Ein Geschlecht* is also ambiguous as the remaining members of the family return to the valley, and, hopefully, to a new and better world, leaving the red cloak of autocratic authoritarian rule to bleach in the mountain sunshine. Only in *Die Bürger von Calais* do we have a visual presentation of the triumph of the "New Man" as the English king and his followers kneel (unintentionally, it must be stated) before his dead body in the church. In Zweig's play the Jews leave Jerusalem with heads held high, although defeated: "Wir wandern den heiligen Weg unserer Leiden,/ Von Prüfung und Prüfung zur Läuterung. [. . .] "Heimwärts zu Gott" (*Dramen* 508; We walk the holy path of our suffering/ from trial to trial, onwards to purification. [. . .] Home to God). The Chaldean soldiers look on in amazement: "Haven't we destroyed their God's altars, haven't we defeated them?' asks the captain and receives the reply: "Man kann Menschen töten, aber nicht den Gott, der in ihnen lebt. Man kann ein Volk bezwingen, doch nie sein Geist." (*Dramen* 508; You can kill men but not the God within them. You can vanquish a people but not its spirit.)

This final scene from *Jeremias* will remind us of the aforementioned quote from Stephen Beller's article, and we should ask how the play was seen after November 1918. The play was still considered to be primarily an anti-war play and, even before its staging in Zurich, it had been read by such men as Heinrich Lammasch and Ignaz Seipel, who were key figures in the Austrian movement for a negotiated peace.[53] Zweig describes his meeting with Lammasch in his autobiography and also comments on the changes in the government's attitude towards Germany, although he claims he was unaware of these key shifts in policy (*WvG*, 294–98). With the war at an end, anti-war drama could now be performed in Vienna and, in September 1919, Unruh's *Ein Geschlecht* was performed at the Burgtheater, followed in May 1920 by Franz Werfel's *Die Troerinnen* (with two new scenes emphasizing the misery of war). The Deutsches Volkstheater, under Alfred Bernau, staged Hasenclever's *Antigone* in June 1919 and Zweig's *Jeremias* on September 9 of that year. Originally, it was only slated for one performance, but it was so successful that Bernau kept it in the repertoire for several more performances, alternating it with his production of Goethe's *Torquato Tasso*. The reviews were very positive.[54] Raoul Auernheimer, in the *Neue Freie Presse* (October 10), wrote that Zweig's play illustrated quite directly the political situation in Vienna during the war and furthermore suggested that this pessimistic tragedy would be one of the few literary works of the war that would last, and that the cry it sends forth would echo for years to come, as it stemmed from the painful experience of a poet's deeply shattered spirit ("gehört zu den wenigen bleibenden Dichtungen diese Krieges. Der Schrei, der sich ihm entringt, wird lange nachhallen, weil er aus dem durch schmerzlichstes Erleben zutief erschütterten Gemüte eines Dichters quillt."). Otto König, writing an unusually long feuilleton review in the *Arbeiter Zeitung* (October 11), ranked Zweig with Shaw, Hasenclever, Barbusse, Goering, Feutchtwanger und several others who had dared to question the war, and concluded that he had not only made the plot topical, but had brought what is ever present in human destiny and human suffering into contemporary events. ("Er hat auch nicht nur gewaltsam aktualisiert, sondern nur das Ewige im Völkerschicksal und Menschenleid in den Vordergrund des zeitlichen Geschehens gerückt.") Nevertheless, both reviewers would no doubt have been surprised at the play's subsequent history. For unlike the other German pacifist plays, it has lived to fight again.

It was brought back out of retirement after the Second World War and performed in Salzburg with such success that they "guested" the drama in Vienna. Somewhat to my surprise, in 2007, it was again revived, at Oberammergau as a "festival drama" in the gap between the ten-year cycle of the Passion Play, using the amateur village actors and their biblical costumes to great effect on the large Festival stage. Christian Stückl, who produced the play, is artistic director of the Munich Volkstheater, and director of the last two "Passion Plays" in Oberammergau. He also produces the Salzburg Festival's production of Hofmannsthal's *Jedermann*. As Jeremiah, he cast Martin Norz, the villager who performed the role of Christ at Oberammergau in 2000, and the play was performed very successfully with new music by Markus Zwink, three choirs, and a sensibly trimmed-down text. Stückl apparently did not cut scenes as had happened in Zurich and Vienna, but trimmed excessive verbiage to reduce its length to a managable two-and-a-half hours. Apparently, what interested this experienced producer of festival drama was the pacifist rather than the Jewish element of the play. "How does one face up to the idea of a God-given war?" he asked, stressing that this was a contemporary theme, because, in his words, both George Bush and Osama bin Laden have called on God to justify their wars. With more than 500 actors, singers, and musicians, he produced what one German critic called a "parable about the senselessness of war." He placed the emphasis of his production on the youngsters who refuse to listen to Jeremiah and, as the critic Georg Kasch wrote,[55] the cry of "Krieg, Krieg, Krieg" (War, war, war) resounded like a hurricane from the stage, accompanied by the stamping of spears and the raising of fists, all of which made a tremendous and irresistible impact on him. The producer even managed to maintain this anti-war mood in the closing scene of the play, wrote Kasch. As the music faded away, the defeated people of Jerusalem were seen disappearing into the darkness offstage. They left Jerusalem in flames behind them, a deserted city. The final scene, the critic suggested, was both a warning in symbolic form and a testament to an impressive, convincing and living theatrical tradition. It would seem that Stefan Zweig's most personal play lives on.

Notes

[1] Bernhard Diebold, *Anarchie im Drama: Kritik und Darstellung der modernen Dramatik* (Frankfurt: Frankfurter Verlagsanstalt, 1922), 431–33.

[2] Robert Dumont, *Le Théâtre de Stefan Zweig* (Paris: Presses Universitaires de France, 1975).

[3] Judith Beniston, "Drama in Austria," in *A History of Austrian Literature 1918–2000*, ed. Katrin Kohl and Ritchie Robertson (Rochester, NY: Camden House, 2006), 23, 34–35.

[4] In a letter from Zweig to Ellen Key dated August 12, 1905, cited in D. A. Prater, *European of Yesterday* (Oxford: Clarendon Press, 1972), 33–34.

[5] Stefan Zweig, *Die Welt von Gestern* (Frankfurt am Main: Fischer, 1970), 196–203 (hereafter cited in text as *WvG*).

[6] Stefan Zweig, *Die Dramen*, ed. Richard Friedenthal (Frankfurt am Main: Fischer, 1964) (hereafter cited in text as *Dramen*).

[7] Raoul Auernheimer. *Neue Freie Presse*. November 7, 1926: 2.

[8] Details of the controversy caused by the performance and the reactions of both Zweig and Strauss can be found in Prater 234–36 and 240–41, and in *Die Welt von Gestern*, 378–87.

[9] Hanns Arens, ed., *Stefan Zweig im Zeugnisse seiner Freunde* (Munich: Langen Müller, 1968), 84.

[10] *Hundert Tage* (One Hundred Days) co-written with the Italian dramatist Giovacchiono Forzano and premiered at the Burgtheather in Vienna with great success on April 22, 1933, starring Werner Krauss.

[11] Werner Krauss (famed for his various performances in the role of Napoleon) had wanted to play the part in Vienna, and a delegation was sent to confer with Zweig, then in Italy, without success.

[12] Stefan Zweig, *Die Welt von Gestern* (Frankfurt am Main: Fischer, 1970), "Die ersten Stunden des Krieges," 246–71 and "Der Kampf um die geistige Brüderschaft," 272–90, and, in Anthea Bell's new translation, Stefan Zweig, *The World of Yesterday* (London: Pushkin Press, 2009), 237–60 and 261–77 (hereafter cited in text as *WvG* and *WoY*, respectively).

[13] Donald Prater, *European of Yesterday: A Biography of Stefan Zweig* (Oxford: Clarendon Press, 1972), 65–107.

[14] Friderike M. Zweig, *Stefan Zweig wie ich ihn erlebte* (Stockholm: Neuer Verlag, 1947).

[15] C. E. Williams. *The Broken Eagle: The Politics of Austrian Literature from Empire to Anschluss* (London: Elek., 1974).

[16] Edward Timms, *Karl Kraus: Apocalyptic Satirist* (New Haven: Yale University Press, 1986), 299.

[17] It was performed in a shortened version at the Stadttheater on February 27, 1918. For Zweig, the play's theme was the need "to seek the renewal of the spirit in defeat itself." See Prater, 103.

[18] The article is reprinted in *Die schlaflose Welt*, 30–33. Unless otherwise noted, all translations from German are my own.

[19] Stefan Zweig, *Tagebücher* (Frankfurt am Main: Fischer, 1984), 93 (hereafter cited in text as *T*).

[20] Johann Peter Eckermann, *Gespräche mit Goethe* (Zurich: Artemis, 1949), entry of March 14, 1830, 731–32. Goethe, discussing attacks on his "lack of patriotism" with Eckermann, told him that he would not have been able to bear weapons unless full of hatred, and only as a young man, a twenty-year-old, could he have felt that hate. Zweig obviously felt the same.

[21] Stefan Zweig, *Briefe 1914–1919* (Frankfurt am Main: Fischer, 1998) (hereafter cited in text as *Briefe*).

[22] It is worth noting that Arthur Schnitzler and the satirical journalist Karl Kraus were the only two major Austrian writers who refused to support the war. As it happens neither was liable for military service.

[23] This term refers to a pro-war article by Bahr.

[24] Stefan Zweig, *Die schlaflose Welt: Aufsätze und Aufträge aus den Jahren 1909–1941*, ed. Knut Beck (Frankfurt am Main: Fischer, 1983), 52–67.

[25] Berta von Suttner was the recipient of the first Nobel Peace Prize in 1905, having published a novel *Die Waffen nieder* (1894) and later edited the international pacifist journal with the same name. She was known in popular parlance as "Die Friedens Berta" and was acquainted with Zweig.

[26] The essay was not published in Vienna, but in the July/August 1918 issue of the Berlin-based pacifist journal, *Friedens-Warte. Blätter für zwischenstaatliche Organisation*. Reprinted in *Die schlaflose Welt*, 122–25.

[27] Stefan Zweig, *Jeremias: Eine dramatische Dichtung in neun Bildern* (Leipzig: Insel, 1918). All references to the play are taken from Stefan Zweig, *Die Dramen*, ed. Richard Friedenthal (Frankfurt am Main: Fischer, 1964) (hereafter cited in text as *Dramen*).

[28] See, for example, his letter of July 19, 1915, to Julius Bab (*Briefe* 78), or the Schnitzler letter mentioned earlier. His diary entry of May 18, 1915, (*Tagebücher* 172) records the start of his work on the play; that of June 1, 1915, indicates that has drawn up a plan for the drama.

[29] Stephen Beller, "The Tragic Carnival," in *European Culture in the Great War*, ed. Aviel Roshwald and Richard Stiles (Cambridge: Cambridge University Press, 1999), 150.

[30] This slogan was first coined by Philipp Wilhelm von Hörnigk in 1684, used again as Prinz Eugen's battle cry, then picked up by the polemicist Franz Schuselka in the revolutionary year 1848. Much used in Imperial Austria, it was finally taken up by the right-wing chancellor, Dollfuss, in the 1930s.

[31] Reading the play, one feels that there was no need to excise whole scenes, but rather to curtail their length and wordiness!

[32] Alfred Polgar, *Die Weltbühne*, vol. 2 (1919): 545.

[33] Bernhard Diebold, *Anarchie im Drama: Kritik und Darstellung der modernen Dramatik* (Frankfurt: Frankfurter Verlagsanstalt, 1922), 432.

[34] Georg Heym, "Der Krieg," in *Menschheitsdämmerung: Ein Dokument des Expressionismus*, ed. Kurt Pinthus (Reinbek bei Hamburg: Rowohlt, 1959), 79–80.

[35] I use the title given to the play in the translation by J. M. Ritchie and J. D. Stowell in *Vision and Aftermath: Four Expressionist War Plays* (London: Calder & Boyars 1969).

[36] Hauptmann makes this statement in a letter of August 29, 1914, to Romain Rolland, cited in Gerhart Hauptmann, *Sämtliche Werke*, Vol. 11 (Frankfurt am Main: Propyläen, 1974), 847–49.

[37] One wonders whether Zweig was aware of the fraternization between German and English soldiers on the western front at Christmas 1914.

[38] Reinhart Goering, *Seeschlacht*, in Günther Rühle, ed., *Zeit und Theater 1* (Berlin: Propyläen, 1973), 362–77.

[39] "Das neue Pathos," in Stefan Zweig, *Émile Verhaeren* (Frankfurt am Main: Fischer, 1984), 139–40.

[40] The frequency with which this occurs can be seen by checking the following page references in Zweig, *Die Dramen*: 369–71, 422–31, 453–57, 477–80, 485–87, 489–90, 497–508.

[41] Reviews of the plays by Schickele, Kaiser, Goering, Unruh, and Hasenclever can all be found in Günther Rühle, *Theater für die Republik 1917–1933* (Frankfurt am Main: Fischer, 1967).

[42] Aine McGillicuddy, "Controversy and Censorship: René Schickele's 'Hans im Schnakenloch,'" *German Life and Letters* 60, no. 1 (2007): 59–74.

[43] Paul Goldmann, *Neue Freie Presse*, March 12, 1918: 1.

[44] Georg Kaiser, *Werke 1*, ed. Walther Huder (Berlin: Propyläen, 1971), 541.

[45] Günther Rühle, *Zeit und Theater: Vom Kaiserreich zur Republik 1913–1925* (Berlin: Propyläen, 1973), 446.

[46] Walter Hasenclever, *Gedichte Dramen Prosa*, ed. Kurt Pinthus (Reinbek bei Hamburg: Rowohlt, 1963), 173.

[47] Rühle, *Zeit und Theater*, 407.

[48] Hasenclever, 181–82.

[49] Rühle, *Zeit und Theater*, 406.

[50] Hasenclever, 170–71.

[51] Hasenclever, 165.

[52] Alfred Polgar, *Die Weltbühne*, vol. 1 (1921): 661.

[53] Lammasch (1853–1920) was a senior statesman and lawyer, and there are several important references to him in Zweig's letters. Seipel (1876–1932), a Catholic priest, was later to be an uncompromising right-wing prime minister.

[54] Suffice it to say that the latent anti-Semitism, notoriously ubiquitous in the *Reichspost*, emerges in Brečka's review (October 10) where he notes, "Das Umbiegen am Schluß der Dichtung in eine rein jüdische Angelegenheit wirkt gleichfalls unangenehm" (The shift at the conclusion of the work into a purely Jewish affair also has an unpleasant effect).

[55] Georg Kasch, "*Jeremias*—Christian Stückl choreografierte Stefan Zweigs," originally published in *Die Welt* and the *Berliner Morgenpost*, Jun 15, 2007. Accessible online at: http://www.nachtkritik.de/index.php?option=com_content&view=article&id=259:jeremias-christian-stueckl-choreografierte-stefan-zweigs-mammutwerk-mit-hundertschaften-und-kamelen&catid=129:passionstheater-oberammergau, accessed September 4, 2014.

3: "That Voice in the Darkness!": Technologies of the Tropical Talking Cure in Stefan Zweig's *Der Amokläufer* and *Verwirrung der Gefühle*

Geoffrey Winthrop-Young

THE FOLLOWING READING OF STEFAN ZWEIG'S novellas *Der Amokläufer* ("Amok," 1922) and *Verwirrung der Gefühle* ("Confusion," 1927) attempts to tackle a question related to the intermedial dynamics of modernism.[1] The decades between the early 1880s and the late 1920s saw the appearance of numerous literary texts dealing with—and at times obsessing over—new sound recording and storage devices such as the phonograph and the gramophone. There are lesser-known texts by well-known authors (Arthur Conan Doyle's non-Sherlock Holmes stories "The Voice of Science" and "The Japanned Box," or Jules Verne's truly McLuhanesque media novel *The Carpathian Castle*); there are famous texts by authors whose other writings have been forgotten (most notably, Bram Stoker's *Dracula*); and there are famous texts by authors whose fame dwarfs even that of Zweig (think, for instance, of the gramophone séances in Thomas Mann's *The Magic Mountain*). To be sure, the literary engagement with the impact of a given media technology does not require that the technology itself be clearly depicted in the text. The artifact may be distorted almost beyond recognition, as in the case of the lethal(ly) legal apparatus in Franz Kafka's "In der Strafkolonie" (In the Penal Colony, 1919) which some say is modeled on a phonograph.[2] Or it may be completely absent, as in Joseph Conrad's *Heart of Darkness*. There are no phonographs in Conrad's tale, and yet it depicts a plethora of phonographic tropes related to the cultural and epistemological problems posed by mechanical sound reproduction: from the horror over the disembodied voice and an awareness of far-reaching changes in the relationship between background noise and foreground message, to the dreaded suspicion that the ability to sever voice and language from body and mind has revealed that we did not have any control over our language in the first place. As we shall see, much of this applies to Zweig's *Der Amokläufer*.

Many of these texts take place in surroundings that are depicted as non-Western, exotic, primitive, and backward: remote penal colonies, the jungles of Africa and Indonesia, the Transylvanian fringe of civilized Europe. Western settings, in turn, are frequently either isolated or dilapidated leftovers from earlier times. Mann's phonographically facilitated return of the dead takes place in the far-off Swiss Alps, while Doyle's "Japanned Box" plays out in "a very, very old house, incredibly old," a pre-Norman castle that exudes "the smell as from a sick animal."[3] Phonographs appear to thrive in ruins and jungles, on mountain tops and remote islands. Why? How are we to explain this association of backward setting with forward technology? The following remarks on two of Zweig's texts—*Verwirrung der Gefühle* and *Der Amokläufer* will serve as a point of departure to unfold the question.

At the beginning of *Verwirrung der Gefühle* the philologist Roland v. D. is presented with a "Festschrift" celebrating his thirty years of academic writing. Though the occasion invites a sense of achievement, the honoree remains subdued. He is honest enough to recognize the importance of his work, yet his honesty also forces him to admit that he cannot recognize himself. As an author he was able to shed light on the lives of others, but nothing he wrote reveals his own past. What he put to paper is *his*, but it is not *him*—an uncomfortable insight that he illustrates with a seemingly offhand comparison:

> Mir gings genau so, als da ich zum ersten Mal meine eigene Stimme aus einem Grammophon sprechen hörte: ich erkannte sie vorerst gar nicht; denn wohl war dies meine Stimme, aber doch nur jene, wie die andern sie vernehmen und nicht ich selbst sie gleichsam durch mein Blut und im innern Gehäuse meines Seins höre.[4]
>
> [I felt exactly as I did when I first heard my own voice on a recording: initially I did not recognize it at all, for it was indeed my voice but only as others hear it, not as I hear it myself through my blood and within my very being, so to speak.][5]

The remaining one-hundred-thirty pages attempt to produce a narrative which, unlike scholarly production and phonographic reproduction, remains true to this authentic voice of the blood. Roland recounts how as a young student he fell under the spell of a charismatic instructor, how he had a short affair with his revered teacher's wife, and how, finally, his teacher revealed to him in a long monologue that he was gay and had fallen in love with him. Roland left his agonized mentor, never to return, but he concludes his narrative with the admission: "Keinen habe ich mehr geliebt" (*K* 487; I have never loved anyone more, *C* 141).

We are deep in Stefan Zweig territory. Reduced to its basic outline, *Verwirrung der Gefühle* exhibits two features that figured prominently in the decades-long academic "Mißachtung" (disdain) for Zweig,[6] a disdain that recently resurfaced in Michael Hofmann's take-down of Zweig in the *London Review of Books*.[7] First, Zweig's novellas tend to assume the shape of conventional nested narratives. A lengthy confession, invariably containing some shameful secret, is addressed to an invariably male narrator who, in turn, passes it on to the reader. (In Zweig's world women are far better speakers than listeners.) Time and again critics have scorned the mismatch of form and content. Zweig's deeply distraught nested narrators may be writhing in suicidal anguish, but like a blissful cloud floating across a battlefield their tales unfold with all the serenity of a nineteenth-century novella. Second, the novellas tend to pillage and recycle ideas and concepts borrowed from Freudian psychoanalysis. The oedipal drama of *Brennendes Geheimnis* (The Burning Secret, 1911), the repressed homosexuality of *Verwirrung der Gefühle* with its didactic arrangement of compensations and displacements, and the domestic sado-masochism that afflicts so many of Zweig's married couples have prompted critics to charge Zweig with a pathetic display of intellectual vassalage, culminating in the indictment that his texts are nothing but easily digestible Freudian case studies that may even have interfered with the spread of psychoanalysis.[8]

No doubt the critics have a point. Formal conservatism and a conspicuous indebtedness to Freud are as much part of Zweig as his inability to create convincing portrayals of anybody from outside his own social and geographical background, not to mention his tendency to reduce the complexities of history to the stage-like interaction between representative figures. However, some of these maligned features become substantially more interesting once they are read in light of recent developments in media and literary theory that focus on the very innovation invoked by Roland while trying to illustrate his alienation from his own voice: phonography. It is not an offhand comparison. Rather, it sets the stage for a complex pattern of aural exchange and deferral in the course of which writing and phonography, transcribed and recorded speech, inner and outer voice play off each other in a bewildering intermedial *mise-en-abîme*.

The first twist is that Roland's own voice, the one he has set out to capture in his more personal narrative, turns out to be someone else's. Not Roland's voice is absent from the *Festschrift* but that of his teacher: "Von allen ist *gesprochen*, nur von ihm nicht, der mir die Sprache gab und in dessen Atem ich *rede*."[9] (*K* 404; The book speaks of everything else, but not of the man who have me the gift of language and with whose tongue I speak, *C* 11).[10] Roland is in search of the voice of the other hiding underneath layers of impersonal academic discourse; he wants to provide a written voice for the voice that gave him a voice in the first place. Not surprisingly, his account revolves around scenes of dictations and aural rapture in which Roland is enveloped and permeated by his master's voice: be it listening to the latter's intoxicating "jagende Lippe" (*K* 414; quick tongue, *C* 25)—"[n]iemals noch hatte ich einen Menschen so begeistert, so wahrhaft mitreißend reden gehört" (*K* 414; I had never heard anyone speak with such enthusiasm, *C* 25)—or taking down his ecstatic dictations that, not coincidentally, include the "barbarischen Hymnen Walt Whitmanns" (*K* 442; barbaric hymns of Walt Whitman, *C* 70). And then there is the final night in which the teacher reveals his passion for Roland. As happens frequently in Zweig's novellas, the pivotal confession takes place in darkness; that is, in a confessional setting that diminishes visual while enhancing aural input.[11] The invisibility of the speaker amplifies the impact of the voice: "Diese Stimme im Dunkel, diese Stimme im Dunkel, wie fühlte ich sie eindringen bis in das innerste Gebälk meiner Brust!" (*K* 486; That voice in the darkness, ah, that voice in the darkness, how I felt it penetrate my innermost breast! *C* 138). So overwhelming is this voice that the physical union between teacher and student is transformed into oral/aural intercourse: "Und ich nahme diese heiß vorstoßende, diese glühend eindringende Stimme in mich auf, schauernd und schmerzhaft, wie ein Weib den Mann in sich empfängt" (*K* 486; And I received that fervent, ardently urgent voice pressing on with its tale into me with a shuddering and painful sensation, as a woman takes a man into herself, *C* 138).

At first glance the text deploys a series of conventional synecdoches and metonymies. The teacher is reduced to "Stimme" (voice); "Stimme" in turn, is replaced by "Lippe" (tongue). However, it is soon no longer clear—and this is the second crucial twist—whether voice and tongue can stand in for a whole or whether they are independent objects. This ambiguity is already apparent in a minor gap between indefinite article and possessive pronoun:

> Dunkel fiel über uns. Ich fühlte, daß er nahe war, fühlte es an seinem Atem, der schwer und wie röchelnd irgendwo im Unsichtbaren ging. Und plötzlich stand zwischen uns eine Stimme auf und erzählte mir sein ganzes Leben. (*K* 479)

> [Darkness fell over us. I sensed him near me, knew it from his breathing which somewhere passed into the unseen heavily, almost stertorously. And suddenly a voice rose in the air between us and told me the whole story of his life.] (*C* 127)

A voice emerges that narrates *his* life. Is the voice part of the man or is it a third party? Can the voice be referred back to the speaker, or is it so removed from its physical source that it has become an independent entity—just like a phonographic traces that remain audible long after the disappearance of their original sources? Roland is engaged in the paradoxical attempt to recapture by means of writing an estranged inner voice that was estranged by writing in the first place. To confound matters even further, this estrangement of voice through writing is illustrated by the alienation of voice through phonography. As a result, a set of questions emerges that is of pivotal concern to the art of storytelling in the age of mechanical sound reproduction. When is one's own voice no longer one's own? Was it ever? If not, can it still be used to reveal something about the speaker? And how did literature—in particular: the notion of a personal voice on paper—react to the advent of recording technologies that were able to capture voices in ways writing could not emulate? *Verwirrung der Gefühle* is helpful when it comes to formulating these questions, but in order to arrive at some answers we need to turn Zweig's most impressive voice text, *Der Amokläufer*.

Everything meticulous borders on self-parody. *Der Amokläufer* is a meticulously crafted tale exhibiting all the features Zweig's critics love to scorn. Once again, a neatly packaged narrative eruption full of scandalous and ultimately suicidal secrets is passed on to the reader by a male mediator. Once again, the confessional discharge is informed by (and cries out for) psychoanalytic exegesis. And once again, the soliloquy takes place in a nocturnal environment that emphasizes the speaker's voice. But there is something artificial about the story, as if it were mocking its paper-mâché exotic locale. All the threadbare props and tropes of William Somerset Maugham's South Sea tales are on display: jungle melancholia, meek natives, colonial banquets, the nocturnal glory of the Indian Ocean and the Southern Cross, sexually compliant child-like Malayans, the inscrutable Chinese crone, the Great Regression of the Solitary White Man, and so on. *Der Amokläufer* confirms that the main purpose of exotic settings in Zweig's writing is to serve as an exaggerrated mirror image that will help Western readers to learn something about their own achievements and afflictions. According to Klaus Zelewitz "Das Exotische wird mit dem Bekannten verglichen, gleichgesetzt oder als die mehrfache Steigerung des Bekannten definiert" (The exotic is compared or equated with the known, or defined as its manifold increase).[12] Little expertise is needed to realize that the novella hinges on an isomorphy of time and space. The farther you move away from the center of civilization, the further back in time you go. The journey to the Far East is a travel back in time, offering Western observers the opportunity to come face to face with their collective childhood, when passions and afflictions were not yet covered up by neurotic layers and amok was still a matter of violent action instead of violent words and directed outward rather than inward.

A brief note regarding the ambiguous depiction of amok in Zweig's text:[13] the rise of cultural psychiatry has resulted in a growing willingness to classify amok as a culture-specific syndrome, as opposed to the traditional tendency to subsume it under established Western medical categories. Emil Kraepelin, one of the founding fathers of psychiatry, simply equated it with epilepsy and catatonia.[14] Yet the question remains as to what cultural and historical dynamics ensured that amok came to be recognized as a disease (and given its own name) in the Indonesian region but not elsewhere. One intriguing explanation is to link amok to regionally specific forms of suicidal warfare.[15] Zweig's novella holds the middle ground: On the one hand the doctor's behavior is clearly *not* a case of amok. The switch from jungle brooding to frenzied pursuit of his female patient may roughly mirror the sequence of *sakit hata* (phase of brooding) and *mata gelap* (darkened eyes), but little else fits the picture. With the exception of striking a boy he does not inflict any physical injury on anybody; throughout his pursuit he remains acutely conscious of what he is doing; his actions are in part very deliberate; and he is later able to recall everything in great detail. On the other hand, it *is* amok (especially if we consider his frenzied confession a case of verbal amok), albeit a civilized, highly neurotic form. It is, ironically, the racially-tinged Eurocentric temporal divide between West and Far East that allows Zweig to both respect the specificity of amok and incorporate it as useful tool for Western diagnosis. However, the point I want to make is that Zweig's exotic locale is not only (as in so many other tropical tales) representative of a still-lingering jungle past that may erupt into Western lives, it also represents a looming future.

Let us begin with a literary parallel that, strangely enough, has not yet been discussed. The frame narrative of *Der Amokläufer* takes place on a ship. An unnamed man is listening to a fellow passenger tell the story of a highly symbolic and ultimately lethal breakdown suffered by an isolated male European professional in the tropics. The tale is told at night; hence the invisible speaker is no more than a "Stimme im Dunkeln"[16] (voice in the darkness).[17] Given this pithy description it is hard not to think of Joseph Conrad's *Heart of Darkness*, that other, more famous tale of a tropical breakdown. Whether or not Zweig was influenced by Conrad is of little concern. Quite apart from the fact that literary influences can be difficult to prove, the concept itself is overrated. Influence has too much influence in literary studies. Instead we should tackle what biologists call convergent evolution: that is, the emergence of similar structures in taxonomically diverse organisms in response to similar external conditions. Much as unrelated marine predators like ichthyosaurs, dolphins, and sharks all developed deceptively similar bodies, texts from vastly divergent traditions and conforming to equally distinct genre rules may display eerily similar textual features. How do these two narratives about voice, identity, obsession, and death both end up telling similar tropical tales?

In his illuminating account *Voice and the Victorian Storyteller* (2005) Ivan Kreilkamp places *Heart of Darkness* at the tail end of the Victorian obsession over authorship and voice.[18] His point of departure is Walter Benjamin's famous essay "Der Erzähler" ("The Storyteller," 1936) with its mournful assurance "daß es mit der Kunst des Erzählens zu Ende geht"[19] (that the art of storytelling is coming to an end).[20] Benjamin—and this is just one of the many strange twists in his poignant account—is trying to communicate to his readers that they are experiencing the end of communicable experience.[21] Social changes and media shifts have eroded a storytelling tradition that was woven into the communal fabric and featured narrators capable of dispensing advice to audiences able to integrate the communicated wisdom into their lives. Rather than accept Benjamin's obituary Kreilkamp argues that during the nineteenth century the supposed displacement of the voice was countered by an array of literary strategies designed to ensure "that voice is heterogeneous and thriving within modern print culture" (*V* 1). Of the many reconfigurations of the old storyteller in the new, market-driven literary habitat, probably the most successful was the promotion of the novelist to the status of charismatic storyteller. "By defining a novel as the utterance of a powerfully authentic speaker, authors and critics can claim that novelistic language generates the same kind of community supposedly once defined by face-to-face oral exchange" (*V* 3). Rather than accepting the obsolescence of the classic storyteller, "Victorian fiction based its authority on its ability to preserve endangered speech or to conjure the illusion of vocal utterance" (*V* 181). Endowing novelists with such bardic prowess, however, only works if reading protocols are in place that program audiences to automatically convert printed texts back into an authorial voice. Large sections of modern hermeneutics rest on this suppression of typographic mediation. But if it was the introduction and growing dissemination of print technology that made these reading protocols necessary, it is the introduction and dissemination of phonography that threatens to render them obsolete. For what does phonography do? More precisely, what does it do to writing? There are four major points, all of which will play their part in the following discussion. First, by capturing real voices "with an unheard-of precision and fidelity" (*V* 181), phonography highlights the fact that writing operates merely by way of symbolic mediation. Second, by storing voices that can be replayed at any time, phonography severs the connection between voice and speaker. R. Murray Shafer famously coined the term "schizophonia" to describe this formerly truly unheard-of split between an original sound and its electroacoustic reproduction.[22] Third, the phonographic replay of encoded analog traces undermines traditional notions of time as a homogenous, linear movement. New media facilitate a short circuit between past and present that defies continuous time. Fourth, by offering the possibility to scrutinize recorded speech, phonography gives rise to the notion that language was not even at the command of the speakers when they were speaking.

One of the most consequential events, then, in the struggle of the Victorian novel to simulate a regenerated storyteller is the introduction of sound recording. "Edison's tinfoil phonograph, a rather unprepossessing instrument, divides history into two halves, a before and an after. Prior to 1877, all sounds died."[23] In Edison's words, after 1877 speech became immortal. *Heart of Darkness* was written after this divide; and though it contains no explicit reference to sound recording technology, Kreilkamp makes a compelling a case that it "can be seen as one of the Victorian period's final tests on the efficacy and functioning of the storyteller paradigm in a new regime of reproducible speech" (*V* 193). The verdict is mostly negative, for the text records a journey into a tropical nightmare in which "schizophonic" voices overcome listeners precisely because they are no longer clearly linked to speakers. The impact of Marlowe's disembodied nightly voice on the unnamed frame narrator is but a prelude to the impact of Kurtz's voice on Marlowe, whose exclamation, "A voice! A voice! It rang deep to the very last!"[24] anticipates Roland's "Diese Stimme im Dunkel, diese Stimme im Dunkel!" Indeed, the realization that language may function independently of the human speaker is part of the final "horror" glimpsed by Kurtz. The praise heaped on Edison's invention is counterbalanced by "the pessimistic vision of the voice without the body as a demonic agency, a sign not of progress but of an inhuman 'horror,' a frightening break between the voice and its human source" (*V* 182). And just as in the third point described above, *Heart of Darkness* hints at the terrifying possibility that words and voice may never have been at the command of speakers in the first place. Supposedly intelligent and intelligible speech may be no more than a temporary condensation of sounds within a broad spectrum of noise. In the eyes—or ears—of the frame narrator, Marlowe's tale "seemed to shape itself without human lips in the heavy night-air of the river" (*HD* 27), while Marlowe, reflecting on his acoustic memories of Kurtz, concludes:

> A voice. He was little more than a voice. And I heard—him—it—this voice—other voices—all of them were so little more than voices—and the memory of that time lingers around me, impalpable, like a dying vibration of some immense jabber, silly, atrocious, sordid, savage, or simply mean without any kind of sense. (*HD* 48)

Something very similar occurs in *Der Amokläufer*. Throughout the night the narrator exhibits an acute awareness of sounds produced by the doctor's mouth that do not amount to articulated speech: "Ein leises, trockenes Husten hart neben mir ließ mich aufschrecken" (*A* 103; A light, dry cough nearby startled me, *RG* 45). "Nur den Atem meinte ich zu hören und das fauchende Saugen an der Pfeife" (*A* 103; I thought I could hear his breathing and the sucking noise of his pipe, *RG* 45).

"Ein Schluck gluckste leise" (*A* 112; I heard him take a gulp, *RG* 52). "Wieder stockte die Stimmen. Und was dann ausbrach, war mehr ein Schluchzen als ein Sprechen" (*A* 139; His voice stopped again. And then what he uttered was more like sobbing than speech, *RG* 71). "Und jetzt sprach er nicht mehr—er schrie, geschüttelt von einem heulenden Zorn" (*A* 140; And now he was no longer speaking—he was shouting, shaking with raging anger, *RG* 72). In addition to all this coughing, rasping, hissing, sucking, gurgling, stuttering, sobbing, screaming, and howling, the confession is punctuated and enveloped by other noises, from the clinking of the glasses and the tolling of the ship's bell to the "ferne, dumpe Herzstoß" (*A* 112; distant dull heartbeat, *RG* 51) of the engine and the sound of the sea——"das leise, unaufhörliche Rauschen, das unter dem Kiel und zwischen der leidenschaftlichen Rede beharrlich mitlief" (*A* 128; the light, ceaseless rushing noise that ran under the bow and constantly accompanied the passionate discourse, *RG* 63). Here, "rushing noise" is used to translate German "Rauschen," a key term that is deployed several times in the text. A cognate of English "rustle," the verb *rauschen* refers to the sound of waves, trees, and hedges; it is easily one of the poetically most over-used and -charged words in the German language primarily because of the way its onomatopoetic qualities conjure up natural sounds rife with poetic significance. But in one of most remarkable extensions ever undertaken in any language, German scientists started to use the noun "Rauschen" to denote what their English counterparts referred to as white noise, that is, a disturbance variable with a broad frequency spectrum. The nocturnal setting of *Der Amokläufer* is an aural canvas, a broad spectrum of acoustic data in which meaningful sounds are embedded in— and appear to arise from—noise, "das leise, unaufhörliche Rauschen" (the light, ceaseless rushing noise). As a result, the boundaries between meaningful articulations and meaningless background noise "without any kind of sense" (*HD* 48) start to shift and blur. Hitherto worthless acoustic signals are upgraded and reconceptualized as revealing traces, while a lot of meaningful articulation is revealed to be disposable babble. No epistemological innovation indicates this more strongly than the late nineteenth-century promotion of clues, which according to Carlo Ginzburg is as evident in the rise detective fiction as it is in the work of Freud.[25] Zweig's doctor may insist on the plenitude and unflinching veracity of his confession—"Ich muß ihnen alles direkt erzählen, von Anfang an [. . .] Da gibt es keine Scham, kein Verstecken" (*A* 109; I must tell you everything straight, from the beginning, otherwise you won't understand [. . .] That way there is no shame, no concealment, *RG* 49)—, but he does not divulge everything, and what he does relate does not amount to a truthful confession. *Der Amokläufer* insinuates that humans are incapable of knowing themselves well enough to speak the truth when speaking about themselves. In order to grasp what is really going on, it becomes necessary for trained listeners to perceive, store, and analyze all the accompanying noise as clearly and analytically as the allegedly meaningful discourse. This, however, requires new auditory practices that in Zweig's day were pioneered by two entities: phonographs and psychoanalysts.

Freud himself had already drawn a connection between the modus operandi of the analyst and the new mechanical recording and communication gadgetry:

> [Der Arzt] soll dem gebenden Unbewußten des Kranken sein eigenes Unbewußtes als empfangendes Organ zuwenden, sich auf den Analysierten einstellen wie der Receiver eines Telephons zum Teller eingestellt ist. Wie der Receiver die von Schallwellen angeregten elektrischen Schwingungen der Leitung wieder in Schallwellen verwandelt, so ist das Unbewußte des Arztes befähigt, aus den ihm mitgeteilten Abkömmlingen des Unbewußten dieses Unbewußte, welches die Einfälle des Kranken determiniert, wiederherzustellen.[26]

> [The doctor] must turn his own unconscious like a receptive organ towards the transmitting unconsciousness of the patient. He must adjust himself to the patient as a telephone receiver is adjusted to the transmitting microphone. Just as the receiver converts back into sound waves the electric oscillations in the telephone line which were set up by sound waves, so the doctor's unconscious is able, from the derivatives of the unconsciousness which are communicated to him, to reconstruct that unconscious, which has determined the patient's free associations.][27]

For those working at the intersection of discourse analysis and media archeology, this is a classic instance of the return of the repressed technology. Just as Plato's *Phaedrus* condemns writing as insufficient for philosophical purposes only to have it reappear in metaphorical guise to illustrate the philosophically more satisfactory inscription of the soul, Freud elides the fact that nineteenth-century storage and communication media precede and prepare the ground for psychoanalysis, only to have them illustrate the dynamics of his talking cure. One of the most ingenious contributions of Friedrich Kittler has been to read passages like this much like Freud himself listened to his patients.[28] Just as the analyst privileges unintentional and sublexical clues over intended utterances in order to decode what the patient is repressing, Kittler takes literally what Freud reduces to the status of metaphorical illustration. Psychoanalysis is not *like* phonography; psychoanalysis *is* phonography because the introduction and internalization of impassive mechanical sound recording technologies constitutes the main enabling factor for a fundamental reassessment of language. Freud's talking cure is based on the realization that language is not an instrument. Neither is it the faithful outward expression of an inscrutable inwardness. It is a data stream of clues and signals that allow the trained listener to analyze all that in pre-phonographic days was dismissed as noise and remained unrecorded: slips, silences, miscues, parapraxes, stuttering, hemming and hawing. The most intriguing aspect of Zweig's much-maligned Freudian connection, then, is not the recycling of psychoanalytic concepts but of one of its main techniques—the talking cure.

With this in mind we can sketch two readings of *Der Amokläufer* that pull the text in different directions, endowing it with the kind of ambiguity that is indicative of the ambiguity of Zweig's tropical setting. The first reading—one more in line with the mainstream of Zweig criticism—is a contained reading that centers on the twin strategies of narrative closure and deferred diagnosis. More than in any other Zweig text, the well-structured frame narrative of *Der Amokläufer* anchors and domesticates the framed confession. Counterbalancing the fairytale-like "sieben Jahre" (*A* 108; seven years, *RG* 49) that the doctor spends in his generic "höllischen Einsamkeit" (*A* 108; hellish loneliness, *RG* 49), the frame narrative provides exact time and date—"Im März des Jahres 1912 ... im Hafen von Neapel" (*A* 100; [i]n March 1912 ... in the harbour of Naples, *RG* 42)—and punctuates the tale with the tolling of the ship's bell and periodic glances at the "Radiumzifferblatt" (*A* 105; luminous dial, *RG* 47) of the frame narrator's watch. More importantly, the narrative ends in death. Death is not only the ultimate narrative closure; in line with Benjamin's association of death and authority, it also provides a certain gravitas that acts as an added incentive to the reader to explain why the doctor behaved as he did. As Joseph Strelka points out, the failure of the frame narrator as well as of the doctor himself to furnish a satisfactory diagnosis compels the reader to step in.

> Da [der Arzt] nicht psychoanalytisch geschult ist, geht er nur bis zu dem ihm bewußten frühesten Punkt zurück, an dem er aus Liebe für eine ebenso hochmütige und kalte Frau ein Vergehen auf sich lud. An Stelle der Dreizeitigkeit Freuds, die bis zu dem meist unbewußten frühen Kindheitserlebnis zurückgeht, das die wirkliche Enthüllung und Spannunglösung ermöglicht, geht er vom frischen Anlaß nur bis zum ersten parallelen Anlaß zurück und die dadurch entstehende Zweizeitigkeit verhindert auch eine heilende Lösung.
>
> [Since [the doctor] is not schooled in psychoanalysis, he only goes back to the earliest conscious instance at which he committed a crime out of love for an aloof, cold woman. Replacing the tri-temporality of Freud, which allows for true revelations and a sense of relief by going all the way back to the predominantly unconscious childhood experiences, the doctor merely refers the recent incident back to the first parallel incident; and this bi-temporality precludes any cure.][29]

In other words, the lack of information provided by the doctor about his early adult life is designed to prompt readers to diagnose the events in the tropics as a repetition of an event which itself was already a repetition of childhood events that the doctor is either unwilling or unable to talk about. Once again, the tropics offer nothing new. Their main purpose is, first, to stage an exotically enriched constellation that will trigger a pre-existing behavior pattern and, second, to provide an equally exotic label: amok. The text pulls out all the stops to ensure that readers get the point. On the one hand, there is a diachronic sequence of events that clearly mirror each other: The encounter with the English woman repeats the hospital incident involving a similarly strong and domineering woman, who, in turn, mirrors the prostitute to whom the doctor loses his money. All three incidents or women, it is understood, derive their impact from some unnamed childhood affliction. The doctor may not talk about his childhood, but his amok takes place in a country which appears to be devoid of indigenous adults. The only real adults are foreigners (Europeans or Chinese), while the natives are depicted as children or child-like. We must, therefore, also consider the doctor's childhood to understand the origin of his ailment.

This diachronic sequence is complemented by an equally didactic synchronic set of similarities that link the narrator to the doctor. A set of cleverly deployed lexical clues blurs the boundary between frame and nested narrative, thus enabling the reader to understand one by way of the other. Entranced by the Southern night sky, "so stahlblau und doch so funkelnd" (*A* 101; so shining, so steel-blue hard, *RG* 44), that it appears to him "als verhülle dort ein samtener Vorhang ungeheures Licht" (*A* 101; as though a velvet curtain of overwhelming light was hanging there, *RG* 44), the frame narrator is overcome by the temptation to lie down on the deck and "meinen Körper weibisch hinzugeben" (*A* 102; [yield myself] physically like a woman, *RG* 44) to the sky's embrace. Similarly, when the doctor first encounters the English woman in the nested narrative, her face is "verhüllt" (*A* 113; hidden by a thick veil, *RG* 52), and she exudes "eine stählerne, eine männliche Entschlossenheit" (*A* 116; steely masculine determination, *RG* 54). The word *stählern* (steely) appears three times on as many pages; and just like the "steel-blue" sky prompts the male narrator to feel like a woman, the "steely" demeanor of the English woman triggers the doctor's predisposition to adopt a submissive "feminine" part, that he initially, and tragically, tries to overcompensate by blackmailing her into sex.

As in many of Zweig's novellas, then, there is a conspicuous affinity between frame and framed narrator. *Schachnovelle* (1942) ("The Royal Game," 1944) is an obvious example. The frame narrator admits that "[a]lle Arten von monomanischen, eine einzige Idee verschlossenen Menschen haben mir zeitlebens angereizt"[30] ([I have always been] attracted by every kind of monomania, by people obsessed with one single idea, *RG* 6). In other words, he is obsessed with obsessions, a second-order obsessive who falls for two first-order obsessives, the chess maniacs Dr. B. and Mirko Czentovic. Ultimately, this approximation of frame and nested narrator is a literary manifestation of Zweig's belief that practicing psychoanalysts should only treat patients with whom they share the mental predisposition they are trying to cure. Bluntly put, only an analyst with paranoid or masochistic inclinations (now or in the past) can effectively treat a paranoid or a masochist. Zweig is applying the homeopathic logic of *similia similibus curentur* ('like cures like') to psychoanalysis. Freud took exception to this very restrictive approach,[31] which was based on a misunderstanding of his teachings (not to mention the obvious fact that it would result in poor business practices since it would severely limit the number of patients for each individual analyst). In Zweig's world, the listener/observer needs to be like the object of his attention in order to understand the problems of the latter. In Freud's world analysts need not be like their patients, but they must undergo analysis themselves.

More importantly, the text performs the aforementioned reconceptualization of language. The traditional relationship between speaker and language appears to be inverted. Language is not an instrument of the speaker; speakers are shaped by language. Rephrased in Lacanian fashion, the subject is a product of a chain of signifiers. In order to arrive at a successful diagnosis, then, readers/analysts must forfeit the signified and follow the play of the signifiers staged by the text. They must be able to listen to printed noise, as it were. Consider, for instance, the fact that the doctor's narrative outburst is triggered by the frame narrator's well-meaning remark concerning the duty to help those in need: "Wenn man jemanden in Bedrängnis sehe, da ergebe sich doch natürlich die Pflicht zu helfen" (*A* 107; If a man saw another in distress, then naturally it was his duty to help, *RG* 48). "Pflicht" triggers the story. As the doctor informs the frame narrator, "Nur das Wort, das Sie sagten, hat mich so merkwürdig berührt . . . so merkwürdig, weil es gerade das ist, was mich jetzt quält, nämlich ob man die Pflicht hat . . . die Pflicht . . ." (*A* 107; the word you spoke struck me as so remarkable . . . so remarkable, because that is precisely what is troubling me, that is to say, whether one has a duty . . . a duty, *RG* 48), only to add at the end of his story: "Aha . . . Ihre famose Pflicht zu helfen . . . aha . . . Mit der Maxime haben Sie mich ja glücklich zum Schwatzen gebracht" (*A* 152; Aha . . . your splendid duty, to help. Aha . . . you certainly loosened my tongue properly with that principle, *RG* 80). In much the same way as the analyst-reader is forced to retrace a tapestry of gliding words (from steely emasculating skies to steely emasculating women), it is possible to provide a Lacanian reading of *Der Amokläufer* by analyzing it as an eruptive enchainment of signifiers pulled along by the volatile master signifier "Pflicht." Somewhere in the Indian Ocean, the great Kantian philosophy of duty expires in a verbal amok run.

At this point we have slipped from a contained into a more decentered or unchained reading that undermines the twin strategies of narrative and diagnostic closure. It will, in conclusion, allow to us briefly discuss the assumption that texts like Stoker's *Dracula*, Verne's *Carpathian Castle*, Conrad's *Heart of Darkness*, and Zweig's *Der Amokläufer* choose exotic and/or backward locales to address the impact of phonography on literature and the constitution of the subject. As mentioned above, these emphatically non-Western (or non-modern) settings result in an isomorphy of time and space: to travel to these un(der)developed countries is to travel back in time. The Dutch East Indies with its childlike natives are the past—the childhood—of the West, hence Westerners keen on understanding their own neurotic afflictions have the opportunity to observe a world not yet deformed by the neuroses of civilization.

However, leaving aside the questionable racist and culturalist assumptions underlying this construction, we should be careful using words like "travel" or "movement" in this context. They tend to connote uniform motion along an absolute time axis that neatly separates past, present, and future. Zweig's novella, however, treats time differently. The text stages a choronoclasm: time is dramatically folded in such a way that the deep past directly touches upon and on occasion invades the present, thereby annihilating or at least temporarily suspending all that occurred in between. As a neurotically distorted form of amok erupts in its original habitat, the modern world suddenly comes up against its past that never faded away. Similarly, the conduct of the doctor can only be understood if it seen as a compulsive reappearance and repetition of a past that is still present. This is, of course, vintage Freud—or at least the conveniently streamlined Freud crafted by Zweig. The whole psychoanalytic enterprise (and this includes the analysis of the unconscious as well as the possibilities of treatment) presupposes this absence of linear time from the psychic apparatus. But if theorists like Kittler are correct to assume that "Freud's materialism reasoned only as far as the information machines of his era,"[32] then this means that the nonlinear time of the psychic apparatus is a discursive effect of *machine time*. To be precise: it arises from the time of phonography—a time fundamentally at odds with our notions of conventional time. As Wolfgang Ernst has emphasized, if at some point in the past analog recording devices store physical effects of the real (sound waves) which are then replayed in the present, "there is a media-archeological short circuit between otherwise historically clearly separated times."[33] And this is precisely what happens in Zweig's text: *Der Amokläufer* offers a Freud-inflected vignette of mechanized *madeleine*-moments.

But in the case of Conrad and Zweig this implicit attention to media is not only related to the sudden reappearance of the past, it also offers an equally unsettling glimpse of the future. In Kreilkamp's reading of *Heart of Darkness* the unease over the question of the disembodied voice—that is, the question whether or not voices severed from speakers are "successful" or "failed" (*V* 202) synecdoches—is itself a synecdoche for a greater breakdown and disintegration of what should be a whole. To quote Marlowe's disembodied voice:

> I had to lean right out to swing the heavy shutter and I saw a face amongst the leaves on the level with my own looking at me very fierce and steady, and then suddenly, as though a veil had been removed from my eyes, I made out deep in the tangled gloom, naked breasts, arms, legs, glaring eyes—the bush was swarming with human limbs in movements, glistening, of bronze colour. The twigs shook, swayed, and rustled, the arrows flew out of them, and then the shutter came to. (*V* 45)

Shutters, twigs, breasts, arms, eyes: Marlowe's jungle is a pandemonium of "potentially inhuman synecdoches" (*V* 195), the site of a comprehensive breakdown of the corporeal and spiritual totalities that have assembled themselves in the West. Of course it is possible (though also slightly escapist) to apply the standard interpretation and view this in terms of atavism or regression, as something Westerners could fall back into. But I want to suggest that the more the focus is on technology and its impact on the conceptualization and deconstruction of the subject, the more the alleged regression can also be read as a movement forward into an equally subject-defying bondage to technology. Conrad's Africa and Zweig's Far East bracket the West; they do not only stand in for its ever-present past but also for its possible future. In much the same way as the new invention of sound recording was said to have inspired a new orality, a short-circuit is established between the "immense jabber" of primitive orality and the increasing noise of severed and reified voices. Already in Zweig's day these voices—stored, replayed, and scrutinized far from their sources—were starting to add to the "immense jabber" of the airwaves. Europe—Zweig's humanist Europe composed of subjects seemingly in command of tongues and words—is not a zenith of cultural evolution, but a temporary constellation bracketed by the "Eingeborene und Tiere" (*A* 108; natives and animals, *RG* 49) of the tropics on the one hand and the ship's engines and recording devices on the other. As a transient arrangement of signals into patterned clues, the controlled discourse of the subject too must fade and disintegrate into white noise, exactly like the doctor's tale. "Wieder nur dies Rauschen, als ob das Mondlicht strömte" (*A* 123; Another silence, again, there was only a rustling sound as though the moonlight were pouring down, *RG* 60).

Notes

[1] This paper is the revised and extended version of an essay published in *A Transatlantic Gathering: Essays in Honour of Peter Stenberg*, ed. Marketa

Goetz-Stankiewicz and Thomas Salumets (Munich: Iudicium, 2007), 139–50. I wish to thank the editors and press for permission to reprint parts of the essay. Unless otherwise noted, all translations are mine.

[2] See Wolf Kittler, "*In dubio pro reo*. Kafkas 'Strafkolonie,'" in *Kafkas Institutionen*, ed. Arne Höcker and Oliver Simons (Bielefeld: Transcript, 2007), 33–72.

[3] Arthur Conan Doyle, "The Japanned Box," in *Round the Fire Stories* (San Francisco: Chronicle Books, 1991), 54.

[4] Stefan Zweig, *Die Kette* (Vienna: Herbert Reichner, 1936), 403 (hereafer cited in text as *K*).

[5] Stefan Zweig, *Confusion*, trans. Anthea Bell (London: Pushkin Press, 2002), 10 (hereafter cited in text as *C*).

[6] See Guo-Qiang Ren, *Am Ende der Missachtung? Studie über die Stefan Zweig Rezeption in der deutschen Literaturwissenschaft nach 1945* (Aachen: Shaker, 1995); Vivian Liska, "A Spectral Mirror Image: Stefan Zweig and his Critics," in *Stefan Zweig Reconsidered: New Perspectives on his Literary and Biographical Writings*, ed. Mark H. Gelber (Tübingen: Niemeyer, 2007), 203–17.

[7] Michael Hofmann, "Vermicular Dither," *London Review of Books* 32, no. 2 (January 2010): 9–12.

[8] See Thomas Haenel, *Stefan Zweig: Psychologe aus Leidenschaft* (Düsseldorf: Droste, 1995), 198–212.

[9] Italics mine.

[10] Translation amended.

[11] Dominique Bona offers a concise account of this recurring *ur*-scene in Zweig's novellas: "Le narrateur ne peut ni voir le visage ni discerner les traits de l'homme dont l'histoire, pareille à la vieille catharsis d'Aristote, est une tentative—qui échouera—de se libérer lui-même, se purifier de son horrible secret. Sans la nuit, il serait resté muré dans son silence. Mais la nuit, apparemment, le délivre. La délivrance des héros de Zweig, par l'aveu du secret, a toujours lieu grâce à cette lumière plus ou moins obscure ou tamisée, qui évoque celle des confessionnaux ou des cabinets de psychanalyse, et qui atteint dans *Amok* l'opacité quasi totale" (The narrator can neither see the face nor discern the features of the man whose story, similar to Aristotle's classical notion of catharsis, is an attempt to unburden and purge himself of his horrible secret—to fatal ends. If not for the nighttime, he would have maintained his silence. But the night apparently unburdens him. This unburdening of Zweig's heroes, by the disclosing of the secret, is always due to this light source that has been darkened or dimmed, calling to mind the confessional box or the study of the psychoanalyst, and attaining a near-total opacity in *Amok*), Dominique Bona, *Stefan Zweig, l'ami blessé: Biographie* (Paris: Plon, 1996), 162–63; editors' translation. Freud got it right when, after analyzing three of Zweig's novellas, including *Verwirrung der Gefühle*, he described the author as a *Lauscher*—an eavesdropper. See Stefan Zweig, *Briefwechsel mit Hermann Bahr, Sigmund Freud, Rainer Maria Rilke und Arthur Schnitzler*, ed. Jeffrey B. Berlin, Hans-Ulrich Lindken, and Donald A. Prater (Frankfurt am Main: Fischer, 1987), 179.

[12] Klaus Zelewitz, "Stefan Zweig: Exotismus versus (?) Europhilie," in *Die letzte Partie: Stefan Zweigs Leben und Werk in Brasilien (1932–1942)*, ed. Ingrid

Schwamborn (Bielefeld: Aisthesis, 1999), 149. See also Jennifer Ann Gosetti-Ferencei, *Exotic Spaces in German Modernism* (Oxford: Oxford University Press, 2011), 90–103.

[13] For an excellent summary of the discussions of the concept "amok" in Zweig's day (as well as of the importance of Zweig's text for popularizing the term), see Heiko Christian, *Amok: Geschichte einer Austreibung* (Bielefeld: Aisthesis, 2008), 196–219.

[14] Roland Littlewood, "Russian Dolls and Chinese Boxes: An Anthropological Approach to the Implicit Models of Comparative Psychiatry," *Transcultural Psychiatry* 37, no. 58, ed. John L. Cox (London: Croom Helm, 1986), 48.

[15] See John C. Spores, *Running Amok: An Historical Inquiry* (Athens, Ohio: Center for International Studies, 1988).

[16] Stefan Zweig, *Amok: Novellen einer Leidenschaft* (Frankfurt am Main: Fischer, 1950), 112 (hereafter cited in text as *A*).

[17] Stefan Zweig, *The Royal Game and Other Stories*, trans. Jill Sutcliffe (New York: Holmes & Meier, 2000), 51 (hereafter cited in text as *RG*).

[18] Ivan Kreilkamp, *Voice and the Victorian Storyteller* (Cambridge: Cambridge University Press, 2005) (hereafter cited in text as *V*).

[19] Walter Benjamin, "Der Erzähler. Betrachtungen zum Werk Nikolai Lesskows," in *Gesammelte Schriften* 2.2, ed. Rolf Tiedemann and Hermann Schweppenhäuser (Frankfurt am Main: Suhrkamp, 1972), 439.

[20] Walter Benjamin, "The Storyteller," in *Illuminations*, ed. and introduced by Hannah Arendt, trans. Harry Zohn (New York: Schocken, 1968), 83.

[21] The fascination exerted by Benjamin's "The Storyteller" essay rests to no small degree on a peculiar form of self-reflexive necrolatry. Its authority derives from the fact that it talks about the death of a craft that itself derived its authority from death. "Death is the sanction of everything the storyteller can tell. He has borrowed his authority from death" (94). But, like most obituaries, "The Storyteller" mourns the loss of qualities greater than the deceased possessed; it tells more stories than the departed ever lived up to. It is, for instance, not clear whether the decline of storytelling is primarily linked to social changes, media shifts or literary evolution; it is not clear how we are to understand the relationship between the collective, quasi-medieval tradition "which goes from mouth to mouth" (84) and the authority of great individual storytellers; and it is not clear how print-savvy authors (including Benjamin's prime exhibit Johann Peter Hebel), who were adapting orality to print, can be transfigured into epitomes of a story-telling tradition conceptualized in oral terms. See also Geoffrey Winthrop-Young, "Luhmann und Kannitverstan im Druck. Zur Evolution typographischer Subjekte und alemannischer Sprachmaschinen," *Germanic Review* 33, no. 7 (2002): 195–217.

[22] R. Murray Schafer, *The New Soundscape: A Handbook for the Modern Music Teacher* (Don Mills: BMI Canada, 1969), 43–47.

[23] John Durham Peters, "Helmholtz, Edison and Sound History," in *Memory Bytes: History, Technology, and Digital Culture*, ed. Lauren Rabinovitz and Abraham Geil (Durham, NC: Duke University Press, 2004), 177.

24 Joseph Conrad, *Heart of Darkness*, ed. Paul B. Armstrong (New York: Norton, 2006), 67 (hereafter cited in text as *HD*).

25 Carlo Ginzburg, "*Morelli, Freud*, and Sherlock Holmes: Clues and Scientific Method," in *The Sign of Three: Dupin, Holmes, Peirce*, ed. Umberto Eco and Thomas Sebeok (Bloomington: University of Indiana Press, 1983), 81–118.

26 Freud, quoted in Friedrich Kittler, *Aufschreibesysteme 1800/1900* (Munich: Fink, 2003), 342.

27 Sigmund Freud, *The Standard Edition of the Complete Psychological Works of Sigmund Freud*, vol. 12, ed. and trans. J. Strachey (London: Hogarth, 1962), 115–16.

28 Friedrich Kittler, *Discourse Networks 1800/1900*, trans. Michael Metteer and Chris Cullens (Stanford: Stanford University Press, 1990), 273–304. See also Geoffrey Winthrop-Young, *Kittler and the Media* (Cambridge: Polity Press, 2011), 66–71.

29 Joseph Strelka, "Psychoanalytische Ideen in Stefan Zweigs Novellen," *Literatur und Kritik* 169/170 (1982): 46.

30 Stefan Zweig, "Schachnovelle," in *Meisternovellen* (Frankfurt am Main: Fischer, 2012), 434.

31 See Zweig, *Briefwechsel*, 193.

32 Friedrich Kittler, "The World of the Symbolic—A World of the Machine," in *Literature Media Information Systems*, ed. John Johnston (Amsterdam: G+B Arts, 1997), 134.

33 Wolfgang Ernst, "Media Archaeography: Method and Machine versus History and Narrative of Media," in *Media Archaeology: Approaches, Applications and Implications*, ed. Erkki Huhtamo and Jussi Parikka (Berkeley: University of California Press, 2011), 240.

4: Narrating Alterity: Stefan Zweig, Emmanuel Levinas, and the Trauma of Redemption

Robert Weldon Whalen

GERONTOPHAGY IS THE FATE which awaits the illustrious dead. It is, as historian C. Vann Woodward explains, the "primitive ritual of eating one's elders."[1] What Woodward is referring to is the sort of symbolic mastication we inflict on politicians, public figures, and artists after their deaths. Today's celebrities are tomorrow's dinner; we gnaw at their every flaw, and when we're sated, there often isn't much left. Consider, for example, the fate of Stefan Zweig.

In the years between wars, Stefan Zweig was one of the world's most popular authors. Since his death in 1942, though, his reputation has endured repeated attacks. In 1943, Hannah Arendt wrote what Michael Steinberg calls a "withering review" of Zweig's memoir, *The World of Yesterday*; as Steinberg points out, Arendt rejected not just this one book but Zweig's whole approach to life and art.[2] In 1984, Sylvia Patsch bemoaned the fact there was so little discussion of Zweig's relationship with British literature; Patsch noted that one obvious reason for this was that so little of Zweig's work was available in English translation.[3] Indeed, a 1987 bibliographic study of Zweig's work in English produced "disconsolate results."[4] While Zweig's work was, of course, available in German, very little of was still available in English, at least not in the United States. Not only was Zweig's work difficult to find, the bibliographer also sadly reported that, "not one of my students had ever heard of Stefan Zweig, and only a few of my colleagues knew anything about him."[5] Another observer, in 1999, noted Zweig's disappearance, and remarked that "the reception of Zweig's work has suffered immensely since the Second World War rendered anachronistic his dream of universal humanity."[6] Probably the most thorough critique of Zweig's art occurs in an article by Leon Botstein, in which he notes that Zweig's work "appears to us moribund, anachronistic, naïve, and superficial."[7] Though somewhat sympathetic to Zweig, Botstein nevertheless argues that Zweig's importance is not in his ideas, but precisely in "the evident bankruptcy of Zweig's views of history and politics" (B 81). Zweig is important, then, not as an artist but as a specimen of an extinct species (the central-European, cosmopolitan, assimilated, progressive-minded, Jewish intellectual), and as an advocate of a failed dream (non-violent, pan-European humanism). The gerontophagists, it would appear, have picked Zweig's bones clean.

And yet, life still stirs in those bones. True, Zweig has not returned to anything like his inter-war celebrity. Zweig has, though, proved remarkably durable, and he still appears, sometimes in the most unexpected places. Alex Ross, the *New Yorker*'s music critic, noted in 2009 that the classical pianist Mitsuko Uchida included Zweig's autobiography in her summer reading.[8] Conferences are regularly dedicated to Zweig's work; a simple Internet search turns up hundreds of articles devoted to him; many of his novellas have been re-printed in handsome paperback editions and have found a whole new generation of readers. No doubt, Zweig's resilience is a result of the continuing power of his art, what one reviewer refers to as his "deep [. . .] social reach" and "detailed [. . .] human sympathy."[9]

This essay argues that another equally important reason that Zweig's presence remains powerful is the acuity of his concerns, and that what is especially striking about these concerns is their similarity to those of his contemporary, the French philosopher Emmanuel Levinas. In fact, this essay will show that Zweig, the habitué of Viennese café society, and Levinas, the visionary philosopher, share a basic understanding of their time and the human condition, an understanding centered on the themes of alterity, trauma, and redemption.

Alterity

In Stefan Zweig's novella, *Geschichte eines Unterganges* ("Twilight," 1910), Madame de Prie, French aristocrat and salonière, steps into her salon to find the king's courier awaiting her with a message that will radically change her life.[10] In Zweig's *Die Mondscheingasse* ("Moonbeam Alley," 1914), a traveler is delayed; his ship is late arriving in France, so he misses the train to Germany and must spend an "unerwarteter Tag" (unexpected day) in a French port.[11] That "unexpected day" plunges the traveler into tragedy. In *Phantastische Nacht* ("Fantastic Night," 1922), a man, after returning home, sorts through his mail and discovers an astonishing document. In *Schachnovelle* ("Chess Story," 1942) a passenger on a ship encounters a chess master with a shocking story.[12] Reading a Zweig novella is a bit like watching a Hitchcock film; everything seems normal until the utterly unexpected intrudes. Zweig's novellas are typically memory stories. One narrator first frames the story by explaining that on one normal day something very odd happened, then a second, more important narrator steps in to tell the tale. Anthea Bell, one of Zweig's translators, remarks:

> The framework device is a favorite of Zweig's; the narrator, usually anonymous, is not personally involved in the story, or only very distantly so, but hears the central character recount his or her own tale [...] the protagonists themselves [...] [then] recount tales of acute moral or emotional dilemmas. (*TW* 99)

Interruptions of all kinds occur in Zweig's stories. Sometimes the intruder is an object—a letter, for example, or a racetrack ticket—which then sets in motion an unexpected chain of events. Often the intruder is a person—sometimes known, sometimes unknown—who enters and disrupts the narrator's life. Sometimes, oddly enough, the protagonist encounters himself or herself as a shocking "other." The glamorous Madame de Prie, for example, in *Geschichte eines Unterganges*, sees herself in a mirror and is horrified: "War sie das wirklich? Ihre Wangen schienen ihr eingefallen und ohne Frische, ein böser Zug um den Mund höhnte sie an, die Augen lagen tief in den Höhlen und sahen schreckhaft, wie hilfesuchend, heraus" (*GU* 29; Was that really herself? Her cheeks looked hollow and dull, a bitter set to her mouth mocked her, her eyes lay deep in their sockets and looked out in fear as if searching for help, *TW* 41). In Zweig's world, alterity is odd, weird, often erotic, and always dangerous.

Zweig's stories do not simply *include* interruptions; his stories *are* tales of interruption. To be sure, an obsession with the eruption of the "other" into the mundane is hardly unique to Zweig. Fin-de-siècle Viennese culture is filled with unexpected and horrifying interruptions, from the dreams that disrupted the sleep of Freud's patients to Crown Prince Rudolf's suicide or to Empress Elizabeth's and Archduke Franz-Ferdinand's assassinations. More generally, twentieth-century European culture was a culture of dislocation and disruption. Zweig's great skill is his ability to articulate with economy and precision the obsession he shared with his contemporaries. In this regard one thinks of Franz Kafka, James Joyce, and Samuel Beckett, for instance. Zweig's expression of alterity is distinctive; it has a very Viennese accent. If, as Karl Kraus famously remarked, turn-of-the-century Vienna was a "Versuchsstation des Weltuntergangs" (experimental station for the end of the world),[13] then understanding Vienna in this context is important; according to Wilma Iggers, there is no better guide to turn-of-the-century Vienna than Zweig. She wrote: "I know of no author whose life, work, concerns, and style can give us more insight into [Vienna] than Stefan Zweig."[14] Between the World Wars Zweig's readers included most of Europe's intellectuals; he maintained a vast correspondence in several languages; that he was a eulogist at the funerals of Sigmund Freud, Hugo von Hofmannsthal, and Rainer Maria Rilke suggests the respect afforded him as an intellectual elder statesman.[15] His many admirers praised especially his psychological insight; he thought of himself a kind of "Freud of literature" (D 13). Zweig's immense productivity and enormous popularity—he was, according to Lynda King's calculations, the most translated German-language writer of his era—made him a leading representative of both Viennese-tinted modernism and literary Freudianism.[16]

If Stefan Zweig is the narrator of alterity, Emmanuel Levinas is alterity's philosopher. Though twenty-five years separated the older Zweig from the younger Levinas, both were profoundly shaped by the era of the World Wars. Zweig remained linked to fin-de-siècle aestheticism, something quite foreign to Levinas, and Levinas was a religious believer, while Zweig was not. Both, though, were Jewish intellectuals whose ideas were shaped by Central-European culture. Zweig was an Austrian; Levinas, born in Lithuania and a citizen of France, was profoundly influenced by European philosophy, especially the work of Edmund Husserl and Martin Heidegger. Though Zweig did not survive the disaster of the 1940s and Levinas did, both of their lives were fundamentally shaped by catastrophe. As Levinas would later remark, his life and work were "dominated by the presentiment and memory of the Nazi horror."[17] Simon Critchley writes that every philosopher has a "big idea," and he argues that Levinas's big idea was "that ethics is first philosophy, where ethics is understood as a relation of infinite responsibility to the other person."[18] As a simple enough proposition, it would—as Jacques Derrida remarked in his funeral oration for Levinas—change the course of modern philosophy.[19]

"First philosophy" since Aristotle has always been talk about "reality," that is, about "being"; metaphysics, one usually learns in school, is "first philosophy." Even that fearsome critic of the Western philosophical tradition, Martin Heidegger, agreed that understanding the meaning of being was philosophy's first task. Levinas disagreed. Ethics, Levinas argued, is fundamental to human experience and therefore, in a sense, "prior" to metaphysics. In his 1962 essay, "Transcendence and Height," Levinas contends that "moral consciousness is primary and the source of 'first philosophy.'"[20] And central to ethics, Levinas insists, is the experience of alterity. Thought typically means relating the particular to some more general "horizon," but it is precisely this sort of thinking that Levinas rejects. Ethics does not subsume persons, and as Levinas prefers to say, "faces" within some general horizon. On the contrary, Levinas writes in his 1951 essay, "Is Ontology Fundamental?": "to comprehension and signification grasped within a horizon we oppose the signifyingness of the face" (*BPW* 10). Against the "totality" of all horizons and systems, Levinas contrasts the "infinity" of the other, the different, the face. The aim of his influential book, *Totality and Infinity* (1969) is "to distinguish between the idea of totality and the idea of infinity, and affirm the philosophical primacy of the idea of infinity."[21] The encounter with the other, alterity, is not simply one possible experience among many. Alterity is the primal experience, the fundamental human phenomenon, which triggers ethical reflection, and from ethics all else—metaphysics, politics, social thought—flows.

Levinas begins with a familiar claim which goes back, through Edmund Husserl and Franz Brentano to the medieval Scholastics: that thought itself is always thought about something, even if only about itself. Thus, thought structurally includes otherness. I encounter myself as other; more joltingly, I encounter minds that are not my own, a world I did not make. This encounter with otherness is incessant and inexorable, and it imposes on me the necessity of responding or at least reacting. Alterity thus produces a kind of fundamental obligation imposed on me by the "other," which becomes for Levinas the basis of ethics. Thus ethics arises not from metaphysical speculation, but from this foundational encounter with otherness. As Levinas said in 1962: "The very principle of my enterprise, giving value to the relation of infinite responsibility which goes from the I to the other [. . .] is our most valuable everyday experience [. . .] but this is an illuminating experience, metaempirical" (*BPW* 23). As an "illuminating experience," the infinite responsibility regarding the other derives from neither deduction nor induction. According to Hilary Putnam, "what Levinas wants to remind us of is precisely the underivability of what I called the fundamental obligation from any metaphysical or epistemological picture" (*C* 43).

Ethics, then, is prior to metaphysics, and ethics is rooted in an encounter with an "other." Levinas is not simply restating Kant's categorical imperative with its claim that I must treat others as ends, and not means. Nor is he merely repeating Martin Buber's famous advocacy of dialogue between an "I" and a "Thou."[22] Levinas has little patience for Kant's stress on the autonomy of the subject. He is far more interested in relationships than in autonomy (*C* 161–62). Buber and Levinas are similar in many ways. For example, both focus on relationships, not autonomy, as the basis of ethics. Levinas acknowledged his debt to Buber and others: "Many of the ideas that we have developed come perhaps too late after the work of Gabriel Marcel and [Martin] Buber; but our effort does not so much consist in identifying the originality of the I-Thou relation as in showing the ethical structures of this relation" (*BPW* 20). In some ways, Levinas is much more radical than Buber. For Levinas, an "I" does not even exist until it responds to the call of the "other" and in the relationship with the "I" the "other" never loses its "totally otherness" (*C* 37). Ethics, Levinas insists, cannot assume that basically all humans share the same essence and therefore should treat each other as each would like to be treated. If "we are all alike," if we prioritize "sameness," then we run the risk, to our peril, of marginalizing difference. What Levinas calls for is not some genial acceptance of "sameness," not some grudging "tolerance" of difference, but an understanding that the "other" is profoundly "other," and as such, as "other," intrudes into my life and inevitably, thereby, shapes the narrative of my life (*C* 38).

According to Levinas, Descartes's picture of the autonomous ego is deeply misleading. No ego is ever alone; if nothing else, each ego is haunted by its own thoughts which stand over and against the ego as an "other." Self-awareness, in which "I" am aware of "me," implies otherness. "I" is never "innocently alone"; "to be," Levinas writes, is a "reflexive verb," that is, a verb always in relationship.[23] Alterity of one sort or another is part of the very structure of human beings. Alterity is the source of human longing and eros; even our sense of time emerges from the experience of alterity (*EE* 96).

Levinas is alterity's philosopher; Stefan Zweig is alterity's poet. The primal relationship between "self" and "other" is, in Zweig's imagination, endlessly complex, sometimes catastrophic, and always dangerous. One example is the unhappy protagonist of his novella *Geschichte eines Unterganges*, Madame de Prie. Exiled from the Parisian court, she is suddenly separated from all the people who formerly made up her universe. She is plunged into solitude, into herself alone: "Madame de Prie, die verzweifelt wie ein wildes Tier in dem Gefängnis ihrer inneren Einsamkeit auf und ab irrte" (*GU* 12; Madame de Prie, pacing up and down like a wild animal in the prison of her inner solitude, *TW* 20) becomes desperate to escape not only her exile but the prison of her "I." Not every escape from solipsism, Zweig warns, is either successful or healthy. For instance, she begins to prey on a young provincial boy just the way she might have preyed on a young courtier back in Paris. But she cannot escape from own ego: "sie war zum erstenmal mit sich allein [. . .] und [könnte] in der entsetzlichen Stille ihr eigenes Schluchzen hören" (*GU* 16; She was alone with herself for the first time [. . .] [and] heard her own sobbing in the terrible silence, *TW* 25).

Another example is *Der Amokläufer* ("Amok," 1922), a story that deals with "ein merkwürdiger Unfall" (strange accident) which occurred in Naples.[24] The narrator is aboard a ship sailing from India back to Europe. On one strange night, the first-person narrator sits alone on deck, and suddenly notices an "other" right beside him: "Ich kann nicht sagen, wie seltsam und schaurig das war," the narrator explains, "dies stumme Nebeneinandersitzen im Dunkeln, knapp neben einem, den man nicht sah" (*M* 91; I can't say how strange and eerie it was to be sitting next to someone like that in the dark, very close to a man I couldn't see, *A* 16). This "other's" face "schien grauenhaft verzerrt, finster, und koboldhaft" (*M* 91; seemed dreadfully distorted, dark, and goblin-like, *A* 17). The narrator then recounts this "other's" strange story. A third example is *Der Stern über dem Walde* ("The Star above the Forest," 1904), Zweig's poignant tale about a waiter, François, who is infatuated with "eine exotische, ewig unerreichbare Gräfin"[25] (*A* 83; an exotic Baroness who would be forever unattainable). In the novella, François discovers just how painful yearning for an unattainable "other" can be.

Zweig's project is not, however, equivalent to Levinas's. A poet/writer and a philosopher do not necessarily aim to accomplish the same things in the same way. Yet what they share in this case is a fascination with the relationship between the "I" and the "other," in which each is profoundly alien to the "other." Furthermore, they also share a sense that this phenomenon of alterity is the key to understanding reality.

The experience of alterity, as Levinas argues in *Time and the Other*,[26] must be the foundation of ethics, and ethics is for him "first philosophy." Metaphysics, our basic understanding of being, flows from ethics, which concerns our sense of the good. Levinas was intrigued by Plato's Delphic comment that in some mysterious sense the Good is "beyond being" (*EE* xxvii). Being is what we share with objects; being is a kind of universal horizon against which we interpret particularity. As such, Levinas finds the notion of "being" suspicious. Modern philosophy's task, Levinas argues, is to "liberate human beings from categories adapted uniquely for things" (*BPW* 8). Moreover, we ought not erase particularity by understanding it strictly within the context of some universal horizon, but we ought to attempt to encounter particularity precisely as particularity. Levinas calls this an encounter with a specific and unique "face"; it aims for "comprehension and signification grasped within a horizon." As Levinas writes: "We oppose the signifyingness of the face" (*BPW* 10). An encounter with the "other" wherein one becomes an "other" to the "other" is what Levinas understands as the ethical. If Plato's cryptic observation is correct, then the "other," by inspiring the ethical, carries us both to the Good, which is beyond Being.

Trauma

In Zweig's *Geschichte eines Unterganges*, Madame de Prie struggles to overcome her isolation. She tries to seduce a young provincial boy; she throws a spectacular party, much like the parties she knew back in Paris. She fails to find others, or even an "other," who can fulfill her life. Shockingly, the "other" she eventually discovers is her other self, which she experiences as grotesque. Then she hits on a desperate solution—suicide. Her death will shock the court! Everyone, grief-stricken, will realize how unfair her banishment has been. She takes poison, but alas, even death betrays her. She is found with a ghastly expression on her face: "Ihr gesicht [war] zu einer entsetzlichen Grimasse verzerrt" (*GU* 48; Her face was distorted into a terrible grimace, *T* 65) while back in Paris her death is scarcely noticed. In this story and elsewhere, Zweig's "other" appears in many different guises, sometimes as another person, sometimes as unsettling and disruptive news, sometimes as another self.

However "otherness" appears, its intrusion is dangerous, traumatic, and often lethal.

Suicide is a recurring theme in Zweig's novellas, both as possibility and event. Astrid Heyer notes: "In Stefan Zweig's novellas and his one novel, five male characters and four female characters commit suicide. Victims of situations that seemingly no longer permit them a way out, Zweig's characters are desperate human beings who can only find an end to their sufferings by committing suicide."[27] Suicide is not the only outcome for Zweig's characters, but even his non-suicidal characters are profoundly shaken by their strange encounters. Zweig is a narrator of trauma. However, the concept of "trauma" requires elucidation.

Trauma is not an external phenomenon—not exterior, not "out there"; rather it is interior or "in here." No event is in itself traumatic. Trauma occurs within an event's perceiver; it is the perceiver who translates an event into trauma. Trauma, James Berger writes, "is not simply another word for disaster."[28] What is peculiar about trauma, as Sigmund Freud argued, is its incomprehensibility, its unrepresentability. We experience an event; we cannot assimilate the event to our categories and values, we cannot comprehend it, and though we see it, we cannot even picture it to ourselves. Such an event is nameless. Because we see it physically but cannot picture it mentally, the event is both nameless and, in an odd sense, invisible. This nameless and invisible thing "destabilizes language" (Berger 569) and psychically overwhelms us. We respond to this threatened destruction of our subjectivity with terror. This response is what makes an event traumatic.

We respond to the shock of trauma with grief and mourning, the work through which we struggle to stabilize our subjectivity by naming and picturing the event. If we fail at this work, mourning becomes chronic melancholia, and we are haunted by the unnamable and invisible. The act of naming and picturing involves assigning meaning to the event, situating it within a moral universe, and transforming the unnamable and invisible thing that terrifies us into a symbol that inspires us. Our psychic work transforms terror into awe.

This transformation is possible because the traumatic unnamable and invisible other that threatens to destroy us is also potentially the means by which we transcend ourselves. The death of the I directly parallels the transcendence of the I. The unnamable is called the "*totaliter aliter*," the totally other, which some writers, such as Karl Barth and Rudolf Otto, identify with the divine. Otto refers to the unnamable and unrepresentable both as the "*tremendum*," the terrifying, but also as the "*tremendum fascinans*," the fascinating tremendum.[29] Horrified by the tremendum that overwhelms us, that threatens to abolish our subjectivity, we are also attracted by the tremendum which exceeds the frontiers of our subjectivity and thereby promises transcendence. Our mourning work requires that we translate threat into promise, disaster into transcendence, the incomprehensible into the symbolic. As it is expressed in the Hebrew Bible: "The fear of the Lord is the beginning of wisdom" (Prov. 1:7).

Zweig's characters are, alas, more often than not overwhelmed by their reality. The famous novelist "R.," we learn from an unnamed narrator in *Brief einer Unbekannten* ("Letter from an Unknown Woman," 1922), had been off on holiday; upon his return to Vienna, he found waiting for him a "einen Brief, der fremde Schriftzüge trug und zu umfangreich schien" (*M* 151; a bulky packet addressed in a strange hand-writing)[30] The packet contains a manuscript that begins with the words: "Mein Kind is gestern gestorben" (*M* 152; My boy died yesterday, *FN* 71). The story the manuscript tells is utterly shocking. A woman wrote the manuscript; as a girl she had been a passionate fan of novelist R. As a young woman, she had followed him everywhere, and once, finally, had had an intimate encounter with him. R. had long since forgotten that encounter, but the young woman never forgot it because she became pregnant and bore a child who was the novelist's son. She never made any effort to reveal herself to R. and he, of course, had no idea about the pregnancy, the birth or who she was. But she writes now to inform him: "Mein Kind ist gestorben, unsere Kind—jetzt habe ich niemanden mehr in der Welt, ihn zu lieben, als Dich. Aber wer bist Du mir, Du, der Du mich niemals, niemals erkennst, der an mir vorübergeht" (*M* 194; My boy, our boy, is dead. I have no one left to love; no one in the world except you. But what can you be to me—you who have never, never recognized me . . . you who went on your way unheeding, *FN* 102). The woman then makes reference to her own imminent death; the manuscript never in fact reached R. until after she had already died. R. puts down the manuscript. According to the narrator, "Er schrak zusammen: ihm war, als sei plötzlich eine Tür unsichtbar aufgesprungen, und kalte Zugluft ströme aus anderer Welt in seinen ruhenden Raum" (*M* 197; he shuddered, feeling as if an invisible door had been suddenly opened, a door through which a chill breeze from another world was blowing into his sheltered room, *FN* 104).

This story is close to Levinas's thought in some ways. Levinas argued that an encounter with an "other" is inevitably traumatic. If the "other" can fit neatly into one's pre-existing categories, then the "other" is obviously not other. If the "other" is genuinely other, then the "other" escapes or even explodes our pre-existing categories. To Levinas, as Simon Critchley writes, "the 'other' is not a phenomenon but an enigma, something ultimately refractory to intentionality and opaque to the understanding" (*C* 8). Not only is it opaque; as Critchley reminds us, Levinas, in his later work, frequently referred to the encounter with the 'other' as "traumatizing" (*C* 13).

Levinas spent much of his career exploring the encounter with, or the avoidance of the encounter with, the "other." In *Totality and Infinity* he argues that Western thought, since the Greeks, has tried to discover some "total" system that explains everything. Every such attempt, though, is exploded by what Levinas calls "infinity," that which is inherently beyond any totality. In *Otherwise than Being* (2008), Levinas explores, among many other things, the linguistic ramifications of alterity.[31] Levinas makes a distinction between "*le dit*," the "said" (that which is said), and "*le dire*," the "saying" (what one is saying). We instinctively struggle toward the "said," the finished, the closed, the comprehensible. At the most abstract level, philosophers who make claims about "being" are most often, according to Levinas, attempting to capture being in the "said." "Saying," on the other hand, is expression not yet limited by concept; "saying" is not yet finished; "saying" remains open-ended and unfinished. The "said" is static, fixed; "saying" engages one in an unpredictable process. The "said" is ontological; "saying" is ethical (*C* 17). Levinas does not see this differentiation as a distinction between good and bad; without the "said," thinking-in-concepts would be impossible. But Levinas does insist that there is a horizon beyond the given, infinity beyond totality, something other than being. There exists a "saying" that precedes the "said," and this "saying" is foundational to, and in some way prior to, the "said." If there is any freedom for us, any redemption possible for us, Levinas argues, it is to be found in the saying, which reveals the infinite, that which is beyond being. The encounter with the infinite, though, the encounter with that which is "beyond being," which is radically other, is inherently "traumatic" (*BPW* 131).

Trauma can take many forms; it need not be operatic. In "Sommernovellette" ("The Fowler Snared," 1906), for example, Zweig tells a bleak story which evolves into a story within a story within a story. As is typical for a Zweig novella, an unnamed narrator encounters an odd fellow with an odd story to tell—"wovon ich glaube," the odd fellow says, "dass es eine hübsche Novelle wäre"[32] ([which might] be worked up into a novella, *FN* 109). Once, while travelling, this odd fellow—and older gentleman—noticed in his hotel a pretty young girl sitting demurely with her rather plain mother. A fancy struck the older gentleman; perhaps he could inject love into the girl's life not by approaching her himself— he is far too old for that—but by writing her an anonymous love letter. He writes one, then another, and is delighted to see the girl's excitement increase daily. A handsome young man appears at the hotel; he and the girl shyly exchange glances; the older gentleman writes yet another letter, this one confirming the girl's hopes that the young man is flirting with her. But, all ends in disaster. Somehow the mother had been intercepting the letters, and the tearful girl is hurried away. The older gentleman's fake letters did not lead to love but to heartbreak. The narrator re-enters the story and suggests other possible endings. The older gentleman admits that in the end he too was heartbroken by this incident. Quoting Balzac, he remarks that "*L'amour coûte cher aux vieillards*" (*PN* 18; love is costly for the old, *FN* 117). The sad old man wanders away. It is night, but the narrator is not tired; he writes: "Aber die Müdigkeit, die sonst von der Wärme der weichen Nächte mich früh befing, war heute zerstreut durch die Erregung, die im Blute aufklingt, wenn einem Seltsames widerfährt oder wenn man Fremdes für einen Augenblick wie Eigenes erlebt" (*PN* 18; The fatigue I might have felt this sultry night was kept at bay by the stir of the blood that comes when something strange has happened, *FN* 117). In the black sky, a meteor catches the narrator's eye and it seems to him that, like the meteor, we too are "von blinder Kraft geschleudert wie ein Leben in die jähe Tiefe unbekannter Geschicke" (*PN* 19; driven by a blind force as our lives are driven into the abysses of unknown destinies, *FN* 118).

Zweig's sad and often traumatic stories, are not, however, merely exercises in melancholy. In each story, a frozen world, a rigid life, a "said" narrative, is suddenly disrupted by the unknown, by a surprise, by something dangerous, by some "saying." Formally, of course, Zweig makes this point by beginning a narrative, then interrupting it by some "story," by a telling, a "saying" which interrupts the "said." Here Zweig's writing parallels Levinas's thinking. To use Levinas's terms, Stefan Zweig is a narrator not of the "said," but of the "saying," and if there is redemption in Zweig's fictional universe, it is revealed in the saying which reveals the infinite that is beyond being.

Redemption

Zweig's characters normally face very hard lives. In their world, invariably, "das Unerwartete [geschieht] plötzlich" (*M* 485; the unexpected suddenly happen[s], *CS* 76). The body of the strange passenger in *Der Amokläufer* washes ashore, drowned, in Naples Bay. The obsessed waiter, François, in "Der Stern über dem Walde," throws himself under a train. The maidservant in "Leporella" (1929) drowns in the Danube. The despairing Russian prisoner of war in "Episode am Genfer See" ("Incident on Lake Geneva," 1919) when he realizes just how far away Russia is, drowns himself. These four tales, like so many other Zweig texts, are narratives of destruction. The odd, the eerie, and the strange traumatically interrupt mundane life, with catastrophic results. However, as Zweig's translator Anthea Bell points out, "one might reasonably suppose, then, that Stefan Zweig, like Webster in T. S. Eliot's famous line, was much possessed by death. Yet although the elegiac note prevails, in all these four suicides there are gleams of light, certain redeeming features" (*A* 142).

It is fair to ask if there is redemption in Zweig's fictional world. Astrid Heyer, comparing Zweig to the French novelist Georges Bernanos, argues that "Zweig has not integrated [in his work] the component of spiritual salvation. There is not a hint of God's presence."[33] Still, as Anthea Bell has noted in the aforementioned quote, even in Zweig's often suicidal narratives, there are traces or hints of happier possibilities. In *Phantastische Nacht*, for example, the first-person narrator explains that a packet of papers from one Baron von R., who was killed in battle in 1914, has fallen into the narrator's hands. The papers recount Baron von R.'s "fantastic night." As an aristocrat and as something of a misanthrope, Baron von R. had few human contacts. But, thanks to a typically Zweigian chain of odd events, Baron von R. becomes engaged with a series of different people in Vienna. Suddenly, the icy Baron von R. feels that he is at long last engaged with other human beings: "[Ich] spürte ich die Masse, [Ich] spürte Menschen all seine Macht" (*PN* 214; [I] felt the crowd, [I] felt human beings as a force," the Baron writes (*FN* 45). He becomes entangled with the very dregs of Viennese society, while he understands the magnetic power that drives prostitutes and their clients together: "Und mit einmal verstand ich, was Männer zu solchen Wesen treibt, verstand, daß es selten nur Hitze des Blutes ist, ein schwellender Kitzel ist, sondern meist bloß die Angst vor der Einsamkeit, vor der entsetzlichen Fremdheit, die sonst zwischen uns sich auftürmt" (*PN* 224; Suddenly I understood what drives men to such creatures, I saw that it is seldom just the heat in the blood, a growing itch, but is usually simply the fear of loneliness, of the terrible strangeness that otherwise is between us, *FN* 52). Shadowed by two criminals, the Baron is shocked that he does not hate or fear them: "In diesem Augenblick überkam mich plötzlich ... ein so unendliches, ein brüderliches Mitleid mit diesen beiden Menschen" (*PN* 234; I was suddenly overcome by an infinite, fraternal sympathy for these two men, *FN* 59). In the story, the "other" is terribly other, and yet when the Baron surprisingly experiences concern, sympathy, and even love for that "other," he is transformed. At the end of this story, the Baron called his experience "das Wunder meiner Erweckung" (*PN* 243; the miracle of my awakening, *FN* 66).

Doomed love and inexorable obsession lead to self-destruction, but Zweig's protagonists rarely act out of malice. Their dreadful fates are interspersed with powerful lines of affection, wonder, and care. Zweig's aim is usually not simply to relate a sad story. Perhaps Peter Gay has it backwards when he writes in his introduction to Joel Rotenberg's translation of *Schachnovelle* that Zweig's aim is to "unriddle the mystery" (*CS* 10) that shaped his characters' lives. It could be that Zweig's wish is to "riddle with mystery" the mundane lives of his predominantly bourgeois protagonists. Perhaps his aim is not so much to answer questions as it is to question answers. If there were to be a motto for Zweig's stories, it might well be, as it is said in *Schachnovelle*: "Doch nun ereignete sich etwas Unvorhergesehenes" (*M* 449; But now, something unforeseen happened, *CS* 31). Zweig's invariable narrative move is to shiver the fixed back into the mobile, the certain into the uncertain. Zweig's play-within-a-play structure, in which a first narrator recounts another's story, is designed to destabilize the "said"—that is, the fixed narrative structure—by injecting into it, a "saying"—that is, a second narrative, centered by the unexpected. Zweig's controversial essay, "Die Monotonisierung der Welt" (1925), in which he severely criticizes "Americanism," functions in a similar fashion. Zweig's skepticism about "Americanism" is much more than European snobbery. Zweig saw in "Americanism" a relentless drive toward conformity, homogeneity, and totalism; Americanism is in this sense the "said."[34] Europe, with its fierce heterogeneity and diversity, is thus the "saying" to America's "said." The recurring rupture of the "said" by the "saying" in Zweig's work is not simply a storytelling technique; it is, rather, to speak with Levinas, the road to redemption.

For nearly five years, from 1940 to 1945, Levinas was a prisoner of war. During those years, he thought out what he would later publish as *Existence and Existents*, his first book. A student of Husserl and Heidegger, Levinas brooded about reality, existence, and being. Life in the prison camp, he came to think, was not unlike life in freedom. Life is life, being is being, and according to his experience: "Being is essentially alien and strikes against us. We undergo its suffering embrace like the night, but it does not respond to us" (*EE* 9). The oddest thing about being, Levinas thought, was that though real, being is no-thing, nothing; being is a kind of "anonymous rumbling" (*EE* 23) we hear with our peripheral hearing; no-thing being is the "it" in "it's going to rain"; the "there" in the "there will be trouble"; the "*il*" in "*il ya a*" ("there is"), and the "es" in "es gibt" ("there is"). Levinas writes: "The rustling of the *there is* . . . is horror. We have noted the way it insulates itself in the night, as an undetermined menace of space itself disengaged from its function as receptacle for objects, as a means of access to being" (*EE* 55). This sense of being is much like the protagonist's "nothing" in Zweig's *Schachnovelle*. The protagonist, Dr. B., recounts the imprisonment he endured, and says: "Aber niemand kann schildern, kann messen, kann veranschauen, nicht einem anderen, nicht sich selbst, wie lange eine Zeit im Raumlosen, im Zeitlosen währt, und keinem kann man erklären, wie es einen zerfrißt und zerstört, dieses Nichts und Nichts und Nichts um einen" (*M* 461; There's no way to describe, to gauge, to delineate, not for someone else, not for yourself, how long time lasts in dimensionlessness, in timelessness, and you can't explain to anyone how it eats at you and destroys you, this nothing and nothing and nothing around you, *CS* 47).

Philosophy's great struggle, Levinas thinks, at least in the West, has been to tame this ominous being by enclosing it in clear concepts. The process of hunting and capturing being, ontology, is for all its merits doomed to defeat because being eludes its concepts, conceptualization. Concepts are that which can be "said"; but being constantly escapes the frozen said and returns to elusive "saying." As Rudolf Bernet points out, Levinas here is much like the psychoanalyst Jacques Lacan: "Levinas comes very close to the Lacanian notion of the 'Real' as that which remains 'beyond signification.'"[35]

But this comparison is not quite accurate, for Levinas insists that if "the Real," which is beyond our concept of being, cannot be "said," we are capable of "saying" something about it, and that it is quite capable of "saying" something to us. To be sure, "saying" disrupts the "said"— a more compelling second story disrupts a first story—and the result is traumatic. Yet, as the protagonist of *Schachnovelle* explains: "In dieser äußersten Not ereignete sich nun etwas Unvorhergesehenes, was Rettung bot" (*M* 462; At this moment of greatest need, something unforeseen happened that promised to save me, *CS* 48). The unforeseen, so often the trigger of trauma and disaster, is simultaneously the only thing—which is beyond "thingness"—which can transport us from the "no-thing" of being to the Good which is beyond being.

Of course, Stefan Zweig is not Emmanuel Levinas. Zweig is no philosopher, and Levinas is no storyteller. Yet, these two very different writers experienced different aspects of the same catastrophe; both looked to alterity, trauma, and redemption as three keys to finding their ways through dark times. For Levinas, this may mean that his seemingly arcane and obscure thoughts actually have a wide resonance. For Zweig, this may mean that his work has a philosophical depth yet to be explored. Perhaps this recognition is one reason why, having survived an extensive season of gerontophagy, Zweig has again become the focus of serious study. Perhaps Zweig has himself now become the "other" who haunts us.

Notes

[1] C. Vann Woodward, *Thinking Back: The Perils of Writing History* (Baton Rouge: Louisiana State University, 1986), 4.

[2] Michael Steinberg, "Hannah Arendt and the Cultural Style of the German Jews," *Social Research* 74, no. 3 (Fall 2007): 879.

[3] Sylvia Patsch, "Stefan Zweig and English Literature," *Modern Austrian Literature* 17, no. 2 (1984): 59.

[4] Randolph J. Klawiter, "The Reception of Stefan Zweig in the United States, a Bibliographical Account," *Modern Austrian Literature* 20, no. 3/4 (1987): 53.

[5] Klawiter, "The Reception of Stefan Zweig in the United States," 53.

[6] Ken Frieden, "The Displacement of Jewish Identity in Stefan Zweig's 'Buchmendel,'" *Symposium: A Quarterly Journal in Modern Literatures* 52, no. 4 (Winter 1999): 232.

[7] Leon Botstein, "Stefan Zweig and the Illusion of the Jewish European," *Social Studies* 44, no. 1 (Winter 1982): 63 (hereafter cited in text as B).

[8] Alex Ross, "The Music Mountain," *New Yorker*, June 29, 2009, 64.

[9] William Deresiewicz, "Dead Letters," *Nation*, June 9, 2008, 11 (hereafter cited in text as D).

[10] Stefan Zweig, "Geschichte eines Unterganges," in *Der Amokläufer: Erzählungen* (Frankfurt am Main: Fischer, 1984) (hereafter cited in text as *GU*). English-language translations cited from Stefan Zweig, *Twilight and Moonbeam Alley*, trans. Anthea Bell (London: Pushkin Press, 2005) (hereafter cited in text as *TW*).

[11] Stefan Zweig, *Die Mondscheingasse: Gesammelte Erzählungen* (Frankfurt am Main: Fischer, 1989), 336.

[12] This novella has been translated into English as *The Royal Game*, trans. Ben Huebsch (London: Pushkin Press, 2001); as "The Royal Game," in *The Royal Game and Other Stories*, trans. Jill Sutcliffe (New York: Holmes & Meier, 2000), 7–71; and as *Chess Story*, trans. Joel Rotenberg, with an introduction by Peter Gay (New York: New York Review of Books, 2006). Since Rotenberg's translation (hereafter cited in text as *CS*) is the novella edition that is most readily available to American readers, his translation has been referenced throughout this essay.

[13] Karl Kraus, "Franz Ferdinand und die Talente," in *Grimassen: Auswahl 1902–1914* (Berlin: Volk & Welt, 1977), 557.

[14] Wilma Iggers, "*The World of Yesterday* in the View of an Intellectual Historian," in *Stefan Zweig: The World of Yesterday's Humanist, Today*, ed. Marion Sonnenfeld (Albany: State University of New York Press, 1983), 18.

[15] Oliver Matuschek, *Stefan Zweig: Drei Leben, Eine Biographie* (Frankfurt am Main: Fischer, 2006), 325.

[16] Lynda King, "The Parallel Lives of Two Austrian Superstars: Vicki Baum and Stefan Zweig," *Modern Austrian Literature* 37, no. 3/4 (2004): 13.

[17] Howard Caygill, *Levinas and the Political* (New York: Routledge, 2002), 5.

[18] Simon Critchley and Robert Bernasconi, eds., *The Cambridge Companion to Levinas* (New York: Cambridge, 2002), 6 (hereafter cited in text as *C*).

[19] Jacques Derrida, *Adieu to Emmanuel Levinas*, trans. Pascale-Anne Brault and Michael Naas (Stanford, CA: Stanford University Press, 1999), 4.

[20] Emmanuel Levinas, *Emmanuel Levinas: Basic Philosophical Writings*, ed. and trans. Adriaan T. Peperzak, Simon Critchley, and Robert Bernasconi (Bloomington: Indiana University Press, 1996), 20 (hereafter cited in text as *BPW*).

[21] Emmanuel Levinas, *Totality and Infinity*, trans. Alphonso Lingis (Pittsburgh: Duquesne University Press, 1969), 26 (hereafter cited in text as *TI*).

[22] Martin Buber, *I and Thou*, trans. Walter Kaufman (New York: Scribners, 1970).

[23] Emmanuel Levinas, *Existence and Existents*, trans. Alphonso Lingis (Pittsburgh: Dusquene University Press, 1988), 16 (hereafter cited in text as *EE*).

[24] Stefan Zweig, "Der Amokläufer," in *Meisternovellen* (Frankfurt am Main: Fischer, 2012), 86 (hereafter cited in text as *M*). English translation cited from Stefan Zweig, *Amok and Other Stories*, trans. Anthea Bell (London: Pushkin Press, 2006), 11 (hereafter cited in text as *A*).

25 Stefan Zweig, "Der Stern über dem Walde," in *Verwirrung der Gefühle* (Frankfurt am Main: Fischer, 2009), 9.

26 Emmanuel Levinas. *Time and The Other*, trans. Richard Cohen (Pittsburgh: Duquense University Press, 1990).

27 Astrid Heyer, "Suicide in the Fiction of Georges Bernanos and Stefan Zweig: The Death of Two Female Adolescents," *Christianity and Literature* 56, no. 3 (Spring 2007): 442.

28 James Berger. "Trauma and Literary Theory" *Contemporary Literature* 38, no 3 (Fall 1997), 572. Hereafter cited in text as Berger.

29 Rudolf Otto, *The Idea of the Holy*, trans. John Harvey (New York: Oxford University Press, 1969), 31.

30 Stefan Zweig, *Fantastic Night and other Stories*, trans. Anthea Bell et al. (London: Pushkin Press, 2007), 71 (hereafter cited in text as *FN*).

31 Emmanuel Levinas, *Otherwise than Being*, trans. Alphonso Lingis (Pittsburgh: Duquesne University Press, 2008), 37.

32 Stefan Zweig, *Phantastische Nacht: Erzählungen* (Frankfurt am Main: Fischer, 2009), 8 (hereafter cited in text as *PN*).

33 Heyer, 447.

34 Robert McFarland, "Migration as Mediation: *Neue Freie Presse* American Correspondent Ann Tizia Leitich and Stefan Zweig's 'Die Monotonisierung der Welt,'" *Seminar* 42, no. 3 (September 2006): 242.

35 Robert Bernet, "The Traumatized Subject," *Research in Phenomenology* 30 (2000): 160–79.

Part III. Criticism and Essays

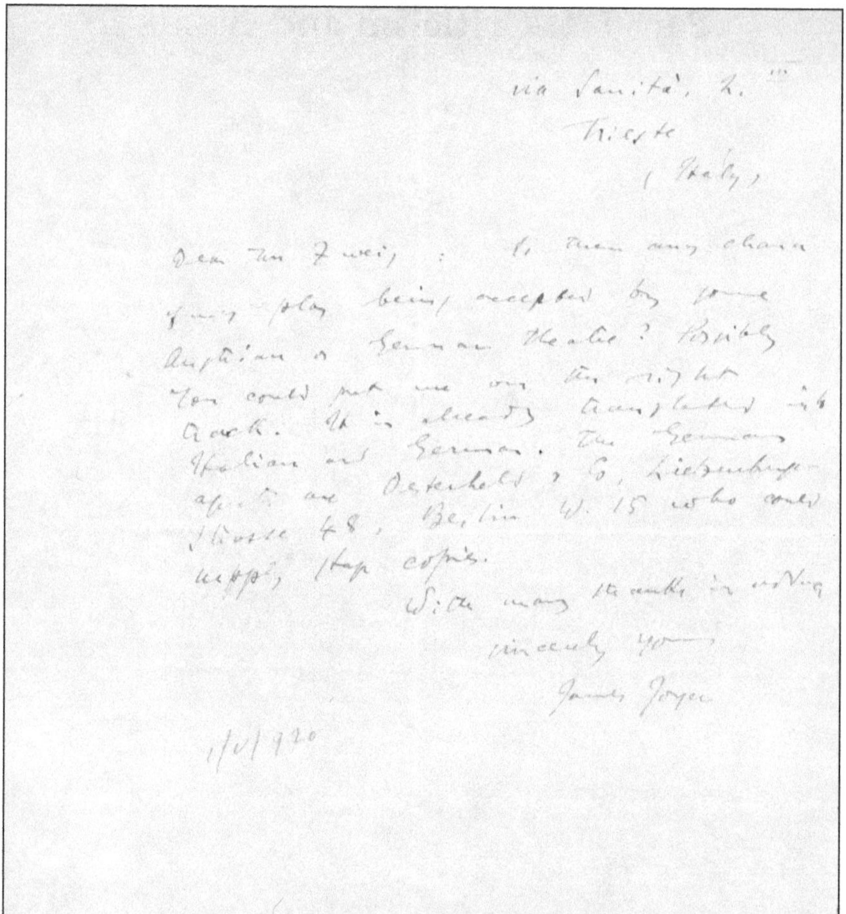
via Sanità, 2. III
Trieste
(Italy)

Dear Mr Zweig: Is there any chance of my play being accepted by some Austrian or German theatre? Possibly you could put me on the right track. It is already translated into Italian and German. The German agents are Oesterheld & Co, Lietzenburgerstrasse 48, Berlin W. 15 who could supply stage copies.

With many thanks in advance
sincerely yours
James Joyce

1/V/920

Fig. 5.1. Letter from James Joyce. Courtesy of the Stefan Zweig Collection at Reed Library, State University of New York at Fredonia.

5: Stefan Zweig and the Concept of World Literature

Mark H. Gelber

THE GAP IN TIME BETWEEN STEFAN ZWEIG'S 1942 suicide and the present provides us with the possibility of attaining a fair vantage point for an assessment of his contribution to "world literature." Before doing so, however, it will be important to delimit a workable concept of world literature which can be utilized for this analysis. In the first part, which is the bulk of this essay, it is important to describe and measure Zweig's contribution to world literature as it was registered or acknowledged during his lifetime. The time frame extends from the date of his first publications at the end of the nineteenth century, through the interwar years, when he reached the apex of his career as a writer and was celebrated as the most widely read and translated serious German-language author in the world, until his suicide in February 1942 in exile in Brazil. One goal of this essay is to position Zweig within the context of world literature and to assess how important a writer he was during his lifetime within this specific framework. In the second part, which is brief in contrast to the first, a depiction of his place within world literature in the time period after his death is provided. The status and reception of writers are subject to ever-changing constellations of factors which exert an impact on world literature, and Zweig's place or rank invariably changes as critical reflections about his writings and stature negotiate their way through newly emerging and different conceptions of literature and culture.

One factor that renders a fair assessment of Zweig's place within the framework of world literature somewhat problematic is his fluctuating popularity over time and in different places, especially taking into account the dramatic decline in his stature during the last half-century in German-speaking Central Europe and in the Anglo-American literary and cultural world. This decline is particularly noticeable among the academic and intellectual elites, from whose ranks the arbiters of literary taste, canonicity, and sometimes plain popularity emerge. Because the English language has established itself as the global lingua franca, in face of the technological and communications revolution of the last thirty years, failure to secure or maintain true literary stature in the English-language cultural world would seem to have serious international literary implications.

While it is generally acknowledged that during his lifetime Zweig was widely considered one of the towering figures of European letters, with an extended international readership, his status dropped precipitously following his death, especially in Central European, German-speaking and -reading Europe. For example, in 2003, Marcel Reich-Ranicki, one of the most influential literary critics and arbiters of German-language culture with an extensive, indeed mass, public following, was asked to comment on the amply lauded German-language literature of the Weimar Republic, that is, the literature of the years between the World Wars, the very time of Zweig's greatest popularity. Reich-Ranicki recalled in his response the following names: Rainer Maria Rilke, Hugo von Hofmannsthal, Stefan George, Thomas Mann, Franz Kafka, Hermann Hesse, and Arthur Schnitzler, first and foremost, followed by Bertolt Brecht, Gottfried Benn, Alfred Döblin, Ödon von Horwath, Robert Musil, Kurt Tucholsky, and Joseph Roth.[1] The name of Stefan Zweig evidently did not even come to mind. One may fairly ask what were the evaluative or critical principles, explicit or implicit, that led Reich-Ranicki to mention the specific writers he cited. He does not in fact elaborate those principles; thus, one can only surmise what they may have been. It appears likely that he attributed primacy in his response to literary innovators with a particularly nuanced relationship to the German language and an acute interest in the problematics or crisis of expression. Judging from the specific names listed above, it could be that for Reich-Ranicki Zweig was not skeptical enough about literary expression, or he was not polysemic enough in his works, not ambivalent enough, or not ironic or mysterious enough. Zweig did not produce literature as a result of intense personal suffering; he was not an expressionist, and he was not politically motivated. He never cultivated a symbolic or mythic discourse. He was sentimental, wealthy, and his creative sensibilities were aesthetically conservative and not sufficiently modernist. He celebrated authors and the zeitgeist that informed their works; in fact, he tended to idealize authorship in general, viewing authors and their works as unities. Any or all of these explanations might help explain his absence from Reich-Ranicki's list, which is in a way tantamount to a fall from grace, as it means banishment from the circle of writers of first rank. As a matter of fact, virtually all of the above criticisms had been expressed on occasion or sporadically during Zweig's lifetime, even during the time of his greatest popularity, and sometimes by important literary and cultural figures. But, following his suicide in 1942, an act which was also criticized sharply within the community of German language authors in exile from Nazi controlled Europe, the negative criticism of Zweig came to dominate his reception, especially in Germany and in German-speaking Europe, but also in the Anglo-American world.

While it is true that Zweig's decline in stature in the second half of the twentieth century was precipitous, a very different trajectory of his reputation may be traced in other locations and languages. For example, Zweig's immense popularity has continued or even increased since his death in France, in Russia and throughout Eastern Europe, in Brazil, in China, and in the Far East. In these places he and his writings in translation continue to enjoy enviable stature and they also command serious respectability in academic, literary, and intellectual circles. It very well may be that different evaluative criteria have been awarded primacy in the different cultures, or that his works read differently in various languages and locations. I call these criteria the underlying nationalist factors in international reception. For example, Zweig's popularity in France was, and continues to be, exceedingly strong. Studies about him and his writings are regularly published in French; his works are available and often republished in French translations; there are numerous Stefan Zweig clubs which are visible in French cultural life; films of his works are often screened, public lectures and international conferences about him and his work are frequently organized; the last major international conference, perhaps, was the Colloque international: Actualité(s) de Stefan Zweig, which took place at the Université de Haute-Alsace, Mulhouse in March 2010. The organizers of the conference were keen to explore the reasons for Zweig's extended and loyal French readership, as well as the factors which keep him very much present on the French cultural scene, whether in print or on screen. Evidently, he was and continues to be the most widely read German-language author in France.

Some of the reasons for this phenomenon may be found in Zweig's privileged relationship to French language and letters. It is fair to label Zweig a francophile; he spoke and wrote French fluently in a country where *francophonie* and *francophilie* are very important cultural values for the literary establishment. Also, he worked tirelessly during his lifetime to promote French poetry, literature, and culture throughout German-speaking Europe. This task was not an easy one, given the political and military enmity and tense economic, industrial, and cultural competition between France and Germany that characterized the period of Zweig's lifetime. Zweig was a frequent guest in Paris and he cherished numerous French writers, artists, and intellectuals as his close friends. He regularly translated from French into German, edited volumes of French literature for German publishers, reviewed French literature for German-language periodicals, wrote biographies, historical miniatures, and literary studies of leading French authors, thinkers, and historical personalities, both those living and those long dead, including (just to mention a handful): among the authors, Stendhal, Balzac, Rousseau, Chateaubriand, Baudelaire, Rimbaud, Renan, Taine, Sainte-Beuve, Verlaine, Romain Rolland, and Proust; or among the historical figures: Marie Antoinette, Joseph Fouché, and Napoleon. In a sense, the French public has appreciated and continues to appreciate Zweig for all of these myriad efforts, in addition to their establishing ever new bonds of affinity with him through his literary work. In this way, the French reception of Zweig may be understood partially as an expression of gratitude to him.[2]

In two recent books, however, David Damrosch has invited us to reconsider world literature, that is, the *concept* of world literature in different ways, some of which may shed light on the issue of Zweig, his variable or varying popularity and stature in different languages and cultures, and also on the issue of his contribution to world literature in general. In *What Is World Literature?* (2003)[3] and *How to Read World Literature* (2009),[4] Damrosch formulated the following definition of world literature: world literature is comprised of literary works that circulate beyond their culture of origin, either in translation or in their original language (*WWL* 4). Damrosch thus focused his attention on literary production, publication, and circulation, but also on global reception. It is generally agreed that the concept of "Weltliteratur" (world literature) derives from Goethe, who introduced the concept in 1827 in a conversation with Eckermann, his primary interlocutor in the latter part of his life, who dutifully recorded and later published their conversations (*WWL* 2). According to Eckermann's record, Goethe opined that the concept of "national literature" had lost its meaning and that, in any case, the epoch of world literature was at hand to replace it. Readers familiar with Goethe's *Faust I*,[5] for example, may recall the "Prelude in the Theater," one of the three prologues which introduce this classic work, and the fact that this Prelude is closely modeled on one found in a play by the ancient Indian Sanksrit writer, Kalidasa: namely, the play *Shakuntala*.[6] Goethe, who read literature in the original in several European languages, also read world literature in translation, and he had read Kalidasa in translation. In this same manner, Goethe read Serbian poetry, Chinese novels, and Persian verse, and much of his "global reading" finds its way, sometimes obliquely but sometimes explicitly, into his own literary production. His ambitious poetry collection, *West-Östlicher Divan* (1819, 1827)[7] is regularly cited in this regard. For Goethe, the concept of world literature was based on improved access to literature from traditions and cultures based far away from the European continent. Damrosch employed the term "glocalism" to help explain the phenomenology of literary works crossing national boundaries, especially in terms of the exportation of local situations abroad or the importation of global situations home. Damrosch writes: "In literature, glocalism takes two primary forms: writers can treat local matters for a global audience—working outward from their particular location—or they can emphasize a movement from the outside world in, presenting their locality as a microcosm of global exchange" (*HRWL* 109). Furthermore, Damrosch argues that literary works may manifest themselves differently abroad than they do at home, or in fact, that works change when they move from a national to a global context. For Damrosch, world literature refers preeminently to works that gain something in literary translation. While the nature of this gain needs to be investigated critically, it may very well be that the case of Zweig's enormous continuing popularity and stature in France, in Brazil, in China, and elsewhere, as well as the vagaries of his reception in German-speaking Central Europe, might be explained accordingly.

When we bring these perspectives regarding the concept of world literature to bear on the case of Stefan Zweig and his contribution to it, it would be fair to label him as one of the truly outstanding proponents, producers, and facilitators of world literature in the twentieth century, with perhaps one important caveat. The latest observations concerning world literature, formulated by Damrosch and others, are normally careful to resist Eurocentric notions of world literature, which are often based on the notion of the enduring value, indeed the inviolability, of European literary masterpieces. Zweig, for all of his internationalism and cosmopolitanism, remains by and large a grand European with a decidedly Eurocentric focus. Thus, his authorial orientation is partially at odds with the truly global spirit which informs the most recent meditations on the topic of world literature, and it is important to keep this fact in mind. Nevertheless, his reception and impact have been and continue to be truly global, extending in translation far beyond the confines of Europe.

In order to convey the entire picture and to set the record straight, some biographical information must be introduced into this discussion. Already as a young man, Zweig travelled widely throughout the world, as far as India to the East and the Panama Canal to the West, well beyond the boundaries of the European continent. He took world cultures very seriously. He wrote travel pieces, historical miniatures, and books that place non-European locales and literary, historical, and cultural figures associated with them at the center of interest. Towards the end of his life, during the period of his exile from Nazi-controlled Europe, that is, after he departed from Austria and left Great Britain, he lived in the United States and in Brazil, and he traveled throughout North and South America. He also incorporated parallel (non-European) aspects of this experience—which he called a "nomadic" experience—into his writings. But taking his total literary production into account, despite his sporadic interest in and regular exposure to non-European texts, personalities, societies, and cultures, he remained very much within the European orbit, intellectually and spiritually close to European ideas, institutions, and literary establishments, despite the physical distance which separated him from the European continent during the last phase of his life. He never really managed to break out of the European framework or to distance himself from it sufficiently in order to embark on a more globally oriented career within the framework of world literature.

During his lifetime, Zweig's contribution to world literature consisted of prolific authorship, editorship, and literary and cultural mediatorship, which crossed national boundaries. His activities in these areas crossed several national and linguistic boundaries, and not merely the borders between France (and French-speaking Belgium) and German-speaking Central Europe. He authored an extensive corpus of literary and critical works, spanning several genres, including poetry, drama, fiction, including both short texts (the Novelle) and the legend, and longer ones (the novel). Some of these works, especially his short fiction, which often manifests keen psychological insights and subtle characterizations within tightly knit or dramatic plot structures, are literary gems in their own right. He authored full-length biographies, an autobiography, historical miniatures, travelogues, book reviews, eulogies, and essays on a wide range of cultural and literary topics. Much of his literary output, and certainly the more substantial items, were translated into thirty or forty or more languages, thus guaranteeing their international dissemination. In fact, his work proved to be supremely translatable. He commented on this aspect of his writing in his late memoir, *Die Welt von Gestern*,[8] linking it to his dislike or even disdain for excessive verbiage and redundancy in a literary work. Zweig opined that his talent for condensation rendered his works eminently suitable for translation on a global scale:

> ... der ständigen Ausschaltung aller überflüssigen Pausen und Nebengeräusche ... Verzichten-könnens, denn ich klage nicht ... und ... als die durchgesiebte Essenz zurückbleiben. Wenn irgend etwas, so hat mir die strenge Disziplin, mich lieber auf engere Formen, aber immer auf das unbedingt Wesentliche zu beschränken, einigermaßen die Wirkung meiner Bücher erklärt, und es wurde wahrhaft beglückend für mich, dessen Gedanken von Anbeginn einzig auf das Europäische, auf das Übernationale gerichtet gewesen, daß sich nun auch aus dem Ausland Verleger meldeten, französische, bulgarische, armenische, portugiesische, argentinische, norwegische, lettische, finnische, chinesische ... und eines Tages las ich ... daß ich zur Zeit der meistübersetzte Autor der Welt sei. (*WvG* 365–56).[9]

[that steady elimination of all superfluous stops and starts ... being able to forego ... and only—the essence—survive[s] the sifting. If anything, the strict discipline of restricting myself rather to the more limited forms of expression and always to the absolutely essential partially accounts for the effect of my books. It made me extremely happy, who had always thought in terms of the Continent, of the super-national, when publishers from abroad announced their interest, French, Bulgarian, Armenian, Portuguese,

Argentinian, Norwegian, Latvian, Finnish, Chinese, . . . and one day I read . . . that I was then the most translated author in the world.] (*WoY* 321)

Zweig thus became recognized early on and widely as an important voice or authority on various aspects of European culture, especially poetry, prose, theater, and art. He was celebrated by some as a master of the German language; he perfected, a highly stylized, even poetical German prose, to be sure, which appealed seductively to the cultured taste of the German "Bildungsbürgertum"—that is, the well-educated, middle-class readership of Central Europe which prized and idealized literacy, while it cultivated art and literature as primary cultural values. At the same time that his own writings were crossing national and linguistic borders in the original and in translation, Zweig assumed a visible and important role as a literary mediator between cultures. His mediatorship encompassed his work as a translator or adapter of numerous writings, mostly from French and English into German, as well as his sustained efforts as an editor. He was also the author of countless book reviews and introductions to the translated works (into German and French) of a wide variety of writers from their native tongues into German. In this respect, Zweig proved himself to be a devoted disciple of Goethe, who expressed the view that any literature left to itself would soon exhaust its vitality. Any given national literature, in order to stay vibrant and vital, needed to be refreshed by interest in, and the contributions of, foreign literatures, according to Goethe.

In addition, Zweig was for many years very close to numerous influential publishers, especially to Anton Kippenberg, the owner of the Insel publishing house, one of, if not the most, prestigious German publishing firms of its day. Zweig wrote about Insel and Kippenberg in glowing terms in *Die Welt von Gestern* (*WvG* 195–97). According to Zweig's retrospective account, Kippenberg had complete confidence in Zweig's own sense of literary value and the former relied heavily on his evaluative judgments; in this way Zweig was able to influence decisively publication policy at Insel, as well as initiate publication projects and book series. Perhaps the most important one in the context of world literature was the "bibliotheca mundi," or world library project. Zweig's idea, which he was subsequently able to realize at least partially, was to publish world literature, that is, literary masterpieces in their original languages both for a multilingual German-language readership, as well as, when exported, for a wider European or international readership beyond Central Europe. Works by Stendhal and Baudelaire in French, by Byron and Keats in English, but also an anthology of Hungarian literature in Hungarian, and one of Hebrew literature in Hebrew, for example, were published in this series before it ceased to issue new volumes. This internationally oriented project is a perfect example of Zweig as a major propagator and proponent of world literature.

At this point it is helpful to narrow the focus of this essay to specific examples of Zweig's mediatorship, in order to underscore the importance of this aspect of his place in world literature and to amplify it a bit. Two examples from English-language literature have been chosen for this purpose. Despite Zweig's erudition and exposure to English literature, and despite the fact that he resided for several years in London and in Bath, as well as his having spent significant blocks of time in the United States, that is, in New Haven, in Ossining (New York), and in New York City, he never really became intimate or comfortable with American literature and culture, but also perhaps, to an extent with British literature and culture. Towards the very end of his life, in an effort to explain why he preferred South America over the United States or Britain, he confided in letters that the English and American world remained foreign to him. He probably would not have ventured to say the same thing about French literature and culture; in a way, he felt that it was also his, despite the fact that he was not a native speaker or a citizen of France.

Still, one would not necessarily be aware of the fact that Zweig felt somewhat estranged from or uncomfortable with English literature and culture, when evaluating Zweig's numerous writings on English language authors, because he appears to express himself on English topics with as much authority and insight as he exhibits regarding Central European-German or French topics. In the following I focus briefly on the examples of Lord Byron and Charles Dickens. In an essay he wrote on Lord Byron in 1924, he compared Byron astutely with Percy Bysshe Shelley, whose poetry was for Zweig more noble than Byron's, and with John Keats, whose poems reflected more purely poetical genius, when contrasted with Byron's own verse.[10] Evidently, Zweig was quite familiar with English Romanticism. In his essay, he employed an essentialist approach, which drew on Byron's biography and emphasized dimensions of his personality and his character. This orientation led him to conclude that Byron was, in short, more of a fascinating historical figure, or a charismatic hero, or more of a dramatic and captivating personality than a poet (*LB* 603). For Zweig, Byron's true essence, thus, resided outside of his poetic endeavors. In the course of his essay, Zweig contrasted Byron with an entire range of poets and poetic personalities, including Shakespeare and Milton (English tradition), Klopstock, Goethe, and Hölderlin (German), Dante (Italian), and Baudelaire (French). Also, the examples of Nietzsche and Delacroix, a philosopher-poet, on one hand, and a painter, on the other, are integrated into the essay in a comparative sense, specifically regarding the psychological commentary which Zweig offers concerning Byron. Thus, Zweig exhibits impressive international range and comparative, interdisciplinary insights which cross national boundaries. Zweig was attracted to, and intrigued by, Byron's titanic spirit, his pride and strength of will, but also his melancholy. Despite Zweig's numerous references to Byron's writings and obvious familiarity with his works, he avoids employing a literary-critical approach; he never attempts a close reading of Byron's poetry. It is simply not his way of assessing the stature of Byron or other poets and writers.

In his study of Dickens, whom Zweig positioned alongside two other great nineteenth century novelists, Balzac and Dostoyevsky[11]—a study he later included in a collective volume entitled *Baumeister der Welt: Versuch einer Typologie des Geistes* (Master Builders of the World: An Attempt to Classify the Spirit, 1930)—Zweig utilized different evaluative criteria and different analytical categories (in contrast to the essay on Byron), in order to determine the essence of Dickens and his supreme importance as an encyclopedic genius and universal artist. Zweig's approach in this study relies on aspects of Dickens's reception in general; he was fascinated by the relationship of Dickens to his adoring readership, especially in Britain, but also abroad. Zweig digressed at length on the widespread and impassioned anticipation which awaited the monthly installments of Dickens's early work, as it appeared in popular and accessible British journals. In this same vein Zweig cited the well-known example of Dickens's public reading tours. For example, he described enthusiastically how in the United States Dickens's fans lined up days in advance in front of the box office in order to guarantee being able to purchase tickets; people slept on mattresses through bitter-cold winter nights (arranging to have food and drink brought to the line from nearby restaurants so people would not lose their place in line). During the famous American tours, Zweig reported, the lecture halls were inevitably too small, and alternative venues had to be located at the last minute in order to accommodate the huge crowds. Zweig reported that in Brooklyn, New York a massive church was secured at the last minute as a substitute for the original lecture hall, which, although by no means modest in size, could never have accommodated the tumultuous throngs of admirers who waited patiently to listen to, and to experience personally, a public reading by the beloved English writer.

In his extended reflection on Dickens, Zweig in fact employed a significantly different critical approach, in contrast to the essay on Byron, although some aspects are similar. As in the essay on Byron, Zweig situated Dickens in relationship to a plethora of other writers. In the case of Dickens Zweig mentions first and foremost other novelists, but some poets as well, mostly but not exclusively from the tradition of the English novel. Thus, he positioned Dickens not only alongside of the accomplishments of Balzac and Dostoevsky, the two other towering novelists of the nineteenth century who formed the triumvirate of the larger study on the truly outstanding creators, not of one or a few excellent novels, but rather creators of an entire novelistic world, comprised of many first-rate, epic-length texts. Thus, Zweig also contrasted Dickens with Walter Scott, Thackeray, Fielding, Smollett, Oscar Wilde, and Swift, whose achievements, while significant in their own right, were for Zweig inferior to that of Dickens. Zweig also referred to Shakespeare, Shelley, and Byron in the same study. While Zweig was keen on revealing the essential genius of Dickens, parallel to the essentialist thrust of his essay on Byron, he undertook to achieve this goal by relating Dickens to Victorian England, especially in terms of the unique qualities of the English nation resident in Britain, its national home, but also in relationship to the particular time of Dickens's literary activity: the Victorian Age. Zweig claimed that Dickens's novels were in perfect harmony with English literary taste at the moment of their composition, and that his writing was the realization of the English tradition (DM 371). For Zweig, Dickens's humor, his powers of observation, his morality, and his aesthetic and spiritual form belong to and derive from, in effect, the English nation, from sixty million Englishmen (and women) (372). In a highly stylized formulation, Zweig argued that Dickens, in fact, was not the one who produced his corpus of literary works, but it was rather the English and their tradition which created it: "Nicht er hat dieses Werk gedichtet, sondern die englische Tradition" (372). What the writings of Dickens reflected was the will of the nation in the process of becoming—almost in an unconscious manner—works of art (372). At the same time, Dickens, or his writings, succeeded in transforming the everyday experiences of the most unpoetic of all nations into poetry.

It is important to classify or categorize this type of writing about literature and culture. As a matter of fact it is very close to or even characteristic of the work of a nineteenth century French philosopher, literary historian, and cultural critic, Hippolyte Taine, who is not very well remembered anymore, especially outside of France. Nevertheless, Taine was a commanding intellectual figure of the late nineteenth century and quite prolific; he wrote, among many other works, an ambitious *History of English Literature*.[12] Furthermore, the connection between Zweig and Taine is patently obvious, because Zweig wrote his doctoral dissertation on "The Philosophy of Hippolyte Taine," which he submitted to the University of Vienna in 1904. Taine claimed that it was possible to explain literary works as products of three basic contextual categories: "race, moment, milieu." When Taine employed the term "race" in this sense, he did not primarily or necessarily mean "race" in the biological or anthropological sense of the term. Rather it signified the various collective, national, and cultural characteristics, which authors shared with others. "Moment" signified time or timing in the larger sense, either regarding the author's life or the period of time in history, or the zeitgeist, the spirit of the time. "Milieu" was the factor of geographical or cultural space, which also, according to Taine, exerted certain impact on literary creation. Thus, in order to understand a work of literature, all that was ostensibly necessary, according to this methodology, was to comprehend the specificity of race (that is, the national, racialist, or cultural uniqueness or particularity) of the author, the exact time or timing of the creative act, and the specific location of literary genesis, since these three factors were central to the production of literary works and, in fact, to the nature of any aesthetic object. Obviously, Taine's theory is deterministic, positivistic, and reductive. In the nineteenth century, it may have appeared to many to be scientific or quasi-scientific, since it employed to a degree the depersonalized technical discourse and sober rhetoric of scientific inquiry. Consequently, it seemed to represent a modern approach to literature. Furthermore, Taine tended to minimize or even marginalize subjective value judgments which informed much of the common writing on literature in the late nineteenth century. When Zweig wrote that Dickens was basically identical to the English nation, that this reciprocal identity was in fact his (and their) genius, or that his work was the realization of the English tradition, as it came to expression during the Victorian period, Zweig employed the critical categories of Hippolyte Taine. In a doctoral dissertation on Stefan Zweig and Hippolyte Taine, Natascha Weschenbach argued that in wake of his doctoral dissertation virtually all of Zweig's subsequent essayistic and biographical writings were heavily indebted to Taine.[13] In terms of his commentary on Byron and the study of Dickens, though, one can see that he employed Taine inconsistently each time. However, regarding the issue of world literature, as explicated by Damrosch and emphasizing the crossing of national and linguistic boundaries, Zweig has in these cases drawn significantly on a French positivist thinker in order to explore English language authors for a German language (and international) audience, and in turn, in translation for a global readership. This contextualization positions Zweig squarely in the center of the enterprise called world literature.

It must be added that Taine's categories, which cannot provide reliable guidelines for precise literary analysis, may have encouraged Zweig to avoid close reading of literary texts, while he formulated instead hopelessly speculative pronouncements and empty generalizations. In a sense, he became—perhaps partially owing to the tutelage of Taine—a master of sometimes acute, but more often gross generalizations. It may be that these types of formulations appeared intriguing, witty, and exceedingly attractive to his middle class readership, the "Bildungsbürgertum" already referred to at the beginning of this essay. These formulations must have resonated powerfully with this readership, because otherwise it would be very difficult to explain his stupendous popularity during his lifetime. While these generalizations may have struck a chord of sympathetic understanding and knowing approbation in diverse readerships during his lifetime, it is doubtful that they could continue to fulfill this function in the long run, especially after his death. To give specific examples, in the essay on Dickens where Zweig compares the English to the Germans, he states: "Jeder Engländer ist mehr Engländer als der Deutsche Deutscher" (DM 372; Every Englishman is more English than the German is German). This sort of empty nationalistic rhetoric is typical in this regard. Another similar apercu: "Auch als Künstler ist der Engländer mehr rassepflichtig als der Deutsche oder der Franzose" (DM 372; Also as an artist the Englishman is bound more to principles of race than the German or the Frenchman). Zweig was certainly not immune from employing the seductive, but ultimately meaningless racialist jargon of his time—indeed it was part and parcel of the heritage he adopted from Taine.

What I have tried to demonstrate so far in this essay is that Zweig's literary and cultural mediatorship was just as important, if not more important, in terms of his contribution to world literature, than his plain authorship of some very fine literary works. It is not possible within the framework of this essay to give justice to the range and variety of Stefan Zweig's impressive achievements in this regard, although I have already mentioned some of them. Zweig either translated, edited, introduced, promoted, eulogized, and reviewed the following, to name just the most important figures (whom I have not mentioned so far): Heinrich von Kleist, E. T. A. Hoffmann, Jean Paul, Rainer Maria Rilke, Jens Peter Jacobsen, Walter Rathenau, Karl Emil Franzos, Jakob Julius David, E. M. Lilien, Theodor Herzl, Sholem Asch, Joseph Roth, Sigmund Freud, Gerhard Hauptmann, Thomas Mann, Klaus Mann, Jakob Wassermann, Max Brod, Oskar Baum, Ernst Weiss, Felix Braun, Peter Altenberg, Elias Canetti, Eugen Relgis, Gustav Mahler, Alexander Moissi, Berta von Suttner, Hugo von Hofmannsthal, Hermann Bahr, Arthur Schnitzler, Ernst Toller, Michel de Montaigne, Henri Barbusse, Émile Verhaeren, Dante, Ben Jonson, William Blake, Walt Whitman, James Joyce, Leo Tolstoy, Maxim Gorki, Ivan Goncharov. This list goes on. It includes German playwrights, humorists, and politicians; Austrian short-story writers, dramatists, and novelists; English poets, French philosophers, American and Italian poets; Russian realists; Rumanian, Scandinavian, and Yiddish writers; Prague thinkers and polemicists; Zionist artists, stars of the European stage, composers, theater critics, just to name a few. It is fair to say that during his lifetime, Stefan Zweig mediated single-handedly a good portion of the Western canon within German-speaking Central Europe, with a decided emphasis on French, Russian, and English literatures, in addition to German. However, while these activities comprise a substantial element in his contribution to world literature, they naturally lose their importance over time. Thus, after his death, his mediatorship continued to be perceived or to leave its mark to some degree, since the impact of what he had accomplished did not disappear overnight. However, within a generation or less, Zweig's impact in this area faded from the eye or memory of the public in Central Europe and internationally, and he disappeared in this sense from the consciousness of those engaged in the enterprise of world literature.

As a consequence of this situation, in the decades since his death, Zweig's stature and contribution to world literature have been largely judged on the narrow basis of a limited notion of authorship, on one hand, and perhaps on the basis of his propagation of the European idea, his eurocentricity, on the other. Both aspects, while having been subjected to various kinds of trenchant criticism, have allowed him to maintain a hold, even if a tenuous one, within the greater context of world literature in the last so many years. To some degree, a significant resurgence of critical interest in Zweig has depended on a reorientation and a new serious engagement with the idea of authorship itself. Critical approaches which decades ago argued for the "death of the author," typical of Roland Barthes for example, while exerting tremendous influence in literary scholarship for a generation, have, I believe, already exhausted themselves.[14] They need to be, and are being, replaced with other approaches that reevaluate and revalue authorship and authors in relationship to literature and culture. This reevaluation may not follow the guidelines or methodology practiced by Zweig as a follower of Taine in his own writings. But, by attributing more serious scholarly concern to different concepts of authorship and authors, Zweig is likely to gain ground and perhaps reestablish himself as a writer deserving more serious and new critical consideration in the twenty-first century. On March 1, 2011, a graduate student conference entitled "Concepts of Authorship" was held in Israel, and a dozen papers were listed on the program. This example is but one of several which lend credibility to a new tendency to reconsider authors and to reevaluate authorship precisely in this sense.

Furthermore, there have been some noticeable, practical efforts recently, both in the United States and in the Central European-German speaking world, to place Zweig's writings and the issue of his contribution to literature and culture back on the agenda of topical interest. The retranslation in Great Britain and the republication of some of Zweig's fiction, for example, spearheaded by the *New York Review of Books*, are two examples.[15] Another is the organization of several major international conferences on Zweig, in the United States, in Great Britain, and in China. Another initiative is the inauguration of a bi-annual Stefan Zweig lecture in Fredonia, site of the American Stefan Zweig archive. In Central Europe, the recent publication of a new scholarly Stefan Zweig biography and the establishment of the Stefan Zweig Centre in Salzburg, with its ambitious program of events and publications, are additional indications that may be cited. It could very well be that a new phase of Zweig reception and appreciation, precisely in those places where his stature and reputation have suffered the most since his death, is already underway.

Notes

[1] Marcel Reich-Ranicki, "Was charackterisiert die vielgerühmte Literatur der Weimarer Republik?" *Frankfurter Allgemeine Zeitung*, October 26, 2003, 25.

[2] An additional index of Zweig's status in France is the impressive popularity of a recently published novel by Laurent Seksik: *Les derniers jours de Stefan Zweig* (The Last Days of Stefan Zweig) (Paris: Flammarion, 2010). This novel depicts the last few months of Zweig's life, before he committed suicide with his second wife in Brazil. Over 45,000 copies were sold in the first year and publishing rights were negotiated for translations into German, Russian, Turkish, Spanish, Chinese, Korean, and Hebrew.

[3] David Damrosch, *What is World Literature?* (Princeton: Princeton University Press, 2003) (hereafter cited in text as *WWL*).

[4] David Damrosch, *How to Read World Literature* (Oxford: Wiley-Blackwell, 2009) (hereafter cited in text as *HRWL*).

[5] Johann Wolfgang Goethe, *Faust 1. Der Tragödie erster Teil* (Ditzingen: Reclam, 1986).

[6] Shakuntala, *Translations of Shakuntala and Other Works* (Stockbridge, MA: Hard Press, 2006).

[7] Johann Wolfgang Goethe, *West-Östlicher Divan* (Munich: DTV, 1979).

[8] Stefan Zweig, *Die Welt von Gestern* (Frankfurt am Main: Fischer, 1970) (hereafter cited in text as *WvG*). All English translations cited in the text are from B. W. Huebsch and Helmut Ripperger's 1943 translation, reprinted as *World of Yesterday: An Autobiography by Stefan Zweig* (Lincoln: University of Nebraska Press, 1964) (hereafter cited in text as *WoY*).

[9] In this section of *Die Welt von Gestern*, Zweig lamented the "überflüssigen Schilderungen, geschwätzigen Dialogen und unnötigen Nebenfiguren" (*WvG* 363; the superfluous descriptions, talky dialogues, and unnecessary minor characters, *WoY* 319) characteristic of even classic texts of the Western tradition. He wrote: "Selbst bei den berühmtesten klassischen Meisterwerken stören mich die vielen sandigen und schleppenden Stellen, und oft habe ich Verlegern den kühnen Plan entwickelt, einmal in einer übersichtlichen Serie die ganze Weltliteratur von Homer über Balzac und Dostojewskij bis zum *Zauberberg* mit gründlicher Kürzung des individuell Überflüssigen herauszugeben, dann könnten alle diese Werke, die zweifellos überzeitlichen Gehalt haben, erneut lebendig in unserer Zeit wirken (*WvG* 363–64; Even in the most celebrated classics the many sandy and dragging passages disturb me, and often I have laid before publishers the bold notion of a comprehensive series of the literature of the world from Homer through Balzac and Dostoyevsky to *The Magic Mountain* thoroughly curtailing the superfluous in each; then all of those works whose timeless value is undoubted could acquire new life and influence in our day, *WoY* 319). This notion of a strictly edited series of world literature, with an eye toward extreme abbreviation, was fortunately never adopted by any of Zweig's publishers.

[10] Stefan Zweig, "Lord Byron. Das Schauspiel eines großen Lebens" in *Stefan Zweig. Essays*, ed. Dietrich Simon (Leipzig: Insel, 1983), 598–606 (hereafter cited in text as *LB*; unless otherwise noted, all translations are mine).

[11] Stefan Zweig, "Drei Meister" in *Stefan Zweig: Essays*, ed. Dietrich Simon (Leipzig: Insel, 1983), 338–97 (hereafter cited in text as DM).

[12] Hippolyte Adolphe Taine, *The History of English Literature*, trans. H. Van Laun (New York: Holt and Williams, 1872).

[13] Natascha Weschenbach, *Stefan Zweig und Hippolyte Taine* (Amsterdam: Rodopi, 1992).

[14] Roland Barthes, "The Death of the Author" in *Image-Music-Text* (New York: Hill & Wang, 1977), 142–48.

[15] "Stefan Zweig," *New York Review of Books*, accessed April 20, 2014, http://www.nybooks.com/books/authors/stefan-zweig/.

6: Landscape, "Heimat," and Artistic Production: Stefan Zweig's Introduction to *E. M. Lilien: Sein Werk*

Richard V. Benson

EPHRAIM MOSES LILIEN WAS NOT YET THIRTY YEARS OLD when a monograph appeared chronicling his work and celebrating him as one of the greatest artists to emerge during a period of cultural renaissance among European Jews. This 1903 monograph, titled *E. M. Lilien: Sein Werk, mit einer Einleitung von Stefan Zweig* (E. M. Lilien: His Work, with an Introduction by Stefan Zweig, 1903) included an introductory essay by an even younger Stefan Zweig along with reproductions of bookplates, drawings, and book and magazine illustrations spanning Lilien's career up to that point.[1] In his introductory essay, Zweig detailed major stations in Lilien's artistic development and discussed Lilien's artwork as central to the emergence of Jewish national consciousness.

Lilien's work is scarcely known outside specialist circles today, but there can be little doubt of his historical prominence as a major figure in European-Jewish art. Significantly, the beginning of Lilien's artistic output coincided with the so-called "Jewish Renaissance," which began at the fin-de-siècle and marked a renewed engagement with Jewish history and culture.[2] Although the exponents of the Jewish Renaissance, including most prominently Martin Buber, shared many beliefs with members of the Zionist movement, the Jewish Renaissance remained a cultural movement focused on the creation of modern, self-consciously Jewish art and thought, rather than on the foundation of a Jewish nation-state. The monograph thus served as an ideal vehicle for taking stock of recent developments in Jewish art and, ultimately, for exploring some of the most prominent debates within Zionism around 1900. It is Zweig's rich introduction to this text, however, which deserves special attention from scholars today, particularly because of the way Zweig characterizes Lilien's talent and importance. The introductory essay unfolds around a biographical sketch of the artist outlining three major stages in his creative development: his youth in the Galician city of Drohobycz, where he was apprenticed to a sign painter; his failed attempt at artistic success in Vienna, and his ultimate breakthrough in Munich with the journal

Jugend; and his collaborations with two radically different poets: the *völkisch*-nationalist German aristocrat Börries von Münchhausen, and the Galician-born poet of the sweatshops of New York and London, Morris Rosenfeld.

Throughout the essay, Zweig engages with central topics of concern for Jewish culture in German-speaking Europe, including questions about the nature of Jewish art and about the role of culture in the Zionist project. Because these questions marked a major division in the movement around 1900 it would have been difficult to avoid addressing them in an essay on Lilien's work at the time. Perhaps no other artist was situated as squarely in the middle of these debates as Lilien, a fact underscored by his many roles at the Fifth Zionist Congress in Basel in 1901, during which tensions flared between cultural Zionists campaigning for a more central role assigned to modern Jewish culture in the Zionist project, and political Zionists concerned primarily with the formation of a Jewish state. In a speech at that conference, Lilien's friend and collaborator Martin Buber cited Lilien's work as a prime example of the importance of modern Jewish culture for Zionism.[3] At the same conference, Lilien delivered a speech of his own, in which he attempted to find common ground between both camps by trying to clear up apparent misunderstandings on both sides of the issue (S 108–9). He even designed a commemorative postcard for the conference, which bore one of the most enduring images of fin-de-siècle Zionism, based perhaps on the most stable "common ground" available to these two camps.[4]

Significantly, "ground"—common and exotic—is a central concern in Zweig's assessment of Lilien's work and its role in Jewish national consciousness. In the essay he repeatedly turns to images of landscapes, to which he attributes a special influence on Lilien's creative process. In other words, in Zweig's analysis, Lilien's art was deeply rooted in specific images of place. Scholars, including Mark H. Gelber and Markus Helmut Lehnhart, have shown that Zweig's interest in the intersection of place and artistic production was heavily influenced by his engagement with the nineteenth-century French literary critic Hippolyte Taine, whose thought was the subject of Zweig's doctoral dissertation.[5] Zweig even cites Taine in his essay, and their common emphasis on race and milieu—two of Taine's categories for understanding aesthetics—is hardly subtle. Nevertheless, Zweig's particular reliance on notions of place and landscape and images of landscape to explain artistic production deserves closer attention, especially within the context of the Jewish Renaissance and the broader discourses on culture and place prevalent around 1900.

Zweig appropriates two distinct paradigms for understanding the intersection of physical space (that is, location) and the production, dissemination, and reception of culture. First, he engages with a dominant fin-de-siècle discourse on East European Jewish culture in order to position Lilien as a cultural intermediary, an "Ostjude" (East European Jew) with special access both to authentically Jewish culture and to West European civilization. In the process, Zweig draws from the deep, yet notoriously conflicted, wellspring of meaning conveyed by the German notion of "Heimat." This term provided him with a second major discourse on the relationship between location and culture. It served Zweig by helping him explain both the authenticity of Lilien's art and its role in Jewish national consciousness. Through the use of landscape images and these two prominent paradigms of place, Zweig's characterization of Lilien provides clues about the kind of common ground that might have existed for the two sides of the Zionist debates on Jewish culture. This article subjects Zweig's engagement with these two paradigms for understanding space and culture to closer examination as a vehicle for evaluating Zweig's response to the key questions of culture that divided Zionism around 1900.

Lilien and the Discourse of the "Ostjude"

Zweig's introduction provides some context for grasping the importance of Lilien's work. Rather than offering interpretations of individual works or a synthesis of the collection as a whole, Zweig claims in the opening paragraph merely to want to lend to the Galician-born artist's name "einen Strahl jener schöpferischen Liebe zur Kunst, die ihn aus dem Dunkel eines östlichen Dorfes in den Blickpunkt aller Kultur und eines ganzen sehnsüchtigen Volkes erhoben hat" (Z 10; a ray of that creative love of art which raised him out of the darkness of an Eastern village into the focal point of all of culture and of an entire yearning people). This passage suggests that Drohobycz, the East European village of Lilien's youth, offered the young artist scant opportunity to encounter "true" culture. Only his extraordinary love of art allowed him to escape the "darkness" of this village (specifically labeled as an East European location) and emerge into the light of culture. The implicit distinction between East and West in this passage clearly privileges the latter as a site of art and civilization—a place where artistic talent might develop—while situating the former as an obstacle to be surmounted.

The image of Drohobycz as an "Eastern village" that Zweig creates, however, is not quite accurate. As Michael Stanislawski has noted, the community was hardly as small and impoverished as Zweig suggests, but was rather "a bustling center of the petroleum trade with a population of nearly 20,000" (S 101). Moreover, the Jewish population of the small city was hardly homogenous; it reflected the diversity of modern Jewry elsewhere in Europe (S 101–2). The city was thus a far cry from the dark, cultureless "Eastern village" that Zweig describes. In fact, his characterization of Lilien's hometown takes up and perpetuates a romanticized image of East European Jewish life as a kind of ghetto existence, secluded from both culture and modernity in a region that one can only escape through extraordinary effort and fortunate exposure to external "Western" civilization.

This image of the extraordinary "Ostjude" pursuing culture and raising himself from the poverty and "darkness" of *shtetl* life is neither new nor surprising. It fits neatly into what became a standard paradigm in German culture for imagining East European Jewish life. This paradigm was popularized most prominently a generation earlier by the cultural sketches of Karl Emil Franzos, especially his multivolume collection *Aus Halb-Asien* (From Half-Asia).[6] In this 1876 text and throughout much of his career, Franzos used the term "Halb-Asien" to describe the Eastern edges of the Austro-Hungarian Empire, a region he famously characterized as "ein seltsames Zwielicht" (a strange twilight) caught between the light of civilization and the darkness of barbarism.[7] For Franzos, only West European culture offered a means of escaping this situation. If we consider Zweig's essay in light of this popular paradigm for understanding East European Jewish culture, it becomes clear that even as he celebrates Lilien's originality and exemplarity, Zweig strategically situates the artist within a popular discourse that maps culture onto privileged locations. He thus suggests a particular reading of Lilien's artistic achievement: Lilien, the Jewish artist from Galicia, must struggle against local cultural darkness in order to develop his innate talent. All the more remarkable, then (so this story goes), is his art in light of his humble background.

Near the end of the text Zweig takes this view of Lilien a step further. After establishing him as an artist of both the "ghetto" and the highest levels of "Kultur," Zweig assigns him the role of cultural intermediary, a mediator between the world of art and civilization that he eventually entered, and that of "den zahllosen Entfremdeten der Bildung, von denen er gekommen" (Z 27; countless number of those who are estranged from the cultural education from which he came). This view, too, should come as no surprise, for it is a position that many authors and intellectuals with Galician ties claimed for themselves. Franzos himself, in order to legitimate his own writings on Galicia, assumed the role of a privileged insider familiar with the incommensurable worlds of "Bildung" and the *shtetl*. For his part, Lilien's collaborator Martin Buber likewise justified his retellings of the Chassidic legends by claiming an analogous position between East and West in his early work, including *Die Geschichten des Rabbi Nachman* (The Tales of Rabbi Nachman, 1906).[8]

In their writings on East European Jewry, authors such as Franzos and Buber were most concerned with transmitting images of the *shtetl* or of traditional Jewish life to a modern, acculturated, bourgeois (and in some cases non-Jewish) readership. In his essay on Lilien, however, Zweig credits the artist with also bringing culture *into* the *shtetl*: "In seiner Hand hat sich für viele zum erstenmal die Flamme der Kunst entzündet. Die Kongreßkarte, die ferne im teifsten Rußland irgend einer empfängt und staunend im Dorfe umherzeigt, ist der erste Strahl künstlerischer Kultur, der ihnen von allem Anbeginn in die Augen geleuchtet" (Z 27; For many, the flame of art ignited for the first time in his hand. The [Fifth Zionist] Congress card—which someone far away in deepest Russia receives and shows around the village in amazement—is the very first ray of artistic culture that has ever illuminated their eyes). Here again, Zweig assigns familiar roles to East and West in this passage, and in doing so he once again positions Lilien as a kind of "ghetto" artist. Moreover, the deterministic paradigm that he adopts in his discussion of Lilien's origins imbues images of place or location with crucial value vis-à-vis artistic production. However, unlike many texts that draw on such a framework to describe East European Jewish culture—especially those by Franzos—Zweig's rendering of that community is not wholly negative. While the Eastern village is a source of hardship for Lilien, it is also a source of ostensibly authentic Jewish cultural material and it provides a foundation on which Lilien eventually creates nationally-conscious Jewish art. Thus, Zweig's essay depicts Lilien as a true cultural intermediary, crossing boundaries and exerting influence on two distinct cultural worlds.

Landscape, "Heimat," and Artistic Production

As the first paragraph of Zweig's essay already makes clear, notions of place or location are central to his understanding of Lilien's career. However, his discussion of the role of place in Lilien's biography extends beyond the East/West dichotomy that marks so much of the writing in German about Galician Jewry from that period. In order to explain the "Jewish" quality of Lilien's art and its role in Jewish national consciousness, Zweig draws on another major discourse of place in German culture at the beginning of the twentieth century: *Heimat*. The idea of "Heimat," which has undergone significant changes since the early nineteenth century, is notoriously difficult to pin down, particularly in Zweig's youthful, even ebullient prose, and it requires brief contextualization here. The concept rose to particular prominence in Germany in the decades following unification in 1871. During that time, it bore specific associations both with often romanticized notions of local or provincial life and with the more broadly conceived idea of a German nation. In the words of historian Celia Applegate in her classic study of the term: "The utility of *Heimat* lay in its capacity to obscure any chasms between small local worlds and the larger ones to which the locality belonged."[9] Drawing on Applegate's work, Alon Confino shows that multiple local notions of "Heimat" in the German lands became instrumental in crafting a national German identity where none had previously existed.[10] This specific employment of the concept of "Heimat" to bridge the local with the national suggests that, in many ways, "Heimat" is a specifically German expression of broader European responses to modernity. These responses are akin to what Eric Hobsbawm famously termed "the invention of tradition."[11] In Zweig's essay on Lilien, "Heimat" is indeed closely linked to the intangible, even imagined, bonds among people.

Zweig's introduction removes the notion of "Heimat" from its specifically German context in order to refer simultaneously to the Habsburg crownland and to a Zionist vision of Jewish nationalism. Still, his use of the term encompasses the abstract concepts of the local and the national that are usually associated with it. Zweig develops his notion of "Heimat" through descriptions of specific landscapes, which are concrete expressions of abstract ideas about place. They tend to exert decisive influence on artistic production. For instance, Zweig identifies two qualities that contribute to Lilien's inspiration and creative faculties: his deep connection to Jewish tradition, and his upbringing in a Galician landscape. He discusses both of these factors in terms of "Heimat." On one hand, Lilien's "schöpferische Idee" (creative idea) is particularly meaningful according to Zweig, "weil ihre Wurzeln tief eingegraben sind in das ganze blutende Herz eines weltverstreuten *heimatlosen* Volkes" (Z 11, because its roots are deeply entrenched in the entire bleeding heart of a homeless people, dispersed throughout the world).[12] Zweig notes of Lilien: "sein schöpferisches Weltbild ist kein zufälliges und erborgtes, seine Eigenart blüht aus eigenster *Heimatsscholle*, aus Volksmythe und Rassenwerten, aus nationaler Umgebung und persönlichem Schicksal ins Leben empor" (Z 12; his creative world view is neither random nor borrowed; his originality blossoms forth into life from his own native soil, from folk mythology and racial values, from national ambience and personal fate).[13] According to Zweig, Lilien's artistic creativity and his artistic importance are thus rooted in his engagement with Jewish tradition and with Jewish nationality. Zweig describes this people as at once "heimatlos" (without a "Heimat") and yet Galicia appears able to offer "Heimatsscholle" (native soil, literally: a furrow-slice of "Heimat") on which Lilien's creative impulses take root.

It is tempting to attribute the tension in this description—that is, the gap between the lack of "Heimat" that drives Lilien's "creative idea" and the "Heimatsscholle" that allows for his "creative world view" to develop—to Zweig's youthfully energetic but imprecise prose. Perhaps "Heimatsscholle" is simply a metaphor that gestures toward the two abstract concepts that Zweig later associated with it: "Volksmythe" and "Rassenwerte." But in the very next paragraph of his essay, there appears a precise description of the landscape of Lilien's childhood home—the locale that Zweig also refers to as Lilien's "Heimat":

Lilien ist zu Drohobycz in Galizien geboren. Das Land ist arm und traurig. Die *grauen* kalten Felsen der Karpathen sinken dort langsam hinab in die öde *eintönige* Fläche, die sich weit in die russischen Steppen hinüberdehnt. Und das Leben ist ohne Schönheit und hinreißende Gewalt in diesen rauhen unwirtlichen Gegenden. Ein Künstler empfängt dort nicht die wundersame Gabe, die Welt als einen Fächer jubelnder und lockender *Farben* zu sehen, die sich in verrauschenden Formen falten; nie lehrt ihn das Leben, die tausendfach abgetönte *Skala koloristischer Nuancen* in seinen Schöpfervisionen aufklingen zu lassen. Wie ein schmaler Rest bleibt die plastische Silhouette, das flüchtige Bild der Form *ohne den opalisierenden Tanz der farbigen Werte.* (Z 12) [14]

[Lilien was born in Drohobycz in Galicia. The land is poor and desolate. The *gray*, cold cliffs of the Carpathians sink there slowly down into the barren, *monochromatic* expanse, which stretches out far into the Russian steppes. And life is without beauty and captivating force in these harsh, inhospitable regions. An artist will never receive there the wondrous gift of seeing the world as a fan of jubilant and seductive *colors* that fold themselves into intoxicating forms; never will life teach him to allow the thousandfold-tinted *spectrum of coloristic nuances* to echo in his artistic visions. The plastic silhouette persists like a moldy remnant, the fleeting image of form *without the opalescent dance of chromatic values.*]

Lilien's artistic production is clearly tied to landscape in this passage, and the landscape in question—like the "Heimatsscholle"—represents an actual, physical location with definite, fixed geographic borders. Zweig's text asks: How could Lilien possibly develop any kind of artistic vision in this place, devoid as it is of both beauty and color? Indeed, the gray, monochromatic landscape of Drohobycz appears here as something that an artist must overcome, and Zweig's subsequent description of Lilien's failed attempt to establish himself as an artist in Vienna certainly reinforces such a reading. Zweig likens Lilien to a drowning man, who searches for purchase on the nearby shore, "aber alles zerbröckelt unter seinen blutenden Fingern, und jenes dunkle Meer der Not, das Tausende in sein tiefes Schweigen reißt, schleudert ihn in die Heimat zurück" (Z 13; but everything crumbles beneath his bleeding fingers, and that dark sea of hardship, which drags thousands into its deep silence, hurls him back to the "Heimat"). At first, Lilien the artist strives but fails to secure a foothold in the world of culture beyond Galicia. Thus, he is forced to return to his colorless "Heimat" with a renewed longing for high culture—that is, for the metropolitan "Western" culture of Vienna, Munich, or Berlin.

Zweig's description of Lilien's hometown and his narrative of the artist's failed attempt to escape it fit neatly into the familiar ghetto paradigm that Franzos popularized and that has been discussed already. Despite this overtly negative image of Drohobycz and of Lilien's initial failure to escape it, however, Zweig's image of Lilien's gray "Heimat" harmonizes perfectly with his ultimate choice of medium. Zweig's characterization of Drohobycz suggests that it is precisely the monochromatic landscape of Galicia—"das öde, eintönige Land"—that makes Lilien such a capable black-and-white artist. Thus, in Zweig's account, the Heimat-as-obstacle becomes a key factor in Lilien's artistic development, even affecting his choice of medium. And Lilien's medium—the grayscale of the illustrator—lends itself ideally to mass circulation; once Lilien arrives at a form of Jewish national consciousness, the landscape of his local "Heimat" perfectly equips him to spread this consciousness. The physicality of this idea of "Heimat" seems to take precedence over any abstract qualities it might represent. However, Zweig's narrative of Lilien's early life consistently leaves the door open for culture—specifically for Lilien's art— to transcend (and thus supersede) such physicality. Still, Lilien cannot achieve this consciousness until he leaves Galicia—at least not according to Zweig's narrative.

If Lilien's first attempt at overcoming the monochromatic landscape of his "Heimat" was akin to the "feverish exertions" of a drowning man seeking to save himself on an elusive shore, then he subsequently resembles Parzival when he achieves his ultimate breakthrough as a nationally-conscious Jewish artist: "dem plötzlich aus Waldeswegen das silberne Heimatsschloß entgegenleuchtet" (Z 16; for whom suddenly out of the paths of the forest the silver *Heimat*-castle shines forth). This awakening occurred abruptly in Lilien's case and through a single work: Börries von Münchhausen's collection of Jewish-themed ballads, *Juda*, published in 1900 and illustrated by Lilien (Z 16).[15] Although Zweig also attributes Lilien's national-cultural awakening to the increasingly prominent Zionist movement, and to a renaissance in the art of book illustration, he clearly privileges the encounter with Münchhausen as the most important factor. Regarding *Juda*, Zweig relies on landscape imagery to help explain Lilien's artistic achievement, although this time he cites Münchhausen's account of the production of *Juda* directly to make his argument:

> Es war auf unserm Thüringer Schlosse Windischleuba. Ein helles Giebelzimmer oben neben dem Turme war dem Zeichner hergerichtet, neben seinem Zeichentische stand mein Schreibtisch. Weit offen die Fenster, Kartoffelfeuer rauchten durchs Thüringerland, und ihr Duft zog ins Zimmer. Auf den Wiesen und Feldern sangen fern die Kinder. (Z 21)[16]

> [It was at our castle Windischleuba, in Thuringia. A bright gable room upstairs next to the tower was prepared for the illustrator; my desk stood next to his drafting table. The windows were wide open,

smoke from roasting potatoes drifted through the Thuringian landscape, and their fragrance wafted into the room. In the meadows and fields children sang in the distance.]

Neither Münchhausen nor Zweig uses the word "Heimat" to describe the Thuringian landscape in which the poet and the illustrator composed *Juda*. However, the image of the artist laboring in a castle gable, open to the sights, sounds, and smells of the idyllic landscape explicitly recalls, and stands in contrast with, the account of Lilien's monochromatic homeland. Furthermore, Münchhausen reinforces this contrast by noting the distinction between Lilien's biography and his own: "die eine voll von unverdientem Leid, die andere eine einzige große Erfüllung jedes Wunsches" (Z 21; the one full of unearned suffering, the other a single grand fulfillment of every wish).[17] The lush landscape of Münchhausen's Thuringia reflects his own personal and artistic biography, just as the gray cliffs of the Carpathian Mountains exert a critical influence on Lilien's artistic production. Here again, Zweig invokes a specific, physical place with fixed geographic boundaries to explain an aspect of Lilien's artistic production. Moreover, Münchhausen's neo-Romantic castle-and-peasant imagery stands in sharp contrast to the standard, romanticized image of the authentic, yet culturally backward *shtetl* with which Zweig frames his narrative of Lilien's youth in Galicia. Finally, Zweig complements Münchhausen's imagery by drawing on the Parzival romance to help illustrate Lilien's national-cultural breakthrough. In this idyllically-depicted Thuringian landscape, how could anything but a castle rising from the forest symbolize Lilien's epiphany?

Once again, physical, geographic space conditions and subordinates cultural production. At the same time, culture seems to challenge the hegemony of location. For Zweig, the work that Lilien produced in this foreign and idyllic landscape marks "das erste Blatt in der Geschichte der nationalen bewußten Kunst" (Z 21; the first page in the history of nationally-conscious [Jewish] art). It is owing to this creative moment in Thuringia that Lilien crosses an important threshold from art to culture. In short, Lilien's artistic production achieves the status of nationally-conscious Jewish culture only after Lilien leaves his gray and barren Heimat in Galicia and enters an exemplary "German" landscape—one located literally at the heart of Europe. The parallel images of Münchhausen's estate and Parzival's "Heimatsschloss" suggest that the collaboration with Münchhausen in Thuringia entails a kind of homecoming for Lilien, in that he comes to an awareness of his Heimat. But the Heimat Lilien realizes in *Juda* is clearly not Drohobycz, nor is it the Thuringian "Heimat" in which the text was produced. Instead, as Zweig makes clear, *Juda* began to open a space for a community (or nation) of Jews to be united through shared culture and shared experience—a "Heimat" that transcends physical boundaries.

The notion of a transcendent, transnational "Heimat" appears most forcefully in another account of artistic production that Zweig provides in his essay, namely the account of Lilien's illustrations of Morris Rosenfeld's *Lieder des Ghetto* in a German translation from the Yiddish by Berthold Feiwel. Published in 1902, the same year in which Lilien, Feiwel, and others co-founded the *Jüdischer Verlag* (Jewish Publishing House) in Berlin, *Lieder des Ghetto* marks another major book project for Lilien. In Zweig's analysis, this text surpasses *Juda* in terms of both its cultural significance and the "native truth" that it represents. He attributes this significance to the biographical parallels between Lilien and Rosenfeld: "Erst in diesem Buch ist die *heimatliche Wahrheit* ganz in ihm erstanden, weil der fremde Dichter ihm sein eigenes Leben erzählt" (Z 22, emphasis added; the *truth of Heimat* first arose in [Lilien] with this book, because the foreign poet told him his own life story). For Zweig, that Lilien and Rosenfeld both hail from Eastern Europe was crucial, and just as Lilien overcame the monochromatics of his Galician "Heimat" in order to produce great culture, Rosenfeld drew poetical inspiration from his own proletarian tribulations: he had worked as a tailor in the sweatshops of New York and London. While Lilien was creating his art in Berlin, Rosenfeld was writing poetry across the Atlantic, and the common bond that poet and artist shared transcended local origin or even adopted homeland. Since, according to Zweig's conception, Rosenfeld was "der fremde Dichter" (the foreign poet), something other than a shared geographical space or physical location thus united the poet and artist.

The connection between Lilien and Rosenfeld, Zweig contends, is rooted in a shared hope: "der messianische Heimatstraum des verstoßenen Volkes" (Z 22; the messianic dream of *Heimat* of a repudiated people). Here, Zweig suggests a radically different notion of "Heimat" than that posited in the accounts of Lilien's childhood and of his collaboration with Münchhausen. According to this notion of "Heimat," each artist transcends the influence of his own local "Heimat" in the service of a larger Jewish-national "Heimatsidee." Nevertheless, Zweig explains his understanding of each artist's creative vision by once again invoking images of landscape:

> Über dem dunklen *wirren Erdengewühle*, über der *traurigen Einsamkeit des öden Landes* und über *dem Maschinenlärm der großen Städte*, brennt am stillen hohen Himmel die leuchtende Hoffnung des Zionsternes. Und in diesem Verheißungszeichen finden sich zwei treue zerarbeitete Kämpferhände weit über Länder und Meere. Der die Verse schrieb, sang des andern Leben und Sehnsucht und der die Bilder schuf, zeichnet nicht nur eigenes Schicksal, sondern auch das des fernen Bruders. (Z 23)[18]

[Above the dark, *tumultuous throng of the earth*, above the *desolate loneliness of the barren land* and above *the noise of machines in the large cities*, the shining hope of the star of Zion burns in the high, silent sky. And the hands of two loyal fighters, worn to the bone by work, find one another far above nations and seas. The one who wrote verses sang of the life and the yearning of the other, while the other, who created the images, drew not merely his own fate, but also that of the faraway brother.]

The negative image of place ("das öde Land"), which characterized Lilien's "Heimat" in Zweig's description of his earlier career, serves to unite Lilien with Rosenfeld, whose own artwork is a product of locations cast in a similarly negative light ("Maschinenlärm der großen Städte"). But in the section on Lilien's collaboration with Rosenfeld, Zweig does not describe specific locations with definite geographic borders. Instead, the landscapes he depicts are imagined, transcendent landscapes which join the two men as Jewish artists. In this passage, culture completely subordinates geographic location. The abstract notion of "Heimat" that emerges in turn underscores the potential for illumination and dissemination that Zweig attributes to Lilien's work. Accordingly, the Zionist hope opens a channel of cultural influence between Lilien's art and his audience, whether they are acculturated Jews in Vienna or Berlin, or "Ostjuden" "in deepest Russia."

As we have seen, Zweig's essay presents images of landscape to develop notions of "Heimat" which in turn reflect complex relationships to the production and reception of culture. The final image of "Heimat" that emerges in Zweig's essay is rooted in common experience, but it is no longer a lived reality. Instead, it represents a future vision. Such a notion of Heimat indeed encompasses the local and national concepts associated with the term around 1900. However, the ultimate idea of "Heimat" that Zweig presents is in fact transnational. It is a "Heimat" that links disparate landscapes and yet lacks geographic borders. While landscape and Heimat initially seem to condition artistic production in Zweig's essay, this final formulation of a constellation of "Heimat," landscape, and art—which comprise the background for the production of Rosenfeld's *Lieder des Ghetto*—inverts the power structure of this relationship. And, importantly, Zweig privileges the collaboration with Rosenfeld as Lilien's most important work.

That Zweig was later uncomfortable with the overall tenor of his introduction to *E. M. Lilien: Sein Werk* may suggest that he was ambivalent about aspects of Zionism at the turn of the century.[19] In this essay, he grapples with one of the most prominent questions that divided the Zionist organization in this early phase of its existence: the question of the role of culture in the project. In the end, Zweig's essay seems to privilege culture as more important than geography to the Zionist endeavor and to Jewish national consciousness more broadly. Indeed, the complex, transnational image of a "Heimat" united by a messianic hope and by Jewish art seems to transcend politics altogether. A specifically-Jewish "Heimat" can be located most readily in nationally-conscious Jewish art, even in the absence of a specifically-Jewish state. Moreover, if Lilien's journey to national consciousness (as related by Zweig in his essay) is at all exemplary, then Zweig's introduction seems to celebrate non-Jewish spaces as the places in which Jewish national consciousness can emerge. It was, after all, his working in Münchhausen's Thuringian castle, his "Heimatsschloss," that brought about Lilien's own Jewish national awakening.

Throughout his introduction to *E. M. Lilien: Sein Werk*, Zweig links notions of "Heimat" and images of landscape with cultural and artistic production. Through Zweig's repeated appeals to images of landscape, the idea of "Heimat" seems to unfold as a development from a local point of origin that must be overcome, to a transnational cultural community that enables such overcoming. Still, despite the essay's emphasis on landscape and space, and given the implications of territory that these concepts entail, the questions of politics and of the nation-state lurk below the surface in the essay. In one of the essay's few sustained descriptions of an example of Lilien's work—the "Gedenkblatt" from the Fifth Zionist Congress, mentioned above—Zweig invokes the image of "Heimat" as a transcendental cultural realm, only to return to the description of a landscape with a specific geographical location:

> In einem Blatte hat er mit seinem Stifte den ganzen messianischen Traum gestaltet, in einem unvergeßlich schönen Blatt, der Kongreßkarte. Ganz schlicht ist das Symbol. Der zionistische Gedanke als schwingenumrauschter Engel weist dem einsamen Juden in Dornen das Land der alten Verheißung, die sonnige Heimat, die er ackernd durchschreiten soll. . . . Die ganze Sehnsucht lehrt es—und die ganze Erfüllung. (Z 28)

> [On one page, he mapped out the entire messianic dream with his pen, on one unforgettably beautiful page, the [Fifth Zionist] Congress card. The symbol is perfectly simple. The Zionist idea, as an angel encircled by wings, points the way for the forlorn Jew in thorns to the land of the old promise, the sunny *Heimat*, which he should stride across while plowing [the land]. . . . It teaches the entire longing—and the entire fulfillment.]

This description of the "Gedenkblatt" foregrounds the ambiguities and contradictions inherent in the way the Zionist project approached notions of space, belonging, and "Heimat" at the fin-de-siècle. It also indicates Zweig's own ambiguity in approaching these questions. The messianic dream that the card depicts may be merely symbolic, but its symbolism denotes a very particular location—"das Land der alten Verheißung" (the land of the old promise), a historic homeland with a definite geography.

Of course, the landscape that Zweig describes in his reading of the "Gedenkblatt," which is the last of Lilien's works that he mentions, gestures to a location that was highly contested even among Zionists, and the final sentence in his discussion of the card declines to take sides in this controversy, for the exact nature of the fulfillment remains unclear. Certainly the fulfillment of the messianic dream to which the Zionist idea responds involves reclaiming a kind of "Heimat"—a field to be tilled by the forlorn Jew. Given the instability of the idea of "Heimat" in this text and in German culture more broadly, however, one cannot be certain whether the fulfillment of this dream involves a return to a geographic and historic "Heimat" ("das Land der alten Verheißung") or a renaissance of the cultural "Heimat" that Lilien's art embodied.

Notes

[1] Stefan Zweig, introduction to *E. M. Lilien: Sein Werk, mit einer Einleitung von Stefan Zweig* (Berlin: Schuster & Loeffler, 1903), 9–29 (hereafter cited in text as Z. Translations mine).

[2] For a more detailed discussion of the Jewish Renaissance, see Asher D. Biemann, "The Problem of Tradition and Reform in Jewish Renaissance and Renaissancism," *Jewish Social Studies: History, Culture, and Society* 8, no. 1 (2001): 58–87.

[3] Michael Stanislawski, *Zionism and the Fin de Siècle: Cosmopolitanism and Nationalism from Nordau to Jabotinsky* (Berkeley: University of California Press, 2001), 107–8 (hereafter cited in text as S).

[4] For an analysis of Lilien's relationship to the Zionist project, see Milly Heyd, "Lilien: Between Herzl and Ahasver," in *Theodor Herzl: Visionary of the Jewish State*, ed. Gideon Shimoni and Robert S. Wistrich (New York: Herzl Press, 1999), 265–93.

[5] See Mark H. Gelber, "Stefan Zweig und E. M. Lilien: Aspekte der Begegnung von jüdischem Ost und West um die Jahrhundertwende," *Austriaca* 34 (1992): 17–31, and Markus Helmut Lehnhardt, *Du sollst Dir ein Bild machen: Jüdische Kunst in Theorie und Praxis von David Kaufmann bis zur* Kultur Lige (Innsbruck: Studienverlag, 2009).

[6] Karl Emil Franzos, *Aus Halb-Asien: Kulturbilder aus Galizien, der Bukowina, Südrußland und Rumänien*, 4th revised edition, 2 vols. (Stuttgart: J. G. Cotta'sche Buchhandlung Nachfolger, n.d., ca. 1901). I draw here on Steven E. Aschheim, *Brothers and Strangers: The East European Jew in German and German Jewish Consciousness, 1800–1923* (Madison: University of Wisconsin Press, 1982), 27–31.

[7] Franzos, 1: xvi.

8 Martin Buber, *Die Geschichten des Rabbi Nachman* (Gütersloh: Gütersloher Verlagshaus, 1999).

9 Celia Applegate, *A Nation of Provincials: The German Idea of Heimat* (Berkeley: University of California Press, 1990), 10.

10 Alon Confino, *The Nation as Local Metaphor: Württemberg, Imperial Germany, and National Memory, 1871–1918* (Chapel Hill: University of North Carolina Press, 1997), 98.

11 Eric J. Hobsbawm, "Introduction: Inventing Traditions," in *The Invention of Tradition*, ed. Eric Hobsbawm and Terence Ranger (Cambridge: Cambridge University Press, 1983), 1–14.

12 Emphasis mine.

13 Emphasis mine.

14 Emphasis mine.

15 See Börries von Münchhausen, *Juda* (Goslar: F. A. Lattmann, 1900). For an extended discussion of the apparently unlikely collaboration between the Zionist artist Lilien and the *völkisch*-nationalist poet Münchhausen, who would become a prominent cultural figure in Nazi Germany, see Mark H. Gelber, *Melancholy Pride: Nation, Race, and Gender in the German Literature of Cultural Zionism* (Tübingen: Niemeyer, 2000), 87–124.

16 I cite Münchhausen after Zweig here and throughout. The original text of Münchhausen's remarks is found in Börries von Münchhausen, "Wie das Buch 'Juda' entstand," *Die Welt*, April 3, 1901, 21–22, and diverges from Zweig's citations only orthographically.

17 For the original, see Münchhausen, "Buch," 22.

18 Emphasis mine.

19 Michael Stanislawski, *Autobiographical Jews: Essays in Jewish Self-Fashioning* (Seattle: University of Wahington Press, 2004), 118–22.

7: Stefan Zweig's Non-fictional Prose in Exile: Mastery of the European Genre of "Kunstprosa"

Klaus Weissenberger

THE TERM "KUNSTPROSA" has not been widely recognized as an established literary term in English and American literary criticism. A brief definition is thus necessary. The term comes very close to Stephen Minot's classification of "literary non-fiction" as the "fourth genre," constituted by the following three criteria: (a) it refers to real events, persons, and places; (b) it reflects a specific interest in language; and (c) it manifests a tendency to be more informal and personal than other non-fictional forms. Minot derives these criteria from teaching creative writing courses. For that reason he excludes the historical and systematic aspects, as well as specific aesthetic constituents and the intended effect, which characterize "Kunstprosa." Stefan Zweig's exile aphorism, "Who [really] knows 'the' truth—but we [as authors] have to invent it"[1] may serve as an appropriate example to illustrate the multi-dimensionality of "Kunstprosa." This aphorism demonstrates not only the author's dilemma of how to do justice to the experience of exile, but also points to the creative process of exile literature which constitutes itself by conveying the contrast between the reality of exile and the pursuit of timeless meaningfulness. As such, the aphorism addresses a general aesthetic demand which it shares with the other sub-genres of "Kunstprosa," for example, the diary, letter, travel journal, autobiography, biography, dialogue, and essay. All the sub-genres of non-fictional prose represent the literary "trenches" in the struggle to survive persecution and exile—physically and intellectually. Correspondingly, in a letter to Klaus Mann, Zweig outlines as early as May 1933 his poetology of exile literature by stating the necessity to not counter the aggression of the Nazis with their own methods, "aber in unserem stillen, entschlossenen Beharren, in der künstlerischen Kundgabe liegt vielleicht die stärkere Kraft. Kämpfen können die andern auch, das haben sie bezeugt, so muss man sie auf dem andern Gebiet schlagen, wo sie inferior sind und ... in künstlerisch unwidersprechlicher Form die Bildnisse *unserer* geistigen Helden aufzeigen" (but in our quiet, determined insistence, the more effective strength lies perhaps in the artistic message. The others have proven their ability to fight, therefore one must defeat them on a different terrain where they are inferior and . . . demonstrate the images of *our* spiritual heroes in an artistically irrevocable form).[2] With his demand for spiritual heroes, Zweig is directly referring to his Erasmus biography which he had already started and where, "ohne aktuell zu polemisieren, so versuche ich auch hier durch ein Symbol vieles Heutige deutlich und verständlich zu machen" (*BaF* 228; without engaging in present polemics, I was also trying to make clear and understandable many of today's aspects by way of a symbol).

Despite such clear references, scholars have rarely dealt with the literary aspects of non-fictional prose in general, and of exile literature in particular. Instead they have relegated it to the status of a biographical arsenal or to preliminary versions of literary pieces. Some scholars have demonstrated in numerous investigations of non-fictional prose over the last four hundred years that the dividing line between non-fictional "Kunstprosa" and teleological prose—prose written merely for the purpose of providing factual information—runs right through the aforementioned sub-genres. Since in each instance we are dealing with statements about reality—despite tendencies toward fictionalization—only the mode of the relation between the subject and the object of the statement can prove decisive regarding the literariness of the work in question. Unlike fiction, non-fictional "Kunstprosa" is characterized by a failure to resolve the tension between the subjective sensual perception and its objective generalization. Consequently, the depiction of the conflict or tension between the observed object and reflection upon it—that is, between the situated object and its reflection—constitutes a primary formative and structural principle. It is important to note that this conflict is carried out according to the auto-referential rhythm and paradigm of play; in other words, the back and forth movement between observation and reflection appears effortless and the reader, or listener, is the referee who must decide for himself which side to take. This implication corresponds with the principal function of "Kunstprosa" to intend an effect, albeit without losing the transparency of the process. It thus questions the original rhetorical function of *persuasio* via the binary process of *docere* and *movere*, and extends or ultimately re-affirms it in order to activate the dimension of *delectare*. The epistemological quest for knowledge and truth takes on the form of an exploration or adventure with an emphasis on the process rather than the conclusion.[3]

The origins of modern "Kunstprosa" are linked to the discovery of the self, the ego or "I" during the Renaissance. At that time the emancipation of the self from societal, religious, and traditional constraints manifested itself in a dynamic way and found expression in the genres of non-fictional prose, at first especially in the essay. Montaigne and Bacon are considered its founders—the former of its speculative, and the latter of its didactic variant. These two variants represent the antithetical poles of aesthetic production in general. With his emphasis on didactics, Bacon fulfilled the pre-established expectations of society as they appeared in the ideal of the gentleman or "*honnête homme*," while for Montaigne the pursuit of knowledge was open-ended, and did not require taking social expectations into account. Consequently, he classified his literary products as "attempts," that is, "essays." It should be noted that Stefan Zweig belongs to the didactic camp of "Kunstprosa." Ever since Montaigne and Bacon, the genres of "Kunstprosa" have become predominant in times of crisis. The reason for this phenomenon is that the observation of the self normally generates self-recognition as its purpose, and in some instances it may appear to be the only means to affirm one's own identity in view of the challenges presented by a crisis. In exile literature, the oscillation between the depiction of the reality of exile and reflection upon it may culminate in an unresolved paradox. As such it may signify the awareness of the crisis but at the same time it also offers a first step towards its aesthetic resolution. In the case of Zweig, it is astonishing how interrelated his entire oeuvre of "Kunstprosa" is. For this reason, I refer rather often to his letters and essay-like speeches in order to explain the concept underlying his biographies and autobiography.

After the First World War biographies and autobiographies became so popular that they appeared to replace novels as the leading literary genre, because their authors successfully utilized the basic concept of biography and autobiography to recognize and display the "processuality" of life, which manifests itself in an inner consistency and completeness of a subject's life. In view of the political, social, and spiritual turmoil at the beginning of the twentieth century, the most popular biographies and autobiographies were based on the principle of maintaining the bourgeois ideals of safety, success, and a secure standard of living against the adversities of the times.[4] Stefan Zweig benefited from this principle, although his literary biographies differ substantially from many popular versions of it.

While Zweig contributed to the biographical genre with his monograph on Paul Verlaine as early as 1903, his *Sternstunden der Menschheit* (*Decisive Moments in History*, 1927) is a literary milestone in the development of "Kunstprosa" because these historical miniatures actually represent a new genre.[5] Each of these "decisive moments in history" depicts part of a protagonist's biography in a dramatically condensed form resembling the basic structural principle of a novella; however, the formatting agent is not the author, but history itself. Zweig notes this aspect in his speech on "Die Geschichte als Dichterin" (History as Poetess, 1939). Here he refers to the Ciceronian *historia magistra vitae* as follows:

> manchmal treten innerhalb der Geschichte einzelne Episoden, Menschen und Epochen uns entgegen in solcher Höchstspannung,

in so dramatischer Fertigbildung, daß sie als Kunstwerk unübertrefflich sind und in ihnen die Geschichte als Dichtung des Weltgeistes die Dichtung aller Dichter und jeden irdischen Geist beschämt.

[sometimes in the course of history, specific episodes, humans, and eras confront us in such an extreme suspense, in such a dramatic form that they appear as unsurpassed works of art, and that in them history as the poetic output of the world spirit puts to shame the poetry of all poets and of any human spirit.]6

Zweig's biographies of Fouché and Marie Antoinette apply this formative principle to complete the life stories of their protagonists.7 In a letter dated November 11, 1932, Hermann Broch acknowledged Zweig's accomplishment. In contrast to the popular biographies of the time, *Fouché* and *Marie Antoinette* are for him:

vollkommene Tatsachendichtungen, vollkommen in der Phantasie, dennoch sagend "wie es gewesen ist," stehen so ausserhalb des augenblicklichen Biographiewustes ... sie (bilden) eine Kategorie für sich ... man könnte geradezu behaupten, die Kategorie dessen, was bleiben wird.8

[perfect factual poetry, perfect with regard to fantasy, but nevertheless stating "how it had been." As such they stand apart from the present biographical rubbish ... they represent a category of their own, one could even consider them to represent the category of what will stand the test of time.]

But what exactly does history represent for Stefan Zweig and what does he wish to accomplish with his biographical writings? What was Zweig's reason for choosing history as a subject matter and the genre of biography as its medium?

Many scholars have noted that Zweig did not possess a coherent theory of history or that he had not been able to resolve his conflicting concepts of history.9 The reason for this is his differentiation between a chronological and a cyclical historical process, the former referring to the profane or horizontal manifestation and the latter to the sacred or vertical one. This differentiation corresponds to Goethe's classification of history as God's workplace and to Zweig's own coinage "Sternstunden der Menschheit"—which referred not merely to history, but to the history of humanity itself. The vertical dimension of history is Zweig's main interest, and it coincides with his experience of the Austro-Hungarian monarchy as a remnant of a quasi-homeostatic society. As recent scholarship on homeostatic cultures—that is, groups able to maintain an equilibrium of social forces—has shown, only memory can serve to establish a sense of community, legitimacy, and trust. Jan Assmann refers in this context to "cultural memory," as opposed to the "communicative" one, which encompasses memories pertaining to the recent past that humans share with their contemporaries. In the case of "cultural memory," on the other hand, it is the modus of the founding memories which works in oral as well as literate societies, usually in the form of rituals, dances, myths, design, clothes, jewels, tattoos, trails, landmarks, and landscapes.[10] In this context, myth must be understood as a "founding" history seeking to explain the present from its origin in the past. The process of "intentional intensification" provides myths with legitimacy and authority, and they thus attain a sacred character. The latter becomes manifest, on the one hand, in divine myths of creation and, on the other, in the ritual enactment of festivals, which differ categorically from the workday since they suspend profane time and replace it with sacred time. In principle, festivals serve the purpose of disseminating and continuing knowledge, which secures one's identity and reproduces cultural identity. Because of the ritual coherence of oral literature that comes to the fore in festivals, oral literature is based on the interaction of three components: "storage, recall and communication, or poetic form, ritual orchestration, and collective participation" (J.A. 56). This knowledge, which is formative for the continuation of society, is based on two functional principles that complement each other. The first one consists of instructions on how to act appropriately according to common sense, entailing normative implications in the form of everyday pragmatic guidelines as an abridged collective knowledge. This principle stands in contrast to the functioning principle of the formative representation of the unity and character of the community. Formative texts therefore serve as self-definition and convey the continued robustness of identity by way of an illustrative narration of myths in space and time. Normative wisdom impacts life's forms in habits and customs; formative myths, on the other hand, assign meaning to life. This juxtaposition corresponds to the opposition between their distribution or circulation. Normative texts are intended to cope with everyday concerns; formative texts are part and parcel of ceremonial communication. Normative texts answer the question: "What shall we do?" They provide members of the community with guidelines for political and social action. Formative texts like tribal myths, heroic lays, and genealogies, on the other hand, answer questions such as: "Who are we?" or "Where do we come from?" or "What is our place in the cosmos?" The formative texts which assure one's identity, however, necessitate their ritual orchestration, so that the order of the world can be maintained and reproduced in view of the general surrounding disorder and the tendency to disintegration (J.A. 142). In addition to their foundational function, myths also possess a mythomotoric, that is, specifically counter-factual function, which emanates from deficiency experiences in one's own presence and which conjures up the memory of the past by emphasizing what is missing, lost, forgotten, or marginalized. This perspective is especially characteristic of transitional periods. In the extreme case of foreign rule or subjugation, this mythomotoric function can take on a messianic, if not even a revolutionary dimension (J.A. 78–86).

Returning with these reflections to the case of Stefan Zweig, one may convincingly argue that the Habsburg monarchy intuitively represented a quasi-homeostatic society for him owing to its supranational and supra-ethnic configurations. Also, as the successor to the Holy Roman Empire, it embodied the *pax romana* in Central Europe. On account of this legacy it may have appeared to be impervious to political change. Additionally, despite the fact that Zweig's family belonged to the class of acculturated Jews and had only loose religious ties, Zweig would have been familiar with the concept of a homeostatic society through his Jewish heritage—that is, through his awareness of the Covenant and the original religious state of the Jews (Israelites). Consequently, he would have been able to draw parallels between the Jewish upholding of the covenant in the Diaspora and the upholding of the Habsburg myth after 1918. As a result, he saw in the cosmopolitanism exemplified in Vienna under the Habsburgs, together with the leading role played by the Jews in its cultural life, the preliminary stage towards a united post-war Europe. The demise of the monarchy was precisely what created such a feeling of loss that the vision of a united Europe took on the proportions of a messianic goal. Guided by his humanistic ideals and his belief in progress, Zweig was convinced of his literary mission to enlighten his readers accordingly without getting involved in politics as such. Hitler's seizure of power, however, touched Zweig's vital nerve and forced him to "attest" to his identity as a fin-de-siècle Viennese author of Jewish descent, as he had never done before.

Against this background, Zweig's Erasmus biography must be considered a literary turning point. For that reason, it will serve in this context to represent his exile biographies. As late as 1932, Zweig was convinced of the self-regulatory fulfillment of progress according to the historical rhythm of low and high tide, of advances and retreats, and he portrayed an individual's course of life in analogous oscillating patterns between low and high points. But the effect he strives for in the Erasmus biography is markedly different. His letter to Klaus Mann of May 15, 1933, presents a clear indication of what he had in mind:

> Was ich jetzt arbeiten will, ist eine Studie über Erasmus von Rotterdam, den Humanisten auch des Herzens, der durch Luther die gleichen Niederlagen erlitten hat wie die humanen Deutschen heute durch Hitler. Ich will durch Analogie darstellen und auf unkonfiszierbare Weise mit höchster Gerechtigkeit an diesem

Menschen unseren Typus entwickeln und den anderen. Es wird hoffentlich ein Hymnus auf die Niederlage sein. (*BaF* 228)

[What I am now working on is a study about Erasmus of Rotterdam, the humanist also of the heart, who suffered from Luther the same defeats as today the humanistic Germans are suffering from Hitler. I want to portray through analogy and develop our type [of person] and the other one in a way that cannot be confiscated and is doing ultimate justice [to him] as well. Hopefully it will be a hymn to defeat.]

The didactic intent to use history as an analogy to the present is very obvious. It is a method which is rather typical of exile literature.[11] The heralding of defeat, however, is unusual. It is related to the concept of the tragic hero, which Zweig presented in his essay, "Ist die Geschichte gerecht?" (Is History Just?).[12] Here he wishes to offset the deification of victorious heroes, whose fame is embellished by legends, by doing justice to the unsung heroes. In a similar vein he proclaimed in his speech regarding the "Geschichtsschreibung von morgen" (Historiography of Tomorrow), which he delivered in January and February of 1939, that future historiography should demonstrate:

> das Heldische nicht auf den Schlachtfeldern ... sondern in einer einzelnen menschlichen Seele, Heldentum einer inneren Überzeugung und nicht Heldentum unter Befehl eines Korporals, Heldentum des Geistes und nicht der Faust ... jenes Heldentum, das mit seinem Willen nicht nur einer einzigen Nation gilt, sondern der ganzen Menschheit.[13]

> [heroics, but not [that] on the battlefields ... , but rather in an individual human soul, the heroism of an inner conviction and not the heroism ordered by a corporal, heroism of the spirit and not the fist ... that heroism which does not willfully benefit only one nation, but rather all of humanity.]

History should be written from a new perspective, "in einem Sinn, der das Leben der Menschheit nicht als seine stagnierende Erscheinung darstellt, sondern als einen Fortschritt ins Humane und ins Universelle" (GvM 286; from the perspective which portrays the life of mankind not as stagnant entity, but as a progress towards humanity and universality). Therefore Zweig sees it as:

> unsere Pflicht, eine Umstellung der Heldenverehrung vorzunehmen und diejenigen der Menschheit als Beispiel zu stellen, die sich töten ließen für eine Idee—statt jener anderen, die Tausende und

Millionen in den Tod trieben für den egoistischen Gedanken eigener oder nationaler Macht. (GvM 294)

[our duty [is] to perform a reversal of hero worship and to present to mankind as examples those who let themselves be killed for an idea—instead of those others, who drove thousands and millions to death for the egotistical thought of their own or of national power.]

However, a personal challenge is hidden which Zweig grounds in factual arguments: namely, how to confront Hitler's terror appropriately and effectively. As a person of tolerance and conciliation, he considered hatred and aggression counter-productive, since they would place him on the level of the polemical Nazi propagandist. He also thought such an approach or response to be short lived. Accordingly, in a letter to Klaus Mann he called *Triumph und Tragik des Erasmus von Rotterdam* "eigentlich ein recht privates Buch und keineswegs für den Erfolg bestimmt. Ich habe mir nur selber geholfen, indem ich den heiligen Erasmus als Nothelfer anrief" (*BaF* 249; in reality a rather private book and by no means intended for success. I only helped myself by appealing [as a Catholic would appeal to one of the fourteen saints] to Saint Erasmus as a helper in need). To Hermann Hesse he stated his personal objectives even more precisely:

Ich habe mir Erasmus von Rotterdam als Nothelfer gewählt, den Mann der Mitte und der Vernunft, der ebenso zwischen die Mühlsteine des Protestantismus und Katholizismus geriet, wie wir zwischen die großen Gegenbewegungen von heute. Es war für mich ein kleiner Trost zu sehen, wie schlecht es ihm ging und daß man nicht allein ist, wenn man sich anständigerweise mit schweren Entscheidungen und Entschließungen quält, statt es sich bequem zu machen und mit einem Ruck auf den Rücken einer Partei zu springen. (*BaF* 242)

[I chose Erasmus of Rotterdam to be my [saintly] helper in need, the man in the middle and of reason, who happened to end up between the millstones of Protestantism and Catholicism, just as we [are caught] between the big counter-movements of today. It was a small consolation for me to find out how poorly he fared and that one is not alone, if out of decency one torments oneself with difficult decisions and resolutions, instead of taking the easy way out and jumping on the bandwagon of any one party.]

The political party in question, of course, is the Communist Popular Front. Zweig not only maintained his independence vis-à-vis the political alternatives of his time; he also functioned as the mediator of Erasmus of

Rotterdam, whose accomplishments had been forgotten. Thus he begins his biography as follows: "Erasmus von Rotterdam, einstmals der größte und leuchtendste Ruhm seines Jahrhunderts, ist heute, leugnen wir es nicht, kaum mehr als ein Name."[14] (Erasmus of Rotterdam, the greatest and most brilliant star of his century, is today, we cannot deny this fact, hardly more than a name).[15] A few pages later Zweig enumerates Erasmus's merits, his "Triumph der Vernunft" (*EvR* 16; triumph of reason over unreason, *Erasmus* 11):

> zum erstenmal . . . seit dem Einsturz der römischen Zivilisation war durch die Gelehrtenrepublik des Erasmus wieder eine gemeinsame europäische Kultur im Werden, zum erstenmal nicht die Eitelkeit einer Nation, sondern die Wohlfahrt der ganzen Menschheit das Ziel einer brüderlich idealischen Gruppe. Und dieses Verlangen der Geistigen, sich im Geiste zu binden, der Sprachen, sich in einer Übersprache zu verständigen, der Nationen, sich im Übernationalen endgültig zu befrieden, dieser Triumph der Vernunft war auch der Triumph des Erasmus, seine heilige, aber kurze und vergängliche Weltstunde. (*EvR* 15–16)

> [For the first time . . . since the break-up of Roman civilization, an all-embracing European culture came into being mainly through the instrumentality of Erasmus and his republic of letters. For the first time national vanity was eclipsed and the well-being of mankind as a whole was set up as a goal of a fraternal, idealistic group. And this desire of the educated to bind themselves together in the realm of the spirit, this wish, of [those who speak many] languages to create a [universal] language which would be a supra-national tongue, of the nations to finally come to peace by means of an understanding that superseded individual nations, this triumph of reason over unreason was also Erasmus's own triumph, it was his own short and ephemeral but sacred hour in the tale of mankind's years.] (*Erasmus* 11–12)

The analogy to the League of Nations and to other international organizations of the 1920s is all too obvious as is Zweig's implicit identification with Erasmus at least in the form of a representative of Erasmian philosophy. Consequently, Martin Luther, who is described as "Tatmensch," "Revolutionär," and "[der] dämonisch Getriebenen dumpfer deutscher Volksgewalten" (*EvR* 19–20; a man of action, a revolutionary, [. . .] an emanation of the dark, daemonic forces of the Germanic peoples" *Erasmus* 16), is to be identified with Hitler. The wanton disregard of Zweig's literary mission and worldwide popularity after Hitler's seizure of power is stressed by a telling statement in the biography: "Doctor Martins eiserne Bauernfaust [zertrümmert] was die feine, bloße mit der Feder bewehrte Hand des Erasmus zaghaft zärtlich zu binden sich bemühte"

(*EvR* 20; Dr. Martin Luther's heavy peasant fist destroyed at one blow all that Erasmus's delicate penmanship had so onerously and tenderly put together, *Erasmus* 16). In view of such ruthlessness, Zweig admits Erasmus's and his own helplessness by referring to his earlier stature: "Die Geschichte aber ist ungerecht gegen die Besiegten. Sie liebt nicht sehr die Menschen des Maßes, die Vermittelnden und Versöhnenden, die Menschen der Menschlichkeit" (*EvR* 22–23; History, however, is invariably unjust to the vanquished; she does not appreciate men of moderation, men who play the role of mediators, men who act as reconcilers, in a word, humane men, *Erasmus* 20).

Accordingly, scholars assumed that Zweig was indebted to a Christological concept of salutary suffering which is central to Western civilization.[16] Most likely, however, in order to depict his tragic hero, Zweig drew on a much more specific or more effective paradigm. I suggest that it is based on the memories of minority nations or communities (A. Assmann), which

> often crystallize around devastating defeats. Experiences of defeat can be erected into seminal cores for political memory provided they are emplotted in the matyrological narrative of the tragic hero. Defeats are commemorated with great pathos and ceremonial expense by nations that are founded on a victim identity and whose whole aim is to keep awake the memory of a suffered iniquity in order to mobilize heroic counteraction or to legitimate claims to redress.[17]

The prime example of such a mnemonic culture, with which Zweig was very familiar because of his upbringing in the Austro-Hungarian monarchy, is the heroic memory of the Serbian defeat in the Kosovo region against the Ottoman Turks in 1389, which is commemorated in the Serbian religious calendar and in oral epics. Zweig fulfills this minority criterion with his Erasmus biography in several ways. Firstly, Erasmus did suffer defeat, so devastatingly that Luther considered Erasmus's books, the books of none less than the original reformer, to be the work of "des grimmigsten Feinds Christi" (*EvR* 185; the greatest enemy of Christ, *Erasmus* 217), in other words, the devil. Secondly, Zweig himself belonged to the minority group of humanists prior to 1933. Thirdly, in exile he refrained from being identified with any faction. It is, above all, this threefold affirmation of minority status and the fate connected to it that generates the mythomotoric dynamics which vindicate not only Erasmus and Zweig, but also the reader who identifies with their mission. For that reason, Zweig stressed so much the importance for his exilic writings to constitute "große Darstellungen" (great books)—that is, works whose merit rests solely on "Leistung" (achievement) and demonstrate "hohe und unwiedersprechliche Qualität" (*BaF* 236; high and unequivocal quality).

Correspondingly, Zweig did not wish to produce so-called "popular biographies," although some critics were all too eager to classify his biographies as such.[18] He assessed "popular biographies" succinctly: "In diesen romanhaften Biographien besteht der Kunstgriff darin, die sogenannten 'kleinen' Züge wegzuretuschieren, die heroischen und interessanten zu verstärken. Aber auf diese Art und Weise entstehen Plakate und keine seelischen Porträts im Sinne der großen Meister." (*GD* 353; In these fiction-like biographies, the artistic touch is based on the ability to blend away the so called minor traits and to embellish the heroic and more interesting ones. But that technique results in posters and not in spiritual portraits in the sense of the great masters.) For Zweig "Die getreue Biographie erfindet nichts dazu, sondern deutet nur das Vorhandene aus" (*GD* 353; The true biography does not invent [additional facts], but only interprets the existing ones). Through such interpretations, biography rises above "eine sterile Dokumentensammlung" (*GD* 353; a sterile collection of documents) and substitutes the biographer's dependence on "der sogenannten historischen *Wahrheit*" (the so-called historical *truth*) with his sensitivity towards "*Wahrheiten* der Geschichte" (*GD* 353; historical *truths*). He thereby not only gains the poetic license to integrate his personal engagement into his presentation but also to let history be recognized as a bonding agent for the community: "erst durch die Kunst des Erzählens, durch die Vision des Darstellers wird das bloße Faktum zur Geschichte; jedes Erlebnis und Geschehnis ist im letzten Sinne nur wahr, wenn es wahrhaft und wahrscheinlich berichtet wird" (*GD* 355; Only by way of the art of narration, by way of the imagination of the portrayer does the naked fact turn into history; each event or happening becomes true only when it is being related truthfully and as being probable). Conversely, those facts or aspects which challenge the principal image are forgotten. In this case, memory, or the lack of memory, serves as a censor. This is an aspect characteristic of literature in a homeostatic society, and Zweig reverts to this principle. Most likely he creates the effect which continues the Habsburg myth on a cultural level. Unfortunately, many critics were only too eager to interpret this intuitive suppression of memory as an oversight.

Likewise, those who criticize Zweig for his overuse of temporal adverbs like "always," "in general," "so often," etc.,[19] overlook Zweig's intention to give his principal narration a dimension of timelessness. Similar to the manner in which oral cultures stabilize narratives, Zweig transforms his plots into exemplary messages bridging the gap between past, present, and future. Unlike the sensationalistic biographers, Zweig renders the surface plot transparent for its mythical dimension, first by questioning its mythical allusions and then by deepening and ultimately expanding them. In his Erasmus-biography, he accomplishes this by expounding on the positive traits of his protagonists as well as on their flaws. Regarding the former, Zweig heralds Erasmus as the renewer of the pan-European idea in the form of a supra-national republic of letters during the early sixteenth century. Obviously Zweig is also implicitly referring to his own time, documenting the timelessness of Erasmus's humanistic conviction. But, Zweig blames Erasmus and the humanists for their inability to reach the masses:

> Denn gerade dieses Vorbeisehen am Volke, diese Gleichgültigkeit gegen die Wirklichkeit hat von vornherein dem Reich des Erasmus die Möglichkeit der Dauer und seinen Ideen die unmittelbar wirkende Kraft genommen: der organische Grundfehler des Humanismus war, daß er von oben herab das Volk belehren wollte, statt zu versuchen, es zu verstehen und von ihm zu lernen. (*EvR* 108)

> [Such deliberate ignoring of the masses, such studied indifference towards the world of reality, rendered it impossible to provide durability to the kingdom Erasmus hoped to establish, and sapped the vital energy from his ideas. The fundamental mistake of the humanists was that they wished to teach the people from the heights of their idealism, instead of going down among the masses to try to understand them and to learn from them.] (*Erasmus* 123)

It was Zweig's literary *raison d'être* to educate his mass readership, but he realized he was unable to reach the so-called masses the way the Nazis did. Additionally, Zweig's reluctance to speak out in public against the Nazis is reminiscent of Erasmus's unwillingness to side either with the Catholics or the Protestants. As a consequence, Erasmus does fulfill Zweig's notion of the ideal hero:

> Einen wunderbaren Augenblick lang ist Europa einig in dem humanistischen Wunschtraum einer einheitlichen Zivilisation, die mit einer Weltsprache, einer Weltreligion, einer Weltkultur der uralten, verhängnisvollen Zwietracht ein Ende machen sollte, und dieser unvergeßliche Versuch bleibt denkwürdig gebunden an den Namen des Erasmus von Rotterdam. Denn seine Ideen, Wünsche und Träume haben für eine Weltstunde Europa beherrscht, und es ist sein und zugleich unser Verhängnis, daß dieser reingeistige Wille zur endgültigen Einigung und Befriedung des Abendlands nur ein rasch vergessenes Zwischenspiel blieb in der mit Blut geschriebenen Tragödie unseres allgemeinsamen Vaterlands. (*EvR* 92–93)

> [For a wonderful moment in time Europe was dreaming the humanist dream of a united civilization—united in speech, united in religion, united in culture—with the age-long and disastrous contentions laid to rest. [Erasmus's] ideas, his wishes, his dreams, for a

short moment governed Europe; and it was his and is our misfortune that this pure longing for unity and peace among the peoples of the West only constituted an interlude to be soon forgotten in the bloody tragedy of our common fatherland.] (*Erasmus* 105)

It is important to recognize that Zweig attributes Luther's success not so much to his bellicose disposition, "eine kämpferische Natur, ein geborener Raufbold mit Gott, Mensch und Teufel" (*EvR* 120; a pugnacious disposition, a born wrestler with God, with man, and with the devil, *Erasmus* 139), but rather to Erasmus's and the humanists' weaknesses. Zweig's depiction of the historical development thus loses its inevitability and lends credence to a quasi-messianic message:

> Eine Idee, die nicht in Erscheinung tritt, ist darum weder besiegt noch als falsch erwiesen, eine Notwendigkeit, auch wenn sie verzögert wird, nicht minder notwendig; im Gegenteil, nur Ideale, die sich nicht durch Realisierung verbraucht oder kompromittiert haben, wirken in jedem neuen Geschlecht als Element sittlichen Antriebs fort. Nur sie, die nie noch erfüllten, haben ewige Wiederkehr. (*EvR* 208)

> [An idea which is not realized is not necessarily a vanquished idea or a false one; it may represent a need, which, although its actualization is postponed, nevertheless remains no less a need. It is the opposite which is true: only ideals which have never been realized, and are neither worn out nor compromised in any way, continue to work as a ferment in subsequent generations, urging them to the achievement of a higher morality. Only those ideals which have not been fulfilled are capable of eternal return.] (*Erasmus* 243)

Although Zweig provides historical proof of the continuation of the "Erasmian" legacy from Montaigne via Spinoza, Diderot, Voltaire, Lessing, Schiller, Kant, Tolstoy up to Gandhi and Rolland, the optimism with which he pursues his literary mission in the mid-1930s[20] is overshadowed by the expansion of national socialism. This continued through the Anschluss of March 11, 1938, and the Munich Conference of September 29th of the same year, with its devastating consequences for Czechoslovakia. Accordingly, Zweig's letter of October 15, 1938, from London to Alfred Wolfenstein reflects his admission of failure to put the Erasmian idea into effect:

> Ich bin . . . riesig froh, Sie in Paris zu wissen: Prag muß eine wirkliche Hölle sein . . . Ich versuche die Welt so anzusehen, als ob ich in Südafrika wohnte oder in Eskimoland und mir zu suggerieren, daß ein Widerstand und eine Aktivität sofort beginnen wird,

sobald sich eine neue Jugend gefunden hat: wir selbst sind . . . in unserer Gläubigkeit zu stark ramponiert, zu wenig Maniaken und Fanatiker unserer Ideen, zu erasmisch, zu alexandrinisch, um gegen diese Menschen aufzukommen, die einen Prellbock statt Stirn und Herz haben. Gegen diese Besessenen des Nationalwahns können nur selbst Besessene aufkommen; wir sind vergiftet mit Humanität.[21]

[I am . . . immensely happy to know that you are in Paris: Prague must be a real hell . . . I am trying to look at the world, as if I were living in South Africa or in the land of the Eskimos, and to fancy the idea that resistance and activity will begin immediately as soon as a new youth has appeared. We ourselves . . . have been beaten up too much in our confidence, we are not sufficiently maniacs and fanatics of our ideas, too Erasmian, too Alexandrian, in order to prevail against these people who have a buffer instead of a forehead and a brain. Against those obsessed by the mania of nationalism only those who themselves are obsessed can prevail. We have been poisoned by humanism.]

At the beginning and at the end of this letter, Zweig refers to the political reality and the specific situation of exile that results from it. Austria is in the hands of Hitler, and Prague will soon be as well. Paris—with all the refugees from Austria and Czechoslovakia—cannot offer an escape from the escalating misery; it has virtually become Vienna and Prague. Consequently, Zweig is forced to reassess his literary mission. It appears that he soon gives up on his ideal of realizing the Erasmian notion of humanism: being "too Erasmian" and "poisoned by humanism" are very expressive metaphors which convey clearly the weakness of idealism against the overwhelming manifestation of brute force and mass frenzy. Not only Zweig's brand of idealism, but also the British concepts of mutual recognition, fair play, and honor had suffered a defeat at the Munich Conference.

Zweig was thus left to his own devices, or he was forced to withdraw into his own world, searching for a vantage point largely unaffected by reality or offering an escape from this reality. Since his quasi-messianic vision could not be realized under the present political conditions, he reverted to the starting point of his vision, the "golden age" of the Habsburg monarchy. The message of this vision was expressed in such a way as to preserve its underlying idealistic concept and to maintain its function as an implicit guideline for the future. Zweig's speech "Das Wien von gestern" (The Vienna of Yesterday), in which he addressed the exiles in Paris in April of 1940, is the first major document of this almost exclusively counterfactual mythomotoric paradigm. He transfigured Vienna into an object of cultural memory, or a *mnemotopos*, consisting mainly of *lieux de memoires*. This tendency indicates that for

Zweig the *Anschluss* represented the total separation from what Vienna represented to him. He was confronted with the loss of the physical manifestations of his cultural homeland, his "Heimat," and he experienced a void, which he accordingly called "Der Sturz ins Leere" (*BaF* 290; The fall into the abyss).

Zweig's speech is composed along the lines of a biography. It is motivated by the original function of biography to commemorate or eulogize a great hero who has contributed not only to the welfare of the community, but even more so, who has affirmed the community's identity. Although Zweig denies that he is intent on delivering a necrologue or "*oraison funèbre*," he is in fact doing just that throughout most of his speech.[22] He first demonstrates Vienna's unique role from its very beginning as the outpost of a superior Roman civilization and culture against the Germanic and Slavic tribes. In this context he mentions Emperor Marcus Aurelius and his immortal "Meditations." Subsequently, Vienna served as a fortress for the Roman Catholic Church, initially during the counterreformation and later twice against the onslaught of the Ottoman Empire, faithfully fulfilling the highest obligation of a city: "Kultur zu schaffen und diese Kultur zu verteidigen" (Wien 130; to create culture and to defend that culture). It managed to uphold its "European conviction" (europäische Gesinnung) against the most recent attack of (Nazi) barbarism for five years, before "diese kaiserliche Residenz, diese 'capitale' unserer altösterreichischen Kultur, zu einer Provinzstadt Deutschlands degradiert worden (ist)" (Wien 130–31; this imperial residency, this capital of old-Austrian culture was degraded to a provincial city of Germany). For Zweig, Vienna has in effect never been a *German* city, but rather the center of the multi-national empire of the Habsburgs, who dreamt "den alten Traum eines geeinten Europas" (the dream of a united Europe) while "ein übernationales Reich, ein 'heiliges römisches Reich,' [ihnen] vorschwebte—und nicht etwa eine Weltherrschaft des Germanentums" (Wien 131; they envisioned a supranational empire, a 'Holy Roman Empire' . . . and by no means world dominion by the Germanic race). The cosmopolitan mindset of the Habsburgs is not restricted to the aristocracy, but it is reflected in the colorful national diversity of the city and its ethnic inclusiveness. In this context, Zweig singles out the high cultural level among the Viennese, especially with regard to music. The famous composers came and stayed in Vienna because "das kulturelle Klima der Entfaltung ihrer Kunst am günstigsten war" (Wien 136; the cultural climate was the most beneficial for the development of their art). All levels of society were united in their appreciation of music, the theater, and dancing. "Im Burgtheater und in der Oper fließen alle Stände zusammen, Aristokratie und Bürgertum und die neue Jugend. Sie sind das große Gemeinsame." (Wien 139; In the Burgtheater and the opera all social ranks flow together, nobility and bourgeoisie and the new youth. They are the great commonality.) One could feel at home there, and musical artifacts were venerated like religious relics. This identification with culture, especially music, outlasted the empire, and Zweig calls Vienna's reestablishment as a major cultural center between 1918 and 1938 "den schönsten und ruhmreichsten Tag seiner Geschichte" (Wien 148; the most beautiful and glorious day of its history). Vienna had successfully fulfilled once more its historical purpose: "die Freiheit des deutschen Worts, das in Deutschland schon geknechtet war, noch einmal vor der Welt zu bewähren, die europäische Kultur, unser altes Erbe, zu verteidigen" (Wien 147; to once more confirm to the world the freedom of the German language, which was already enslaved in Germany, and to defend our old legacy, European culture). Despite the fact that the Austrians had been eliminated from the ranks of large nations, they had maintained their long-standing place within Europe's culture: "Die Aufgabe, eine überlegene Kultur zu verteidigen gegen jeden Einbruch der Barbarei, diese Aufgabe, die die Römer uns in die Mauern unserer Stadt eingemeißelt, wir haben sie bis zur letzten Stunde erfüllt" (Wien 149; The task to defend a superior culture against the invasion of barbarism, this duty, which the Romans had chiseled into the walls of our city, we have fulfilled it up to the last hour). This statement concludes Zweig's retrospective tribute to Vienna. The "we" in this sentence indicates that this aim had been especially his literary mission after the demise of the Habsburg Empire.

Zweig's analysis results in an assurance that Austrians will continue to fulfill their purpose "auch in der Fremde" (Wien 149; even in foreign lands). The ultimate fate of Viennese culture is directly linked, however, to the outcome of the Second World War, "den ungeheuren Kampf, der heute unsere alte Erde erschüttert" (Wien 150; the enormous battle, which is ravaging today our old planet). Despite these very short prospective remarks, one must take into account that Zweig was addressing an audience of Viennese, Austrians, or former citizens of the old monarchy who shared his sentiments and whose cultural identity was affirmed by this speech. Never again could he count on a repeat of this type of artistic performance, which constitutes or parallels a performance in homeostatic societies: the interaction of text, ritual orchestration, and collective participation, "das große Gemeinsame" (Wien, 139; the great commonality) is driven "zu Pomp und Fest" (Wien 143; towards pomp and circumstance) even in the case of a funeral.

Zweig wrote this speech in British exile, where he also witnessed the beginning of the Second World War. His diary—which he kept for the first three-and-a half months of the war and then from May 22 to June 19, 1940—documents a struggle to continue his literary mission under the increasingly adverse conditions of exile. He realizes that "only [writing] can help (him) in those moments of despair and disgust."[23] But eventually Zweig's attempts to assert himself against political adversaries through literary creativity yielded to total despair as Hitler's seemingly unstoppable military and political successes gradually eroded the basis of Zweig's humanistic ideals and literary mission: "Es wird das furchtbarste Verbrechen Hitlers sein, daß er die Lüge und den Betrug zu einer Respectstellung gebracht hat und man Staatskunst... nennt was seit Jahrtausenden als Verbrechen galt" (*T* 460; It will be Hitler's most terrible crime that he brought respectability to lies and deceit and that one calls now... the art of statesmanship... what one had considered for thousands of years to be a crime). With the fall of France Zweig's worst fears became reality: "die Hakenkreuzflagge auf dem Eiffelturm! Hitlersoldaten als Garde vor dem Arc de Triomphe. Das Leben ist nicht mehr lebenswert" (*T* 471; the Swastika on top of the Eiffel Tower! Hitler's soldiers as guards in front of the Arc de Triomphe. Life is not worth living anymore); "Frankreich ist verloren, für Jahrhunderte zertrümmert, dieses liebenswerteste Land Europas, für wen soll man schreiben, für was leben" (*T* 472; France is lost, devastated for centuries, this most lovable country of Europe; for whom is one supposed to write, what [is there] to live for?); "Europa erledigt, unsere Welt zerstört. Jetzt sind wir erst wirklich heimatlos" (*T* 472; Europe is done with, our world destroyed. Not until now have we really lost our homeland). But Zweig does not stop with this assessment. He regards the defeat of France ultimately as the loss of his efficacy as an author and therefore as the loss of his existential grounding: "unser Leben auf Jahrzehnte zerstört und ich habe keine Jahrzehnte mehr vor mir, ich *will* sie nicht vor mir haben." (*T* 471; Our life has been destroyed for the next decades. I do not have decades ahead of me. I do not *want* to have them ahead of me.)

Not only does Zweig's diary expose his contemplation of suicide in England already during this critical period, but, from a literary perspective, passages from the diary also function as the template for the final pages of his autobiography, *Die Welt von Gestern* (*The World of Yesterday*, 1942), which lead up to the beginning of the Second World War. In them, Zweig reverts to the principles and style of the diary, a paradigm shift that is of significant consequence for the interpretation of *Die Welt von Gestern*. Zweig's autobiography is often criticized for various reasons. Generally speaking, most critics view it solely from the perspective of factual information and consequently point out lacunae and nostalgic misrepresentations. Very few judge it from the standpoint of "Kunstprosa," which is constituted by an aesthetic truth rather than a documentary one. In order to do justice to this work, it is necessary to return to the speech "Das Wien von gestern," discussed above. This speech not only provided Zweig with an idea for the title of his autobiography, which was published posthumously; it also provided the principal criteria to assess his personal development as an author against the backdrop of the historical and political developments between 1939 and 1941. In June of 1939, he wrote that he did not want to write a real "Autobiographie," but rather he conceived his work "als Abgesang jener österreichisch-jüdisch-bürgerlichen Kultur, die in Mahler, Hofmannsthal, Schnitzler, Freud kulminierte. Denn dieses Wien und dieses Österreich wird nie mehr sein und nie mehr kommen. Wir sind die letzten Zeugen" (*Briefe* 250; as a farewell to that Austrian-Jewish-bourgeois culture, which culminated in Mahler, Hofmannsthal, Schnitzler, Freud. For this Vienna and this Austria will not exist any longer and will never come back. We are its last witnesses). Later on, in May of 1940, with Hitler's war underway, he confided to a friend that he was writing his autobiography "aus Verzweiflung," because he had recognized the futility of his original literary conception:

> Aus Verzweiflung schreibe ich die Geschichte meines Lebens. Ich kann nicht concentriert arbeiten. So will ich wenigstens ein Document hinterlassen, was wir geglaubt, wofür wir gelebt haben; ein Zeugnis ist heute vielleicht wichtiger als ein Kunstwerk. Nie ist eine Generation so geprüft, so gepeinigt worden wie die unsere. Sagen wir es der nächsten als Warnung. Vorläufig ist alles fragmentarisch. Aber diese Arbeit tröstet, bald da, bald dort ein Blatt seines Lebens aufzuschlagen. (*BaF* 312)

> [I am writing the story of my life out of desperation. I cannot work in a concentrated manner. Thus, I want to leave behind at least one document about what we believed and for what we have lived; today, a testimonial is perhaps more important than a work of [fictitious] art. Never was a generation so tested, so punished as ours. Let us tell it to the next one as a warning. At the moment everything is still fragmentary. But this labor is comforting by opening sometimes here, sometimes there, a page of one's life.]

Just as he did in his speech about Vienna, Zweig affirms in his autobiography the cultural values of the Austro-Hungarian monarchy as a quasi-homeostatic community that formed and determined his identity. But aside from Vienna and the monarchy representing the "goldene Zeitalter der Sicherheit" (golden age of security) in Zweig's youth,[24] it was much more important that this unique constellation was responsible for his initiation into the world of art on the one hand, and for the course of his own literary development on the other. Accordingly, he describes specifically those encounters with artists who left an imprint on him as an artist, especially Hofmannsthal and Rilke. Zweig saw himself as one of the last successors of "Young Vienna" and, therefore, he concentrated on those figures and encounters which represented to him initiations into the realm of literature and art, and thus provided a standard for measuring his literary accomplishments.

Hitler's seizure of power put an abrupt end to this endeavor and made Zweig realize his failure, not unlike that of the protagonists of his biographies. For this reason, his autobiographical work should be classified as belonging to the "elegiac" type, which distances itself from the present, in contrast to the "picaresque" type, that attempts to distance itself from the past.[25] This preoccupation with achieving distance from the present became the overriding principle for *Die Welt von Gestern*. The degree to which this tendency affects the very act of writing becomes evident in the chapter entitled "Paris, die Stadt der ewigen Jugend" (Paris, the City of Eternal Youth), which covers Zweig's year in Paris from 1904 to 1905. While he is writing this chapter, the Germans are conquering Paris, and he feels compelled to refer to this abominable act. The fall of the city is an emotional experience for him; it grieves him more than most personal misfortunes (*WvG* 151), since the demise of Paris and Vienna together represented the two topographical foci of his cultural eclipse. The cultural reciprocity between Paris and Vienna had beeen for Zweig the outward manifestation of his pan-European vision, as well as his literary creativity. But, the chapter entitled "Incipit Hitler" marks the shattering of both. The man who strove to rise above the sobering or even demeaning sequence of political events by way of his creativity, was being totally controlled by them. This aspect is reflected in the change of intentionality from writing the autobiography as a meaningful retrospection to that of recording the disintegration of one's life at the mercy of fate. This change accounts for the stylistic shift in the autobiography to a diary-like chronicle. It also coincides with the change of his initial status in England since 1934 as a semi-exile (*WvG* 443) to that of a true exile after the Anschluss. With the loss of his Austrian passport, Zweig had lost his "Heimat," and he would soon lose his Central European readership as well. Excluding him from a society for which he could write in his mother tongue was tantamount to depriving him of his literary *raison d'être*. Concluding his autobiography with the day of the British declaration of war, Zweig does not foresee a future for himself as a literary contributor to a totally new world, after his own old one had been destroyed:

> Und ich wußte: abermals war alles Vergangene vorüber, alles Geleistete zunichte—Europa, unsere Heimat, für die wir gelebt, weit über unser eigenes Leben hinaus zerstört. Etwas anderes, eine neue Zeit begann, aber wie viele Höllen und Fegefeuer zu ihr hin waren noch zu durchschreiten. (*WvG* 492)

> [And I knew once more, that the past was done for, everything [that had been] achieved was in ruins. Europe, our home, for which we had lived, had suffered a destruction that extended far beyond our own life. Something different, a new era began, but how many hells, how many purgatories had to be crossed before it could be reached!][26]

The full implication of this statement can only be grasped when placed in the context of Zweig's conception of creativity. Its parameters had been established in his autobiography, and he had presented them in his speech of January/February 1939, "Das Geheimnis des künstlerischen Schaffens" (The Mystery of Artistic Creation), by referring to examples of artists from all artistic realms. From what he wrote it follows with certain inevitability that the loss of reciprocity between author and reader would deprive him of the mystery of artistic creativity altogether.

Despite his pessimistic outlook, Zweig had not forsaken European culture and its values. He had merely given up on their realization within Europe. This change of perspective had been inspired by his first visit to South America in 1936. It was especially Brazil, with its peaceful multi-ethnic co-existence and overwhelming abundance of natural beauty, which convinced him of the possibility for a cultural rebirth: "Hier konnte, was Europa an Zivilisation geschaffen, in neuen und anderen Formen sich großartig fortsetzen und entwicklen. Ich hatte, das Auge beglückt durch die tausendfältige Schönheit dieser neuen Natur, einen Blick in die Zukunft getan." (*WvG* 452; Europe's contribution to civilization could be extended and developed magnificently here in a new adaptation. My vision [is] blessed by the manifold beauty of this bountiful new nature. [It affords me] a glimpse into the future," [*WoY* 400].)

Zweig's second visit to Brazil in 1940 deepened this impression and encouraged him to pursue the idea of writing a book about Brazil. This plan was supported by the Brazilian government, which facilitated extensive travel arrangements for Zweig and his wife Lotte. The title of this travel account, *Brasilien: ein Land der Zukunft* (*Brazil: A Land of the Future*, 1941) reflects his earlier sentiment. Despite the positive tenor of the book, many Latin Americans, especially Brazilians, were highly critical of it. First, it was obvious that Zweig had only rather limited first-hand knowledge of the country. Second, and even more objectionable to them, was the manner in which Zweig stylized Brazil—as if it were similar to one of those heroes of his biographies who fail in the pursuit of their ideals. According to his critics, Brazil had become like a Zweig "hero," but its positive characteristics had hardly been recognized. In effect, Brazil remained a misunderstood country. However, these critics overlooked the fact that in order to be fair, this book had to be viewed from the perspective of Zweig's personal situation of exile.

Zweig was communicating by means of direct and indirect messages in his book on Brazil. The direct ones expressed his gratitude for the permanent residence permit which the Brazilian government had granted him and his wife, and they amounted to a declaration of love for this country. Zweig considered Brazilian society to be the organic result of a will for peace and a basic humanistic attitude of an entire people, upon which "eine unserer besten Hoffnungen auf eine zukünftige Zivilisierung und Befriedung unserer von Haß und Wahn verwüsteten Welt beruht" (one of our best hopes for a future civilizing and pacification of a world that has been desolated by hate and madness is based).[27] Equally important, however, are the indirect messages communicated by the book. One is the polarized reference to Europe, which is typical of a writer in exile—not only as a negative, but also as a positive measure of comparison. By interpreting the present catastrophe in Europe as an age-old syndrome, comprised of its "wahnwitzigen Überreiztheit . . . Gehässig keit im öffentlichen wie im privaten Leben . . . der Politik mit all ihren Perfiditäten . . . der Stickluft des Rassen- und Klassenhasses" (*BLZ* 15–16; insane irritability, . . . malice in both public and private life, . . . the political affairs with all [their] perfidies, . . . the suffocating air of racial and class hatred, *Brazil* 12), including the "fürchterlichen Folgen dieser psychischen Überspannungen" (*BLZ* 16; the horrible results of those insanities, *Brazil* 13), which he had experienced in his own life, Zweig grounds his travelogue about Brazil in his philosophical convictions regarding general cultural developments.

Because of his personal misfortune, Zweig was especially impressed by the harmonic co-existence of the ethnic groups in Brazil. He saw "das Experiment Brasilien mit seiner völligen und bewußten Negierung aller Farb- und Rassenunterschiede . . . [als] den vielleicht wichtigsten Beitrag zur Erledigung eines Wahns, der mehr Unfrieden und Unheil über unsere Welt gebracht hat als jeder andere" (*BLZ* 15; in the experiment we call Brazil, with its complete and conscious negation of all color and racial differences . . . perhaps the most important contribution to doing away with a delusion that has brought more discord and disaster upon our world than has any other, *Brazil* 12). Since Brazil had realized this long desired dream, other constructive mnemonic models from the entirety of Western culture presented themselves to Zweig as a standard of comparison with the Brazilian present. These models provided structure to his description in such a way that his vision of a future Brazil was embedded in archaic or primordial paradigms of stabilization and fulfillment. Already in the letters to Friderike from his first visit in 1936, he referred to Brazil as a "Märchen" (fairy tale), as "Paradiese . . . auf Erden" (gardens of Eden) the harmony of which is due to the missing "Rassenfrage" (race issues).[28] In the Brazil-book itself, Zweig incorporates these *topoi* in an artistic way into the description of his itinerary. For example, his description of the dramatic passage into the harbor of Rio de Janeiro takes on the features of an initiation, which concludes upon finally reaching his destination with the exclamation: "jetzt erst kann das Schiff anlegen und man ist in Südamerika, ist in Brasilien, ist in der schönsten Stadt der Welt!" (*BLZ* 179; Only now can the ship put in, and you are in South America, in Brazil, in the most beautiful city of the world! *Brazil* 157). Having left behind geographically and temporally the countries of Europe which had been at war with each other for thousands of years, the traveler implicitly feels himself to be following in the tracks of the Spanish and Portuguese conquistadores. They had sought to discover the fountain of eternal youth, and accordingly, Zweig's itineraries of discovery reflect a youthful energy. Again and again he is surprised by the contrasts between city and landscape, which can be enjoyed in Brazil "in ihrer einzigartigen harmonischen Gelöstheit" (*BLZ* 202; in their unique and easy harmony, *Brazil* 177). The principle of productive co-existence which he adopts allows him to see the local streets as a picture characterized by a racial melting pot. Not only does it consist of the most beautiful people of the world; in its constant state of flux, it also resembles the artistic principle "die Spannungen zu lösen, ohne sie darum zu zerstören" (*BLZ* 202; of dissolving the tensions without destroying the contrasts, *Brazil* 176).

Zweig's references to the *lieux de mémoire* of Western culture provide the text with the means to illustrate the unique beauty and special development of Brazil and allow for the creation of a stabilizing mnemonic landscape. A street in Rio reminds him of the Cannabière in Marseille, another one of Naples, the cafés of Barcelona or Rome or the cinemas of New York: "Man ist zugleich überall und weiß doch an jenem einzigartigen Zusammenklang: man ist in Rio" (*BLZ* 195; You are simultaneously everywhere, and yet you recognize from the unique harmony: you are in Rio, *Brazil* 171). He compares the drive from Rio and the Copacabana to that between Vienna and the Prater or between Paris and the Bois (*BLZ* 193). The old mining towns Ouro Preto and its sister cities "sind heute das Toledo, das Venedig, das Salzburg, das Aigues-Mortes Brasiliens, bildhaft gewordene Geschichte und dazu noch Geschichte einer eigenartigen nationalen Kultur" (*BLZ* 250; are today the Toledo, the Venice, the Salzburg, the Aigues-Mortes of Brazil, history in visible form, and history of a unique national culture besides, *Brazil* 219). And Bahia "mit seinen mehr als vierhundert Jahren, mit seinen Kirchen und Kathedralen und Kastellen... bedeutete für die neue Welt, was für uns Athen und Alexandria und Jerusalem: ein kulturelles Heiligtum" (*BLZ* 261; with its more than four hundred years, with its churches and cathedrals and citadels... is for the New World what the millennia-old cities are for Europeans, what Athens and Alexandria and Jerusalem are for us: a cultural shrine, *Brazil* 229). Complementing the landscape and city imagery, the *mardi gras* in Rio and a national festival in Bahia remind Zweig of the festivals he experienced in Europe, but he points out the lack of excess in Rio and Bahia. In the chapter about his visit to "König Kaffee" (*BLZ* 231; King Coffee, *Brazil* 201), one may recognize Zweig's nostalgic interest as that of a Viennese coffeehouse-expert, and the terms "Facenda" and "Hacienda" conjure up a youngster's fantasies, which Gerstäcker's and Sealsfield's novels had once aroused in him (*BLZ* 235). But in addition to paying homage to Brazil, Zweig also cautions against emulating the monotonizing craze of the modern world. One chapter is even entitled: "A Few Things That Will Perhaps Be Gone Tomorrow" (*BLZ* 203–7; *Brazil* 177–81).

The conclusion of the chapter on culture indicates Zweig's complex situation of exile around 1941. It shows his longing for rest in old age, while relinquishing a new beginning out of fear that Europe could vanish with its culture, but also with the hope that the European legacy could be continued in Brazil:

> Und sollte . . . die Zivilisation unserer alten Welt sich wirklich in diesem selbstmörderischen Kampf vernichten, so wissen wir, daß hier eine neue am Werke ist, bereit, all das, was bei uns die edelsten geistigen Generationen vergeblich gewünscht und erträumt noch einmal zur Wirklichkeit zu gestalten: eine humane und friedliche Kultur. (*BLZ* 170–71).

> [And if . . . the civilization of our old world should really destroy itself in this suicidal struggle, we nevertheless know that a new one is at work here, ready to realize again all that the most noble intellectual generations at home wished for and dreamed of in vain: a humane and peaceful culture.] (*Brazil* 149)

By then, though, Zweig had most likely already excluded himself from the reconstruction of his world in exile. Accordingly, the last sentence of his book about Brazil must be understood as a condition, at least regarding his own person: "Wer Brasilien wirklich zu erleben weiß, der hat Schönheit genug für ein halbes Leben gesehen" (*BLZ* 284; [Only] a person who really knows [how] to experience Brazil has seen enough beauty for half a lifetime," *Brazil* 250).

Despite Zweig's general despair with regard to both the political situation and the impossibility of his beginning anew himself around 1941, European culture captivated him one more time and provided him with another "saintly helper in need," "ein anderer (besserer) Erasmus ganz ein tröstlicher Gast" (BaF 334; another (better) Erasmus, a totally comforting guest). This reference is to the figure of Montaigne, to whom he dedicated a somewhat fragmentary biographical essay, which more than any other work perhaps addressed the complexity of his exile in Brazil. Although he had acquainted himself with Montaigne in his youth, it is primarily because of the similarity between the atrocities caused by religious fanaticism during Montaigne's lifetime and those caused by the nationalistic fanaticism during his own lifetime which forced him into exile, that Zweig could appreciate Montaigne's unique accomplishment. Montaigne was able "trotz aller Drohungen und Gefahren inmitten der Tollwut der Parteien die unbestechliche Klarheit des Geistes [zu bewahren] wie die Humanität des Herzens unverstört inmitten der

Bestialität" (to maintain [his] unmitigated clarity of the mind despite all threats and dangers in the midst of the raving madness of the parties, [... to maintain] the humanity of [his] heart intact in the midst of bestiality).[29] Just like Montaigne, Zweig had "in seine Hoffnungen, Erfahrungen, Erwartungen und Begeisterungen mit der Peitsche zurückgejagt werden [müssen] bis auf jenen Punkt, wo man schließlich nurmehr sein nacktes Ich, seine einmalige und unwiederbringliche Existenz verteidigt" (10; to be whipped back in his hopes, experiences, expectations, and enthusiasm to the point where one eventually defends only one's naked ego, one's unique and irretrievable existence). It is above all this brotherhood which made Montaigne Zweig's "unentbehrlichen Helfer, Tröster, und Freund" (10; indispensable helper, comforter, and friend). Not unlike Zweig, Montaigne had to witness "[d]iesen grauenhaften Rückfall aus dem Humanismus in die Bestialität ... völlig ohnmächtig ... trotz unbeirrbarer geistiger Wachheit und mitfühlendster seelischer Erschütterung" (11–12; this terrible relapse from humanism to bestiality, being totally powerless ... despite his unwavering mental truth and compassionate emotional shock). Zweig calls this "die eigentliche Tragödie im Leben Montaignes" (12; Montaigne's real tragedy); but it is his as well. Like no other writer, Montaigne had devoted himself to the "höchsten Kunst des Lebens" (15; highest art in life), "rester soi-même," a conviction which Shakespeare adopted from him with his famous advice: "This above all: to thine own self be true."[30] Zweig sees Montaigne as "der Erzvater, Schutzpatron und Freund jedes 'homme libre' auf Erden, als den besten Lehrer dieser neuen und doch ewigen Wissenschaft, sich selbst zu bewahren, gegen alle und alles" (15; the patriarch, patron saint, and friend of every "homme libre" on earth, as the best teacher of this new and nevertheless eternal science, to guard oneself against all and everything). By being "vernünftig [...] für sich selbst, menschlich in einer Zeit der Unmenschlichkeit, frei innerhalb des Massenwahns" (16; reasonable for himself, human at a time of inhumanity, free in the midst of mass madness) and through the process of describing this accomplishment, "er [hat] den Menschen in nuce in sich erhalten, den nackten und überzeitlichen Menschen ... er [ist] unser Zeitgenosse, der Mann von heute und immer, sein Kampf [ist] der aktuellste auf Erden geblieben" (17; he saved within himself the essence of man, the naked and timeless man ... he is our contemporary, forever the man of today, his fight has remained the most pressing one on earth). Reading Montaigne's essays, Zweig feels at once understood and consoled:

> Hier ist ein Du, in dem mein Ich sich spiegelt, hier ist die Distanz aufgehoben, die Zeit von Zeiten trennt ... Jemand atmet, jemand lebt mit mir, ein Fremder ist zu mir getreten und ist kein Fremder mehr, sondern jemand, den ich mir nahe fühle wie einen

Freund... Ein Freund ist gekommen, mich zu beraten und von sich zu erzählen. (17)

[Here is a Thou, in which my ego is reflected. Here the distance, which separates time from times gone by, is transcended... Somebody breathes, somebody lives with me, a stranger approached me and ceased to be a stranger, but has become somebody to whom I feel close as a friend... A friend has arrived in order to advise me and tell me about himself.]

Zweig is so overwhelmed by this unexpected resonance that he portrays Montaigne mainly from the perspective of his own situation in exile. Disregarding all previous scholarly classifications and assessments, Zweig at this point in his life is attracted only to the one concern of Montaigne, namely: "wie er in einer Zeit ähnlich der unsrigen sich innerlich freigemacht hat und wie wir, indem wir ihn lessen, uns an seinem Beispiel bestärken können" (15; how he in a time similar to ours freed himself mentally, and how we, by reading him, can gain strength from his example).

Zweig had to forego writing a systematic biography, partly because he did not have sufficient access to the necessary material (*B* 336), despite the fact that he had established direct contact with the Montaigne-expert Fortunat Strowski in Rio. But Montaigne's life also precluded such an approach. Montaigne's withdrawal into his inner being, as manifested by the retreat into the "tower" of his castle, his "citadelle," prevented him from having a "biography" in the normal meaning of the word (16). He did not become famous for any spectacular deed or act, and he remained suspiciously inactive on the sidelines when the bloody civil war ravaged France during his life:

Jahrelang hatten die Mächtigen Montaigne mit einem gewissen Mißtrauen betrachtet, das die Parteimenschen und professionellen Politiker immer für den freien und unabhängigen Menschen haben. Man hat ihm Passivität in einer Zeit vorgeworfen, in der, wie er sagt, "die ganze Welt nur allzu tätig war." (75)

[For years those in power had viewed Montaigne with a certain distrust, which party members and professional politicians always have towards free and independent men. One accused him of passivity during a time, in which the entire world, according to him, "had been only too busy."]

The parallel to Zweig's situation in exile is only too obvious. When Montaigne twice accepted the role of mediating between Henry III and Henry of Navarre, the later Henry IV, and in doing so contributed to the reconciliation of the feuding sides, he fulfilled Zweig's personal mission. Likewise, when Montaigne rejected Henry IV's offer or request to serve him as an advisor towards the end of his life and proudly responded with a retrospection of his life (80), this résumé could have applied to Zweig as well.

Accordingly, Zweig must have considered it a fitting coincidence to learn that toward the end of Montaigne's life, after he said that "vielleicht die Liebe allein könnte ihn noch erwecken" (81; perhaps only love could reawaken him), the unbelievable happened when he met Marie de Gournay. She was almost the same age as his youngest daughter and had developed a passion for his books: "Sie liebt sie, sie vergöttert sie, sie sucht ihr Ideal in diesem Manne. Wie weit auch die Liebe dann nicht bloß dem Autor, dem Schriftsteller, sondern auch dem Menschen gegolten, ist wie immer in solchen Fällen schwer festzustellen." (81; She loves them, she idolizes them, she is searching for her ideal in this man. To which degree then her love was intended not only for the author, the writer, but also for the man, that, as is common in such cases, is difficult to ascertain.) The phrase in this passage, "wie immer in solchen Fällen," renders the implied reference to Zweig's second wife, Lotte Altmann, all too obvious. Of a similar coincidental nature for Zweig was Montaigne's encounter with members of the indigenous Brazilian population in Rouen, whom Zweig calls even "those Brazilians," as if this fact were well-known. It was for him no coincidence that Montaigne was so fascinated by them, "die keinen Gott, keinen Führer, keine Religion, keine Sitte, keine Moral kennen" (54; who did not know any god, any leader, any religion, any custom, any moral). He does not even shy away from them when he finds out that they are cannibals. The text reads: "[er] finde das viel unbeträchtlicher als lebendige Menschen zu foltern, zu martern, und zu quälen" (59; he [Montaigne] considers this much more negligible than to torture, torment, and afflict living humans). This tolerance and lack of prejudice stand in glaring contrast to Calvin's witch trials and Torquemada's inquisition practices as proof that these actions of inhumanity cannot be excused by being part and parcel of the times: "Immer haben auch in Zeiten der Fanatiker die Humanen gelebt, zur Zeit des 'Hexenhammers,' der 'Chambre Ardente,' und der Inquisition, und nicht einen Augenblick haben diese die Klarheit und Menschlichkeit eines Erasmus, eines Montaigne, eines Castellio verwirren können" (59–60; Always in times of fanatics did also humanists live, at the time of the "Witch Hammer," the "Chambre Ardente" and the Inquisition, and not for one moment have they been able to cloud the clarity and humanity of an Erasmus, a Montaigne, a Castellio). What a personal statement by Zweig, in which the simple reference to these three historical figures comprises the message of his entire literary production in exile! In this context, Zweig contrasts the dogmatic dictum "We know the truth," pronounced by church councils, legates, the Zwinglis, and the Calvins, and enforced by torture and exile, with Montaigne's famous motto: "*Que sais-je*?" (What do I know?). Thus, Zweig adds to its philosophical and essayistic dimension an ethical one, with which he identifies most (60).

The double meaning of "*What* do I know?" and "What do *I* know?" also has implications for the process of obtaining truth and its relation to the process of writing. Since Zweig rejects absolute truth, he relies only on the heuristic process which, through the act of writing, makes a relative truth emerge or find him: "So wird sein Leben ein ständiger Erneuerungsprozeß . . . Die Wahrheiten, die er findet, sind im nächsten Jahr und oft schon im nächsten Monat nicht mehr Wahrheiten." (50; Accordingly, his life turns into a constant renewal process . . . The truths which he finds are next year or often already next month no truths anymore). Consequently, writing is not an end in itself, but it is a means of documenting this process. The writer did not seek it out; it sought him out (46). However, this constitutes the precondition for an aesthetics of creativity, which does not intend to fulfill the expectations of a pre-established norm or standard, but rather strives for self-manifestation. This principle, which Zweig described in his speech "Das Geheimnis des künstlerischen Schaffens" (The Mystery of Artistic Creativity), delivered in January and February of 1939, he admired above all in Balzac, whose biography he was unable to complete prior to his death in 1942, because he considered the scope of the undertaking too great. Montaigne, however, had affirmed its validity for him. He had laid not only the intellectual foundation for it, but had turned the latter into a way of living—either in the seclusion of his tower, or on his nearly two-year journey through France, Germany, and Italy: "Aus Lebenskunst wird Reisekunst als Kunst des Lebens" (66; savoir vivre becomes the art of travel as an art of living). Zweig himself subscribed to this principle, having benefited immensely from the travels in his youth and he had originally envisioned a similar benefit from his travels during the early stages of his exile. But when traveling became involuntary, it had a negative impact on his literary productivity. This lack of freedom must have contributed to the decision to end his life. He also found support in Montaigne's essays in favor of this decision, since he had referred to Seneca's adage about the most important freedom being the freedom bestowed by death: "La plus volontaire mort, c'est la plus belle" (58). Although Zweig misinterpreted this passage from Montaigne's essay "Coutume d'île de Céa,"[31] it must have been this wishful thinking that made him see in Montaigne the "helper, consoler, and friend."

In conclusion I wish to refer to Zweig's lecture "Die Geschichte als Dichterin" (History as Poetess, 1939), in which he justifies his preoccupation with the vertical dimension of history:

Wer die Geschichte als ein Dichterisch-Sinnvolles liebt, der muß auch die Gegenwart und seine eigene Existenz als ein Sinnvolles betrachten, und damit wächst in allen Widrigkeiten in uns das Bewußtsein, daß wir jeder, schaffend und handelnd und schreibend, ein Lebensziel erfüllen... für das Goethe die unvergängliche Formel gefunden hat: "Uns zu verewigen sind wir ja da." (*GD* 360)

[He who loves history as a poetically meaningful [enterprise], must also view his own present and his own existence as meaningful, and due to that, the awareness grows in us despite all adversities that each one of us, by creating and acting and writing, fullfils an aim in life... for which Goethe devised the timeless and valid dictum: "We are here, namely, to immortalize ourselves."]

Did Zweig thus immortalize himself in this way? The answer to this question can be determined only along the lines of his aforementioned aphorism: "Who [really] knows 'the' truth—but we [as authors] have to invent it."

Notes

[1] Mark H. Gelber, "*Die Welt von Gestern* als Exilliteratur," in *Stefan Zweig: Exil und Suche nach dem Weltfrieden*, ed. Mark H. Gelber and Klaus Zelewitz (Riverside, CA: Ariadne Press, 1995), 148–63. This aphorism is from a letter Zweig wrote in English to Richard Friedenthal on September 19, 1941.

[2] Stefan Zweig, *Briefe an Freunde*, ed. Richard Friedenthal (Frankfurt am Main: Fischer, 1978), 228–29 (hereafter cited in text as *BaF*; translations mine).

[3] See Klaus Weissenberger, "Theorien der Kunstprosa" in *Handbuch Gattungstheorie*, ed. Rüdiger Zymner (Stuttgart: Metzler'sche Verlagsbuchhandlung, 2010), 317–20; "Kunstprosa," in *Historisches Wörterbuch der Rhetorik*, vol. 4, ed. Gert Ueding (Tübingen: Niemeyer, 1998), 1506–31; *Prosakunst ohne Erzählen: Die Gattungen der nicht-fiktionalen Kunstprosa*, ed. Klaus Weissenberger (Tübingen: Niemeyer, 1985).

[4] Siegfried Kracauer, "Die Biographie als neubürgerliche Kunstform," in *Aufsätze 1927–1931. Schriften*, vol. 5/2, ed. Inka Müller-Bach (Frankfurt am Main: Suhrkamp, 1990), 195–99.

[5] Other English translations of the title are: *The Tide of Fortune: Twelve Historical Miniatures* (1940), *Stellar Moments in Human History* (1953), *Shooting Stars: Ten Historical Miniatures* (2013).

[6] Stefan Zweig, "Die Geschichte als Dichterin" in *Zeit und Welt: Gesammelte Aufsätze und Vorträge*, ed. Richard Friedenthal (Stockholm: Bermann-Fischer, 1946), 342–43 (hereafter cited in text as *GD*. Unless otherwise noted, all translations from the German are mine).

[7] Doris Wendt, "Stefan Zweig, *Marie Antoinette: Bildnis eines mittleren Charakters* (1932): Eine europäische 'Kontroverse,'" in *Stefan Zweig und Europa*, ed.

Mark H. Gelber and Anna-Dorothea Ludewig (Hildesheim: Georg Olms, 2011), 125–48.

[8] Hermann Broch to Stefan Zweig, November 11, 1932, quoted with permission of the Stefan Zweig Archive at the State University of New York at Fredonia.

[9] Heidy M. Müller, "Castellio gegen Calvin. Stefan Zweigs 'Prinzip Hoffnung' angesichts der postulierten immerwährenden Wiederkehr des Gleichen" in *Stefan Zweig: Exil und Suche nach dem Weltfrieden*, ed. Mark H. Gelber and Klaus Zelewitz (Riverside, CA: Ariadne Press, 1995), 241–51; Lionel B. Steiman, "The Worm in the Rose: Historical Destiny and Individual Action in Stefan Zweig's Vision of History," in *Stefan Zweig, the World of Yesterday's Humanist Today*, ed. Marion Sonnenfeld (Albany: State University of New York Press, 1983), 128–56.

[10] Jan Assmann, *Das kulturelle Gedächtnis: Schrift, Erinnerung und politische Identität in frühen Hochkulturen* (Munich: C. H. Beck, 1997), 52 (hereafter cited in text as J.A.).

[11] On exiled writers, see Alfred Döblin's "Der historische Roman und wir," in *Schriften zu Ästhetik, Poetik und Literatur*, ed. Erich Kleinschmidt (Freiburg im Breisgau: Walter-Verlag, 1989), 291–315. As early as 1936 Döblin wrote an article in which he stated that the linguistic isolation of the exile writer promotes historical novels because they allow the author to justify himself, find solace and take revenge, at least in an imaginary way, by pointing out historical parallels.

[12] Stefan Zweig, "Ist die Geschichte gerecht?" in *Europäisches Erbe*, ed. Richard Friedenthal (Frankfurt am Main: Fischer, 1960), 313–15.

[13] Stefan Zweig, "Geschichtsschreibung von morgen," in *Zeit und Welt: Gesammelte Aufsätze und Vorträge*, ed. Richard Friedenthal (Stockholm: Bermann-Fischer, 1946), 296 (hereafter cited in text as GvM).

[14] Stefan Zweig, *Triumph und Tragik des Erasmus von Rotterdam* (Frankfurt am Main: Fischer, 1958), 9 (hereafter cited in text as *EvR*).

[15] Stefan Zweig, *Erasmus of Rotterdam*, trans. Cesar and Eden Paul (New York: Viking, 1934), 3 (hereafter cited in text as *Erasmus*).

[16] Steinman, "Worm in the Rose," 133.

[17] Aleida Assmann, "Four Fromats of Memory from Individual to Collective Constructions of the Past," in *Fragile Traditions: Cultural Memory and Historical Consciousness in the German Speaking World since 1500*, ed. Christian J. Emden and David Megley (Oxford: Peter Lang, 2004), 27.

[18] See Kraucauer, "Die Biographie als neubürgerliche Kunstform"; see also Leo Löwenthal, "Die biographische Mode," in *Schriften*, vol. 2, ed. Helmut Dehmel (Frankfurt am Main: Suhrkamp, 1980), 231–51.

[19] Löwenthal, 236.

[20] In this vein, he encouraged Joseph Roth: "Wir müssen das 'Trotzdem' zum Leitwort unseres Lebens machen" (*BaF* 247; We have to revert to "nevertheless" as the slogan for our lives).

[21] Stefan Zweig, "An Alfred Wolfenstein," *Stefan Zweig—Spiegelungen einer schöpferischen Persönlichkeit*, ed. E. Fitzbauer (Vienna: Bergland, 1959), 86.

²² Stefan Zweig, "Das Wien von gestern," in *Zeit und Welt: Gesammelte Aufsätze und Vorträge*, ed. Richard Friedenthal (Stockholm: Bermann-Fischer, 1946), 129 (hereafter cited in text as Wien).

²³ Stefan Zweig, *Tagebücher*, ed. Knut Beck (Frankfurt am Main: Fischer, 1984), 421. Original in English (hereafter cited in text as *T*).

²⁴ Stefan Zweig, *Die Welt von Gestern: Erinnerungen eines Europäers* (Frankfurt am Main: Fischer, 1970), 15 (hereafter cited in text as *WvG*).

²⁵ Jean Starobinski, "Der Stil der Autobiographie," in *Die Autobiographie: Zu Form und Geschichte einer literarischen Gattung*, ed. Günter Niggl (Darmstadt: Wissenschaftliche Buchgemeinschaft, 1989), 200–13.

²⁶ Stefan Zweig, *The World of Yesterday*, trans. Benjamin W. Huebsch and Helmut Ripperger (New York: Viking Press, 1961), 436 (hereafter cited in text as *WoY*).

²⁷ Stefan Zweig, *Brasilien: Ein Land der Zukunft* (Frankfurt am Main: Insel, 1981), 19 (hereafter cited in text as *BLZ*); Stefan Zweig, *Brazil: A Land of the Future*, trans. Lowell A. Bangeter (Riverside, CA: Ariadne Press, 2000), 15 (hereafter cited in text as *Brazil*).

²⁸ *Stefan Zweig—Friderike Zweig: "Wenn einen Augenblick die Wolken weichen." Briefwechsel 1912–1942*, ed. Jeffrey B. Berlin and Gert Kerschbaumer (Frankfurt am Main: Fischer, 2006), 306–7.

²⁹ Stefan Zweig, "Montaigne," in *Europäisches Erbe*, ed. Richard Friedenthal (Frankfurt am Main: Fischer, 1960), 14. Despite the fact that Knut Beck edited a new and supposedly definitive edition of Zweig's Montaigne essay in Stefan Zweig, *Zeiten und Schicksale: Aufsätze und Vorträge aus den Jahren 1902–1942* (Frankfurt am Main: Fischer, 1990), subsequent quotes are cited below in text by page number from Friedenthal's edition which includes marginalia excluded from Beck's edition. Beck himself was inconsistent in this aspect of his editorship, so that Friedenthal's edition has the same level of authenticity as Beck's.

³⁰ William Shakespeare, *Hamlet*, ed. Cyrus Hoy (New York: Norton, 1992), 16. This statement is made by Polonius in act 1, scene 3.

³¹ Michel de Montaigne, "Coutume d'île de Céa," in *Essais de Michel de Montaigne*. Présentation, établissement du texte, apparat critique et notes par André Tournon, II, 3 (Imprimerie Nationale Éditions, 1998), 40. Regarding Zweig's misinterpretation of Montaigne, see Hugo Friedrich, *Montaigne* (Bern and Munich: Francke, 2nd rev. ed. 1967), 254–58.

Part IV. Politics and Exile

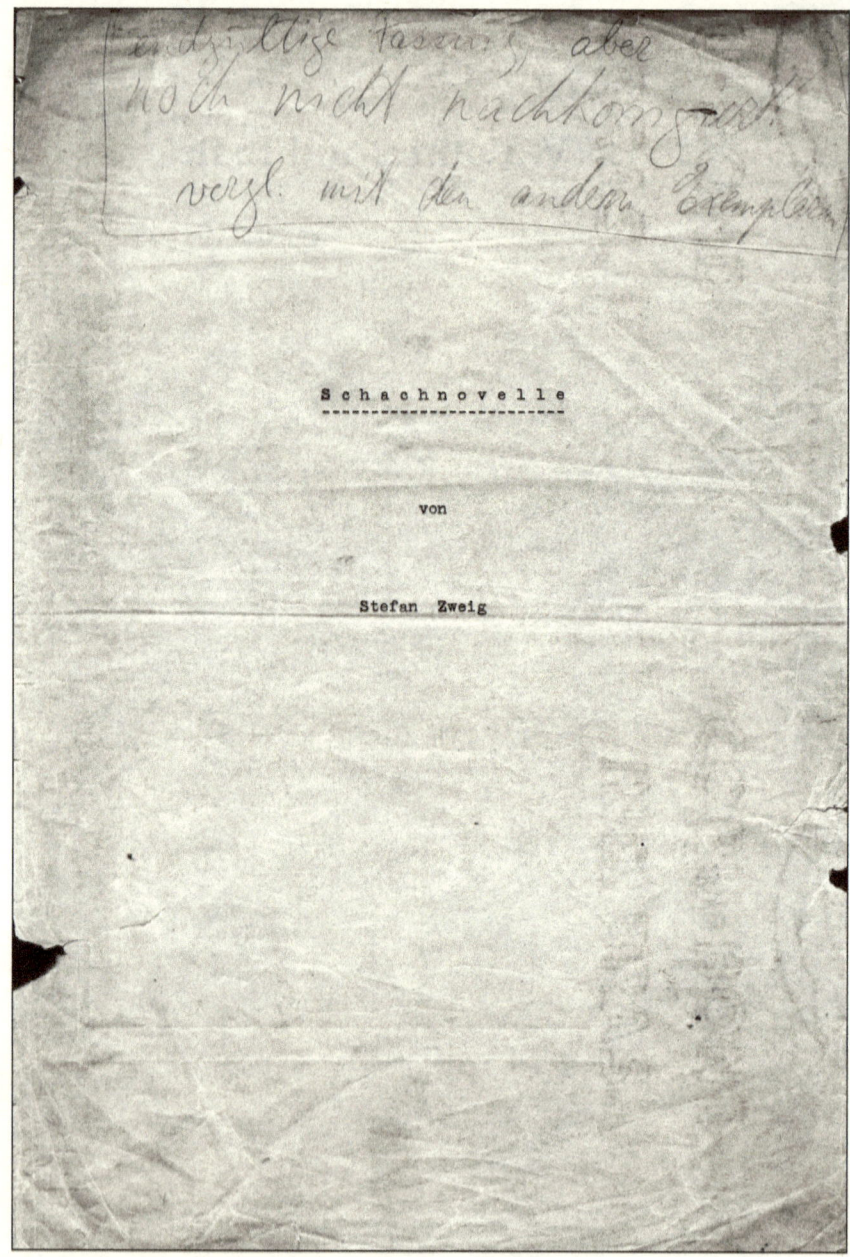

Fig. 8.1. Title page of *Schachnovelle* typescript. Courtesy of the Stefan Zweig Collection at Reed Library, State University of New York at Fredonia.

8: True to Himself: Stefan Zweig's Visit to Argentina in September 1936

Robert Kelz

THE VERY FIRST LINES OF ONE OF STEFAN ZWEIG'S most famous works, *Schachnovelle* ("The Royal Game," 1942), set the novella on a steamer en route to Buenos Aires, Argentina. Twice, in 1936 and 1940, Stefan Zweig himself arrived in the Argentine capital on board an international passenger ship. Argentina, however, has always played second fiddle to Brazil in scholarship on Stefan Zweig, and his relationship to this country remains an underexplored topic. In part this tendency is reflective of the writer's own views. From the very start Zweig himself preferred Brazil to its southerly neighbor and, over time, he developed more profound ties to Brazil than to Argentina.[1]

Yet Stefan Zweig's relationship to Argentina is worth a second look. Zweig's books were widely read in Argentina, and he collaborated closely with Alfredo Cahn, his translator and literary agent there. Alongside Zweig's New York publishers, Ben Huebsch and Gottfried Bermann Fischer, Cahn was one of only three people to whom Zweig mailed copies of his *Schachnovelle* on February 21, 1942, just a day before he committed suicide.[2] In total, Zweig spent approximately six weeks in Argentina. His activities were not confined to the capital of Buenos Aires, but included visits to the cities of Rosario, Córdoba, Santa Fe, and La Plata. Although he never did achieve fluency in Portuguese, by the time of his second visit to Argentina Zweig had become sufficiently proficient in Spanish to lecture almost exclusively in this language, the native tongue of most Argentines.[3] Furthermore, as an exiled Jewish writer, Zweig found much of interest in Argentina. His close friend Paul Zech emigrated to Buenos Aires in 1933, and was only one of over forty-five thousand Jewish refugees received by Argentina during the so-called Third Reich, the highest number of any Latin American country.

Most researchers have focused on Zweig's second trip to Argentina in 1940 and generally made use of two sources on the writer's activities there: his voluminous correspondence and the sympathetic record of his visits left behind by Alfredo Cahn,[4] and Alfredo Bauer's fictionalized biography of Zweig, an informative, though not always factual, source.[5]

In this essay I focus on Zweig's first trip to Argentina on the occasion of the Fourteenth International PEN conference in September 1936. Scholars have paid this sojourn relatively little attention, likely because Zweig was very reserved during these weeks and wrote little about the experience in his correspondence. Drawing from primary sources housed in Argentine archives, I analyze Zweig's first trip to Argentina from within. Although local media were largely disappointed by the writer's reticence, a closer look reveals that Zweig was quite active during this 1936 visit to Argentina, and that it had a lasting impact on many newer members of this country's large immigrant population.

Historical Overview

During the 1930s Argentina experienced a series of governments which were authoritarian, unrepresentative, and tolerant of Fascist agitators and movements.[6] Nominally neutral throughout Zweig's lifetime, Argentina did not declare war on Nazi Germany until March 27, 1945. There were approximately three-hundred-thirty thousand German-speakers already living in Argentina at the time of Zweig's first visit in 1936. The vast majority of them were sympathetic to the Nazi regime, which they associated with the Wilhelminian monarchy. The German embassy capitalized on this situation by funding pro-Nazi media and cultural institutions in the Argentine capital, establishing local divisions of social and labor organizations based in Nazi Germany—such as the German Labor Front and the Strength through Joy program—and exerting heavy influence on the many German-language schools in Argentina. Nationalist German media in Argentina, especially the *Deutsche La Plata Zeitung*, described as early as 1931 by the *Völkische Beobachter* as Hitler's banner in Buenos Aires,[7] were synchronized to National Socialist ideology and received large subventions from Berlin.[8]

Despite its pro-fascist governments and nationalist German population, roughly forty-five thousand German-speaking emigrants, nearly all of them Jews, arrived in Argentina during the Nazi period.[9] Smaller but fervent Jewish and anti-fascist media, as well as social and educational institutions, countered the Nazi presence in Buenos Aires. One crucial anti-fascist German institution in Buenos Aires was the *Argentinisches Tageblatt*, a daily paper with a circulation that reached twenty-eight thousand in the late 1930s.[10] The *Tageblatt* welcomed European refugees to Argentina and gained both readers and writers through this policy. A few of the better-known emigrants on its staff included Balder Olden, a journalist for the *Kölnische Zeitung* and the *Pariser Tagezeitung* whose most popular novels include *Ich bin ich* (I am I, 1927) and *Anbruch der Finsternis* (Advent of Darkness, 1981); Fred Heller, a prolific Viennese author and playwright and theater critic for the *Neue Freie Presse*; Paul

Walter Jacob, founder of the Free German Stage, contributor to the *Neue Weltbühne*, and general manager of the State Theaters of Dortmund from 1950 to 1962; Clément Moreau, a syndicated cartoonist throughout Latin America, whose lampoons were collected in the volumes *Mein Kampf* (My Struggle, 1937) and *Nacht über Deutschland* (Night over Germany, 1940); and Paul Zech, winner of the 1918 Kleist Prize for his expressionist poetry, and whose exilic works include *Nur ein Judenweib* (Only a Jewess, 1935), *Ich suchte Schmid . . . und fand Malva wieder* (I was looking for Schmid . . . and found Malva again, 1941), and *Michael M.* (1985). Other institutions of note for the anti-fascist German colony included the Free German Stage, the only exilic theater worldwide to stage regular productions throughout the Second World War, as well as the Pestalozzi School and the Pestalozzi Society, which were created in 1934 to resist the synchronization of German schools in Buenos Aires to Nazi policy. The cultural landscape of the Argentine capital during the 1930s and 1940s was unique. No other major city saw such fully open competition between Nazi and anti-fascist German-language newspapers, schools, theaters, and other cultural institutions throughout this period.

Expectations and Celebrity

Zweig's first trip to Argentina in 1936 took place in this politically charged atmosphere. In early September of 1936, Zweig left the Brazilian city of Santos on board the British ship the *Highland Brigade* and arrived in Buenos Aires to great fanfare on September 5. Argentina was South America's largest literary market, and both authorized and pirated editions of Zweig's books were becoming increasingly available in Spanish. Furthermore, his drama *Das Lamm der Armen* (The Lamb of the Poor, 1930) had premiered in Argentina that February under the direction of one of the nation's leading playwrights, Edmundo Guibourg. Since Zweig was an invited guest of the Argentine branch of the PEN Club, his arrival in Buenos Aires was a major event which received wide coverage in local media. Not only did Victoria Ocampo write an enthusiastic preview of the upcoming PEN conference in the August 1936 issue of *Sur*, the foremost literary journal in Argentina, but the full spectrum of local media also printed pages of coverage on the conference and its illustrious guests daily.[11] *La Nación*, a widely-read conservative newspaper,[12] hailed the privilege of hosting three globally eminent intellectuals: Stefan Zweig, Emil Ludwig, and Georges Duhamel.[13] A leading liberal paper, *La Prensa*, portrayed Zweig as perhaps the most robust and multifaceted intellect in contemporary Europe.[14] Meanwhile *Crítica*, an influential leftist daily, heralded the arrival of Zweig, Ludwig, and Duhamel in language fit for movie stars: "Impossible not to recognize them. Their faces, continually reproduced in newspapers, books, and magazines, are almost like family."[15] The *Argentinisches Tageblatt* wrote of throngs of local fans who followed the writers everywhere they went, hoping to catch sight of them and, if possible, to gain an autograph.

Many local media and cultural institutions, however, were not satisfied with autographs. Before Zweig had even disembarked from the *Highland Brigade*, a journalist for *Crítica* pressed him to make public declarations against fascism, sharply criticizing him for reserving his opinions and not expressing himself in public, especially considering that he himself was a victim of Nazism (ibid.). Other Argentine media, such as *La Prensa*, insisted that it was incumbent on authors at the PEN conference to steer people toward the paths "of truth and of good."[16] Similar to the Argentine papers, Jewish organizations also put forth a strong message that famous writers, Zweig specifically, had a duty to serve as "geistige Führer. Sie können und dürfen nicht tun, was ihnen angenehm ist, sie haben der Menschheit gegenüber Pflichten . . . denen sie genügen müssen" (intellectual leaders. They cannot and must not do what is pleasant for them. They have obligations to humanity . . . which they must fulfill).[17] The owner and editor-in-chief of the anti-totalitarian *Argentinisches Tageblatt*, Ernesto Aleman, was even waiting for Stefan Zweig and the biographer Emil Ludwig at the docks when their ship arrived in Buenos Aires. Calling Zweig a representative of liberalism in the noblest and broadest sense of the word, the *Tageblatt* demanded from him "Tatbereitschaft" (willingness to act) as well as "selbstlose Einsatzbereitschaft seines Ichs" (selfless deployment of his own person).[18] Along with the status of a star and adulation for Zweig came expectations that he would assume a strong presence in the public sphere.

Zweig resisted this unrelenting pressure from the start. As early as May, before the writer had even left for South America, he expressed his unease to Antonio Aitá, secretary of the Argentine PEN Club as follows: "I don't like to make speeches, to give toasts, and I leave this to others . . . I wish greatly to see Argentina, but I hope you will forgive my weakness in not being a toaster or a conferencer but rather . . . a simple friend amongst friends."[19] More was demanded of Zweig than simple friendship, however, and the conflict between his intentions and the expectations of the local media quickly led to tension. Once in Buenos Aires, Zweig continued to demonstrate his reluctance to make declaratory political statements in an interview with *Crítica*. When the interviewer pressed him to proclaim publicly his outrage against Nazi crimes in Europe, Zweig curtly responded that a writer only had a duty to express himself in his books.[20] Later, he elaborated on this answer, claiming that in *Erasmus* (1934) he had attempted to defend the perspective of pacifism and reconciliation. Adamant that his views were best elucidated in the pages of his books, Zweig stated that he was convinced that the interventions of writers in politics was "useless" (ibid.). To conclude, Zweig firmly requested that the interviewer and Argentine media "let [him] be himself" (ibid.). The public and media expected more, however, and after the first few days of the conference passed without a word from the illustrious author, Argentina media began to graft reactions onto him. *Crítica*, for example, ran a photograph of Zweig with his head in his hands during a speech by Emil Ludwig and printed a subheading in large and bold font for its story about the day's proceedings: "Sobbing, Stefan Zweig follows Ludwig's Appeal."[21] The headline did not escape Zweig's attention, and he later explained in a letter to Raoul Auernheimer that he merely had been propping his head in his hands. Zweig continued to complain to Auernheimer about the "mörderische Interviewtwerden" (murderous interviews) and the Argentine people's overestimation of the possible political impact of writers at the PEN conference.[22] In general, Zweig was disappointed by the conference. He wrote to his first wife, Friderike, that "the air here is not so good as in Rio" and complained to her that the proceedings were "boring."[23]

Over the course of his stay Zweig contributed one short piece entitled, "La unidad en el espíritu" (Unity in Spirit) to *La Prensa*,[24] as well as a note to *La Nación* expressing his gratitude to the Argentine people for their hospitality.[25] He also spoke a few words at the conference in praise of H. G. Wells, the outgoing president of the PEN Club, in anticipation of the British author's seventieth birthday. These represent the only words, spoken or written, that Zweig expressed to a broader public, and they did not satisfy the many groups that had expected so much more of him. *Crítica* was especially harsh. In an article darkly entitled "Epitaph for a Writers' Conference," the newspaper referenced the recent murder of Federico García Lorca in the Spanish Civil War and attacked conference participants collectively for passing their time sightseeing and attending banquets held in their honor rather than recognizing and engaging with the "urgent and terrifying problems" confronting humanity.[26] Disdainful of the proceedings in general, the newspaper singled out Stefan Zweig for particularly acerbic criticism. Although Zweig had been a victim of Nazism in Europe, the journalist asserted, this had not prevented him from declaring himself willing to relocate to Brazil as an official guest of the government, in spite of the fact that the "authorities there, as in Germany, persecute and imprison all people who have the audacity to think freely" (ibid.). For *Crítica*, Zweig's support of Brazil was unacceptable, and it represented yet another instance of his unwillingness to confront the pressing dilemmas facing humanity (ibid.). *Crítica* demanded public action on the part of writers, and Zweig, as one of the most famous and also most taciturn participants at the conference, came in for especially stringent censure.

The anti-totalitarian *Argentinisches Tageblatt* expressed its disappointment with Zweig by implying an unfavorable comparison between him and Emil Ludwig. In contrast to Zweig, Ludwig had been an outspoken and very public critic of fascism throughout the conference. In one session he had nearly come to blows with the Italian Futurist writer Filippo Tommaso Marinetti, who was an active supporter of Italy's fascist leader, Benito Mussolini.[27] Also, Ludwig gave lectures across Buenos Aires urging opponents of fascism to come together to fight the looming threat, and he did not shy away from public controversy, such as the clamor which disrupted his lecture at the Law School of the University of Buenos Aires.[28] Ludwig was an indefatigable crusader against fascism during his stay in Argentina, which the Argentina Teachers' Association recognized with a formal letter of congratulations, praising his "historic appeal for dignity, sincerity, and action by free men."[29] To great acclaim, Emil Ludwig also accepted a request by the Argentine government to undertake a biography of José de San Martin, a national hero renowned for his role in Argentina's struggle for independence from Spain.[30] Furthermore, when he received an invitation to visit the western city of Mendoza, Ludwig proceeded to travel across the Pampa to the Andes mountain range in a well-publicized effort to trace the path of the famous general.[31] According to Alfredo Cahn, the government had first approached Stefan Zweig with this request, but Zweig, invoking his well-known preference for the defeated rather than the victor as hero, declined.[32]

Though it refrained from elaboration, the *Argentinisches Tageblatt* indicated its admiration for Ludwig and disappointment in Zweig. When Stefan Zweig departed Argentina on September 16, 1936, the *Tageblatt* printed a prosaic eighty-six-word paragraph about his departure, a remarkably brief notice considering the great enthusiasm with which the paper had welcomed him eleven days earlier.[33] On the day of Emil Ludwig's departure, by contrast, the *Tageblatt* devoted an entire column to his praise. This publication of this piece underscored the dissimilar public reception of Zweig and Ludwig—to the latter's favor. In his article, the *Tageblatt*'s journalist imagines a conversation between two readers, who contrast Ludwig's exuberance with Zweig's reserve. While one reader admires Ludwig's zeal, the other demurs and draws a thinly veiled comparison to Stefan Zweig: "Na ja, das ist alles schön und gut und macht für ihn Reklame, aber wissen Sie, der Schriftsteller X sagt einem doch mehr zu, so ein stiller, bescheidener Mensch, und bestimmt ein echter Dichter" (Well, that is all fine and nice and generates a lot of publicity for him [Ludwig], but you know, the writer X resonates more with me. Such a quiet, humble person, and certainly a true poet).[34] The journalist then interjects, rejecting these comments as "Gedankenlosigkeit" (thoughtlessness), while claiming that Ludwig's energy shows that unlike some writers, who prefer to remain in the "Gefilden der reinen Kunst, Emil Ludwig ist sich aber der Pflicht und Verantwortung eines Schriftstellers bewusst!" (sanctuary of pure art, Emil Ludwig is aware of the duties and responsibilities of an author!).[35] The *Tageblatt*, like *Crítica* and other prominent Argentine organizations, clearly preferred Ludwig's outspokenness to Zweig's reserve. In media spanning the full breadth of Argentina's political landscape, from the leftist *Crítica* to the far rightwing *La Fronda*, Emil Ludwig was the star of the 1936 PEN conference.[36] Though well-respected as an author, Stefan Zweig failed as a celebrity and public figure to meet the public's expectations.

Spiritual Solidarity

A closer look, however, reveals that a full account of Zweig's stay is more complex than the newspaper reports suggest. As Zweig explained in an interview with *La Nación*, he was drawn in his work to one fundamental quality: "I love the defeated, the forgotten heroes. I never have created a portrait of a victor or of a happy man: not Goethe in literature, nor Caesar, nor Napoleon in war. The defeated—I insist upon this—seduce me."[37] Zweig continued to emphasize that in writing about figures such as Erasmus, Sebastian Castellio, Joseph Fouché, and Marceline Desbordes-Valmore, he believed he could work to achieve a measure of justice for "those whom the world has treated without consideration" (ibid.). In this way, Zweig asserted, he could rectify grave mistakes.[38] Zweig refrained from giving speeches at the PEN conference, where the meetings were attended by high society and the most powerful figures in Argentine politics, including President General Agustin Justo and his entire cabinet.[39] Instead of speaking to the privileged and powerful at the PEN meeting, Zweig mostly devoted his energy in Buenos Aires toward aiding people more similar to the afflicted figures who featured in his literary works.

One such person was Zweig's old friend, Paul Zech, with whom he corresponded regularly for over twenty years. Zech had emigrated from Germany in 1933, and he soon regretted having chosen Argentina, claiming that he would have been happier and more successful in France or Switzerland. Shortly after Zweig arrived in Buenos Aires, Zech sent him a card saying that he had recently suffered a heart attack and could not leave his room. Zweig visited Zech on several occasions during the conference. Unfortunately, scant record remains of these encounters, but we do know that their conversations had a positive impact on Zech.[40] Considered by Donald Daviau as one of the most productive writers of his generation, success remained elusive to Zech in South America (ibid., 160). Nonetheless, he wrote volumes of poetry, contributed frequently to the *Argentinisches Tageblatt* and the Chilean *Deutsche Blätter*, and wrote many works of prose fiction in Argentina. A recent edition of the flagship journal of German studies in Argentina, *Anuario Argentino de Germanística*, suggests a rekindled interest in his exilic writings among South American and European scholars.[41] Furthermore, Zech was instrumental in bringing younger South American writers, such as Jorge Icaza Coronel, to the attention of the German press. A steadfast source of moral encouragement and, on several occasions, financial support, Stefan Zweig played a significant role in Zech's career. In return Zech was very grateful to Zweig and considered him his most loyal friend, as his elegiac "Stefan Zweig: Ein Gedenkschrift" (Stefan Zweig: A Remembrance, 1942) attests.[42]

Although he was skeptical about the PEN conference, Zweig attached great importance to the fact it was being held for the first time in South America. In an interview with *La Nación*, he voiced his hope to find in America "a spiritual solidarity which we have lost" in Europe.[43] Zweig appears to have sought this solidarity with the growing population of Jewish refugees in Buenos Aires. As he expressed in a letter to Paul Zech a few months before his arrival in Buenos Aires, Zweig had never forgotten that his forefathers also had been forced to live in Jewish ghettos. This motivated him, Zweig continued, to make his commitment to Judaism a profound inner duty.[44] Its large Jewish population made Argentina a compelling country for Zweig in which to convert his verbal commitment into action.[45]

In particular, Zweig focused his efforts on assisting the Hilfsverein deutschsprechender Juden (Relief Organization for German-speaking Jews). Moderate in its religious and political positions, the Relief Organization was founded already in 1933. The Relief Organization was the first institution in Argentina dedicated to aiding Jewish refugees, and it offered Spanish language courses, legal advice for illegal immigrants, as well as assistance in finding lodgings and employment. It also published a monthly magazine, the *Mitteilungsblatt des Hilfsvereins deutschsprechender Juden* (News Bulletin of the Relief Organization for German-speaking Jews), about events and services in the community. According to the Relief Organization, a total of ten thousand emigrants were linked to the Relief Organization, or twenty- to twenty-five percent of the total Jewish emigration to Argentina between 1933 and 1945.[46]

The Relief Organization contacted Zweig before he arrived in Argentina and requested that he donate to its annual fundraising campaign, hold a lecture to raise proceeds for the organization, and submit an original, unpublished literary work to its monthly newsletter. Perhaps because many of its members were beleaguered refugees whose only wish was to restart their lives, and who also desired to stay out of politics and avoid contact with the public sphere, the Relief Organization was acutely aware of the imposition it was asking of Zweig. It respectfully characterized his reserve with an apt quote from the scene "Vorspiel auf dem Theater" (Prelude in the Theater) in Goethe's *Faust*: "Verhülle mir das wogende Gedränge, / Das wider Willen uns zum Strudel zieht" (Oh, shroud me from the swirling human eddy / That draws us downward, struggle as we might).⁴⁷ The Relief Organization granted Zweig his wish to be left out of the spotlight as much as possible, heeding his desire that there be neither public advertisements nor media previews in anticipation of the event. Describing its request for a lecture as a great demand which forced Zweig to overcome a strong inner aversion to speaking before a large public, the organization gushed about how "rührend mit welcher Bereitwilligkeit Herr Stefan Zweig [. . .] allen unseren Wünschen entsprach" (touching [it was] with what willingness Mr. Stefan Zweig [. . .] satisfied all of our wishes).⁴⁸ In its review of his lecture, the Relief Organization abstained from criticism altogether, because it felt itself "uns erwiesene Güte so tief verpflichtet, dass, wie wir glauben, ein kritisches Wort—und wäre es auch ein anerkennendes—in diesen Spalten nicht am Platze ware" (ibid.; so deeply indebted for the good deeds done on our behalf that a critical word, even if it were one of recognition, would have no place in these pages). In stark contrast to many other groups, the Relief Organization for German-speaking Jews had nothing but praise for Stefan Zweig.

While his written contribution for the Relief Organization's newsletter was in fact an older unpublished work, written in the form of a speech, it appears that Zweig composed his lecture specifically for his audience of Jewish refugees. Zweig discussed his Jewish legend, *Der begrabene Leuchter* (The Buried Candelabrum, 1937), which he had completed writing earlier that year. *Der begrabene Leuchter* draws from the fate of the sacred seven-armed candelabrum that voyaged from Jerusalem to Byzantium, taking a winding path through Rome and Carthage along the way. According to legend, Roman (Byzantine) Emperor Justinian finally returned the candelabrum to a Christian church in Jerusalem, where it then disappeared. In Zweig's narration, the disappearance is transformed into a mysterious hiding with the possibility of a resurrection. Writing to Alfred Wolf, who was working on a study of Jewish elements in Zweig's works, the author asserted that *Der begrabene Leuchter* represented perhaps his most intensive engagement with Judaism and was for this reason especially important to him.⁴⁹

Speaking to members and beneficiaries of the Relief Organization, Zweig addressed the eternal and acutely relevant question of why God forces Jews to suffer such grave injustices at the hands of people who are no better than themselves. In two of his works, *Der begrabene Leuchter* and his earlier play *Jeremias* (1917), Zweig thematized this question. In *Der begrabene Leuchter*, Zweig hinted that the sufferings of the Jews were perhaps in part due to their increased materialism and, consequently, their neglect of spiritual matters. The Jews' physical and material sufferings, the prophet Jeremiah asserts in Zweig's play, strengthen their souls and bring them closer to God. According to Zweig's lecture in Buenos Aires, the uplifting consolation of these tribulations is that "wir durch die erlittenen Demütigungen nicht härter, sondern friedfertiger, also besser geworden" (seien through the humiliations we have suffered, we have not become hardened but more peaceful—we have become better).⁵⁰ The fact that in Zweig's work the candelabrum has not disappeared forever, but instead merely remains hidden, demonstrates his confidence that the Jews might overcome the trials of the present and look forward to a more hopeful future.

Instead of demanding public political statements from Zweig, the Relief Organization looked to his literary works for insight and guidance. Rabbi Curt Donig emphasized Zweig's talk at the Relief Organization's festivities for Rosh Hashanah the following week. Drawing from Zweig's works and his lecture, Donig invoked a principle of spiritual solidarity similar to that which Zweig had voiced upon arriving in the Argentine capital. Despite his reticence in public, Donig argued that Zweig's lecture and literary works demonstrated his Jewish faith, "denn für den Fragenden ist ja Israel das Volk Gottes, und die Bibel ist Gottes Wort. Der Fragende möchte zwar Gottes Wege, Gottes Ziele und Absichten erkennen, aber er vertraut auf Gottes Gerechtigkeit" (ibid.; because for the questioner Israel is God's people, and the Bible is God's word. The questioner wants to understand God's ways, goals, and purposes, but he trusts in God's justice). Donig concluded his remarks by elucidating a final bond linking Zweig to the Jewish refugee community in Buenos Aires, namely humility. Zweig's expression of solidarity in humility, Donig claims, is wisdom's final word (ibid.). During the high holy days of Rosh Hashanah, Jewish refugees in Argentina found affirmation of Zweig's commitment to Judaism and, in turn, voiced their solidarity with his quest for spiritual unity in the Americas.

Pedagogy for the Persecuted: Stefan Zweig Visits the Pestalozzi School

In the interviews he granted to Argentine media, Zweig devoted considerable attention to the psychology and pedagogy of children in Europe and the Americas. The great tragedy of Europe in the post-First World War period, Zweig declared to *Crítica*, was the inculcation of hatred into the minds of European citizens, especially children: "Day after day, from sunrise to sunset, they were taught hatred, and then at night, they dreamt of it. When the war ended, it was impossible to put an end to the hatred which coursed through everyone's veins. They could not turn it off . . . men, women, and children remained intoxicated."⁵¹ According to Zweig, the European youth of the 1930s evinced the unfortunate results of the pedagogy of hate. They were not intrinsically flawed, but younger Europeans had been steered down misguided paths, "the routes of egoism and the apotheosis of force, which are just as mistaken as the exaltation of nationalism to the extreme of hate."[52] The uplifting discovery of his journey to Brazil and Argentina, Zweig continued, was to have discovered that the foundational humanist values of democracy, tolerance, intelligence, and culture remained valid for the youth in these countries (ibid.). Zweig stated that his most passionate hope was that the youth of South American would never come to live under the sway of the hatred that moved and agitated Europe in the 1930s (ibid.). Skeptical of the grand PEN conference, Zweig believed that its participants could make valuable use of their time in Buenos Aires by cultivating humanist values among the youth in Argentina. And he declared to *La Prensa* that he was committed to achieving this goal (ibid.). Though he fulfilled it in an environment so far removed from the media's eye that his actions passed almost entirely unnoticed, Zweig's promise was not an empty one.

In actuality, Zweig's concern was crucial because the propaganda of hate and its youthful victims were very much present in the Argentine capital. In addition to the anti-fascist *Argentinisches Tageblatt*, the pro-Nazi *Deutsche La Plata Zeitung* also reported on the PEN conference. The *La Plata Zeitung* inveighed against the attendance of Jewish writers, because "diese in dem Schrifttum der verschiedenen Länder niemals eigentlich beheimatet waren, sondern sich in dasselbe eingeschlichen hatten" (these [writers] never were at home in the literature of the various countries, but rather had snuck their way into it instead).[53] Nazism had already infiltrated the German education system in Argentina. In Buenos Aires in 1932 there were twenty German-language schools with approximately four thousand eight hundred students and one hundred twenty teachers, the largest concentration of German language schools outside of Europe.[54] By 1934 nearly all German schools were squarely under the influence of the Nazi propaganda machine. One pupil in the nationalist German school system recalled that the swastika, Hitler's portrait, and the Horst-Wessel Song were ubiquitous in the German schools.[55] A program modeled after the Hitler Youth, the Deutsch-Argentinische Pfadfinderkorps (German-Argentine Scouts), held regular exercises on school grounds; teachers taught from the standard school textbooks used in Nazi Germany;[56] and correspondence among school officials, including the chairman of the German school system in Argentina, Richard Preschel, bore the closing words, "Heil Hitler!"[57] In its yearly report for 1938 the Humboldt-Schule, the largest German language school in Argentina, thanked the German Embassy and the Nazi party for financial support.[58] Within a year after the Nazi seizure of power in 1933, German schools in Buenos Aires had expelled all Jewish pupils.

In 1934 Ernesto Alemann, a Swiss emigrant and owner of the *Argentinisches Tageblatt*, spearheaded the creation of the Pestalozzi School to resist the coordination of German schools in Buenos Aires with

Nazi ideology. Alfred Dang, a socialist educator and journalist exiled in Switzerland, was invited to be the school's first rector. An energetic member of the anti-fascist community on the River Plate, Dang lamented that in Germany "der Geist erschlagen und eingekerkert und der militärische Drill an seine Stelle gesetzt sei" (the spirit has been beaten and imprisoned, and the military drill has been imposed in its stead). He asserted that the Pestalozzi School's objective was "diesem Ungeist, dieser Berauschung zum Mord wahres Menschentum entgegenzustellen" (to confront these demons, this intoxication to murder with true humanity).[59] Incensed by its position in this regard, German Ambassador Edmund von Thermann denounced the Pestalozzi School as "eine ausgesprochene Kampfschule gegen das Gedankengut des neuen Deutschland" (a militant school which was blatantly hostile toward the principles of the new Germany).[60] In 1934 Alfred Dang earned the distinction of being the first German in South America to be denaturalized by the Nazi government.

In 1936 the student body at the Pestalozzi School numbered six hundred, just six percent of the total enrollment at German schools which had implemented or were synchronized to Nazi ideology. When Stefan Zweig and Emil Ludwig received an invitation from the Pestalozzi pupils to visit their school, the writers were intrigued. On the morning of September 18, 1936, the Pestalozzi School received an unannounced visit from two of the most internationally celebrated authors of the day. Zweig spent the entire morning at the school and he later made an audio recording addressed to the Pestalozzi pupils, most of whom, like himself, were exiles from the Third Reich. Zweig's recording, which reinforces the writer's comments to *La Prensa* about cultivating humanist values among Argentina's youth, offers a survival strategy to the Pestalozzi pupils:

> Liebe Kinder, Ihr erlebt jetzt ein kleines Wunder. Passt auf! Ihr hört jetzt meine Stimme, und ich selbst bin nicht da. Ich bin sogar furchtbar weit von Euch, weit über dem Meer und müsste viele, viele Tage reisen, um Eure Hände wirklich fassen zu können [. . .] und doch— Ihr hört es ja—meine Stimme ist da bei Euch im Zimmer [. . .] Ist das nicht ein Wunder? Und Ihr fragt Euch natürlich, wer hat dieses Wunder vollgebracht? Darauf kann ich Euch nur sagen: der Mensch hat es vollgebracht. Und wenn Ihr mich weiter fragt: wieso hat der Mensch das vollgebracht, so kann ich Euch antworten: indem er viel gelernt hat [. . .] Jeder Einzelne, der gut lernt und gut nachdenkt und irgendetwas Neues mit seinem Nachdenken findet, hilft also mit, unsere Welt schöner, vielfältiger und bequemer zu machen. Seht jetzt habt Ihr ein kleines Wunder erlebt, das Wunder [. . .] dass Ihr mich hört und doch nicht seht. Und Ihr, die Ihr jung seid, wie viel solche Wunder werdet Ihr noch erleben! Freut Euch darum, dass Ihr so jung seid, und liebt die Schule, die Euch ins Leben führt, liebt das Leben selbst und liebt Euch, einer den anderen![61]

[Dear children, you are now witnessing a small miracle. Listen! You hear my voice, and I am not there. I am actually frightfully far away from you, far across the sea, and I would have to travel many, many days in order to really grasp your hands [. . .] and yet—you can hear it—my voice is there with you in the room [. . .] Is that not a wonder? And naturally you ask yourselves, who made this miracle come true? I can only answer you by saying that man made it come true. And when you ask me further: how is it that man made it come true? Well, then I can answer you: he made it come true by learning a lot [. . .] Each person who learns well and thinks carefully and finds something new in his thoughts helps to make our world more beautiful, more diverse, and more comfortable [. . .] See, now you have witnessed a little miracle—the miracle that you hear me but don't see me. And you, you who are young, how many more such miracles will you witness! Be happy that you are so young, and love your school, which guides you into life, love life itself and love each other, one unto the other!]

Whereas he remained silent throughout the PEN conference in Buenos Aires, the recording Zweig made for the Pestalozzi pupils testifies to his willingness to speak out. In fact, the recording represents one of the most extensive statements he made during his stay in Argentina. Zweig does not acknowledge the human capacity for destruction nor does he mention Nazi persecution, although these very threats had forced him and his audience into exile, catalyzed the creation of the Pestalozzi School, and brought him together with its pupils. Instead, he advocates faith in the goodness of humanity and encourages the Pestalozzi pupils to focus on their own ability to improve the world. He posits optimism and amity as a means of perseverance amidst the trauma of persecution, conflict, and exile. His message of goodwill and faith in human virtue to the Pestalozzi pupils may be seen as an act of resistance, given the threatening atmosphere of the 1930s. Here, Zweig presents a hopeful view that he himself was ultimately unable to maintain in his own life. Judging from his comments to Argentine newspapers a few days earlier, it seems that Zweig may have believed it incumbent upon himself to communicate a buoyant outlook on the future to his audience of youthful refugees. Indeed, as several of these same pupils expressed to me some seventy years later, Zweig's words were very much the sort of encouragement that many of his traumatized younger listeners needed to hear.[62]

Alfredo Bauer, who in 1936 was an eleven-year-old Jewish refugee recently arrived in Buenos Aires, told me he had been astonished to find Stefan Zweig at the Pestalozzi School. A victim of anti-Semitism for much of his young life, Bauer had begun to view himself as an inferior human being and could not believe that such an international celebrity would pay him and his schoolmates attention. Bauer, who later became a medical doctor and prize-winning author in East Germany, remembers that Zweig's visit to the Pestalozzi School helped him and other children overcome the denigration of Nazi persecution:

> Wer rassisch verfolgt ist und noch dazu als Kind, der verinnerlicht das, und glaubt selber er ist was Schlechteres oder was Anderes. Und sie haben uns beigebracht dass wir Menschen sind, dass das ein Unrecht ist, dass man sich wehren kann. Es ist schwer nachzuvollziehen, was für eine Bedeutung das hatte für uns. Mein Leben wäre was Anderes gewesen ohne diese Menschen. Stefan Zweig war eben solch ein Mensch, der mit Kultur die Humanität propagierten.[63]

> [Somebody who suffers racial persecution, especially as a child, internalizes it, and believes himself that he is something different or inferior. They taught us that we were humans, that racism is wrong, that we could defend ourselves. It is difficult to comprehend what that meant for us. My life would have been something different without these people. Stefan Zweig was a person who propagated culture with humanity.]

As Bauer explains, the encounter with a writer of Zweig's stature transformed the refugees' sense of self-valuation. Moved by the visit of this celebrated author, the pupils deployed Zweig's words to cope with their traumatic experiences, as well as gather strength and confidence to confront a challenging present.

The Pestalozzi pupils' efforts brought life to Stefan Zweig's message of solidarity and intellectual empowerment. The children organized a school festival to raise donations for children who had been displaced by the war and were incarcerated at the Gurs internment camp in Vichy France. Many of the Pestalozzi children had endured similar hardships in Europe, but now they felt empowered to an extent, and could convert their suffering into artistic forms which aided their peers in France, who had not escaped Nazi persecution.[64] Some of the pupils wrote, edited, and published chronicles of their own flights from Europe to Argentina, which they then sold in local bookshops to raise money for children in France. A group of pupils also composed and performed a play in which they imagined themselves to be prisoners in the Gurs concentration camps. Closer to biography than fiction, many of the children on stage were not presenting an imagined script, but rather personal memories of hardships they themselves had experienced firsthand. Frank Nelson noted that he and his classmates at the Pestalozzi School underwent psychological healing by recalling and expressing personal trauma through the embodied memory of dramatic representation.[65] Their efforts raised money to purchase food for Hitler's younger victims across the Atlantic, creating emotional, trans-Atlantic bonds among these child refugees. The pupils in Brazil received many letters from thankful internees, including descriptions of their dreams of finding refuge in the Americas, as well as reports of the strength they gained from learning about the Pestalozzi pupils' own perseverance.[66] Upon his visit to the Pestalozzi School in 1936, Stefan Zweig had written a note to its adult founders: "Die Menschen verdienen Liebe, je mehr sie von bösen Gewalten gedemütigt werden sollen. Aber dringlicher als Alles ist in diesen schweren Tagen, die Kinder . . . für die gute Zukunft zu retten" (The more people are humiliated by evil forces, the more love they deserve. Most urgent of all in these dark days is to rescue the children for a better future).[67] Shortly after Zweig's visit the Pestalozzi pupils themselves were responding to his entreaty.

Upon his arrival in Buenos Aires, Zweig had made clear that he had one imperative during his stay in the Argentine capital: "to be true to [himself]."[68] A few days later, *La Prensa* had published an essay by Stefan Zweig entitled "La unidad en el espíritu."[69] In this short piece, Zweig asserted that a writer's first duty was to put forth a better and more peaceful understanding of humanity (ibid.). It was his obligation to "demonstrate that the spirit is as free and daringly capable as the machine to surmount the borders between peoples and languages" (ibid.; demostrar que el espíritu es tan libre y tan osadamente capaz como la máquina de superar las fronteras entre los pueblos y los idiomas). This statement likely raised expectations that he would adopt a more public profile during the PEN proceedings. However Zweig's writings and deeds during his visit show that he believed the most effective way to achieve this aim was by devoting himself to victims of injustice. In Buenos Aires, his approach gave priority to the more humble religious and educational institutions of refugees over the banquets of the PEN conference. During his visit to Argentina in 1936 Zweig neither gained praise in the Argentine media, nor did he receive the acclaim of prominent national organizations. He did, however, remain true to himself and won the gratitude of adult and child refugees alike.

Notes

[1] Darién J. Davis and Oliver Marshall, eds., *Stefan and Lotte Zweig's South American Letters: New York, Argentina and Brazil, 1940–42* (New York: Continuum, 2010), 9.

[2] Ibid., 35.

[3] "Stefan Zweig llegó ayer procedente de Brasil," *La Nación*, October 27, 1940, n.p.

[4] Alfredo Cahn, *Stefan Zweig, amigo y autor* (Cordoba: Ciudad universitaria, 1966).

[5] Alfredo Bauer, *Der Mann von gestern und die Welt. Ein biographischer Roman um Stefan Zweig* (Vienna: Edition Atelier, 1993).

[6] Ronald Newton, "Das andere Deutschland: The anti-Fascist Exile Network in Southern South America," *The Muses Flee Hitler*, ed. Jarrell C. Kackman and Carla M. Borden (Washington, D.C.: Smithsonian Institution Press, 1983), 306.

[7] Georg Ismar, *Der Pressekrieg: Argentinisches Tageblatt und Deutsche La Plata Zeitung 1933–1945* (Berlin: Wissenschaftlicher Verlag, 2006), 80.

[8] The *Deutsche La Plata Zeitung* had a circulation of 45,000 in 1938 and received 34,000 *Reichsmark* from the German government in 1938 alone (Ismar, 28).

[9] José Alfredo Schwarcz, *Trotz Allem: Die deutschsprachigen Juden in Argentinien* (Cologne: Böhlau, 1995), 60.

[10] Ismar, 14.

[11] Victoria Ocampo, "Congreso Internacional de la Federación de los PEN Clubs," *Sur* 23 (August 1936): 7–10.

[12] Three of the best-selling papers in Argentina, in 1936 were *La Prensa*, *La Nación*, and *Crítica*, with respective circulations of 230,000, 220,000 (340,000 on weekends), and 280,000.

[13] "Eminentes Valores Intelectuales Llegaron Ayer," *La Nación*, September 9, 1936, 10.

[14] "Tres grandes escritores europeos llegarán esta mañana a Buenos Aires," *La Prensa*, September 5, 1936, n.p.

[15] "Cómo son y cómo parecen," *Crítica*, September 5, 1936, 5–6 (unless otherwise noted, all translations are mine).

[16] "Considerose ayer la función social del escritor en el congreso internacional de los P.E.N. Clubs," *La Prensa*, September 8, 1936, n.p.

[17] "Stefan Zweig und Emil Ludwig," *Mitteilungsblatt des Hilfsvereins deutschsprechender Juden*, October 1, 1936, 6.

[18] "Dichter kommen nach Argentinien," *Argentinisches Tageblatt*, September 6, 1936, 7.

[19] Knut Beck and Jeffrey B. Berlin, eds., *Stefan Zweig. Briefe 1932–1942* (Frankfurt am Main: Fischer, 2005), 162.

[20] "La Verdad se Divulga, mas no se Impone" *Crítica*, September 5, 1936, 5.

[21] "Ludwig Hizo el Proceso del Nazismo," *Crítica*, September 8, 1936, 5.

[22] Zweig, in Beck and Berlin, 166.

[23] Darién J. Davis and Oliver Marshall, 9.

[24] "Reflexiones de dos escritores europeos huéspedes de Buenos Aires," *La Prensa*, September 10, 1936.

[25] "Stefan Zweig expresa su agradecimiento por medio de *La Nación*," *La Nación*, September 16, 1936, n.p.

[26] "Epitafio Sobre un Congreso de Escritores," *Crítica*, September 15, 1936, 4.

[27] "Un escándalo en el P.E.N. Club," *La Fronda*, September 8, 1936, n.p.

[28] "Pretendiese interrumpir con un desorden un acto realizado en el facultad de derecho," *La Prensa*, September 17, 1936, n.p.

[29] "La Asociación pro Maestros envió una nota a Emil Ludwig," *La Nación*, September 18, 1936, n.p.

[30] "Emil Ludwig se Propone Novelar la Vida del General San Martín," *Crítica*, September 9, 1936, 5.

[31] "'Lo que hace la historia es la voluntad del héroe, su relieve, más que el hecho,' dijo Emil Ludwig," *Los Andes*, September 20, 1936, 4.

[32] Donald A. Prater, *European of Yesterday* (Oxford: Oxford University Press, 1972), 257.

[33] "Abreise von Zweig," *Argentinisches Tageblatt*, September 16, 1936, n.p.

[34] "Emil Ludwig zum Abschied," *Argentinisches Tageblatt*, September 20, 1936, 6.

[35] Ibid.

[36] "Ludwig Desenmascaró a las Tiranías," *Crítica*, September 9, 1936, 5; "El escritor Emil Ludwig," *La Fronda*, September 19, 1936, n.p.

[37] "Eminentes Valores Intelectuales Llegaron Ayer," *La Nación*, September 6, 1936, 10.

[38] "Internationaler Kongreß der P.E.N. Clubs," *Deutsche La Plata Zeitung*, September 6, 1936, n.p.

[39] "Eminentes Valores Intelectuales Llegaron Ayer," *La Nación*, September 6, 1936, 10.

[40] Daviau, 103.

[41] *Anuario Argentino de Germanística* 2 (December 2010): 8.

[42] Paul Zech, "Stefan Zweig. Ein Gedenkschrift," in *Stefan Zweig, Paul Zech Briefe, 1910–1942*, ed. Ulrich Weinzierl (Frankfurt am Main: Fischer, 1986).

[43] "A la juventud de Europa le importa más el egoísmo que la humanidad, afirmó Zweig," *La Nación*, September 9, 1936, 10.

[44] Daviau, 130.

[45] Darién J. Davis and Oliver Marshall, 75.

[46] Schwarcz, 114.

[47] Johann Wolfgang von Goethe, *Faust*, trans. Walter Arndt, ed. Cyrus Hamlin (New York: W. W. Norton, 2001), 7.

[48] "Stefan Zweig und Emil Ludwig," *Mitteilungsblatt des Hilfsvereins deutschsprechender Juden*, October 1, 1936, 6.

[49] "Zweig to Alfred Wolf," February 4, 1937, cited in Daviau, 177.

[50] "Ein Problem," *Mitteilungsblatt des Hilfsvereins deutschsprechender Juden*, October 1, 1936, 23.

[51] "La Propaganda del odio ha Transformado a Italia, País Pacífico, en País Belicoso, Dice Zweig," *Crítica*, September 5, 1936, 5 (all translations from Spanish are mine).

[52] "A la juventud de Europa le importa más el egoísmo que la humanidad, afirmó Zweig," *La Prensa*, September 9, 1936, n.p.

[53] "Literatur oder Literaturgout," *Deutsche La Plata Zeitung*, September 13, 1936, n.p.

[54] Wilhelm Keiper, *Der Deutsche in Argentinien* (Berlin: Julius Beltz, 1938), 53.

[55] Heinrich Volberg, *Auslandsdeutschtum und drittes Reich: der Fall Argentinien* (Cologne: Böhlau, 1981), 187.

[56] "Die Humboldt-Schule eine naziotische Drillanstalt," *Argentinisches Tageblatt*, April 6, 1938, 3.

[57] Anita Schroer to Richard Preschel, November 13, 1940, Goethe School Archive, Vicente Lopez, Argentina.

[58] Humboldt-Schule Jahresbericht (1939), Goethe School Archive, 23.

[59] Thermann to German Foreign Office, May 10, 1934, Pestalozzi School Archive.

[60] Thermann to German Foreign Office, April 18, 1934, Pestalozzi School Archive.

[61] Stefan Zweig, "An die 'Pestalozzi'-Schüler," *Schülerzeitung der Pestalozzi-Schule*, September 1936, 7–8.

[62] Alfredo Bauer, interview with the author, August 9, 2007; Frank Nelson, interview with the author, January 18, 2009; Robert Schopflocher, interview with the author, August 8, 2012.

[63] Alfredo Bauer, interview.

[64] August Siemsen, "Kinder hinter Gittern," *Das Andere Deutschland*, April 1937, n.p.

[65] Cora Roca, *Días del Teatro: Hedy Crilla* (Buenos Aires: CELCIT, 2001), 336; Alfredo Bauer interview.

[66] Jacques Gniwesch, Ingrid Billigheimer, and Erich Schwamm to the Pestalozzi Schüler, November 5, 1941, Pestalozzi School Archive.

[67] Stefan Zweig to Pestalozzi School, 1936, Pestalozzi School Archive.

[68] "La Verdad se Divulga, mas no se Impone," *Crítica*, September 5, 1936, p. 5.

[69] "Reflexiones de dos escritores europeos huéspedes de Buenos Aires," *La Prensa*, September 10, 1936, n.p.

9: Exile and Liminality in "A Land of the Future": Charlotte and Stefan Zweig in Brazil, August 1941–March 1942

Darién J. Davis

To THOUSANDS OF JEWISH IMMIGRANTS FLEEING EUROPE during the Second World War, Brazil seemed a welcoming social utopia and a peaceful respite from chaos. The country's tropical warmth and its apparent racial and religious tolerance served as a stark contrast to the ravages of war and the official anti-Semitism rampant in Germany and other European nations at the time.[1] Stefan Zweig and his second wife Lotte Zweig (née Charlotte Altmann) had already expressed their positive views about Brazil in letters to family and friends in Europe during their first trip to South America together in 1940. In a letter to his first wife, Friderike, he explained that Brazil is "der einzige Ort, wo es keine Rassenfrage gibt" (the only place where there are no racial issues).[2] Yet it was Brazil's peacefulness that made it

> eines der ... liebenswertesten Länder unserer Welt. Es ist ein Land, das den Krieg haßt ... Darum beruht auf der Existenz Brasiliens, dessen Willen einzig auf friedlichen Aufbau gerichtet ist, unserer besten Hoffnungenn auf eine zukünftige Zivilisierung und Befriedung unserer von Haß und Wahn verwüsteten Welt.[3]

> [one of the most lovable countries in the world. It is a country that hates war ... So one of our hopes for future civilization and peace in our world, which has been destroyed by hatred and madness, rest[s] on the existence of Brazil, whose desires are aimed exclusively at pacific development.][4]

As late as November 1941, just a few months before the couple committed suicide, Stefan Zweig voiced his happiness with Brazil: "... we feel extremely happy here, the little bungalow with its large covered terrace (our real living room) has a splendid view over the mountains ..."[5]

Imagining a peaceful Brazil was important to the Zweigs' dreams, but after they made the decision to settle there, however temporarily, life in Brazil became untenable. Because of their relative economic, cultural, and social privileges—including their British citizenship—the Zweigs did not suffer the same as hardships many other homeless exiles who arrived in Brazil. Yet exile from Europe was psychologically and emotionally challenging.

According to Victor Turner, those who inhabit or traverse liminal spaces are "betwixt and between the positions assigned and arrayed by law, custom, convention, and ceremony."[6] Turner moreover defined the pilgrimage as a form of liminality—as a continuation of a diasporic voyage and the pilgrim as an occupant of an ambiguous, detached space during travel.[7]

While in Brazil the Zweigs occupied a complex liminal space between cultures and languages in which they questioned everything. They were caught between several different worlds (European, North American, and Brazilian) and conflicts, both external (the war) and internal (psychological challenges to their identity and well-being). The Zweigs seemed to be on an incessant pilgrimage for solace. Stefan Zweig best described the couple's state of detachment from country and place when he wrote: "So gehöre ich nirgends mehr hin, überall Fremder und bestenfalls Gast."[8] (I belong nowhere, and everywhere am a stranger, a guest at best."[9] To understand the Zweigs' sense of exile and liminality in the last months of their lives, it is important to examine three critical aspects of their experience: their ambivalence about the political and social issues in Brazil; their isolation in Petrópolis; and their role as translators with complex relationships to the languages of the South American cultures they were exiled in.

Brazil and the Getúlio Vargas Regime

Charlotte and Stefan Zweig traveled to Brazil in an era of intense debate about the direction of national culture in Brazil, or during what Daryl Williams has called its "culture wars."[10] In total, the couple spent less than thirteen months in the country: the first period from August 1940 to March 1941, and the second from August 1941 to February 1942. Both had British passports, Brazilian resident cards, and sufficient finances and contacts to be able to travel in and out of the country. They were invited guests of Abrahão Koogan, owner of the publishing house Editora Guanabara, and of the Brazilian government, headed by President Getúlio Vargas.[11]

The Vargas government's Ministry of Culture and Education officially promoted the celebration of Brazilian cultural syncretism as well as the cultural movement known as "modernism" in education, the arts, and architecture. As a way of thinking, modernism posited that Brazil was unique in contrast to other American countries, particularly the United States, and that it was to be praised because of its relative harmony across racial lines.[12] Some Brazilian writers and intellectuals, such as those associated with the Anthropophagic movement, celebrated the country's presumed ability to assimilate foreign cultures and immigrants and make them Brazilian.[13] However, some writers distanced themselves from this claim. For example, in his satire *Macunaíma* (1928), the modernist writer Mário de Andrade criticized the Brazilian desire to "whiten" the culture and project itself as European, while celebrating cultural syncretism.[14] One of the most important voices of the era was the sociologist, historian, and patriotic writer Gilberto Freyre. Freyre developed the idea of *lusotropicalism* in the 1920s to denote Portuguese adaptation to the tropics and emphasized the centrality of Africans to the formation of what it meant to be Brazilian, or "Brazilian-ness."[15] Freyre, who had studied in the United States, was influenced by his own experiences of living and studying abroad, and by a strong desire to portray Brazil in a positive light. Freyre's *weltanschauung* was clearly influenced by the anthropologist Franz Boas, his advisor at Columbia University in New York, who was a German-Jewish American and a proponent of Jewish assimilation.[16]

Brazil received Jewish immigrants and settlers to its shores from across Europe and the Middle East since the colonial era. From 1824 to 1969, Germans were the fourth largest immigrant group after the Portuguese, the Spaniards and Italians. Of the 250,000 total German immigrants, many of them were of Jewish ancestry.[17] Jews, for example, made up almost five percent of the official immigrants to Brazil between 1926 and 1930, 7.2 percent from 1930 to 1935, and 12.1 percent from 1936 to 1942. As a result of growing nationalist sentiments in the 1930s, however, the Vargas government imposed new restrictions on immigrants in general and on Jews in particular. Ironically, the Brazilian elite and the state often viewed German-speaking Jews (as opposed to Jews from Eastern Europe and the Middle East) as a potentially important part of Brazil's efforts to become an industrialized, cosmopolitan, and modern white country.[18]

Brazil was a land of opportunity for scores of European and Middle eastern immigrants, and many Jews were among the foreigners whom the syncretic country "Brazilianized." At the same time, like the United States, Brazil instituted restrictions on Jewish migration and consciously attempted to discourage the emigration of Europeans of "undesirable" backgrounds.[19] Members of the Brazilian government also flirted with Nazism and dealt with its enemies harshly. The case of the Jewish communist refugee Olga Benário, who was sent back to Germany by the Vargas regime in 1938 and subsequently murdered in a concentration camp four years later, was uncommon but telling.[20] Although neither Stephan nor Lotte Zweig documented any anti-Jewish or anti-immigrant experiences, many working-class immigrants came face to face with the anti-immigrant and anti-Semitic sentiments espoused by local fascist thinkers such as Plínio Salgado and Gustavo Pérez Firmat, and by fascist organizations such as the Integralists (green shirts) even though they were officially abolished by Vargas's government after 1936.[21]

The Zweigs seem to have been mostly unaware of the cultural and political tensions in Brazil. In addition, their publisher and state officials shielded them from any unpleasant experiences. By the time Stefan and Lotte Zweig settled in Petrópolis in August 1941, Brazil was already four years into Vargas's *Estado Novo*, his new proto-fascist state, and the Department of Propaganda had already instituted a number of antidemocratic policies that made it difficult to obtain unbiased information about Brazilian politics inside Brazil. By all accounts Stefan and Lotte Zweig were "desirable Jews." Not only were they German-speaking, secular Jews from Europe, but Zweig was a well-known international figure as well. His decision to reside in Brazil with his wife served patriotic Brazilians well, ironically because of the reverence with which many Brazilians continued to view Europe.

When the Zweigs arrived in Brazil in August 1941, it was a clear rejection of New York and the United States, but their intentions about staying in Brazil were not entirely clear. Even though the Zweigs had resident permits, they did not know how long they would remain in the country. Indeed, despite the low price of real estate, they decided to rent a house rather than purchase one. They chose to stay in Petrópolis because it was sufficiently far from the city of Rio de Janeiro to give them the solitude they desired, but close enough to keep them in contact with urban civilization. Petrópolis was somewhat familiar to them because it was similar to other resort towns Stefan Zweig knew well, such as Bath in England and Semmering in Lower Austria. Petrópolis also had a significant foreign population, giving it a European flare, and its climate was cooler than locations along the coast; it was like an oasis in the midst of the tropics. For the Zweigs, Petrópolis was to Rio as Bath was to London.

Ambivalence and Liminality

The Zweigs' avoidance of politics in Brazil was not unusual. As far as we know Lotte Zweig had never ventured into politics and Stefan Zweig's aversion to overt political involvement has been well documented by biographers. Some Brazilian leftist intellectuals, such as Jorge Amado, interpreted Stefan Zweig's silence to mean that he was a supporter of Getúlio Vargas. Amado and others publicly denounced Zweig's *Brasilien: Ein Land der Zukunft* as government propaganda, forcing Zweig to defend himself in a manner to which he was not accustomed. Despite being ambivalent and at times outright uninterested in local matters, it is clear that Zweig wanted to be accepted by Brazilians, as his response to the critical reception of the volume illustrated. When he wrote about

Brazil he was writing from an emotional space, expressing what he described as his deep gratitude and affection (*MP* 389).

In Brazil, Zweig found elements of his destroyed Vienna. For Zweig, Vienna, before the First World War, had been a multiethnic, multicultural, tolerant yet aristocratic and elegant city with many ethnic groups and peoples. Jews, Germans, Hungarians, Slavs, and others lived there in relative harmony (*WvG* 36, 453–54; *WoY* 20, 401). It seems clear, however, that his comparisons of Austria and Brazil were largely based on his privileged experiences growing up in Vienna, on the one hand, and as a famous European writer in exile, on the other. More importantly, Stefan Zweig's sentimental longing for an idealized world that he could envision in Brazil was also an attempt to re-imagine a mythical youth. Lotte Zweig, as far as we know, was neither nostalgic for her life in Germany, nor did she necessarily share her husband's attachment to Brazil. Apparently, she trusted her husband's judgment and she was genuinely charmed by the attention she received as a European in Brazil and as the wife of Stefan Zweig (*SLZ* 82).

Lotte Zweig's letters to her family in London best articulate the couple's difficulties in adjusting to everyday life in Brazil. Living in Petrópolis meant that Brazil was no longer a distant "land of the future," but a real concrete place to which the Zweigs would have to adjust in the present. They would have to attend to the activities of daily living. Lotte Zweig's longing for family in Great Britain while she resided far away in Brazil, however, was quite powerful. During their first trip to Brazil, Lotte wrote to her brother and sister-in-law about the difficulty she and her husband had in planning for the future. On November 7, 1940, she wrote to Hanna and Manfred Altmann:

> To make plans or even to think ahead for more than 4 or 5 months one does not dare although I always hope for pleasant events and sometimes even have rather premature dreams about being at home again with you. I am surprised to find myself so much more sentimental than I thought, but I discover more and more deeply this habit of living without you for so long, has grown and how much I miss you. (*SLZ* 91–92)

After returning to Brazil in 1941 similar comments about her fond memories of living with her brother and sister in London appear in her letters. On one occasion, after weeks without receiving news or correspondence, Lotte Zweig complained to her sister-in-law Hannah: "I haven't heard from you for quite a while and I really miss your letters. I hope it is just a postal delay and that there was no special reason to keep you from writing" (*SLZ* 151). In another letter to Hanna and Manfred Altmann, dated November 7, 1941, Lotte discussed the general plight of European exiles caught between different worlds as they wrestle with finding a new home outside of Europe:

> We have well arrived on Wednesday and are glad to be here in a somewhat quieter atmosphere . . . we would move up to Petrópolis in about a fortnight and come down to Rio once or twice a week. I do not regret having left the States again. It is strange: nearly all the Europeans down here in South Amer. dream of going to the States while many of those who are there find it very difficult to adapt themselves and wish they could leave and live in South America. (*SLZ* 135)

Lotte did not regret the decision to leave the United States, but neither was she elated to be back in Brazil. Stefan Zweig was somewhat less ambivalent about the move, although he anticipated that he would not have many friends in Brazil. At the same time, he was critical of life in New York and looked forward to a life of solitude. As he wrote in a letter to Hanna and Manfred Altmann:

> We are now four days here and feel allright—happy would be too much because I cannot adapt myself to this nomadic life without a house and without books, we remain Europeans for ever and will feel everywhere strangers. I have no "pep" like the Americans say and also writing will be difficult after the autobiography—all I have to tell is so far away [from] what America likes to read and to hear . . . Our life in Petrópolis . . . will be a solitary one because we do not like more society and I have refused to make public appearance[s] for the next time—we will study Portuguese to feel more sure [*sic*] and I hope to continue to work. In New York we had too many people and here not enough . . . (*SLZ* 136)

From this perspective, Brazil never represented a final destination or a "paradise" as the title of Alberto Dines' biography *Morte no paraíso* (Death in Paradise, 1981) suggests, but rather it was another signpost, a resting spot. Indeed, it was to be their last.

The Zweigs were able to travel and remain in Brazil because the government and the country benefited from having them in different ways. Both Zweigs received a great deal of attention in the press, and they were treated like royalty. The presence of a world-renowned author of Zweig's stature and his wife in Brazil helped to elevate the country's status on the world stage. Lotte's very presence was crucial to Stefan Zweig's respectability in a Catholic country, where marriage tended to secure an individual's place in society. Moreover, Lotte Zweig's skills as a linguist, translator, typist, secretary, and research assistant were obviously invaluable to her husband, not to mention her companionship. The Zweigs' presence also fed into Brazil's nascent inferiority complex vis-à-vis Europe and the Brazilian need to be validated by Europeans as a modern nation.

Lack of Social Attachments: Another Form of Ambivalence?

In Brazil, the Zweigs did not affiliate with any particular political or cultural groups, whether religious or civic, although they attended benefits for Jewish refugee organizations as they had done in Britain and the United States. As already noted, both Zweigs had shunned overt political activism prior to their arrival in Brazil, and Stefan Zweig had been clear about his discomfort with public activism. They nonetheless worked tirelessly to help friends and family financially and to secure exit visas from Europe. Brazil served as safe space for the couple trying to escape the war, but they continued to engage with the world even as they lamented their powerlessness and inability to do much to change contemporary conditions (*SLZ* 12).

Initially, the decision to settle in Petrópolis was predicated on the belief that the small resort city could be a place of rest and solitude. It was not a place where they intended to live to deepen their understanding about Brazil. Nonetheless, the Zweigs wrote constantly about their impressions of the people, the landscape, and the climate (*SLZ* 24–26). Before Stefan Zweig's arrival in Brazil in 1941, he wrote to his Brazilian publisher Abrahão Koogan that he wanted to avoid festivities and the hectic schedule of his previous visit. In a letter from New York, Stefan informed Koogan that he had reserved a cabin on the *Uruguay*, and asked him not to tell anyone since he was exhausted and only wished to rest in Rio de Janeiro and Petrópolis.[22] In a follow-up letter, Zweig repeated this same message: "I am very tired, I have worked a great deal and the idea of resting in Brazil is a great temptation." But he was also optimistic about his and Lotte's ability to accommodate to a new life in Brazil, and he planned to learn to speak Portuguese, believing that "because [he] read it without great difficulty [learning it would] not be very difficult" (*Briefe* 311–12).

In his essay on the pilgrimage, Turner does not only focus on the voyage and the destination but also on the critical importance of the "communitas" among the pilgrims en route, the camaraderie, and the shared experience of travellers.[23] Given the Zweigs' unique situation as privileged guests of a dictatorship that officially limited Jewish entrance into Brazilian territory, as well as his fame, if there were any *communitas* it was made up of two persons, Charlotte and Stefan, whose bonds revolved around family and work.[24] The Zweigs had received numerous invitations to travel and give talks around South America. They kept their British passports, secured Brazilian residency cards, and thus kept all options open in a manner understandable for two people who were compelled to go into exile.

While Arendt emphasized Stefan Zweig's privileged status no matter where he traveled, Leo Spitzer focuses on the tensions between assimilation and marginality, underscoring Zweig's flight from what he calls subordination.[25] Initially, Brazil released Zweig from some of the tensions characteristic of his situation as an exile, by allowing him to imagine a comfortable life outside of Europe. Zweig himself seemed to be very pleased or even impressed by how popular he was in the tropical haven and by how well the Brazilians treated him and his wife. Likewise, Charlotte was pleasantly amused by the attention given her by the Brazilian press, while she followed her husband's lead dutifully, in a way that was typical of the times. But she was by no means a quiet or submissive wife, as her letters from Brazil to her family clearly indicate.[26]

Although the Zweigs had physically escaped the war, news of the worldwide conflict was constantly around them. If they avoided information or were ignorant about local politics in Brazil, the same could not be said about life in Europe and the details of the war. In addition to letters from their friends and family that supplied them with news and a connection to Europe, they read the newspapers to stay abreast of what was happening in the conflict. While Stefan Zweig generally maintained a calm disposition, according to his Brazilian lawyer Samuel Malamud, he was "always" complaining about the "times," that is to say, what was happening in the world.[27]

It would be incorrect to claim that the Zweigs had not made any deep personal connections or serious contacts in Brazil. They often received visitors who lived in Petrópolis or the neighboring town of Teresópolis, or from Rio de Janeiro, and occasionally from elsewhere in South America. The Zweigs were fond of resident intellectuals such as the Chilean poet Gabriela Mistral, and particularly the Cuban diplomat Hernández Catá. Their circle of friends was much smaller than the one they enjoyed in Europe or in New York. While these new connections sometimes seemed ephemeral, they could occasion new and unexpected sorrows. When Herández Catá died unexpectedly in a plane crash, both Zweigs were deeply saddened as well as indignant. Stefan best expressed these emotions when he wrote in a letter to Hanna and Manfred Altmann dated November 12, 1940:

> We have refused, Chile, Paraguay, Colombia, Cuba, we have enough for the moment—enough of success, fees, flowers, people and refugees. How we are longing to sit quietly again in Bath!
>
> A sad news was that our best friend in Rio, Hernandez Catá, the ambassador of Cuba has been killed in a stupid aeroplane accident.

Three days after his death a letter had reached me here, saying, that he would wait with his car on the aerodrom, when we arrive—and he lost his life meanwhile in a plane excursion. He was the kindest man I have met since years and he garanties for Eisemann in Cuba—I hope they did send the visa to Eisemann from Havanna. You understand that the only way to be grateful for the preference and happiness which we enjoy is that we try to use here our influence to help to others [sic]. (SLZ 80–81)

The Zweigs wanted solitude but they also wanted access to an intellectual community and to good libraries. For many people, religion may provide a sense of community, but neither of the Zweigs was particularly religious. Nonetheless, Abrahão Koogan recalled that he accompanied the couple to the synagogue in Rio (the temple on Rua Tenente Possolo) on the holy Jewish day of Yom Kippur in 1941, and he recalled exchanging ideas about the events of the world and about the situation of the Jews. According to Koogan, Zweig felt "aliviado por estar entre os seus" (relieved to be among his own), as if being among Jews from all over the world brought him solace.[28] Whether or not Koogan correctly interpreted this expression of sentiments or was merely projecting his own feelings onto Stefan Zweig, we know that Lotte and Stefan Zweig only rarely attended synagogue (SLZ 3). If Koogan is right, however, this synagogue visit would signal an important change in understanding the relationship between Zweig's "European-ness" and his "Jewishness."

Petrópolis as a Space of "Trance"

Stefan Zweig was so enthralled by Brazil and its potential that he wrote his first book-length travelogue about it, calling it "a land of the future." Zweig's deep longing for a pre-Hitlerian Europe clearly influenced his writing and his relationship to Brazil, even while he lived there. He and Lotte had spent a greater part of the 1930s crossing national borders, immersing themselves in different cultures and languages as their families had decades before. Lotte's family had moved from Katowice in modern-day Poland, to Germany and then to England, for example. Stefan's family had moved from Bohemia (in the modern-day Czech Republic) to Vienna, where Zweig was born, and throughout his life he traveled and lived in many places in Europe.

Petrópolis was a comforting place because it was somehow familiar to them. It had a European air and was similar to the resort towns that the Zweigs had enjoyed throughout the thirties, but it was also isolated and sufficiently removed from the intellectual circles to which they were accustomed. In Petrópolis, the Zweigs' image of Brazil as a lush tropical multicultural paradise would shift. In their last home, they contemplated these conflicts and often experienced new insights, as well as times of joy and periods of deep sadness. They praised what they saw as the Brazilian ability to be happy with so few possessions. Yet they complained about the lack of conveniences, the absence of friends and of libraries (*SLZ* 24–34).

Ironically, the Zweigs settled on 34 Rua Dias Gonçalves, a street named after the Brazilian poet Antonio Dias Gonçalves, best known for his "Song of Exile," in which he implores God not to let him "die without getting back to where I belong."[29] Their house seemed to them to represent Brazil, and it was also a symbol of the Zweigs' liminality and exile in a place where they ultimately felt that they did not quite belong. Moreover, the Brazil that the Zweigs imagined initially as a peaceful, harmonious place far from the ravages of war became a liminal space in which they negotiated their sense of "European-ness" and "Jewish-ness," and at the same time a place where they could hold on to their internationalist, humanist, and pacifist ideas far away from the war. Although they remained appreciative of Brazil and Brazilians until their suicides, Brazil, with its tropical landscape and quaint ways, remained forever an exotic place to which the Zweigs never really made a final commitment. It was a "paradise," to use the term from the title of Alberto Dines's biography, in contrast to the "hell" Stefan and Lotte Zweig had left in Austria and Germany respectively. But, over time the land that Stefan Zweig called "a land of the future" became a locus in which his sense of exile and liminality was exacerbated. It could not bring him any lasting solace in the last months of his life.[30]

In many ways, the Zweigs' state of liminality while in Petrópolis may be described as a kind of trance. For anthropologist and filmmaker Maya Deren, "trance" describes the phase of altered consciousness of those who are possessed or experiencing some type of epiphany, a phenomenon she explored in her seminal work *The Divine Horsemen: The Living Gods of Haiti*.[31] While the Zweigs were certainly in an altered state of consciousness, one can hardly describe their experience as an epiphany. Rather, Deren's concept of movement, transience or suspension gives us insight into the Zweigs' sensibilities and their internal conflicts. Stefan and Lotte Zweig faced competing interests among family, friends, work, and cultures and languages. In this context, without a clear direction or purpose both Zweigs remained in a state of "trance," or transience. They were fleeing Europe, the war, and the United States, and being actively courted or seduced by the Brazilian government, Zweig's publisher, and his Brazilian audience. At the same time they left all doors open for the possibility of escape or new travels. This tense situation was barely perceptible under the calm surface of the externally peaceful and isolated town of Petrópolis.

The concept of a "trance" as a voyage, as a type of crossing over and yet not quite arriving, is both a metaphor and literal state for the Zweigs as they repeatedly made decisions about where they would live after they left Great Britain in 1940. As already mentioned, both Zweigs were seasoned travelers. They had arrived in New York City on June 30, 1940. While in New York, they were also making preparations for a trip to South America; they organized his research schedule and travel agenda for the book he planned to write on Brazil. Once in Brazil, they made plans to travel around the country and to go to Argentina, among other places (*Briefe* 278). In contrast, Petrópolis was a physical resting place, a safe house, but it did not allay their fears or rescue them from the psychological wounds of exile and war. On the contrary, to a couple accustomed to travel, the quiet and calm of Petrópolis may have magnified or intensified their anxieties and concerns.

As modern travelers, the Zweigs were accustomed to the short-term liminality of travel, which entailed the art of temporarily suspending customs and cultural expectations as the traveler enters new cultural spaces. Brazil represented a qualitatively different place of exploration because they truly enjoyed Brazil and its people. The Zweigs remained there longer than in any other territory outside of Europe. Also, they had secured resident cards that allowed them to come and go as they pleased. Sometimes, Petrópolis brought out feelings of euphoria and at others it exposed their feelings of isolation and melancholy. Even when Stefan Zweig expressed his insights on humanity and his own privileged upbringing vis-à-vis poor Brazilians, his statements are tempered by sober feelings of detachment from the world in general. In a letter dated August 24, 1941, he wrote to Hanna and Manfred Altmann,

> I believe I was right to go to Brazil where I have a right for permanent stay while in America I was only a visitor and in case of war I would have had all these little annoyances as a foreigner (a friendly one in this case). I hope you have got my letter about the house, it is important for me that you dispose in such a way that you can take it over completely—Don't think about me, I have written all in the chimney. (*SLZ* 134)

The expression "written . . . in the chimney," coming from the German idiom "etwas in den Rauchfang schreiben" (write something in the chimney), means that he had tried to prepare himself to lose everything. It illustrates the detachment that Stefan Zweig attained or wanted to attain, but also his realization that he could lose everything at any minute.

Most importantly, Zweig could envision a land of the future while he was in transition, traveling from town to town and obtaining a glimpse of the Brazilian land and its people as a tourist and outside observer. Only when we understand Stefan Zweig's complicated liminal world and the couple's psychological mindset does his following idealized assessment of Brazil, though factually inaccurate, make sense:

[Brasilien] scheint mir eines der vorbildlichsten und darum liebenswertesten Länder unserer Welt. Es ist ein Land, das den Krieg hasst und noch mehr: das ihn soviel wie gar nicht kennt... Als einzige der iberischen Nationen hat Brasilien keine blutigen Religionsverfolgungen gekannt, nie haben hier die Scheiterhaufen der Inquisition geflammt, in keinem Lande sind die Sklaven verhältnismässig humaner behandelt worden. Selbst seine inneren Umstürze und Regierungsänderungen haben sich beinahe unblutig vollzogen. (*BLZ* 17–18)

[Brazil seems to be one of the most exemplary and therefore most loveable countries in the world. It is a country that hates war, and what is more, practically does not know it at all... Brazil is the only Iberian nation that has not known bloody religious persecution; the stakes of the Inquisition were never ablaze here, in no other country were the slaves treated more humanely. Even its inner overthrows and changes in government took place in an almost bloodless fashion.] (*BLF* 14)

Liminality, Translation, and Language

Like many interlocutors, translators, and guides before them—including Paul Claudel, Darius Milhaud, Blaise Cendrars, Filippo T. Marinetti, Benjamin Peret, Georges Bernanos, and Henri Michaux—Stefan Zweig and to a lesser extent Lotte Zweig served as translators of Brazil to European audiences. However, they did not establish many permanent attachments to Brazilians outside of government contacts or certain writing circles. Like the Zweigs, Belgian-born writer Henri Michaux traveled extensively in Brazil in the late 1930s. Unlike them, he wrote candidly about his difficulty meeting ordinary Brazilians, a fact that certainly affected how and what he would write about them in 1939.[32] The Zweigs met many Brazilians and foreigners through Koogan and other contacts, but in some respects, like Michaux, their contacts were limited. Other European observers such as Blaise Cendrars and Giuseppe Ungaretti wrote about the general elation of most Europeans who saw Brazil in general and Rio de Janeiro in particular as "paradise on earth."[33] For these travelers Brazil represented some aspect of Europe that they had lost or that they deemed deficient. It is not surprising, for example, that the Italian poet Giuseppe Ungaretti compared Rio to his experiences in the Mediterranean, and Zweig's framework was the Vienna of his youth.[34]

While translating Brazil, the Zweigs were absorbed in their own liminal condition, which led to a "confusion of the senses," to borrow a term from the title of one of his novellas.[35] Brazil represented an idea that corresponded in their minds to a certain need. Zweig faced a challenge about how to convey his personal view of the country while avoiding generalizations for an audience ignorant of Brazil or with an entirely different set of expectations about the southern, tropical underdeveloped country? In his introduction to his travelogue Zweig attempted to respond to this challenge by informing readers that he changed his opinion "über den Wert der Worte 'Zivilisation' und 'Kultur'" (*BLZ* 17; about the value of the words "civilization" and "culture," *BLF* 13) He was no longer "willens, sie kurzerhand dem Begriff 'Organisation' und 'Komfort' gleichzustellen" (*BLZ* 17; willing to equate them unhesitatingly with organization and comfort, *BLF* 13), amenities which he had enjoyed for most of his life. Thus, the confusion of the senses resulted from a radical change in sensibilities, in addition to the angst involved in exile.

While both Zweigs were adept linguists and prepared to learn both Spanish and Portuguese, neither ever felt secure in the languages that were around them. In fact, at one point Lotte lamented that Brazilians did not speak Spanish, because it would be so much easier for her. She felt that it was impossible for her to keep Spanish and Portuguese apart. In an October 19, 1940, letter to Therese Altmann, she referred to Portuguese as an "ugly language" (*SLZ* 72–73). Both Zweigs had to face the fact that owing to the war the market for German writing had dwindled, and furthermore, they had to write letters to their family in English to avoid the wartime censorship. Life in Brazil often brought out mixed feelings and conflicting emotions. They did begin to learn Portuguese in earnest, but regretted that they had to learn and use another language altogether. They seemed to enjoy the Brazilian people, but they tended to complain, either about the lack of resources for work or about the weather that "made people lazy." In one letter to the Altmann family Lotte wrote about her own laziness as a result of the heat. In another, Stefan Zweig commented about how the weather affected his wife's health (*SLZ* 97, 102, 163–64). These complaints and comparisons between life "at home" (in Europe) and life in exile (in the tropics) are typical of trans-national people, particularly for those who can look back, observe, compare and are privileged enough to be able to travel. For the Zweigs this privilege contributed to their mood swings and to the sense of continually living in a liminal state.

Translation can be regarded as a liminal art or profession, independent of whether one believes the translator is a technician or a co-creator. As Walter Benjamin so eloquently put it, the content of translation is "like a royal robe with ample folds. For it specifies a more exalted language than its own and thus remains unsuited to its content, overpowering and alien."[36] Thus, it seems crucial to re-emphasize the multilingual cultural heritage of both Zweigs. Stefan learned German, Italian, and French at an early age. Lotte was fluent in German, English, and French. They also spoke or understood a number of other languages—including Yiddish and Esperanto, but probably communicated with each other mostly in German and English—even in Brazil (*SLZ* 17).

In South America, they took Spanish and Portuguese lessons, although it seemed they were more proficient in the former than the latter. Indeed they probably communicated the least in Portuguese, the language of Brazil, even after they had secured residency cards and returned to live in Petrópolis in late 1941. Both Zweigs wrote letters in English so as not to raise the suspicions of the censorship during the war, and at some point they began to feel uneasy about their relationship with the German language and culture. Stefan Zweig reportedly spoke French and Spanish with Gabriela Mistral, the Chilean poet, and with Hernández Catá, the Cuban consul in Brazil. He also seemed to prefer to communicate and write to his publisher Brazilian Abrahão Koogan in French. Ironically, the Zweigs rarely had opportunities where they had to use Portuguese or where they were without someone who could translate. The only exceptions were their interactions with the domestic help and other Brazilian workers.[37]

Even though Stefan Zweig was a master of the German language and even though Lotte, his wife, secretary, and researcher, organized, typed, and often commented on the German manuscripts they worked on, they were constantly traversing language barriers. Their correspondence from Brazil was full of German, French, Yiddish, Viennese, Portuguese, and Spanish phrases, representing a world in which they were constantly translating, code-switching, interpreting, and re-interpreting. In addition, they were constantly being exposed to concepts, objects, and foods that only existed in Brazil.

It is indeed remarkable that, despite these complexities and complications, the Zweigs wrote that they felt "at home" in Brazil, at least from time to time. They valued the peace and quiet, and they continued to be fascinated by Brazil's people and its landscape. In Stefan Zweig's handwritten suicide letter, which he entitled "Declaracão," the Portuguese word for "declaration" (presumably also written on behalf of Lotte even though it is in the first person singular), the couple's admiration for Brazil is clear. He thanked the country that taught him and gave him much. But he ended his suicide note as follows:

> So halte ich es für besser, rechtzeitig und in aufrechter Haltung ein Leben abzuschliessen, dem geistige Arbeit immer die lauterste Freude und persönliche Freiheit das höchste Gut dieser Erde gewesen. Ich grüsse alle meine Freunde! Mögen sie die Morgenröte noch sehen nach der langen Nacht! Ich, allzu Ungeduldiger, gehe ihnen voraus. (*WoY* 438)[38]

> [So I think it better to conclude in good time and in erect bearing a life in which intellectual labor meant the purest joy and personal

freedom the highest good on earth. I salute all my friends! May it be granted them yet to see the dawn aftern the long night! I, all too impatient, go on before.] (*WoY* 437)

Lotte, on the other hand, explained much differently the impending suicide to her family: She referred vaguely to committing suicide as a "going away like this": "[G]oing away like this my only wish is that you may believe that it is the best thing for Stefan, suffering as he did all these years with all those who suffer from the Nazi domination, and for me, always ill with Asthma" (*SLZ* 185).

Conclusion

Liminality, as a transitory journey and as a phase or a state of being, can, oddly enough, be its own resolution, with elements of enlightenment and euphoria. Certainly there were elements of both in the lives of Stefan and Lotte Zweig in exile. Whereas thousands of Second World War refugees saw themselves forced to accept visas and landing permits from any country that would take them, the Zweigs consciously chose to seek refuge in the small town of Petrópolis in the mountains of the state of Rio de Janeiro—rather than London, New York or Buenos Aires or even Bath or somewhere on the Hudson River outside of New York City.

In spite of Getúlio Vargas's dictatorial rule in Brazil during the 1940s, the Zweigs experienced briefly some rays of hope for themselves and for the world in the future. Many Jews had assimilated into Brazilian society for generations, and they lived in an atmosphere that seemed like paradise compared to the hell that was Europe. As early as 1940, many Jews and refugees in Brazil became politically active, and they joined groups such as the Free Austria Movement, for example. Others awaited the war's end to move elsewhere, including Israel after 1948.[39] Cultural syncretism and the common Brazilian open display of affection camouflaged many of the underlying social and political problems and tensions that characterized the country. Given their status and privileged mobility, the Zweigs were largely unaware of the problematic social and political issues facing Brazil's diverse population.

Ethnic relations in the cities and in the smaller towns of Brazil were far more complex and often hidden from the gaze of the itinerant visitor. But in the end, the external dynamics within Brazil were secondary to the Zweigs' own inner psychological battles. Their life together in exile was an intense liminal experience. They were often ambivalent and harbored mixed emotions about the situation in Brazil and at times they appeared to be indifferent about Brazil and Brazilians. They were not emigrants to Brazil. Rather their experience in Petrópolis was something like being in a trance in the midst of a long voyage or pilgrimage to an uncertain destination. They shared an infatuation with Brazil, but in the end much like Dr. B., the protagonist in Zweig's *Schachnovelle* ("The Royal Game," 1942), whose isolation and mental anguish overwhelm him, their sense of liminality and exile overwhelmed them. In the country that Stefan Zweig called "a land of the future," neither he nor his wife could endure, much less overcome, their isolation and melancholy to experience the future that he had envisioned.

Notes

[1] It is perhaps not surprising that prior to the 1950s Brazil received many more immigrants than it would lose in the second half of the century because of the military dictatorship and economic hardship. According to the Instituto Brasileiro de Geografia e Estatística (IBGE), between 1820 and 1910 Brazil received the following immigrants: 702,690 Portuguese; 1, 254,871 Italians; 332,357 Spanish; 105,341 Germans; immigrants of other nationalities numbering 360,258 entered Brazil, including Turks, Syrians, Lebanese, Armenians, Swiss, Austrians, Japanese (cited in *Nosso Século, 1900–1910*, [São Paulo: Abril Cultural, 1980], xii). Jews were counted as a part of the European national denominations.

[2] Stefan Zweig and Friderike Zweig, "*Wenn einen Augenblick die Wolken weichen*": *Briefwechsel, 1912–1942* (Frankfurt am Main: Fischer, 2006), 307 (translation mine).

[3] Stefan Zweig. *Brasilien: Ein Land der Zukunft* (Frankfurt am Main: Insel, 1981), 17, 19 (hereafter cited in text as *BLZ*).

[4] Stefan Zweig, *Brazil: Land of the Future*, trans. Andrew St James (London: Cassell, 1941), 12 (hereafter cited in text as *BLF*).

[5] Darién J. Davis and Oliver Marshall, eds., *Stefan and Lotte Zweig's South American Letters New York, Argentina and Brazil, 1940–42* (New York: Continuum, 2010), 20 (hereafter cited in text as *SLZ*). All letters from the Zweigs to the Altmann family are in English in the original.

[6] Victor Turner, *The Ritual Process: Structure and Anti-Structure* (Chicago: Aldine Transaction, 2008), 95.

[7] Victor Turner, "Pilgrimage and Communitas," *Studia Missionalia*, no. 23 (1974): 305.

[8] Stefan Zweig, *Die Welt Von Gestern* (Frankfurt am Main: Fischer, 1970), 8 (hereafter cited in text as *WvG*).

[9] Stefan Zweig, *The World of Yesterday*, trans. B. W. Huebsch and Helmut Ripperger (Lincoln: University of Nebraska Press, 1964), xviii (hereafter cited in text as *WoY*).

[10] See Daryl Williams, *Culture Wars in Brazil: The First Vargas Regime, 1930–1945* (Charlotte, NC: Duke University Press, 2001).

[11] Alberto Dines, *Morte no paraíso: A tragédia de Stefan Zweig* (Rio de Janeiro: Rocco, 2004), 336 (hereafter cited in text as *MP*).

[12] Darién J. Davis, *Avoiding the Dark: Race, Nation and National Culture in Modern Brazil* (Aldershot, England: Ashgate International Center for Research in Ethnic Studies, 2000), iii.

[13] Oswald de Andrade, *Manifesto Antropofagista* (1928), translated into English by Leslie Bary as: "Canibalist Manifesto," *Latin American Literary Review* 19, no. 38 (1991): 38–47. This was one of the foundational texts of the anthropophagist theme. It was printed in the first issue of the *Revista de Antropofagia* (Review of Anthropophagy) in May 1928.

[14] In his novel *Macunaíma* (1928), Mario de Andrade treats the question of race directly. Its protagonist is a Black Indian who eventually turns white.

[15] Gilberto Freyre, *The Masters and the Slaves: A Study in the Development of Brazilian Civilization* (New York: Random House, 1964), 278–403.

[16] See Lewis Hanke, *Gilberto Freyre: Vida y Obra. Bibliografía Antología* (New York: Instituto de las Españas en los Estados Unidos, 1939); Jeffrey D. Needell, "Identity, Race, Gender, and Modernity in the Origins of Gilberto Freyre's Oeuvre," in *American Historical Review* 100, no. 1 (1995): 51–77.

[17] Donauschwaben Villages Helping Hands, "German Immigration to Brazil: Periods from 1824 to 1969," http://www.dvhh.org/dta/brazil/1824-1969.htm (accessed August 2, 2014).

[18] Jeffrey Lesser, *Welcoming the Undesirables: Brazil and the Jewish Question* (Berkeley: University of California Press), 180.

[19] Lesser, 88.

[20] Olga Binário's life story is brilliantly presented in Fernando Morais's biography, *Olga: A vida de Olga Benário Prestes, judia comunista entregue a Hitler pelo governo Vargas* (São Paulo: Editora Alfa-Omega, 1986).

[21] Fundacão CPDOC, *Dicionário Histórico Biográfico Brasileiro 1930–1983*, vol. 4, ed. Israel Beloch and Alzira Alves de Abreu (Rio de Janeiro: Editora Forense-Universitaria, 1984), 3051–57.

[22] Knut Beck and Jeffrey B. Berlin, eds., *Stefan Zweig, Briefe 1932–1942*, vol. 4 (Frankfurt am Main: Fischer, 2005), 311 (hereafter cited in text as *Briefe*).

[23] Turner, "Pilgrimage and Communitas," 305.

[24] Jerome Kohn and Ron H. Feldman, 317–28.

[25] Leo Spitzer, *Lives in Between: Assimilation and Marginality in Austria, Brazil, and West Africa, 1780–1945* (Cambridge: Cambridge University Press, 1989).

[26] Hannah Arendt, *The Jewish Writings*, ed. Jerome Kohn and Ron H. Feldman (New York: Schocken, 2008), 317–28; Leo Spitzer, *Lives in Between*, 4, 10; Darién J. Davis and Oliver Marshall, 1–45.

[27] Koogan, n.p.

[28] Abrahão Koogan, "Lembranças do Stefan Zweig," in *Stefan Zweig no país do future* (Rio de Janeiro: Funadação Getúlio Vargas, 1992), n.p.

[29] Antonio Dias Gonçalves, "The Song of Exile," trans. Nelson Ascher, http://allpoetry.com/The-Song-Of-Exile (accessed on August 2, 2014).

[30] See Alberto Dines, *Morte no paraíso: A tragédia de Stefan Zweig* (Rio de Janeiro, Editora Nova Fronteira, 1981).

[31] Maya Deren, *The Divine Horsemen: The Living Gods of Haiti. Divine Horsemen: Voodoo Gods of Haiti* (New York: McPherson, 1983).

[32] Henri Michaux, *Passages* (Paris: Gallimard, 1967), 153–55.

[33] Blaise Cendrars, *Le Brasil* (Mónaco: Les Documents d'Art, 1952), xi, cv.

[34] Leone Piccioni, *Vita di poeta: Giuseppi Ungareti* (Milán: Rizzoli, 1970), 140.

[35] The novella alluded to is *Verwirrung der Gefühle* (literally "confusion of the senses," translated as *Confusion*, 1927).

[36] Walter Benjamin, "The Task of the Translator," in *Illuminations*, trans. and ed. Harry Zohn (New York, 1968), 75.

[37] Ibid., 167.

[38] This edition of *The World of Yesterday* includes a photographic reproduction of the suicide note.

[39] DOPS (Department of Political and Social Order), Folder 1, Austríaco, Arquivo Públio do Estado, Botafogo, Rio de Janeiro, Brazil.

10: Stefan Zweig's Concept of Brazil in the Context of German-Jewish Emigration

Marlen Eckl

> *This region is most delightful, and covered with immense forests, which never lose their foliage, and throughout the year yield the sweetest aromatic odours and produce an infinite variety of fruit, grateful to the taste, and healthful for the body. In the fields flourish so many sweet flowers and herbs, and the fruits are so delicious in their fragrance, that I fancied myself near the terrestrial paradise.*
>
> —Charles Edwards Lester, *The Life and Voyages of Americus Vespucius*

THE ABOVE SENTENCES ARE NOT QUOTED FROM STEFAN ZWEIG'S *Brasilien: Ein Land der Zukunft* (*Brazil: A Land of the Future*, 1941). Amerigo Vespucci made this statement in a letter to his friend and client Lorenzo de Medici. Since Brazil's discovery by European voyagers in April 1500, this land has been as intrinsically linked to the Garden of Eden as it has been believed to be the promise of a great future. Almost from the start, an image of Brazilian society which emphasized its highly cordial and hospitable nature, as well as its apparently harmonious multi-racial society was promoted. These notions were passed down through the centuries and often considered to be the essence of Brazil, which appealed so much to the refugee writers who emigrated there to escape persecution by the Nazis. Many of them dealt with their country of exile in their works. However, there is no portrait of Brazil by an émigré that became as famous as Zweig's Brazil book. His hymn of praise not only decisively shaped the idea of the "land of the future," but, together with his tragic suicide in 1942, it influenced the image of the German-speaking exile in Brazil. The phenomenal impact of his book derives from the prominence of its author. Zweig was undoubtedly the most famous émigré in Brazil—in fact, in all of South America.

In this essay, I compare Zweig's literary image of Brazil with depictions offered in the works of lesser known or even forgotten Brazilian émigré writers such as Alfredo Gartenberg, Hugo Simon, and Richard Katz. Reference will be made as well to statements in the unpublished diaries of Zweig's close friend in Brazil, Ernst Feder. Special attention is accorded to the descriptions of nature, the much-admired cordiality of the Brazilian people, and the depictions of a racially diverse and peaceful democratic society. The political views of émigrés concerning the dictatorial regime of Getúlio Vargas, who served as Brazil's president from 1930 to 1945, will also be taken into account.

Zweig recorded his first impressions of Brazil as follows:

> Angelangt in Rio, das phantastische und anstrengendste Märchen mitmachend, das sich erdenken lässt ... Es ist zum Tollwerden großartig, aber ich werde zerstückelt, zerrissen. Ich nehme täglich ein Kilo ab, aber Brasilien ist *unglaublich* ... Die Schönheit, die Farbigkeit, die Herrlichkeit dieser Stadt ist unbeschreiblich ... Die Menschen bezaubernd ... und eines ist sicher, dass ich nicht das letzte Mal hier war.[1]

> Arrived in Rio ... [T]ook part in [seeing] this fantastic and exhausting fairy tale[-like country, which cannot] be imagined ... [T]he most beautiful landscape I have ever seen. It is enough to drive one out of one's mind, magnificent ... but Brazil is *incredible* ... [T]he people are enchanting ... The beauty, the colorfulness, the splendor of this city is indescribable ... And one thing is sure, this is not the last time that I will be there.[2]

These are Zweig's first impressions of Brazil in 1936, which he enthusiastically shared with his first wife, Friderike. Actually, a state of ecstasy would best characterize the experiences of his first visit in 1936. As a guest of the government, he was given a suite in the world-famous luxury hotel *Copacabana Palace*, a French-speaking attaché to serve as his translator, and a chauffeur-driven car. Zweig was overwhelmed by the effusive cordiality of the Brazilians who received him with a warm-hearted welcome, attended his lectures, and by the hundreds asked for autographs and photos. Indeed, Zweig had not been aware of the extent of his success in Brazil. As a result of the enormous admiration extended to him, he soon spoke to Brazilian journalists about possibly writing a book about the country, and during these early days already began to take detailed notes which were recorded in his diary. Much later they were integrated into the Brazil book.

Four years passed before Zweig was again able to visit Brazil. On this occasion in 1940, he was accompanied by his second wife, Lotte. In view of the so-called *Anschluss* of Austria two years before and the irretrievable loss of his home as well as the outbreak of the Second World War, the writer sought comfort and hope in Brazil. As Zweig candidly commented to a newspaper reporter:

> Erlaubt mir, Europa zu vergessen ... Wie schön und glücklich ist alles hier! Die Gegenwart erweist sich als äußerst schwierig ... Das Leben auf dem südamerikanischen Kontinent erscheint leichter, erfüllter und glücklicher, weil ich darin einem menschlichen Bewusstsein, einer einzigartigen Solidarität in der Welt begegne ... Sie hat eine unerschütterliche Kraft.[3]

> [Permit me to forget Europe ... How beautiful and happy everything is here! The present turns out to be extremely difficult ... Life in the South American continent seems to be easier, more fulfilling and happier because here I encounter a human consciousness, a unique solidarity in the world ... It has an imperturbable strength.]

The development and growth of Rio since his last visit impressed him very much.

> In kurzer Zeit hat sich Rio in eine große Metropole verwandelt, die neuen Gebäude, die neuen Wohnviertel, die unzähligen Wolkenkratzer, die verschiedenen Institutionen ... dies alles offenbart den Grad der Weiterentwicklung, das bemerkenswerte Wachstum.... Uns, die wir aus dem immer mehr zugrunde gehenden Europa kommen, spendet dies Trost und Hoffnung. (*TP* 367)

> [In a short time Rio has turned into a large metropolis, the new buildings, the new residential areas, the innumerable skyscrapers—all this reveals the degree of development, the remarkable growth. Coming from a Europe which is falling more and more into ruin, seeing this gives us hope and comfort.]

Zweig did not realize that the progress had come at a certain political price. Already in 1936 he had been aware that the regime of Getúlio Vargas was a dictatorship. Nevertheless, as he explained to his friend Romain Rolland: "[Glauben] Sie nicht alles, was man über die Diktaturen verbreitet: sie sind ein Paradies, verglichen mit den unsern [*sic*]. Ein Menschenleben hat dort noch einigen Wert und es gibt ... eine ziemlich große Freiheit des Wortes." (Do not believe everything that is written and said about dictatorships. Compared to ours, it is paradise. Human life is still respected and there is ... considerable freedom of speech.)[4] This assessment was based on his superficial impression of the situation in the country during his first visit in Brazil. Four years later he did not trouble himself with the real political circumstances and was content with what he observed on the surface. In regard to the seemingly unstoppable destruction in Europe—which to Zweig still represented his home—he needed or desired to cling to Brazil more strongly than ever before as a glimmer of hope.

Given the exclusionary and prejudicial racial policies of the Nazis, Zweig emphasized in letters to his friends that in Brazil the absurdity of racial differences was demonstrated in a natural way: "Brasilien ist das größte Experiment unserer Zeit in diesem Sinne, und deshalb schreibe ich auch jetzt ein kleines Buch über Brasilien. Wenn sich . . . dieses großartige Experiment vollkommener Rassenmischung und Farbgleichsetzung hier in diesem Land weiter so vollendet bewährt, dann ist der Welt ein Vorbild demonstriert" (In this respect Brazil is the greatest experiment of our time, and therefore I am writing a little book about Brazil now. If this grand experiment of perfect racial mixing and the equality of races proves a success, then it will be a shining example for the world).[5] The fact that the situation in Europe had deteriorated and was continuing to worsen—specifically regarding racism and discrimination—influenced the Brazil book while he was writing it. His travels through the country offered him no reprieve, since Europe was constantly on his mind. He entertained the wishful thought that he had found the "World of Yesterday" in the "Land of the Future."

Of course, the special privileges extended to Zweig played a certain role in his attitude toward the country. For example, an incident reported by the Viennese lawyer Alfredo Gartenberg, who managed to escape to Brazil via France with the help of a temporary tourist visa, may be cited. At that time Gartenberg was dependent on the financial support of the Jewish relief organization, and he desperately tried to obtain a permanent visa and a work permit linked to this visa. But he was unsuccessful. Contrastingly, Zweig immediately received a permanent visa at the Brazilian consulate in Buenos Aires in November 1940. Gartenberg attended a lecture by Zweig in Rio de Janeiro—a version of "Das Wien von Gestern"—and he was indignant that Zweig failed to mention the rich Jewish life which existed in Vienna before the "Anschluss." On the day following the lecture, Gartenberg went to the hotel where the writer was staying so that he might express his anger and disappointment, and they parted irreconcilably. More than a year later, after Gartenberg had learned of Zweig's suicide, he felt obligated to express his last respects. However, owing to his bad conscience regarding his former criticism, he avoided doing so.

This feeling of remorse could have possibly provided the first impetus for Gartenberg to write the novel *O J vermelho* (The Red J), published in 1976. In his portrayal of the exile figures, Max and Eva Maria Bodenheim, Gartenberg related a paradigmatic story of those émigrés who, after having lost their homes Europe, were unable to find a new home anywhere in the world, not even in the apparently paradisiacal Brazil. Zweig's suicide, which influenced the novel to a degree, also impacted Gartenberg's concept of Brazil. Because Gartenberg knew that tragedies such as Zweig's could also happen in this beautiful country, his view of Brazil was diametrically opposed to Zweig's. Indeed, Gartenberg exploded the idea that Brazil represented a land which offered a promising future. Additionally, he warned against the negative aspects of the much vaunted cordiality of the Brazilian people.

The difference between Zweig and Gartenberg becomes most evident from their differing descriptions of nature. In contrast to his compatriot, Gartenberg did not refrain from indicating the dangers inherent in this Garden of Eden. As he wrote in his novel: "For God's sake stop fooling around here. The forests are full of venomous snakes."[6] The paradise Zweig thought to have found in Brazil is, at least for the protagonists of the novel, the equivalent of hell. Hence, the gentile Eva Maria Bodenheim prefers to go back home to the Third Reich. Her Jewish husband Max was unable to find any answer to their dire situation and he decided in the end on suicide. As in the case of Zweig, Brazil did not become the land of the future for Max. From his own experience Gartenberg knew the dark side of Brazil. Yet, despite the adverse circumstances and unlike his protagonists, he did manage to find a new home there.

During his second stay in Brazil Zweig was deeply worried about the difficult situation of the refugees from Nazism who were desperately trying to find a country willing to receive them. Because he could not stop thinking of these people in need, he felt moved by the works of the Russian-Jewish painter Lasar Segall, who had come to Brazil in 1923. The artist had sent Zweig a book of his works. Particularly the painting *Pogrom* impressed him very much. Although Segall was fortunate in that he never had to experience a pogrom in Russia, his touching rendition of the scene moved Zweig to write him a letter in December 1940:

> Könnten Sie, doch, ähnlich wie Sie versuchten, eine Vision des Pogroms zeichnerisch heraufzubeschwören, das ganze Elend der Flüchtenden von heute vor den Konsulaten, auf den Schiffen, in den Bahnen, auf den Wegen zur Darstellung bringen! Es wäre ein gewaltiger Fries, reichend von einem Ende der Welt bis zum andern, und Sie würden damit ein Dokument dieser Zeit schaffen. Ich träume von einem Maler, der so etwas gestaltet, da wir selbst, die Schriftsteller, noch den Dingen zu nahe sind, um sie episch darzustellen. Das Auge des Malers ist da immer rapider.[7]

> [If only you could portray the misery of the refugees of today before the consulates, on the ships, in the trains and on the roads, just as you tried to conjure up a vision of a pogrom graphically! It would be an enormous frieze, reaching from the one end of the world to the

other, and you would create a document of this time. I dream of a painter who [could] create such a work because we, the writers, are too close to the events to describe them epically. The eye of a painter is always faster.]

Zweig did not know that Segall was working precisely on such a painting at that time. The artist was aware that he, as a Jew whose paintings were considered to be "entartete Kunst" (degenerate art) by the Nazis, was very lucky to have found a home in Brazil. Like Zweig he was incapable of forgetting the occurrences in Europe. For him the persecution of the Jews was a repetition of the perpetual cycle of their fate. In his paintings, therefore, he did not want to portray the contemporary suffering only in the form of the persecution of the Jews in the twentieth century. Segall explained his intention as follows: "Everybody is a child of his time and his means of expression are the ones of his time."[8] Furthermore, he put this painful experience in a timeless context. Ernst Feder, the important political journalist of the Weimar Republic, who in Petrópolis became Zweig's closest friend and met Segall in São Paulo in 1945 for the first time, commented in his articles on the painter and his work:

> Das Thema, das ihn am stärksten anzog... war der leidende Mensch, der Verfolgte, der Gequälte, der Märtyrer, und es ist selbstverständlich, dass in diesem Bereich das jüdische Schicksal die erste Stelle einnimmt. Aber all diese Schreckensbilder und Höllenszenen sind in Wahrheit eine Folge von Seelenlandschaften, da Lasar Segall niemals die Ereignisse als solche auf die Leinwand oder in den Marmor projiziert, sondern immer sein ganz persönliches Erleben des Vorgangs in die künstlerische Form überträgt. Das gibt in seinem Werk auch dem aktuellsten Faktum einen zeitlosen, überzeitlichen Charakter.[9]

[The subject that attracted him most strongly was the suffering man, the persecuted, the tortured, the martyr, and it goes without saying that the Jewish fate comes first in this aspect. But all these horror pictures and infernal scenes are in fact a series of inner landscapes, as Lasar Segall never projects only the incidences as such onto the canvas or the marble, but always transfers his very personal experience of the event into an artistic form. Through this, the most current statements in his work of art achieve a timeless, universal meaning.]

Thus, Segall began to deal with the question of refugees artistically. The painting *Navio de emigrantes*, refugee ship, should become, in Feder's opinion, his *Opus Magnum*, not only in the figurative sense, but also in the literal sense of the term. Feder thought it was one of the "stärksten Anklage(n) der Barbarei" (strongest accusations of barbarism, "Tode")

Zweihundertachtzig Figuren füllen den Schiffsraum in statischer Ruhe hingestellt, sie schweigen, bewegen sich nicht und doch rauscht ein Chor der Anklage, ein Hilferuf von ihnen auf, gewaltiger als er je von einer Mayflower scholl, die auf der Suche nach einer neuen Welt den Ozean durchfurchte. Aber neben Klage und Anklage spüren wir in der Haltung, in den verhaltenen Gesten dieser Menschen Glauben, Hoffnung, Zuversicht. ("Besuch")

[Two hundred and eighty people fill the ship, placed there in a static calm. They do not speak, do not move, and yet they raise a chorus of accusation, a cry for help, more powerful than it has ever sounded from a *Mayflower* on its crossing of the ocean in search of a new world. But besides lamentation and accusation we feel faith, hope and confidence in the attitude and the restrained gestures of these people.]

Indeed Segall, in the eyes of many, was able to capture history. He showed the drama of refugees and migration of humankind as a universal, timeless phenomenon. Answering Zweig's request for such a work he wrote:

Ein merkwürdiges Zusammentreffen. Ich arbeite nämlich seit einundhalb Jahren... an einem großen "Emigrantenschiff"... Aus beiliegenden Fotos können Sie die Auffassung und die Komposition ersehen, natürlich nicht die wirkliche malerische Wirkung... Übrigens ist das Thema "Emigranten," "Flüchtlinge" nicht nur ein aktuelles Thema für mich. Ich betrachte die Menschen als ewige Flüchtlinge und habe mich seit je in meiner Kunst mit diesem Problem befasst.[10]

[An odd coincidence! I have been working on a big "refugee ship"... for one and a half years. The enclosed photos may give you an impression of the interpretation and composition, not of course of the real pictorial effect... Besides, the question of emigrants, [or] refugees is not only a current issue for me. I consider people as eternal emigrants and have always dealt with this question in my art.]

Zweig was duly impressed by Segall's work and expressed his admiration in a letter written in January 1941: "Ohne mir ein autoritäres Urteil zu erlauben, möchte ich Ihnen sagen, dass Sie hier einen Herzschuss getan haben: Es ist auf diesem Bilde eine wirklich visionäre Zusammenfassung des zeitlichen Elends, für uns in der empfindlichsten Form. Wie gerne würde ich das Original sehen!" (Although I am unqualified to give an authoritative judgement, I would like to tell you that you hit the bull's eye: This painting is a truly visionary summary of the contemporary misery, and for us, in the most sensitive form. How much would I love to see the original work).[11] However, despite this wish expressed by Zweig, the two would never meet again in Brazil.

For some time Zweig was incapable of deciding to take up residence in Brazil and to make it his permanent country of refuge. In mid-January 1941, after having finished research for his book on Brazil, he and Lotte returned to the United States, where he wrote the book, starting in July of 1941. It was published in six languages, among them a Portuguese version printed in Brazil. At that time, he finished a short biography of Amerigo Vespucci and made drafts for his memoir, *Die Welt von Gestern* (*The World of Yesterday*, 1943). Before Zweig would have to make a serious effort to change his legal status in the United States, he had already decided to return to Brazil. Accordingly, he wrote his Brazilian publisher and friend Abrahão Koogan in a letter in mid-August 1941:

> Wir stellen uns vor . . . nach Petrópolis zu gehen, wenn Sie für uns ein Appartement oder ein kleines Haus ausfindig machen können. Ich bin sehr müde, ich habe viel gearbeitet, und die Vorstellung, mich in Brasilien auszuruhen, ist eine große Verführung . . . Wir wohnen seit Monaten, seit mehr als einem Jahr ständig in Hotels, und Sie können sich vorstellen, wie sehr wir uns wünschen, in einem "Zuhause zu leben."[12]

> [We are thinking of going to Petrópolis, if you can find an apartment or a small house for us. I am very tired, I have worked long and hard, and the idea of resting in Brazil is very tempting. I think it is better to stay in Petrópolis for six months. . . . We have been living in hotels for months, continuously for more than a year, and you can imagine how much we would love to have a "home."]

When Zweig arrived in Brazil for the third time at the end of August 1941, he did not visit it as a guest of the government, as a celebrated writer or as an explorer. He also did not announce himself as the author of the *Brazil* book which later was recognized as a classic. Instead, he entered Brazil as an émigré who sought refuge from the criminal racial policies and the cruel war unleashed by the Nazis. This does not imply that Zweig had lost his prominent and privileged position. But now he had become a part of the refugee community and, as such, was in closer contact with the other émigrés.

Only a few of the sixteen- to nineteen-thousand mostly Jewish refugees Brazil received between 1933 and 1945 deliberately chose this country as their country of exile. In the refugees' opinion, Brazil, like most of the Latin-American countries, was considered second choice—if it is possible to use the word "choice" in this context at all. Before taking Brazil into consideration, the refugees had for the most part unsuccessfully applied for an immigration visa to the United States. Thus, exile in

Brazil was coincidence or fate for the majority of them. Only very few refugees succeeded in obtaining a permanent visa without any difficulties like Stefan and Lotte Zweig, since the dictatorial Vargas regime, like many other governments, pursued a most restrictive immigration policy, especially towards the Jews during these years.

On June 7, 1937, five months before the coup d'état that established Vargas's fascist-inspired *Estado Novo* (New State), Secret Circular 1,127 was issued by the Ministry of Foreign Relations and authorized personally by President Vargas. This circular prohibited the concession of visas to persons of "Semitic origin." Strict application of the few clauses that would permit Jews to enter further reduced the number and "in 1938 just five hundred Jews immigrated legally to Brazil, the lowest number in years ... Brazil steadfastly refused to admit large numbers of refugees ... Circular 1,249 was anti-Jewish without prohibiting all Jews from entering. Rather, it created visa categories based on economic benefit."[13]

According to this circular, visas were granted only to Jewish capitalists who could pay a minimum of five hundred thousand *milreis* (US $29,000), or technical experts, scientists, and Jewish artists or intellectuals of international renown. So it was mainly a loophole in the law regarding granting temporary visas that saved the lives of thousands of refugees who did not fit into the above-mentioned categories. In the end Brazil became the second country of refuge in South America after Argentina. Having successfully immigrated, a refugee might "receive permanent status; this was granted only with difficulty before August 1939, and forbidden by law thereafter."[14] Therefore, many refugees were forced to live with an unresolved legal status and, still worse, the permanent fear of deportation to Europe.

One of Zweig's old acquaintances from Berlin, the banker and patron of the arts Hugo Simon, was threatened with deportation after he managed to arrive in Brazil. Zweig had been a most welcome guest in Simon's Berlin villa and had also visited him in Paris, where the banker found refuge after he was forced out of Germany in 1933. After the Nazis occupied France, his life was again in danger. He and his wife only succeeded in fleeing to Brazil by using forged documents and a temporary visa. They arrived in Rio de Janeiro in March 1941 under the names Hubert Studenic and Garina Studenicova. A decree passed at the end of July 1941 granted refugees who immigrated with a temporary visa a provisional permanent residence permit for the duration of the war, so no deportation was pursued against them. Of course, Simon's living conditions in Brazilian exile were significantly different from Zweig's, especially since Simon and his wife had to continue living under the false identity used to enter the country. Apart from Zweig, only their mutual friend Ernst Feder and his wife Erna knew the couple's real identity.

Despite these problematic circumstances and the fact that he came to Brazil involuntarily, Simon found a new home in the country. He even had the chance to realize a childhood dream by taking a course in sericulture, the cultivation of silk worms, in Barbacena, a small town located in the state of Minas Gerais. He enjoyed life there and considered the country a paradise in which one can obtain what one needs and people are always kind. He was fascinated by its nature.[15] As Feder wrote of him: "Er liebte Brasilien und seine Menschen und fühlte sich wohl und heimisch in diesem begnadeten Lande." (He loved Brazil and its people. He was happy and felt at home in this blessed country.)[16]

Inspired by the course in sericulture, the banker began writing the educational novel *Seidenraupen* (Silkworms) which has never been published. According to Simon, writing the novel was a personal necessity since he had seen and experienced so much in his turbulent life. It seemed to him to be a great pity if his memories were to be lost.[17] His novel was strongly influenced by autobiographical experience and contemporary historical developments. Unfortunately, Simon was not able to finish it because he died prematurely of cancer in 1950. But until the end, writing the novel was an important activity in his life.

In his novel he portrayed Brazil as a "Wunderland" (wonderland),[18] blessed with a landscape which looks like a terrestrial Garden of Eden and with a promising future. In his opinion, the country was the ideal land for immigrants, as it had vast unsettled territories and it allegedly granted freedom to refugees. His enthusiastic description of Brazilian flora and fauna is exceptional among the émigré writers, apart from Zweig's own hymn of praise. Simon omitted negative characterizations regarding the much vaunted but flawed Brazilian cordiality, while he emphasized only the positive aspects, especially the naturalness of racial diversity and local readiness to help foreigners.

> Nun erinnerte ich mich, dass mir mein Bruder einmal geschrieben hatte, dass er zwei prächtige junge Burschen hätte, einen weißen und einen schwarzen, die für ihn, und, wenn ich käme, auch für mich, durch dick und dünn gehen würden... "Sie müssen unsere Gäste sein," sagte Dr. Metellus, auf ein nahe gelegenes Haus weisend... Ich zögerte... Wir hatten uns auf einen längeren Aufenthalt hier eingerichtet, und ich glaubte deshalb, wir könnten eine solche Gastfreundschaft nicht ohne weiteres annehmen. Bevor ich aber meine Bedenken aussprach, sagte Dr. Metellus: "So lange Sie auch hier bleiben, sind Sie uns willkommene Gäste."[19]
>
> [Now I remembered that my brother had once written a letter, telling me that he knew two splendid fellows, one white and one black, who were willing to stick with him through thick and thin, and if I came, would also do so with me... "You must be our guests," said

Mr. Metellus pointing at a house nearby . . . I hesitated . . . We had prepared for a long-term stay . . . Before I could express my doubts, Mr. Metellus said: "Regardless of how long you stay here, you are our most welcome guests."]

In connection with the question of racial equality and democracy, he merely alluded to the widespread myth of the "humane slavery," which had allegedly existed in Brazil in contrast to other countries.

Unlike Zweig, who was unable to muster new courage to face life and continue his writing, Simon was inspired by the beautiful Brazilian landscape and faith in the great future of Brazil. He knew how to take comfort in the tropical climate and its natural bounty, and he sensed the potential of the country's promising future. He, therefore, did not give up, but rather started a new life in his country of exile despite the adverse circumstances of the initial phase.

Zweig probably heard from his fellow émigrés about the difficult everyday work circumstances that they experienced in Brazil. Yet, of even more significance are the remarks he heard about unfavorable changes taking place in Brazil under the authoritarian government of Getúlio Vargas. These developments go unmentioned in Zweig's *Brasilien: Ein Land der Zukunft*: "heute, da es als Diktatur gilt, [kennt Brasilien] mehr individuelle Freiheit und Zufriedenheit als die meisten unserer europäischen Länder"[20] ("Today, though considered to be a dictatorship, Brazil knows more individual freedom and contentment than most of our European countries"[21]). In December of 1941 Zweig shared his thoughts with Feder about political occurrences in the country. In turn, Feder recorded Zweig's opinions in his diaries: "[Stefan Zweig] findet Brasilien vollkommen verändert . . . das Minderwertigkeitsgefühl gegenüber allem Fremden, auch Argentinien, durch betonten Nationalismus, der alles Neu-Erreichte [*sic*] auf Getúlio Vargas zurückführt, ersetzt. . . . Brasilien wird durch die rasche Umwandlung viel vom Besten verlieren" ([Stefan Zweig] thinks that Brazil has completely changed . . . the feeling of inferiority towards foreigners has been replaced by marked nationalism that attributes all the latest achievements to Getúlio Vargas . . . Brazil will lose much of its best by this rapid change).[22]

Like Simon, Feder only came to Brazil by chance since his application for an immigration visa to the United States proved unsuccessful. In fact, Brazil was the only country from which Feder, the former leading political editor of the *Berliner Tageblatt*, obtained a valid visa. It was the humanity of the Brazilian ambassador in France, Luiz Martins de Souza Dantas, which saved the lives of the journalist and his wife Erna. In light of the tragedy of the desperate refugees from Nazism, Souza Dantas was not willing to accept the inhuman immigration policy of his native country and he ignored it by granting visas after his arrival in Rio de Janeiro.

According to Feder, he gained "Einzug in die große brasilianische Presse" (*Diary* 111; entry into the large Brazilian press) through his article about Columbus, which had just appeared in the Brazilian newspaper *Jornal do Brasil*. Over the next years Feder played a significant role in Brazilian journalism, evidenced by the fact that in the Brazilian newspaper *Diário de Notícias* he had his own daily column entitled: "Assim fala o radio de Berlim" (That's what the Berlin radio broadcasts). After Zweig's suicide Feder even achieved international renown as the chronicler of the Austrian writer's last weeks in Brazil.

Imparting knowledge about Europe and Brazil to the readers in the respective countries was one of the most important goals of Feder in his articles for the Brazilian and Swiss press, as well as for German-language exile journals. While Zweig clung to the notions of "Land of the Future" and the "World of Yesterday" by believing to have found in Brazil a better Europe and finishing his memoirs in Petrópolis, Feder built a mental bridge between the Old and the New Worlds by means of his journalistic work. The Paraguayan Secretary of State, Juan Benitez, expressed his admiration for this exceptional successful second career of the émigré with the following words:

> Ernst Feder, the famous former editor of the *Berliner Tageblatt* came to Brazil with his wife and the pen as his only aid . . . Without leaving the fundamental doubts of a liberal European thinker behind, he knew how to adjust to the American environment. He is interested in and writes about episodes and the problems of our Americas . . . his horizon is the world . . . a steadfast Liberal, a modest master.[23]

Owing perhaps to Feder's varied Brazilian experiences, he—significantly better than other émigrés—recognized the drawbacks of the superficial cordiality typical of the Brazilians. German friends who already lived in Brazil for some time warned him to be careful:

> Brasilianer [sind] sehr empfindlich, tadeln dürfe man nichts. Die Brasilianer sind nicht aufrichtig, sie sind ganz anders als die Europäer . . . Der Brasilianer sagt einem nicht gern etwas Unangenehmes, nimmt es deshalb mit Wahrheit und Zuverlässigkeit nicht genau.[24]

> [Brazilians [are] very touchy, nothing should be criticized . . . The Brazilians are not sincere, they are completely different from the Europeans . . . The Brazilian does not like to inform somebody of something unpleasant. Thus, he is not very receptive to truth and [or the concept of] reliability.]

The fact that Feder later recorded Brazilian ideas and views of Brazil and its people predominantly in his diaries might have been a consequence of that warning. In this regard, Zweig had already observed Brazilian sensitivity regarding criticism. Feder attributed this characteristic to an incapacity to criticize unemotionally. Experience had taught Feder that discrimination and prejudice against people of color and native inhabitants still prevailed in Brazil. He was the only one of the émigrés mentioned in this paper to become acquainted with the attitude of the lower classes toward the Vargas-regime. As a result, he was able to understand the deep internalization of the myth of Getúlio Vargas as "father of the poor" and their admiration of the dictator. Specifically, because he possessed this "insider information" he could not see the country in the same favorable light as did the other émigrés.

Nevertheless he managed to feel at home in Brazil, because he was able to find intellectual and cultural links between his German homeland and his country of refuge. Goethe played a key role in this context since he had also been highly interested in Brazil. Hence, Goethe had been in touch with famous German and Austrian researchers on Brazil, among them Carl Friedrich Philipp von Martius. Not in the least because of the comforting knowledge of "Goethe's love of Brazil," as Feder termed it, did this journalist come to the same conclusion as Goethe, who wrote in his review of Martius's book on the palms of Brazil: "So empfinden wir uns in einem entlegenen Weltteil durchaus anwesend und einheimisch" (So we feel quite present and at home in this distant part of the world).[25]

Despite the close contact with Zweig during the last weeks before his suicide, Feder was not able to impart confidence or sufficient encouragement so that the writer could learn to accept Brazil as a new home and think in more positive terms. Absorbed in memories of happy days in the past and mourning for his lost home, Zweig could not develop faith in a new future. As he confided to his friend Felix Braun:

> I am so frightfully depressed by the present as well as by the future and feel superfluous—what is a writer without its own language, without a country, without its past, without its future? The values we have lived for are destroyed, the men we have loved dead or in misery, the [*sic*] mankind in madness—what have I to give and to whom?[26]

Richard Katz, another Jewish-born émigré in Brazil and one of the most successful journalists and most famous German-speaking travel writers at the end of the 1920s, had no illusions about the fact that postwar Europe would be completely different from the continent he had left behind. Nonetheless, he did not lose courage to face life. He and Zweig never met in Brazil. In January 1942, when Katz was asked by Werner Richter if he was in contact with Zweig in Brazil, he replied as follows: "[Mit] Stefan Zweig stehe ich nicht in Verbindung, da ich hier sehr zurückgezogen lebe und möchte auch daran nichts ändern" (I am not in contact with Stefan Zweig, as I am leading a secluded life here and do not want to change anything in this regard).[27] As Katz was well aware and distrustful of the negative consequences of media interest, he disapproved of Zweig's dealings or transactions with the Brazilian public, and especially its media. Regarding this point he remarked in his second book written in Brazilian exile in 1942:

> [Ich] befand mich in jenem Übergangszustand vom Touristen zum Einwohner... Das war die Folge meines Bestrebens, dem Jahrmarkt der papiernen Eitelkeiten zu entgehen, der sich um einen Schriftsteller selbst nach seiner Auswanderung abspielt. So fern hatte ich mich von Hafen-Reportern, Pen-Club, Lesern und Übersetzern gehalten, daß ich allein auf einer fremden Insel saß.[28]

> [I was in that transitional stage from being a tourist to becoming a resident... That was the consequence of my effort to flee the journalistic vanity fair that accompanies a writer even after his emigration. I kept myself so far away from harbor-reporters, the P.E.N. Club, readers and translators that I was left alone on a foreign island [that is, the island of Paquetá, M.E.].

Conversations with Katz most probably would not have prevented Zweig's tragic end, but they could have shown him that the pain of the irretrievable loss of one's homeland could be overcome. Like Zweig, Katz was one of the very few privileged émigrés who had no financial difficulties. Additionally, he, again like Zweig, deliberately decided in favor of Brazil as country of refuge, although he had at his disposal a valid immigration visa for the United States. He chose Brazil as his exile home because he knew it from his travels and had fond memories of it. However, an important difference between Zweig and Katz should not be overlooked. As Katz observed in retrospect: "Das Schicksal war mir wohl: ich suchte eine Zuflucht und ich fand eine Heimat..." (Fate was well-disposed to me: I sought a refuge and found a home...).[29]

When Katz arrived in Brazil in April 1941 after a dramatic odyssey through Europe and two failed escape attempts, he was so traumatized that he chose a secluded life on the island of Paquetá, situated in Guanabara Bay near Rio. There he began to write his first book in Brazilian exile called *Mein Inselbuch* (My Island-book). Although he felt that he was writing this book in order to come to terms with painful experiences of the recent past, he wanted to familiarize himself with the country of his exile. Just as Katz's heart was torn between his former home in Europe and this happy country of his exile, memories of flight and a Europe shattered by war merge with depictions of life on a Brazilian island in his book:

Also wurde mir, als ich in einem Paquetá-Garten eine *Platane* sah, mit *einem* Male schwer ums Herz. Denn ich sah nicht nur diesen hellen Stamm ... sondern ganze lange Reihen solcher Stämme ... ich bin lange Stunden im Autobus durch die Platanen-Alleen Südfrankreichs gefahren. Ja, ich sehe ihre dicken Stämme ... und ich sehe den Autobus ... vollgestopft mit müden schaukelnden Menschen. Einen ganzen Tag lang fuhr er so, eine Nacht und nochmals einen Tag, von Genf bis an die Pyrenäen. Das war mein erster Fluchtversuch aus Hitlers Europa ... dieser Versuch misslang ... Als ich die Platane sah, versank die Insel vor mir und die Sicherheit, die sie mir bietet, und vor mir sah ich den Specknacken des Gestapobeamten in Perpignan ... So eng also gehört eine Landschaft mit ihrem typischen Baumwuchs zusammen. Paquetá hingegen—es wird Zeit, daß wir auf die friedliche kleine Insel zurückkehren—hat nicht nur einen typischen Baum, sondern deren viele und dazu noch Palmen. (*MI* 142–44)

[So all of a sudden my heart grew heavy as I saw a plane tree in a garden on Paquetá, because not only did I see this one pale trunk, but also long rows of such trunks ... I travelled through the plane tree avenues of Southern France by bus for long hours. Yes, I see their thick trunks ... and I see the bus ... crammed full with tired ... people. All day it drove on like that, one night and another day, from Geneva to the Pyrenees. That was my first attempt to escape Hitler's Europe ... this attempt failed ... When I saw the plane tree, the island vanished from view and along with it the security she provides me, and in my mind's eye I saw the fat neck of the Gestapo officer in Perpignan ... Thus, a landscape is closely connected with its typical stock of trees. On Paquetá, however—it is time to return to this peaceful little island—there is not only one typical tree but several, and moreover palm trees.]

This manner of writing about his experiences helped Katz cope with the loss of his home and opened up possibilities for a new one. Katz's awareness that "das Paradies überall verloren ist" (everywhere paradise is lost)[30] allowed him entry or access to Brazil, as well as to its people, and furthermore it enabled him in more than ten different book publications to portray the country more realistically than Zweig did. For example, when Katz described Brazil's nature, he directed attention to neglected regions and also expressed criticism and dismay about the destruction that had been caused by human actions. There is also a difference regarding their views towards the extensive unsettled territory. Zweig was inclined to stylize the uninhabited regions as symbols of vital strength and a promising future: "Raum ist auch seelische Kraft. Es erweitert den Blick und erweitert die Seele ... wo Raum ist, da ist nicht nur Zeit, sondern auch Zukunftspace"; (*BLZ* 135; [S]pace ... is also spiritual strength. It enlarges the outlook and it enlarges the soul ... Where there is space, there is not only time, but also the future, *BLF* 133).

However, Katz discussed this aspect mainly in connection with the Nazi ideology of "Lebensraum" (living space) and "Blut und Boden" (blood and soil). Contradicting Zweig, Katz maintained:

> Solche Größe ist freilich nicht nur ein Vorteil ... Der Lebensraum-Fanatiker frohlocke nicht zu früh: Also an Menschen fehlt es in Brasilien! Die werden *wir* liefern!' Sondern er versuche erst *selbst*, im Hinterland zu siedeln, im Amazonas-Sumpf etwa oder in der Steppe Nordostbrasiliens. Aber das will er ja gar nicht ... wenn dieses Buch erscheint, wird Hitler—so hoffe ich—am eigenen Leib die Erfahrung gemacht haben, daß weiter Raum nicht Leben bedeutet. (*BR* 228–29)

> [Such a great space is not only an advantage ... The *Lebensraum* fanatic should not rejoice too soon: "There is a lack of people in Brazil! *We* will provide them!" He should rather try to settle in the hinterland, in the swamps of the Amazonas for instance or in the northeastern Brazilian prairie land. But he does not want to do this at all ... [When] this book is published, Hitler—I hope—will have experienced first hand that open space does not necessarily mean life.]

For Katz the promising future was based on the generous, always polite Brazilian people rather than on the country's size. And in contrast to the other émigrés, he often wrote about political occurrences in Brazil and the actions of the Vargas regime. In so doing—and even if only between the lines—Katz also dared to voice criticism. Although emphasizing the racial tolerance of the Brazilians and explaining "daß es gesetzwidrig ist, den Farbigen minderes Recht zu geben" (*GH* 318; that it is against the law to deny rights to people of color), he had to admit that even in Brazil—and seventy-five years after the abolition of slavery—the equality of rights had not been completely put into practice.

It was easier for Katz to express his opinions than for Zweig, since he did not want to publish any of his books during the war. Katz's decision was proven correct by the harsh critiques, which though few in number, nevertheless still had been written about Zweig's *Brazil* book. In June 1942, Feder and Katz spoke about Zweig's suicide and about the latter's decision not to publish during the war. As Feder noted in his diary, Katz "[w]ill hier nichts veröffentlichen, hält es [für] überhaupt nicht richtig, in portugiesischer Sprache über Brasilien zu schreiben, ob Lob, ob Tadel, wird immer Anstoß erregen" (*Diary* 519; [Katz] does not consider it proper to write about Brazil in Portuguese, whether praise or reproach, it will always cause offence).

Zweig was hurt by the criticism published about him and his *Brasilien: Ein Land der Zukunft*. In particular, the accusation that his book had been contracted by the Vargas regime offended him greatly. Despite the fact that the book sold exceptionally well, and even though there were only relatively few negative discussions of it, the few negative criticisms did not allow him a moment's rest. As he let his Argentinian editor and friend Alfredo Cahn know: "Das Brasilienbuch ist inzwischen hier erschienen und sehr gut aufgenommen worden. Geärgert hat mich dabei nur . . . dass hier ein dummes Gerede umherging, als ob ich dieses Buch im Auftrag oder sogar mit besonders guter Bezahlung der Regierung geschrieben hätte. Gegen solche Dinge kann man sich aber nicht wehren." (The Brazil book has been published here in the meantime and has been very well received. I was only annoyed by the fact that a silly rumor was spread that I wrote the book on behalf of—or for payment by—the government. But one cannot defend oneself against such things.)[31]

The mental state of émigrés and refugees from Nazism that influenced the conception of Zweig's book was largely incomprehensible to his Brazilian critics. Indeed, they were unable to realize that he had to write his hymn of praise to Brazil in the manner he did, since he urgently required hope that a better, still undamaged world existed. Zweig did not leave the readers in the dark about this. Already in the introduction he made clear that Brazil represented a new version of his beloved homeland, which was destroying itself with war and hate:

> So one of our greatest hopes for future civilization and peace in our world, which has been destroyed by hatred and madness, rests on the existence of Brazil, whose desires are aimed exclusively at pacific development. Wherever ethical forces are at work, our task is to strengthen the intentions. Wherever in our troubled times we find hopes for a new future in new zones it is our duty to point out this country and these possibilities. And that is why I am writing this book. (*BE* 13)

In 1936 Zweig had already noticed the lack of people and capital in Brazil. In view of the arrival of refugees whose numbers had been steadily growing in the five years between his first visit and the writing of the book, he considered Brazil an ideal host country for the masses of people who were mostly unwanted nearly all over the world, and also in Brazil. Consequently, Zweig made an indirect appeal to Brazil to receive more refugees and by this appeal he hoped to be able to save their lives: "Brazil suffers from anaemia, from too few people in too large a space. The cure for the Old World and, at the same time for this New World, would be a thorough, patient and wisely carried out transfusion of blood and capital" (*BE* 130).

This cautious appeal died away unheard. Instead, several critics expressed contrary and negative opinions. Zweig was not prepared for these accusations and especially for comments which implied that he had insufficiently discussed the drawbacks of the dictatorial Vargas regime or that he failed to offer commentary about Brazil's deficient industrial progress. He felt hurt, despondent, and misunderstood. As a consequence, the isolation in the small bungalow in Petrópolis, which he himself had desired and at first found restful, became increasingly more depressing. As Segall commented to his friends after having met Zweig by chance shortly before his suicide: "Dieser Mann wird an Traurigkeit sterben" (*TP* 529; This man will die of sadness). The artist could not know then that they had met for the last time.

Zweig sought reminiscences of his lost European home in Petrópolis, and, at first, thought to have found some there. However, it soon became clear that desire could bear no comparison with reality. Petrópolis was not an Austrian summer resort, and in the letters to his friends Zweig's lamentations about the lack of intimate and intellectual conversations as well as the unavailability of well-equipped libraries became more and more frequent. Furthermore, he felt that the literary work he had longed for at the beginning had become a burden. He suffered deeply from the loss of his German-speaking readers. "Ich selber arbeite weiter, aber ohne das alte Vergnügen am Werk. Ich fühle beim Schreiben, dass ich kein rechtes Publikum mehr habe wie früher. Und zuweilen werde ich etwas nachlässig, weil ich doch nur für den Übersetzer schreibe." (*BaF* 333; I continue writing, but without the joy of working as in former times. While writing I feel that I do not have a proper readership anymore. And sometimes I become a little bit careless since I am only writing for the translator.)

Yet, in his last months Zweig finished the two works for which he will always be remembered by his readers: his memoir *Die Welt von Gestern* (*The World of Yesterday*, 1942) and his most famous novella *Schachnovelle* (*The Royal Game*, 1942). He was well aware of the special quality of this last work. How much the novella concerned him can be seen by the fact that he worked on it until the very end. He committed suicide only after having finished it and dispatching copies of the typescript to his publishers in the United States, Sweden, and Argentina. Concern about the publication of his works could not obscure the fact that a deep depression had already gripped him. Nonetheless, the writer attended the carnival in Rio de Janeiro in mid-February 1942, because he wanted to experience this spectacle once in his life. But, the reality of the war prevented any joyful celebration. At this time, the newspapers announced the fall of distant Singapore to the Japanese. Also, after the Vargas regime had broken off diplomatic relationships with the Axis Powers, German submarines began sinking Brazilian ships off the Brazilian coast. This action brought the war close to his Brazilian doorstep. These occurrences also confirmed Zweig's feeling that life for his generation was sealed, a matter of the past.

On February 23, 1942, Stefan and Lotte Zweig were found dead in the bedroom of their bungalow in Petrópolis. The double suicide shocked the Brazilian and international public as well as émigrés all over the world. The Vargas regime paid its last respects by allowing a state funeral for this Austrian-Jewish writer. Feder's diary entry reveals that Zweig's death deeply moved the Brazilians who were united in mourning:

> Die ganze Stadt steht unter dem Eindruck der Feierlichkeit . . . Während die Wagen durch die Stadt rollen . . . schließen spontan alle Geschäfte. Auf dem Friedhof die Fülle so stark, dass wenig zu sehen und zu hören, ein ergreifendes Bild, diese Menge, die alle Schichten, Rassen und Klassen umfasst und sichtlich ergriffen ist. (*Diary* 121)

> [The entire city stands under the impression of solemnity. While the hearses roll through the town, all the shops spontaneously close. At the cemetery the crowd is so full that there is little to see and to hear, a moving scene, this crowd that comprises all social strata, races and classes and that is visibly moved.]

Only one time thereafter, on the occasion of the death of Segall fifteen years after Zweig's suicide, did Feder witness such deep and extensive mourning.

> Niemals seit dem Tode Stefan Zweigs hat der Hingang eines Künstlers die brasilianische Öffentlichkeit so bewegt und erschüttert, wie die Nachricht vom Tode des Malers . . . Lasar Segal . . . Die Beisetzung auf dem jüdischen Friedhof in São Paulo zeigte die Teilnahme aller Kreise der Bevölkerung—in der Deputiertenkammer entwarf der Abgeordnete Carlos Lacerda ein ebenso tief empfundenes wie intimes Bild des Menschen und des Künstlers. Der Redner . . . sprach diesmal im Sinne aller Parteien. ("Tode")

> [Since Stefan Zweig's death never has the passing of an artist moved and shocked the Brazilian public so deeply as the news of the death of the painter . . . Lasar Segall . . . All circles of the population expressed their sympathy during the burial at the Jewish cemetery in São Paulo . . . in the Chamber of Deputies the representative Carlos Lacerda drew a deeply sensitive as well as intimate picture of the person and artist Segall . . . On this occasion the speaker gave voice to the opinion of all parties.]

Thus, Zweig and Segall were united not only by how they dealt with issues faced by refugees from Nazism; their respective deaths also led to public displays of grief by the Brazilian people. Moreover, they both shared a sincere love of Brazil. Although Zweig experienced some disappointments in Brazil, his love of the country remained unchanged. Hence, before departing from this world of his "own free will and in right mind," as he stated, Zweig urgently wanted to fulfill one last responsibility: to thank Brazil. As he wrote, he was obligated

> diesem wundervollen Lande Brasilien innig zu danken, das mir und meiner Arbeit so gute und gastliche Rast gegeben. Mit jedem Tage habe ich dies Land mehr lieben gelernt und nirgends hätte ich mir mein Leben lieber vom Grunde aus neu aufgebaut, nachdem die Welt meiner eigenen Sprache für mich untergegangen ist und meine geistige Heimat Europa sich selber vernichtet. Aber nach dem sechzigsten Jahre bedürfte es besonderer Kräfte nun noch einmal völlig neu zu beginnen. Und die meinen sind durch die langen Jahre heimatlosen Wanderns erschöpft. (*TP* 71)

[to give heartfelt thanks to this wonderful country of Brazil which afforded me and my work such good and hospitable repose. From day to day I have learned to love the country more and nowhere else would I have preferred to rebuild my life again, now that the world of my native language has perished for me and my spiritual home Europe is destroying itself. But after one's sixtieth year special powers would be needed in order to make a wholly new beginning. And mine are exhausted by the long years of homeless wandering.]

Notes

[1] Stefan Zweig and Friderike Zweig, *Wenn einen Augenblick die Wolken weichen: Briefwechsel 1912–1942*, ed. Jeffrey B. Berlin and Gert Kerschbaumer (Frankfurt am Main: Fischer, 2006), 306–8.

[2] Stefan and Friderike Zweig, *Stefan and Friderike Zweig: Their Correspondence 1912–1942*, trans. and ed. Henry G. Alsberg and Erna MacArthur (New York: Hastings House, 1954), 289–91 (translation amended where necessary). Unless otherwise noted, here as elsewhere, all translations are mine. In instances where a work or text has already been translated, the printed version is cited. However, if available translations are inaccurate, corrections have been made and noted by square brackets.

[3] Quoted in Alberto Dines, *Tod in Paradies: Die Tragödie des Stefan Zweig* (Frankfurt am Main: Edition Büchergilde, 2006), 366 (hereafter cited in text as *TP*).

[4] Stefan Zweig to Romain Rolland, September 28, 1936, in *Romain Rolland/Stefan Zweig, Briefwechsel 1910–1940*, ed. Waltraud Schwarze et al., vol. 2, *Briefwechsel 1924–1940* (Berlin: Rütten & Loening, 1987), 635.

[5] Stefan Zweig to Berthold Viertel, October 20, 1940, in Stefan Zweig, *Briefe an Freunde*, ed. Richard Friedenthal (Frankfurt am Main: Fischer, 1978), 320 (hereafter cited in text as *BaF*).

[6] Alberto Gartenberg, *O J vermelho* (Rio de Janeiro: Editora Nova Fronteira, 1976), 381.

[7] Stefan Zweig to Lasar Segall, December 13, 1940, in Vera d'Horta, ed., *Lasar Segall: Navio de emigrantes* (São Paulo: Imprensa Oficial, 2008), 27.

[8] Lasar Segall, quoted in Maria Luiza Tucci Carneiro and Celso Lafer, *Judeus e Judaísmo na obra de Lasar Segall* (Cotia: Ateliê Editorial, 2004), 82.

[9] Ernst Feder, "Zum Tode des Malers Lasar Segall," 1957. Ernst Feder Collection. AR 7040, Leo Baeck Institute, New York; Ernst Feder, "Besuch bei Lasar Segall in São Paulo," *Argentinisches Wochenblatt*, January 18, 1947 (hereafter cited in text as "Tode" and "Besuch").

[10] Lasar Segall to Stefan Zweig, December 27, 1940, in d'Horta, *Lasar Segall*, 28.

[11] Stefan Zweig to Lasar Segall, January 7, 1941, in d'Horta, *Lasar Segall*, 31.

[12] Stefan Zweig to Abrahão Koogan, August 1, 1941, in Stefan Zweig, *Briefe 1932–1942*, ed. Knut Beck and Jeffrey B. Berlin (Frankfurt am Main: Fischer, 2005), 311–12.

[13] Jeffrey Lesser, "Jewish Refugee Academics and the Brazilian State, 1935–1945," *Ibero Amerikanisches Archiv: Zeitschrift für Sozialwissenschaften und Geschichte* 21, no. 1 (1995): 224, 230–31.

[14] Robert M. Levine, "Brazil's Jews During the Vargas Era and After," *Luso-Brazilian Review* 5, no. 1 (1968): 54.

[15] Cf. Ursula Rike, personal interview with the author, June 1, 2004.

[16] Ernst Feder, "Hugo Simon," *Aufbau* 4 (August 1950): 14.

[17] Cf. Eva Maria Rimpau, personal interview with the author, January 23, 2004.

[18] Hugo Simon, "Seidenraupen," unpublished typescript, Hugo Simon Collection, Deutsche Nationalbibliothek, Deutsches Exilarchiv 1933–45. Frankfurt am Main, E2005/63, 528.

[19] Simon, "Seidenraupen," 40–41.

[20] Stefan Zweig, *Brasilien: Ein Land der Zukunft* (Frankfurt am Main: Insel, 1981), 18 (hereafter cited in text as *BLZ*).

[21] Stefan Zweig, *Brazil: Land of the Future*, trans. Andrew St. James (New York: Viking Press, 1941), 13 (hereafter cited in text as *BLF*).

[22] Ernst Feder, diary entry of December 30, 1941, quoted in Marlen Eckl, "'Die Blüte des Exils': Ernst Feder und sein Brasilianisches Tagebuch," *Martius-Staden-Jahrbuch 54 (2007): 120 (hereafter cited in* text as *Diary*).

[23] Juan Pastor Benitez, "A flor do exílio: Ernesto Feder e Fabrice Polderman," *O Jornal*, March 14, 1946.

[24] Ernst Feder, diary entries of August 8 and 15, 1941, quoted in Marlen Eckl, "Das Paradies ist überall verloren," in *Das Brasilienbild von Flüchtlingen des Nationalsozialismus* (Frankfurt am Main: Vervuert 2010), 313.

[25] Ernst Feder, "Goethes Liebe zu Brasilien," in *Goethe: Jahrbuch der Goethe-Gesellschaft* 13 (1952): 176.

[26] Stefan Zweig to Felix Braun, July 8, 1941, Felix Braun Collection, Wienbibliothek im Rathaus, I.N. 198.121 (original letter in English; grammatical and stylistic errors left uncorrected and intact).

[27] Richard Katz to Werner Richter, January 1942, Werner Richter Collection, Deutsches Literaturarchiv, Marbach am Neckar, A: Richter 69.3823/2.

[28] Richard Katz, *Mein Inselbuch: Erste Erlebnisse in Brasilien* (Zurich: Schweizer Druck- und Verlagshaus, 1950), 138 (hereafter *cited in text as MI*).

[29] Richard Katz, *Gruß aus der Hängematte: Heitere Erinnerungen* (Rüschlikon: Albert Müller, 1958), 306 (hereafter cited in text as *GH*).

[30] Richard Katz, *Begegnungen in Rio* (Erlenbach-Zurich: Eugen Rentsch, 1951), 7 (hereafter cited in text as *BR*).

[31] Stefan Zweig to Alfredo Cahn, September 19, 1941, in Zweig, *Briefe 1932–1942*, 316–17.

11: Stefan Zweig: Life in Cities of Exile

Klemens Renoldner

Last Years in Europe

"[A]LLES HÄNGT JETZT VON DER NEUEN WELT AB" (from now on everything will depend upon the New World). Stefan Zweig wrote this line in mid-June 1940 to his friend, writer and translator Joseph Leftwich, who was living in London.[1] Zweig wanted to explain to him why he had hesitated so long to leave England. He made it clear that he had now finally decided to make the journey to New York and from there go on to Latin America. He informed his friend that he hoped to be back in Great Britain by the end of October. But the farewell at Euston Station in London, where Lotte and Stefan were seen off by Hannah and Manfred Altmann and his friend Heinrich Eisemann, turned out to be a final farewell to Europe. In March he had written to the German writer Hermann Kesten that whoever left Europe now would never again return: "Hier können wir durch unsere bloße Anwesenheit eine Aufgabe erfüllen. Amerika würde uns verschlingen" (Here we can serve at least a purpose by simply being present. America would devour us).[2]

Lotte and Stefan Zweig had found a new home in Bath, about 120 miles from Britain's capital. They resided there for less than a year. After leaving Salzburg in 1934, it was here where he allowed himself to feel at home again. Bath even seemed to have triggered certain memories of the view from Salzburg's Kapuzinerberg or of the Salzkammergut. Later, Stefan Zweig would use similar comparisons for the house in Petrópolis. "Bath ist bezaubernd, die reizendste Stadt, die ich in England kenne—ein Erszatz-Salzburg" (Bath is amazing, the most charming place I know in England—an Ersatz-Salzburg)."[3] He now had a library at his disposal, even if it was only a tenth of the size of the library he had in his home in Salzburg. Thus, it was finally possible to carry on with his work, even though with the outbreak of war there was a permanent fear of a possible German invasion.

These were his last, but also quite disturbing months in old Europe. There was permanent waiting and enquiring in vain at the authorities about their British citizenship. Prominent friends tried to intervene—but without success. It took nearly a whole year before Lotte and Stefan

Zweig finally received British citizenship. Now they had succeeded at last: the prolonged farewell from his Salzburg home had dragged on for years. The house was finally sold in May 1937, so this period of his life lay behind him once and for all. His divorce from Friderike had finally been completed after countless negotiations. He acquired a new citizenship, married a second wife, lived in a new home, and was free to travel again. His destination was the United States, but the American government only issued Zweig and his wife transit visas, which stipulated a certain date for leaving the country. Their new home was thus found—and lost.

Zweig's letters and his diary entries from those years clearly reveal that he was very depressed by the reports of Jewish refugees coming to London. He received countless pleas for help in the letters sent to him. After all, Hitler's regime had already been in power in Central Europe for six long years. Jews in Germany, Austria, and in the occupied countries endured horrific humiliations. Many had been displaced, tortured, and murdered, even before the death camps would finally continue this genocidal process, which affected thousands and, ultimately, millions of people. Not infrequently, he received terrible news in this regard in letters addressed to him at Hallam Street 49 in London and then at Lyncombe Hill in Bath. It is against this background that one has to understand what was meant by his phrase: "From now on everything will depend upon the New World."

Retreat from Big Cities

In contrast to his earlier journeys—and their various literary or journalistic descriptions—Zweig in the last phase of his life showed little interest in the cities that he visited in the New World. He seems to have experienced cities like London and New York as collective places of helplessness or of great poverty and, for himself, as places of perpetual depression. All those countless lives of refugees from the Old World weighed heavily upon him. Accounts by his friends and contemporaries seem to confirm this. Especially in New York he seems to have suffered more because of the numerous people he met and the sad news he received, which put extra pressure on him. There were many friends whom he had been able to help, and he continued to help many more of them. People appear to have expected him—and perhaps he himself expected as well—to carry ever more new emigrants on his shoulders. His letters provide some of the details of the countless efforts he made to help newcomers. But given the fact that he had sufficient difficulties regarding his own matters during the years in England, he yearned for some peace and quiet for his own sake. The route to the U.S. and Latin America should have signalized some kind of escape or clearance of vital significance. As he wrote: "From now on *everything* will depend upon the New World."[4] Zweig yearned for a situation that would again allow him to concentrate again on work. He wished be in control and take hold of his personal life again, just as he had in former years.

Typically for Zweig, whenever he felt the urge to return to intensive work he retreated from big cities. This pattern of behavior established itself early in Zweig's career, when the conditions were much more advantageous: "Die Großstadt ist purer Irrsinn" (Big cities are pure madness!), he wrote to his first wife Friderike from Berlin.[5] As early as 1915, he had moved with her from central Vienna to the outskirts of the city into two small pavilions in Rodaun. From 1917 to 1919 he declined to live in the city of Zurich because he found it too distracting in the German-speaking Swiss city. He preferred to live in Rüschlikon on Lake Zurich instead, in order to be able to work there. Concerning Vienna, he never considered returning there after the war but rather chose Salzburg as his new home from 1919 on. And from there he would retreat—if the commotion of the Salzburg Festival orchestrated by Max Reinhardt and Hugo von Hofmannsthal became all too distressing—to the quiet countryside around Salzburg. He tended to reside in the mountains in Thumersbach on the shores of the Zeller See. After his farewell to Austria in 1933/1934, London appeared to be merely a temporary resting place for him. His new home in Britain was to be the quiet town of Bath, where he bought a house with a garden again. When Zweig wrote his book on Magellan, he was not living in central Lisbon, which he sincerely enjoyed, but rather outside the city in Estoril.

At the end of their lives, Lotte and Stefan decided not to live in metropolitan Rio, a place that would have gladly received him "like a lover," but rather in Petrópolis, a comparatively secluded place.[6] In the last year of his life, in 1941, the sixty-year-old writer Stefan Zweig retreated from urban New York City and tried to give voice to his memories in New Haven and in Ossining.

European Identity

Life in the cities of exile made it clear to him in no uncertain terms that he, along with thousands of others, had in reality become a refugee. Even if not in need financially—he could still pay for lodging in good hotels—a nomadic life of restlessness forced him to carry his suitcase from one country to the next and from one city to the next. The fact that he was constantly confronted with uncertainty and had to make provisional or temporary arrangements weighed heavily upon him. To a degree, in exile he lost his position as an internationally acclaimed and successful man of letters. Because the work that once served as his personal zone of freedom was hindered by politics and forces beyond his control, his European mission had become a matter of absurdity.

His farewell to Europe and attempt to begin life anew in the "New World" emphasized in a shocking manner that his very own philosophy of individual freedom had been destroyed. In Europe aggressive nationalist ideologies provoked a world war. Fascism extinguished the pan-humanist and pan-European idea of peaceful co-existence without national boundaries or religious animosities, which he had promoted. In a letter to Paul Zech, Zweig explains this process as follows:

> Wonach ich strebte, schon in meinen frühesten Jünglingsjahren, war die Betonung des "Europäischen Menschen" und der "Europäischen Geisteshaltung." Soll das jetzt vorbei sein? Total und unwiderbringlich? Nach all den jahrhundertelangen Anstrengungen unserer geistigen Größen?[7]

> [What I was striving for, even in my earliest youth, was an emphasis on the "European Man" and the "European Mind." Should all that have been in vain now, totally and irretrievably? After all those efforts that our greatest minds have made over centuries?]

Zweig's enthusiasm for Europe has its roots, as Donald Prater has convincingly shown, in his family background, in Zweig's urban Viennese identity, in his Austrian and, above all, Jewish identity. The roots of his family, reached as far as the Ukraine, Bohemia, Italy and France, and are of utmost importance in this respect. Zweig's European identity is not, as one might be led to believe, an identity that had been acquired by learning, or one that developed as a result of years of intense dialogue with his friends in Switzerland between 1917 and 1919. Rather, his European identity has its roots in his disposition, a deeply personal identification that goes back to the days of his childhood and youth in Vienna. Bearing this fact in mind it is not difficult to understand why Zweig was so terribly shaken and severely threatened in exile, given the threatening political situation in the 1930s and 1940s, and the helplessness and impotence of Europe on the verge of its demise.

The Old World and the New World

Stefan Zweig seemed to be able to perceive the New World only in relation to the process of destruction going on in Europe. In his 1936 essay "Kleine Reise nach Brasilien" Zweig chose the term "Anomalie" (KRB 292) when referring to a fundamental difference between Europe and Brazil after his first journey across South America. For him, Brazil had not arrived at a point where the question of race might be an issue. Instead, it had precluded the possibility of race becoming a problem "auf die einfachste und glücklichste Art . . . indem es seit Jahrzehnten den Unterschied von Rassen,

Hautfarben, Nationen und Religionen bei seinen Bürgern völlig ignoriert" (KRB 292; in the easiest and most fortunate way just by having completely ignored for decades any difference as regards race, color, nation, and religion among its citizens). In Brazil he found a general acceptance of people as they are, which makes it possible to avoid disputes of this kind.

Zweig's position in regard to cities and urban life, from which he himself had profited so much in younger years, was characterized in the last phase of his life by much ambivalence, as well as paradoxes and contradictions. One major paradox is that after arriving in the New World he uses all the energy he has at his disposal to look back at the Old World, on which nothing much can depend any more. Tragically, he clings to this world more at this point, probably because he once had been so sure about it. But now he must give it up, for example, the safety of a world exemplified by the metropolitan capital of Austria, Vienna. Furthermore, he definitely will never be able to appreciate fully the New World and its big cities.

The process of idealizing the example of Brazilian society as a historical reply to an authoritarian and racist Europe, as formulated by Zweig, seems to represent an astonishing contradiction to his own experience in the cities of Brazil. An especially interesting example is São Paulo, which, in Zweig's description, is constructed "improvisatorisch, hastig, auf Geratewohl" (KRB 302; in an improvised fashion, hastily and randomly) so that "man unwillkürlich an Liverpool, und Manchester erinnert [ist]" (KRB 304; one is involuntarily reminded of Liverpool, or Manchester). According to Zweig "Diese Stadt weiß, daß sie sich ihre Form erst erobern muß" (KRB 304; this city is aware of the fact that it has not yet found the shape it might be looking for); its sights have "einen fatalen Beigeschmack" (KRB 305; an embarrassing aftertaste).

It is with obvious European disappointment that Zweig speaks about the fact that this city has extinguished its own history of three hundred years. He laments the development of the city, namely that it has not grown—as European cities have—"gradually and in a ring-like fashion . . . around a centre"—like Vienna, Paris, Rome. What irritates him is the provisional or temporary character of town planning, the uncontrollable, spontaneous and individual quality of new developments, the hard to imagine speed with which everything grows, the purposelessness in regard to all that. In contrast, European cities have, at least in his view, grown as organic wholes. The metaphors Zweig uses draw on the sphere of natural laws. He had already suggested these comparisons in his 1913 essay "Der Rhythmus von New York" (The Rhythm of New York). But in São Paulo he sees chaos, pure chance, and actions of caprice, dissonance and manifestations of an uncivilized character.

In contrast, in a speech given in the Theatre Marigny in Paris on April 26, 1940, entitled "Das Wien von gestern" (The Vienna of Yesterday) Zweig remarked that the highest task for a city is

Kultur zu schaffen und diese Kultur zu verteidigen. Wien hat als Vorposten der lateinischen Zivilisation standgehalten bis zum Untergang des römischen Reiches, und dann wieder aufzuerstehen als das Bolwerk der römisch-katholischen Kirche . . . In ihr ist immer wieder der alte Traum eines geeinten Europas geträumt worden; ein übernationales Reich, ein "heilig römisches Reich," schwebte den Habsburgern vor—und nicht etwa eine Weltherrschaft des Germanentums.

[to create cultural achievements and to defend culture. Vienna stood firm as an outpost of Latin civilization until the decline of the Roman Empire, only to be resurrected as the stronghold of the Roman Catholic church . . . Vienna has always been the place where the ancient dream of a united Europe has been dreamed again and again, the dream of an empire beyond national boundaries and not of a worldwide domination of Teutonism.][8]

Nostalgic images and memories of "cultural capital" Vienna came into his mind at this moment. It is an act of complete transfiguration, an idealized image of the place of his birth, the capital in which he spent his childhood, because in April of 1940 Austria has been occupied by German soldiers for two years and has become part of National Socialist Germany! Soon France will be occupied as well! How different Vienna suddenly appears to be, especially since he often expressed his misgivings and felt hostility toward the city. He abandoned it at the end of the First World War and he repeatedly referred to it in a pejorative way.

Zweig's Paris lecture of 1940 is dominated by a retrospective leaning on the history of ideas and a personal report and evaluation. Wistful images of nostalgia work as a life-sustaining principle from abroad. And it is the old Europe, the old Vienna and Austria, the Salzburg years and the intellectual shape of Europe before Hitler's rise which preoccupies him during these months and years. Finally he begins to prepare materials for his rightly famous autobiography, which with logical consistency will be called *Die Welt von Gestern* (The World of Yesterday).

First Brazilian Impressions

After attending the PEN conference in Argentina and touring in Latin American, Zweig returned to Europe, and he wrote an informative and telling letter to Romain Rolland in September 1936:

Mon cher ami, rentrant, de l'Amérique du Sud je veux vous écrire un peu des [!] mes impressions. Elles sont excellentes. Les pays sont profondément pacifique[s], le terrible fléau du nationalisme n'est pas

encore virulent et entre les hommes il y a—grâce à l'espace entre eux—moins de haine. On nous regarde en Europe comme des fous: et ils ont bien raison, de voir, combien de terre est encore disponible, on en comprend pas, pourquoi les gens s'ac[c]rochent à notre Europe—il y a ici une intensité de l'optimisme et d'idéalisme, qui était un tonique pour moi . . .
(*Briefe* 167–68)

[My dear friend, upon returning from Latin America I would like to give you some impressions of what my experiences were. They were excellent. These countries are utterly peaceful and have not yet been affected by the epidemic of nationalism, and there is less hatred among the people just because of the distance between them. They see us Europeans as madmen, and right they are! If one bears in mind how much land there is still left at their disposal one simply does not understand why people still should be clinging to our Europe. There is optimism and idealism in such an intensity that it was really refreshing . . .]

The fact that Brazil alone is as large as the whole European continent makes it "a land of the future." Furthermore, a surge of communal energy can be recorded there. As Zweig wrote: "wer Augen hat, um Werdendes zu sehen, und Nerven, um Schwingungen aufzufangen, spürt hier das Wachwerden eines neuen Typus, einer neuen Gemeinschaft" (KRB 294; Whoever has an eye for change and a sense for vibrations must perceive the awakening of a new model of community). A special idea of national pride was developing in Brazil, according to Zweig, and it was based on a peaceful kind of nationalism. Even in the mostly rather liberal United States, Zweig perceived regrettably that "eine Farbengrenze gezogen [wird]" (KRB 292; a color line has been drawn) between black and white people. However, during his first visit to South America in 1936 Zweig praised the Brazilian "model" as an alternative to Europe, and later, after several journeys across the country, he dwelled upon this issue more extensively in his book *Brasilien: Ein Land der Zukunft* (Brazil: A Land of the Future, 1941).

Brazil—Land of the Future

There is a contradiction between Zweig's nostalgic words about the long lost cultural metropolis of Vienna and his description of the proletarian Brazilian cities of the future. In 1936 Zweig views São Paulo as "das Werdende und nicht das schon Vollendete" (KRB 304; an emerging process instead of any completion or perfection). For him it is a place for workers, one of those "Nurarbeitsstädte" (KRB 305; cities of labor only) which are, after all, not necessarily focused on art and beauty:

Wenn man also auf dem Begriff der Schönheit durchaus beharren will, so kann man die São Paolos nicht eine vorhandene, sondern eine werdende nennen, eine nicht so sehr optische als energetische und dynamische, eine Schönheit und Form von morgen, die man durch das Heute eben jetzt mit einer ungeduldigen Gewalt durchbrechen fühlt. (KRB 304)

[But if one may not do without the concept of beauty, one can at least call São Paulo's beauty one that has not yet been fully developed. But actually [it] will slowly but surely be emerging and developing, a beauty not so much on a level of the perceiving eye, but an energetic and dynamic kind of beauty and form of tomorrow that may be felt at the actual moment of breaking through today with an impatient force right now.]

For Stefan Zweig the city seemed to be all too proletarian and ugly. But he was definitely fascinated by its speedy pace, and the process of urban development seems to point at something new for him, namely a "World of Tomorrow"—a utopian tomorrow about which one cannot know very much. It escapes our experience and lies beyond it. But experience continually seems to shape all his perceptions and texts, although a connection with the "Old World" is never erased. In this sense, his Brazil book can be held up against the "Old World," as a kind of positive and utopian position against the swan song conveyed by *Die Welt von Gestern*. São Paulo thus appears to represent the "World of Tomorrow." Stefan Zweig was convinced that Brazil could serve as an example for the world and make a contribution in regard to its renewal, but at the same time he remained somehow detached from its promise because it was too unspecific in his mind. In the end Zweig was unable to gain vitality. His conception of Brazil was based on merely a glance at what one day might emerge, that is, a utopian view of the "New World." But it was no real home, as it turned out.

A second urban example in Brazil is Rio de Janeiro, which he called "die schönste Stadt der Welt" (KRB 310; the most beautiful city in the world), referring to a phrase originally used by Alexander von Humboldt. The city "breitet sich auf mit weichen, weiblichen Armen, es empfängt, es zieht an sich heran, es gibt sich mit einer gewissen Wollust dem Blicke hin" (KRB 310–11; spreads its soft, female arms, embraces, draws one near, abandons itself with a certain voluptuousness to the perceiving eye). Using a female persona to represent the city makes an exciting and fertile subject for anyone interested in the history of civilization—much more so if a city abandons itself like a voluptuous lover. And it is only a short step from a lover's embrace to the field of music: harmony, rhythm, dance, and sense of time—all in all essential coordinates in his lecture on Vienna.

One can also find very similar phrases and rhetoric in Zweig's earlier descriptions of Salzburg.

> Alles ist hier Harmonie, die Stadt und das Meer und das Grün und die Berge, all das fließt gewissermaßen klingend ineinander... und diese Harmonie wiederholt sich in immer andern Akkorden: anders ist diese Stadt von den Hügeln gesehen und anders vom Meer, aber überall Harmonie, gelöste Vielfalt in immer wieder völliger Einheit, Natur, die Stadt geworden ist, und eine Stadt, die wie die Natur wirkt. (KRB 310–11)

> [Everything here is harmony, the city and the sea and the green spaces and the mountains... and this harmony repeats itself with perpetually changing chords. The city looks different if viewed from the hills, and different again if viewed from the sea, but everywhere there is harmony, a relaxed kind of variety in a completely integrated whole, again and again, nature turned into a city and a city which seems like nature.]

What should be kept in mind in this context is that Zweig did not plan to live for an extended period of time in these cities. Mostly, he experienced them only as a visitor. The visitor's eye glances over the past and present surface and tends to maintain a distance from zones of social conflict. Zweig perceived the cities of the "Old World" as shaped by historically established urban centers. In these centers he paid his visits to major cultural institutions like libraries or museums. He met with outstanding representatives of the arts. The picturesque or sinister aspects of urban life may have fascinated the visitor for an evening, may even have made him shudder for one night, but there was always the hotel room to which he might retreat. When many years earlier, Zweig, using another name and pretending to be unemployed went out looking for a job in New York as a kind of experiment, he was surprised that he was able to receive more than one job offer. He rejoiced about the fact that this was all so easy in the big American city.

Let us take a final look at Stefan Zweig's way of perceiving cities in exile: his perception aims back at the past. He aims at the political situation in Europe; he is concerned with his worries, about not being able to return and the fact that he has actually lost his only recently set up new home in England—a home in the "European mind."

Zweig sometimes reacted to his situation in exile with serious bouts of depression. There was a psychic fixation on the past that fatigued him, sometimes even paralyzed him, and from which he found it difficult to escape. Historical subjects with which he had been dealing since the time of his Erasmus-book had facilitated the expression of only vaguely concealed comments on the dangerous and hopeless political situation facing Europe. Towards the end of his life, Zweig's perceptiveness and attention were primarily directed towards the fact that he was continually experiencing some kind of anxiety or loss. Whatever his real life experiences, what was always lurking in the background was a world-threatening situation connected to the tragic decline of Europe.

The New World—Land of No Hope

Stefan Zweig was fascinated by the vitality of metropoles around the world during his entire life. He often recorded and published his impressions as a visitor, explorer, and stroller in the city in his travel accounts, in letters and in *Die Welt von Gestern*. With acute insights, he observed London, Zürich, Moscow, New York, São Paulo, Rio, and—again and again—Paris, the only city granted a chapter of its own in *Die Welt von Gestern*.

But why—and this is a question that puzzles and confounds us no matter how often we ask it—why was Stefan Zweig not able to find refuge and a new home in the cities of the "New World" just as numerous other emigrants did? There was no shortage of possible locations where likeminded people, who were also the victims of persecution and exile, were gathering to represent their own interests, continue their work, found magazines and publishing houses, places that offered shelter from solitude and depression. These places, of course, these cities, they did exist, and not only on the East coast of the United States. So why did Zweig after all leave the United States again? Why was he so depressed in New York that he felt he had to leave?

When he departed from Europe and wrote that "from now on everything will depend upon the New World," he may not have realized how true, but also how daring it was to articulate such a sentence! He definitely did not make this statement easily. In fact, it required a long process for him to arrive at a situation that made such a statement possible. Zweig was led to believe and he had hoped that the New World would turn out to be his anchor in case of an emergency. But this wish was not one that could be fulfilled!

Notes

[1] Quoted in Donald A. Prater, *Stefan Zweig: Eine Biographie* (Reinbek bei Hamburg: Rowohlt, 1991), 294.

[2] Ibid.

[3] Stefan Zweig to Ben Huebsch, June 8, 1939, in Stefan Zweig, *Briefe 1932–1942*, ed. Knut Beck and Jeffrey B. Berlin (Frankfurt am Main: Fischer, 2005), 248 (hereafter cited in text as *Briefe*). All translations, unless otherwise noted, are mine.

[4] Quoted in Prater, *Stefan Zweig*, 389.

[5] Stefan Zweig to Friderike Zweig, Berlin, December 10, 1926, in Stefan Zweig, *Briefe 1920–1931*, ed. Knut Beck and Jeffrey B. Berlin (Frankfurt am Main: Fischer, 2000), 174.

[6] Stefan Zweig, "Kleine Reise nach Brasilien," in *Begegnungen mit Menschen, Büchern, Städten* (Vienna: Herbert Reichner, 1937), 310 (hereafter cited in text as KRB).

[7] Quoted in Prater, *Stefan Zweig*, 293.

[8] Stefan Zweig, "Das Wien von gestern," in his *Zeit und Welt: Gesammelte Aufsätze und Vorträge*, ed. Richard Friedenthal (Stockholm: Bermann-Fischer, 1946), 130–31 (hereafter cited in text as "Wien von gestern").

12: The Writer's Political Obligations in Exile: The Case of Stefan Zweig

Jeffrey B. Berlin

> *Ganz begreiflich ist dein Wunsch nach einer Weltreise. Eine Mondreise wäre freilich noch vorzuziehen, weil man da ganz bestimmt keine Zeitungen und Radionachrichten bekäme...*[1]
>
> [Your wish to undertake a trip around the world is completely understandable. Of course a trip to the moon would be preferable, since there one definitely would not receive any newspapers or radio news reports.]
> —Stefan Zweig, unpublished letter of June 23, 1933, to Emil Jannings

I.

THE PURPOSE OF THIS ESSAY is to discuss Stefan Zweig's characterization of the zeitgeist in Europe in the 1930s and early 1940s, and especially the still controversial issue regarding whether or not he had an ethical and personal obligation to voice his opinions regarding political matters before and after he willingly became an émigré in Great Britain.[2] This context also prompts consideration of the socio-political and literary-historical position advanced during these turbulent times by other prominent Austrian and German intellectual émigrés,[3] including Hannah Arendt, Klaus Mann, Thomas Mann, Joseph Roth, Felix Salten, Ernst Toller, Arnold Zweig, and Ernst Weiss. What is most interesting about these and other German-speaking émigrés is their often differing attitudes toward the same set of circumstances. Nevertheless, they all denounced or rejected Zweig's professed reluctance to express his viewpoints publicly regarding the worsening situation in face of Hitler's rise to power and the dire situation caused by the outbreak of the Second World War.

The current investigation concerns equally important related matters: Zweig's thought and activities from 1933 to 1940, a period in which Zweig spent most of his time residing on British soil.[4] The positions and posture displayed by Great Britain's senior officials concerning political, social, and economic matters greatly affected him. The following discussion of several of the most salient incidents he witnessed and the manner in which he responded to them expands our understanding of the significance of Zweig's career.

The extent to which a writer—particularly an émigré writer—has a responsibility regarding political matters is open to question. What motivates one individual to assume a stance of active political involvement as opposed to one of partial or total silence? At the same time, is silence the equivalent of irresponsibility and apathy? Does silence have other inferences? Is passivity the same as counter-reality, and what voice is used to express passivity? Does the professional writer have the option to express a viewpoint—or an obligation and political duty to do so? What relationship exists between the émigré and the host country? Are the political obligations of a citizen and an émigré, who presently resides in the respective country, the same?

Also, on whose terms are such assessments to be made? Furthermore, are we to ignore Zweig's consistent declarations that he never wanted to become a political commentator? These and related considerations are central to the following inquiry. To develop and corroborate my argument, it is useful to draw on a variety of published and as yet unpublished primary source materials, especially Zweig's lectures, formal speeches, and essayistic writings of the 1930s and early 1940s, which shed light on his experiences in Britain.[5] Certainly, letters to and from him, as well as diaries and interviews, are pertinent.[6] His biographical writings during this period, such as *Joseph Fouché* (1929), *Erasmus* (1934), and *Castellio and Calvin* (1936) also deserve attention in this same framework.[7]

II.

Otto Zarek, one of the few friends with whom Zweig was close enough to use the familiar German "Du"-form (you/thou), stated that Zweig "was not a politically-minded thinker [and] often said [. . .] he loathed the 'political outlook,' refusing to accept the doctrine that even his apolitical approach to the human problem had a political meaning, by way of implication."[8] Zarek remarked: "It was in vain to try and convince him of the necessity to take sides in the struggle for European survival which [. . .] was the meaning of the war against Hitler" (185). Zweig had always explicitly stated that his position on humanitarianism, that is, his concern about human welfare or his ethic of kindness, benevolence and sympathy, extended universally and impartially to all human beings. To be sure, Zweig adhered to the doctrine that humane people and societies are concerned wholly with the welfare of the human race or human condition, and a state which remains peaceful retains superiority over one which relies on brute force. Zweig summed up his view in a reflective letter written to Romain Rolland on December 18, 1932. In his formulation, there is an ominous premonition regarding the fate of Europe and particularly the outlook for European Jews: "Für mich ist alles, was heutzutage politisch geschieht, der pure Irrsinn: ob man Hitler oder den Sozialisten wählt, es ändert nichts. Der Grund ist faul." (For me, all political events today are pure madness: whether the choice is Hitler or the socialists, that changes nothing. The basis is rotten.)[9]

Zweig's assessment was of course accurate. Unrest predominated, the vicious Nazi terror accelerated, and politics were becoming more corrupt, brutal, and demoralizing by the irrational frenzy caused by the assault of pseudo-legality brought on by Hitler. By March 9, 1933, the situation had deteriorated, as Zweig's comments on this date to Friderike indicate: "Der Panik der Intellectuellen ist recht groß, die Hetzartikel gegen die jüdischen Schriftsteller wiederholen sich jeden Tag mit neuer Heftigkeit, und angeblich geschieht mehr als in den Zeitungen steht." (There is really great panic among the intellectuals, provocatory articles against Jewish writers appear daily with new vigor. Evidently more is happening than what is reported in the newspapers.)[10]

As Zweig's letters substantiate, around February or March 1933 it was becoming increasingly difficult for him to ignore the enormous obstacles that faced him and others owing to the threatening political developments. Zweig usually responded to the news as if he were being threatened by boundless tempests of loneliness and hopelessness. The impact of these situations was at times ravaging, and Zweig experienced them in an emotional manner. His reactions, which were clear signs of a depressive temperament, now and again jolted him with such tremendous force that he was incapable of defending himself. The effects of some incidents also seemed more potent than others, so that eventually he resolved to end his life. This decision, which he later implemented, was criticized disapprovingly by some of the same individuals who for years had opposed and criticized his reluctance to take a public stance against National Socialism.

Study of Zweig's life and work reveals that he repeatedly declared his reluctance to engage in politically related issues. After his youthful enthusiasm at the outbreak of the First World War subsided—he had gotten caught up briefly in support of the war—he permanently altered his thinking, dedicating the balance of his life in support of pacifist causes.[11] Just as he remained a declared opponent of war and an advocate of international reconciliation, he was very much committed to humanitarian and humanistic principles. He expressed his abhorrence toward politics in a letter to Richard Strauss on September 3, 1933: "Der Politik seit je geekelt" (politics always disgusted me).[12] Or, as he claimed in a letter to Hermann Hesse, dated January 30, 1935, "Ich habe gelernt die Politik [...] das Wort an das Schlagwort verraten, das Dogma an seine

Übertreibung, redlich zu hassen als den Widerpol der Gerechtigkeit" (I have learned to hate [...] politics, which must exaggerate, betray words in favor of catchwords and carry dogmas to extremes; it is the opposite of justice).[13] He normally stood aloof from politics, and as he wrote in his autobiography, he did not even vote. Friderike Zweig observed succinctly that politics were her husband's "arch enemy."[14] In this regard, an unpublished diary notation, dated October 14, 1945, penned by Siegmund Warburg, with whom Zweig first became acquainted in 1923 and who may be counted as one of Zweig's trusted friends, provided a unique description about his complex individuality:

> Sein Idealismus bedeutete nicht den Glauben an irdischen Fortschritt, sondern die feste Überzeugung von der ewigen Macht irrationaler Kräfte und Werte, die unabhängig von äusseren Siegen oder Niederlagen ihren Ausdruck finden in guten Taten, in künstlerischen Schöpfungen, und vor allem in den Gestalten grosser und edler Menschen. Er war alles andere als ein Cyniker und doch hatte er einen kühl-skeptischen Realismus, wie man ihn selbst unter Cynikern selten findet [...] Das ging soweit, dass er oft fast absichtlich im Gegensatz zu dem, was er sich erwünschte, seine Prophezeiungen aussprach [...] Er fühlte mit Schrecken, dass wir durch eine über Generationen dauernde dunkle Übergangszeit gehen müssten, bis diese neuen Gebilde sich geformt haben würden. Seine Hoffnung war, dass nach einem langen Interregnum des Tumults und der Unordnung und inmitten der Planwirtschaft und der neuen Beamtenstaaten, die er herankommen sah, doch am Ende ein Raum für individualistische Lebenskultur sich ergeben würde, und dass dieser Individualismus der Zukunft zugleich nüchterner und härter sein würde als der Individualismus der Jahrhundertwende.
>
> [His idealism did not include faith in earthly progress, but a firm belief in the eternal power of irrational forces and values which find expression independently of apparent success or failure in accomplishing good deeds, in artistic creation, and above all in the personality full of greatness and nobility of certain human beings. He was anything but a cynic and yet he had a coldly skeptical realism that is rarely found, even among the most cynical people. [...] This often went so far that, almost intentionally, he would pronounce prophecies in contradiction to his own wishes [...] He had a dreadful presentiment that we should have to go through a dismal transition period, lasting several generations, before new concepts could be established. His hope was that after a long interregnum of turmoil and chaos, and in the midst of the planned management of new bureaucratic states which he saw dawning, a new cultural model of the individual would manage to emerge, and that this individualism would be at once more realistic and more unyielding than that of the end of the last century.][15]

Zweig's weltanschauung championed an affirmation of life and a variety of humanism in which the most value is ascribed to an individual's inner freedom and where individuals could exchange and express views without restrictions. The distinguished American literary critic Lionel Trilling commented that "[Zweig] identified himself with everything in the culture of his time that suggested freedom and democracy, traveling in many countries to seek it out, putting himself at its service as translator and publicist."[16]

Zweig understood that as a public and private figure he had certain responsibilities and societal obligations. Even though he was unable to reduce his absolute hatred toward all political matters, he never ignored the ramifications of the zeitgeist. Still, a number of his colleagues disagreed with his position whereby, for one, his opposition toward Nazism was articulated in his literary writings through the symbolic use of language.[17]

For a lengthy period literary language functioned as Zweig's basic means to oppose in public the ideology of the Third Reich. And as he repeatedly professed and symbolically showed in his literary works, language proper was his weapon. He explained this view well in a letter to Klaus Mann dated May 15, 1933, regarding the shared message found in his *Jeremias*[18] and *Erasmus*: "So wie ich im Kriege durch den *Jeremias* eine jedermann verständliche Stellung nahm, ohne aktuell zu polemisieren, so versuche ich auch hier [in *Erasmus*] durch ein Symbol vieles Heutige deutlich und verständlich zu machen" (Just as I took a stand in *Jeremias* which everyone could understand and which was not polemical, here too [in *Erasmus*], I attempt to make the contemporary situation clear and comprehensible by means of a symbol).[19] In this same letter, Zweig described the essential factors to which he adhered in his writing: "Das rein Aggressive liegt mir charaktermäßig nicht, weil ich an 'Siege' nicht glaube, aber in unserem stillen entschlossenen Beharren, in der künstlerischer Kundgabe liegt vielleicht die stärkere Kraft. Kämpfen können die andern auch, das haben sie bezeugt, so muß man sie auf dem andern Gebiet schlagen, wo sie inferior sind." (KM/SZ, 94; The purely aggressive does not match my character. I do not believe in "victories" but in our intended persistence, and the stronger force probably lies in the artistic pronouncement. As has been shown, others can also fight. But we must strike them in the other area where they are inferior.) Examples of this position are readily found throughout his works, and even in his early writings from the years preceding Hitler's rise to power. But as the zeitgeist changed, so too did Zweig's response to the new political situation, warranting an even more specific statement than the one he had made regarding the connection between his *Jeremias* and *Erasmus*.

The *Erasmus* biography represented an effort to fulfill what he agreed was the responsibility of all individuals to make one's viewpoint known. In December 1933, for example, Zweig told his American publisher

Ben Huebsch that *Erasmus* represented a "Programm für die humane Weltanschauung" (program for the humanistic view of the world), a "Kampfbuch gegen jede Art von Fanatismus" (battle manual against every kind of fanaticism), a "Traktat gegen den Parteigeist und den Fanatismus zur Rechten und zur Linken, den Fanatismus per se" (tract against [political] party spirit and fanaticism both of right and left, fanaticism as such), as well as the "Widerpart der Weltvernunft" (counterpart of world reason).[20] A similar message was conveyed to Richard Strauss on May 17, 1934, in which Zweig claimed that *Erasmus* represented "ein stiller Lobgesang an den antifanatischen Menschen, dem die künstlerische Leistung und der innere Friede das Wichtigste auf Erden ist" (*RS/SZ*, 63; *RS/SZ* Knight, 44; a quiet hymn to the anti-fanatical person who treasured more than anything on earth artistic accomplishment and inner peace). Especially important is the remark which Zweig appended to this letter: "ich habe mir damit die eigene Lebenshaltung in einem Symbol besiegelt" (in this work I have provided [affixed a seal to] a symbol of my own attitude to life).[21]

Zweig emphasized that he was not wavering in his commitment to peace and international understanding. His response to National Socialism was consistent with his life-long position, namely, the striving for understanding between individuals and nations by means of non-violence. Physical confrontation contradicted his principles, and in virtually every feasible manner he remained fundamentally a non-political person—a fact that throughout his lifetime and by a variety of approaches he never attempted to deny. But, in any case, the claim that Zweig was silent about contemporary events and particularly about political matters relating to National Socialism is an inaccurate observation.

Sometimes, Zweig's ostensible response of silence did not imply that one should evade responsibility when confronted with situations that required a reaction. As he remarked in his letter to Rolland on November 11, 1933: "Ich sage nicht, daß der Künstler schweigen muß. Aber er darf im Kampf auch nicht unter sein Niveau herabsinken." (*RR/SZ*, 2:543; I do not say that the artist must be silent. However, in a conflict he is also not permitted to sink beneath his level.) In this same context, in a letter dated November 30, 1933, he wrote Rudolf Kayser that he "count[ed] as a traitor to the exiles."[22]

Zweig defended his symbolic style and his use of analogies between history and literature as a response to contemporary affairs in a letter to Rolland, dated April 26, 1933: "wer zu lesen versteht" (readers will discover), as Zweig remarked, that "die Geschichte unserer Tage" (the history [or current events] of our times) is found in "der Analogie" (the analogy) (*RR/SZ*, 2:510–11). In this same letter he elaborated that the only alternative to this type of writing was emigration: "Uns bleibt kein anderes Mittel mehr, uns vernehmlich zu machen, als durch das Symbol—oder zu emigrieren" (no other means to make ourselves clear is available to us anymore, except the use of the symbol—or [of course] to emigrate). The moralist Zweig remained an exemplary representative of an individual who, through the symbols developed in his literary writing, advanced doctrines of peace and humanitarianism. He was convinced that by writing in this manner he was responding to life issues, which also meant that that he was fulfilling his societal obligations. Zweig intended to be—and he sometimes characterized himself as—a moral leader.

III.

In the early 1930s Stefan Zweig's approach was viewed negatively by some of his contemporaries. Nevertheless, Zweig continued to believe that physical combat and/or polemical statements intended to provoke others were not an effective means of persuasion. Despite sustained criticism, Zweig continued to reason that his symbolic literary works conveyed an obvious message, which promoted democratic principles and humanistic thought. An example of this issue is Zweig's refusal to support Klaus Mann's bi-weekly, *Die Sammlung* (The Collection), which was scheduled to appear in early September, 1933. Shortly after Zweig informed Klaus Mann that he could not lend his name to support the project, which was political and anti-fascist in nature, Klaus Mann responded with an expected degree of frustration and disappointment. On September 15, 1933, Klaus Mann stated that the only conclusions he and other émigrés could draw from Zweig's decision to withdraw his name from those supporting *Die Sammlung* was that "Sie [Zweig] rücken ab [...] um Goebbels nicht zu kränken" (KM/SZ, 135; you [Zweig] are doing everything possible to avoid offending Goebbels). However, Zweig was not the only one to withdraw his name and disassociate himself from this publication. Wholly self-assured that his decision had been correct, Zweig retorted to Klaus Mann that it was not his nature to debate certain issues in public and especially those with any political orientation: "Ich bin keine polemische Natur [...] ich habe mein ganzes Leben immer nur für Dinge und für Menschen geschrieben und nie gegen eine Rasse, eine Klasse, eine Nation oder einen Menschen." (*Briefe*, 4:66; I am not a polemical person. All my life I have always written only for things and for people and never against a race, a class, a nation, or a human being.) Furthermore, the unfriendly interaction concerning *Die Sammlung* did not end with the exchange of words between Stefan Zweig and Klaus Mann.

The resulting quandary led many observers to conclude that Zweig's position was a result of his superciliousness, disloyalty, and an abandonment of his fellow exiles. Zweig was convinced that those who viewed his actions negatively most likely misunderstood his principles. Nevertheless, as his opponents repeatedly announced, Zweig's argument regarding the symbolic meanings presented in his literary writings could never function as a substitute for a public denunciation of National Socialism. The critique of Zweig in wake of the affair surrounding *Die Sammlung* was vicious and unexpected, since almost all those who vociferously rejected his standpoint had been regarded by Zweig as levelheaded, considerate, courteous, and, above all, as appreciated colleagues and supposedly supportive friends.

IV.

The issue of Zweig's reluctance to become involved in contemporary political affairs in an active and public manner in face of the rise of Nazism has continued to interest many critics. Joseph Leftwich, who also may be counted as one of Zweig's closest personal friends, contended that "it was part of Zweig's misfortune that people had acquired the habit of attributing his shrinking withdrawal from anything strident and assertive to personal cowardice."[23] One must ask whether the perception of his reluctance to express his stance against National Socialism in public has exerted a negative impact on judgments of the quality of his writings. Of course Zweig's works were regularly praised in many quarters for their literary excellence. Berthold Viertel, for one, claimed that Zweig was the first writer in Europe to represent "eine[r] Art geistiger Institution" (a kind of spiritual institution).[24] Despite Viertel's accolade and others' praises, Klemens Renoldner explains that

> the rejection of both Stefan Zweig the man and his work has a long history, his contemporaries took to mocking him [. . .] even [. . .] close friends [. . .] contributed to the chronology of Zweig's marginalization. Much of the criticism was borne of the disappointment that Stefan Zweig did not pull his own weight in the anti-fascist effort against National Socialism, attempting instead to survive between and even beyond fronts.[25]

Vivian Liska has argued that "in explaining his reluctance to take political action Zweig consistently invoked values deriving from his liberal humanist creed: freedom, dignity, and a universalist ethos that prevented him from joining warring parties or taking sides for what he perceived to be particularist causes."[26] She maintains: "Even where he argued against the participation of Jews in the public world for their own benefit, his reasons were linked to humanist universals. The preservation of the integrity of a purely spiritual existence among the Jews of his time would, he believed, serve humanity better than their political struggle."[27]

There were those who argued that Zweig remained aloof from politics so that he could safeguard his personal dignity or, as the writer Arnold Zweig (no relation to Stefan) expressed it in a letter to Sigmund Freud, dated September 23, 1934: "[Er] möchte ein Herr über den Parteien sein" (He wishes to be the impartial judge above the parties).[28] Despite all the criticism voiced against him, Zweig's "politically tinged" essays and speeches unequivocally expose the erroneousness of his critics' arguments. They unquestionably refute the claim that silence, which these critics associate with non-action, represented his political watchword.

V.

Before the year 1932 and Hitler's subsequent appointment as chancellor of the Third Reich, Zweig rarely addressed public forums or penned articles and especially shied away from formulating any remarks about the evil of National Socialism. With few exceptions, Zweig declined, when approached, and in most of these instances Zweig refused to engage in any discussion or debate. Almost all requests that urged him to support a political position of one kind or another received the same response; that is, he reiterated his long held position, as he wrote to Klaus Mann on September 11, 1933: "Habe ich beschlossen, nirgendwo mitzuarbeiten, ehe wir nicht alle zu einer endgültigen und einheitlichen Haltung gekommen sind" (KM/SZ, 131; I have decided without exception not to join in unless we have all come to a final and unified position [against Nazism]).

Although his earlier reluctance to become involved had been largely accepted without any major consequences, except perhaps some disappointment, the frequency with which individuals and/or political associations who desired Zweig's support turned to him increased during and after the early months of 1932. Suddenly, Zweig's refusals became especially noticeable to his adversaries. In fact, his unwillingness to participate or join individuals or groups which opposed National Socialism became one of the most frequently cited topics exploited by contemporaries who criticized him.

VI.

Only a few months before January 30, 1933—the date Adolf Hitler was appointed chancellor of Germany—Zweig's lecture, "Die moralische Entgiftung Europas" (The Moral Decontamination of Europe), was presented *in absentia* at the European Volta Congress of the Reale Accademia in Rome.[29] The talk expressed the need for a new concept of history and discussed ways to reduce hatred, political tensions, and collective animosities among peoples and nations. Zweig proposed that the history of culture and of the human spirit, rather than military or political history, be taught in the schools of the world. He also warned about the expression of even a single word which might intensify mistrust between nations, emphasizing that only the intensification of spiritual concerns would permit the deepening of understanding and appreciation for human life.

Zweig's formulations in "Die moralische Entgiftung Europas" constitute a moral stance and also exemplify the good which he desired for humanity. His great dream always had been "die geistige Einigung Europas" (the intellectual union of Europe), as he expressed it in his autobiography (*WvG* 373; *WoY* 351). The progressive and noble thoughts delineated in his lecture are of course Erasmian in nature. They also overtly reveal his highly idealistic perspective. To Zweig's misfortune this idealism became another area which generated much friction between him and some of his contemporaries.

VII.

By spring of 1933 the outlook for peace and tranquility appeared even more dismal, but Zweig was uncertain about becoming an émigré. As he wrote to his friend Frans Masereel on April 4, 1933: "Ich habe die stärkste Abneigung, Emigrant zu werden und würde das nur im äußersten Notfall tun, denn ich weiß, da alles Emigrantentum gefährlich ist, man macht dadurch die Zurückgebliebenen zu Geiseln und erschwert ihnen das Leben." (I have the strongest disinclination to become an emigrant. And I would only do it in an extreme emergency, because I know that existence as an emigrant is dangerous. One takes those who remain behind as hostages and makes their life difficult.)[30] He brought up the issue of exile in letters to several of his friends, mentioning in a letter to Rolland, dated April 10, 1933 a "momentous decision" which awaited him: "Bleiben heißt: leiden. Bedroht sein. Zum Schweigen gezwungen sein. Leben wie ein Gefangener. Fortgehen heißt: die andern im Stich lassen, die nicht vermöge ihrer Arbeit die Chance materieller Unabhängigkeit haben." (*RR/SZ*, 2:506; To stay means suffering. Being threatened. Condemned to silence. Living like a prisoner. To go means abandoning the others whose work does not give them the chance of material independence.)

Tragically, even after Hitler's appointment as German Chancellor not everyone perceived the magnitude of National Socialism's ever increasingly vile practices. Even though Zweig could not possibly comprehend the depths of bestiality to which Nazism would eventually sink, he was nevertheless cognizant that a mysterious threat was poisoning the zeitgeist. Zweig seems to have sensed at this early date that the fate of Austria, and his own fate as a resident in Salzburg, had already been decided.

By mid-1933 Zweig felt the need to emigrate from Austria. Continued residence in Salzburg, where he had lived for fourteen years, no longer seemed desirable. Proximity to the German border and to the ugly political developments in Nazi Germany seemed to have played a role in his decision-making. Not only was his Salzburg home very close to the border,[31] but from it he claimed he could see the mountain where Adolf Hitler's own Berchtesgaden house stood. Thus, as Zweig wrote in his memoirs, Salzburg represented "eine wenig erfreuliche und sehr beunruhigende Nachbarschaft" (*WvG* 429; an unedifying and extremely disturbing [situation in] the neighborhood, *WoY* 402). What was perhaps worse was that living in Salzburg made him feel as if he were living in enemy territory. As he wrote to Rolland on June 26, 1933, he could tolerate "ideologischen Haß, den Haß in geschriebenen Attacken" (ideological hatred and hatred expressed in written attacks), but he found it unbearable to suffer hatred in the eyes of those he encountered daily: "in den lebendigen Augen der Passanten den unterdrückten Haß [. . .] desto böser, je mehr man ihn unterdrückt" (*RR/SZ*, 2:522, suppressed hatred in the living eyes of passers-by [. . .] the more wicked, the more it is suppressed).

For months he vacillated about permanently leaving his Salzburg home, and in this connection he pondered the fate of his library and collection of manuscripts and other collector's items he had amassed over the years. As he wrote to Rolland: "Bücher, Sammlungen [. . .] ich habe für immer die Freude am Besitz und am Stolz darauf verloren. Freiheit, Freiheit vor allem, festen Mut und meine Arbeit—mehr verlange ich nicht!!" (*RR/SZ*, 2:522; My books, my collections [. . .] I've lost forever my joy in their possession and my pride in them. Freedom, freedom above all, courage and my work—I don't ask for more!!) In this letter to his friend, Zweig recorded the difficult process of making a final decision: "Jetzt ist es vorbei [. . .] Das Kapitän muß das sinkende Schiff als letzter verlassen. Aber dieser Schimpf der stupiden Politiker, diese moralische Ohrfeige macht meine Entscheidung legitim. Im Grunde bin ich froh über diese Brüskierung. Sie hat mir geholfen." (*RR/SZ*, 2:522; Now it is over [. . .] like a captain who is the last to leave his ship. But this rebuke by stupid politicians, this moral slap in the face makes my decision legitimate. I am basically happy about this snub. It helped me.) After the search of his home in April 1934 his reflections seemed to become more extreme. In a letter to Thomas Mann dated April 18, 1934, he wrote: "Es ist gleichgütig, ob man schweigt oder nicht schweigt, etwas tut oder nicht tut—so wie man bei Hausdurchsuchungen heute friedlichen Menschen Revolver in die Laden tut oder kommunistische Papiere, so legt man uns Worte und Meinungen unter, die wir nie geäußert haben."[32] (It's all the same, whether one keeps silent or speaks out, acts or fails to act. Just as in house searches today peaceable people have revolvers planted in the drawer or communist papers, so we have words and opinions attributed to us which we have never uttered.)

VIII.

With physical and emotional safety as guiding principles, he voluntarily and happily set foot on British soil on October 20, 1933, where he remained until 1941.[33] Zweig initially told his colleagues that his British sojourn related solely to library research. He explained that a quiet place was required for his current biographical project, and the British Museum represented a perfect choice since it contained all of the necessary reference materials. Zweig may have been convinced that if he explained that he actually went to Great Britain in order to insure his future security, his adversaries might cite this move as another example of his fleeing danger and abandoning his colleagues.

As might be expected, the public burning of books written by Jewish authors also had a tremendous impact on Zweig. Yet the deep despair he suffered stemmed less from anger toward Hitler and Goebbels, who had not prohibited the book-burnings in any way, than from other factors, which are enumerated in a letter to Leftwich dated June 6, 1933: "Nach London komme ich jetzt nicht und halte es auch nicht für gut, wenn einer von den deutschen 'verbrannten' Schriftstellern hinkäme, mir widerstrebt es innerlich, als 'Märtyrer' gefeiert zu werden, der ich menschlich gar nicht bin."[34] (I am not coming to London at this time and do not find it good that any of the German writers whose works have been burned should go there. I have an inner revulsion against being celebrated as a "martyr," which from a human point of view I certainly am not.) As this letter to Leftwich suggests, his apprehension was mostly rooted in concerns very different from those which troubled other individuals. In actuality, Zweig felt that coming at this point to live in London would militate in favor of his being viewed by others as a hero and martyr, which he denied. Above all, he did not want to be the recipient of sympathy. He was uncertain whether or not publicity could be avoided in exile. Would the British and foreign press vigorously attempt to coerce him to discuss his views for their own political purposes? Would the impact of the Nazis in Salzburg have to be explained? Would he be asked to state his position about implications of the book-burnings, not only as they impacted him but also in terms of the manner in which other Jewish writers were responding to the situation?

Zweig lamented that the recent developments in Nazi Germany attracted much more attention abroad than he or anyone else had expected. In this regard, he wrote to Franz Servaes on May 11, 1933: "Ich hätte gern auf diese Reklame verzichtet. Sie wissen, ich bin ein Mensch, dem nichts über die Stille geht."³⁵ (I would gladly have done without this publicity. You know that I am a man who prizes nothing more highly than peace and quiet.) Rather than react publicly, Zweig preferred to wait and remain silent. Even so, many in the émigré community disapproved of his position. Similarly, Zweig was denounced by many for refusing to sever relations with his German publisher for as long as possible.

IX.

Immediately upon his arrival in London in October 1933, Zweig asked Joseph Leftwich to circulate a release to the local newspapers. In it he denied statements that had appeared in the émigré press, which had decried him for refusing "to associate himself with protests against the actions of the Hitlerian regime."³⁶ Zweig told Leftwich that "nothing was further from his mind than the thought of shutting himself out from the common fate of his comrades and brethren-in-blood; and he would despise any attempt on his part to surrender his moral independence in return for any advantages whatsoever. He declared openly and unambiguously that the fate of his brethren-in-blood was obviously a thousand times more important to him than all literature" (93). In fact, years later, in an interview with Robert van Geldner, he said something quite similar: "[Today the mission of the artist] is to feel with the greatest intensity the fate and suffering of his fellow beings."³⁷

Zweig consistently argued that given the political reality, public attention was not advantageous to the Jewish cause: "Speziell für uns deutschschreibende Autoren ist es meiner Meinung nach jetzt nicht tunlich, persönlich oder polemisch hervorzutreten, denn die in Deutschland zurückgebliebenen Juden stellen gewissermassen Geiseln dar, und jede Unternehmung unsererseits, die wir noch frei sind, würde an diesen Wehrlosen gerächt werden."³⁸ (Especially for we [Jewish] writers who write in German, I think it unsuitable [. . .] to come forward in person or in polemical [statements]: for the Jews who have remained behind in Germany represent to some extent hostages [. . .] and every action of ours [. . .] would be avenged on these defenseless people.) However, Zweig's opponents assumed that his pronouncements meant that everyone should avoid speaking about the current situation. Leftwich clarified that Zweig was not was implying that individuals who openly spoke out against the Nazi government were not aiding individuals who were still within the range of Hitler's reach, but rather that such opposition endangered them. Zweig's position was *not* that Jews should refrain from voicing their opinion, but the means by which they articulated their stance needed careful consideration and forethought about its possible implications. As he told Leftwich, it was essential that Jewish opinions regarding the situation in Germany be made public. But he also asserted in this letter that the Jews should not be the only individuals who verbalized their anti-National Socialist position; non-Jews needed to express these views as well: "Wenn nur wir Juden die Aufrufe, die Proteste unterschreiben, schaden wir der gemeinsamen Sache" (If we Jews are the only ones to sign the manifestos and protests that will harm the common cause). In this same letter to Leftwich, Zweig stated that Jews should fight "in der zweiten, der fünften, der zehnten Reihe, und nie an der vordersten, der sichtbarsten Stelle" (in the second or the fifth or the tenth rank, not always on the front line, the most visible place), if they are to have a better chance of victory.

Significantly, the position to which Zweig had long subscribed was the equivalent of that espoused by *The Jewish Chronicle*: "[. . .] the paper responded cautiously once Hitler was made Chancellor. [. . .] They counseled that British Jews should do nothing without consulting German Jews. . . ."[39] Accordingly, Zweig was not only acting in a politically responsible manner, but also his position was in agreement with some of the leading thinkers in Great Britain.

As time passed though, Zweig's concerns and understanding of the situation also altered. Soon he contended that all writers have a duty to take a public stance against Nazism. Zweig finally had realized that the symbolic language woven into the fabric of his literary writings could no longer have the necessary effect and would certainly not function as adequate protection against Hitler. Zweig began to comment on the current situation and now and again he presented lectures which focused on pressing political issues. After his arrival in Great Britain, he also attempted to initiate related Jewish-oriented projects and literary publications.

First of all, his "Jewish Monthly" magazine project was intended to become a "repository of all the best creative work by Jews in all languages."[40] In this connection, Leftwich recalled that Zweig "had no liking for controversies and polemics and [. . .] believed that positive Jewish creative achievement would be the most dignified and [. . .] in the long run, the most valuable reply Jews could make to anti-Semitic calumnies" (95). Another project was entitled "The Joint Manifesto" and represented Zweig's intent to circulate a manifesto which would be a symbolic expression of the zeitgeist in which the Jews lived.

As with his literary writings, Zweig never intended the manifesto to have a functional purpose. As he explained in his letter dated November 16, 1938, to Rolland: "wohl wissend, daß es nichts im wirklichen Leben ändern, aber bleiben würde als ein Dokument" (*RR/SZ*, 2:692; knowing well that it would change nothing in real life, but it would last as a document). As he explained in a letter to Albert Einstein on June 7, 1933, a manifesto would explicitly present the attitude of the artists and writers who had been thrown out of Germany. Zweig envisioned its tone as follows: "das nicht wehleidig jammert und klagt" but as "durchaus positiv, selbstbewußt und dabei mit äußerster Ruhe unsere Situation vor der Welt klarlegt" (a manifesto that would not be full of sniveling moans and complaints, [but] thoroughly positive, self-confident and with utmost calm present clearly our situation to the world).[41]

Zweig wanted the Joint Manifesto to be "ein klassisches und dauerndes Stück deutscher Prosa, als bleibenendes kulturhistorisches Dokument" (a classic and lasting piece of German prose, as a permanent cultural and historical document).[42] However, from the start the project was doomed to failure. As he wrote to Rolland on November 16, 1938: "Ich habe zwei Jahre lang versucht, die besten zusammenzuführen, um ein Manifest herauszubringen [. . .] Aber niemand hatte Zeit, niemand antwortete" (*RR/SZ*, 2:692; I have been trying for two years to get the best people together in order to bring out a manifesto [. . .] But no one had the time, no one replied). Unfortunately, this was not the last occasion when colleagues rejected Zweig's proposed response to the Nazi brutalities.

Zweig experienced the same rejection when he attempted to organize a one-day meeting in Switzerland in order to support writers who had either been expelled from Germany or whose works had recently been burned. He envisaged that the gathering would serve to make it possible for colleagues to discuss their moral obligations regarding the ideological dogmas that threatened them and also to frame a unified response which would unambiguously signal their solidarity and mutual agreement. Despite Zweig's good intentions, all of the individuals whom he had contacted in this regard, including Gerhart Hauptmann and Richard Strauss, either presented different excuses or did not respond at all. Just as many individuals voiced their criticism that Zweig remained silent and was unresponsive to the call of his fellow émigrés. Zweig wrote to Rolland on June 26, 1933 in face of his failure to mobilize his colleagues as follows: "Das Schweigen des geistigen Deutschlands wird historisch bleiben" (*RR/SZ*, 2:522; The silence of intellectual Germany will remain historic).

A remarkable historical document, which pertains to this context, has recently been discovered: a letter that was sent to Zweig from the Amsterdam-based editorial office of *Die Jüdische Stimme. Weltblatt für das Judentum*. (The Jewish Voice. International Paper for Jewry). This document, dated August 29, 1938, may be found at the Stefan Zweig Archive in Fredonia, New York. A two-page, typewritten letter on stationery with the identification *JUDÄA-VERLAG*, it includes at the head of the letter the notation *VERTRAULICH* (confidential). It is addressed to Zweig from the Advocaat-Procureur Mr. D. L. Staal, whose title was head of the editorial department of *Die Jüdische Stimme*. The full text of this document reads as follows:

JUDÄA-VERLAG AMSTERDAM, 29 August 1938
KOMMANDITGS. AUF AKTIEN JAC. OBRECHTSTRAAT 78
FERNSPR. 29044
DIE JÜDISCHE STIMME
WELTBLATT FÜR DAS JUDENTUM Herrn Stephan Zweig.

ABT. Redaktion

VERTRAULICH
Sehr geehrter Herr,

Der Judäa-Verlag zu Amsterdam beabsichtigt binnen kurzem die Herausgabe einer Jüdischen Wochenzeitung in Deutscher Sprache unter dem Namen "Die Jüdische Stimme" und erbittet hierdurch Ihre Zusage zur Mitarbeit.

Dieses Blatt soll in Amsterdam erscheinen und ein Weltblatt für das deutschsprechende Judentum darstellen. Es hofft einen Leserkreis unter denjenigen Menschen zu finden, die Wert darauf legen, ein auf kulturell hoher Stufe stehendes, von keiner politischen Richtung abhängiges Blatt zu lesen, das sie über die jüdischen Angelegenheiten informiert.

Ein solches Blatt ist deshalb dringend notwendig, weil die meisten jüdischen deutschsprachlichen Zeitungen in Deutschland erscheinen, also sowohl hinsichtlich ihrer Berichterstattung als auch hinsichtlich der Personen ihrer Mitarbeiter nicht unabhängig sind.

Unser Blatt soll in der Kritik frei sein, es soll weder einer Partei, noch einer Gruppe, noch privaten Personen dienen. Es wird sich an keiner Hetze beteiligen, sich keinen politischen Vorurteilen unterwerfen, sondern sich nur leiten lassen von dem, was nach seiner Ansicht im Interesse des Judentums liegt.

In religiöser Hinsicht will es neutral sein, ohne den Wert der Religion zu verkennen, da wir der Ansicht sind, dass Einigung und Zusammenfassung für die Existenz des Judentums eine absolute Notwendigkeit sind.

Wir wollen also für das deutschsprechende Judentum ein Blatt schaffen, worin es unparteiische Aufklärung in politischen und wirtschaftlichen Fragen, soweit sie die Interessen des Judentums berühren, finden kann und worin wir auf literarischem und künstlerischem Gebiete die bedeutendsten jüdischen Autoren sprechen lassen werden, so dass wir diesen Schriftstellern Gelegenheit geben können, regelmässig ihre Fähigkeiten in den Dienst des Judentums zu stellen.

"Die Jüdische Stimme" soll deshalb das notwendige Band zwischen den nach allen Richtungen zerstreuten deutschsprechenden Juden bilden, eine Tribüne für diese grosse Gruppe sein und so ihre Kraft verstärken.

In der Erwartung, dass auch Sie die Richtigkeit und Notwendigkeit dieses Blattes anerkennen, bitten wir Sie, uns Ihre Zustimmung zu unserem Vorhaben und Ihre Zusage als Mitarbeiter zukommen zu lassen.

Hochachtungsvoll,
JUDÄA–VERLAG
Geschäftsf.

Mr. D.L. STAAL
Advocaat–Procureur.

Although Zweig was not pleased with the critical positions advanced by his adversaries, he never permitted their displeasure to interfere with his commitments, and he continued to support his fellow refugees in numerous ways. He regularly provided moral, financial, or other forms of support to needy individuals. Also, he mentioned some of these activities in lectures and essays. However, it must be said that the level or intensity of Zweig's activities was less than those of, for example, Thomas Mann during the same period.

X.

As several letters to Rolland and others reveal, Zweig's attitude toward Great Britain, which had been overwhelmingly positive, changed dramatically at a certain point. The intense tone of Zweig's letter to Rolland dated August 14, 1934, reveals that he had become quite disturbed by British pacifism, as well as the British notion that nothing must disrupt the general peace. Zweig tended to interpret British reserve and coolness, which he found to be in marked contrast to the warmth and cordiality of his colleagues in the rest of Europe, as simply a desire to live in peace. It was connected to a British compulsion to exhibit a "kontinuierlichen Optimismus" (eternal optimism). Unpleasant matters in Britain, as Zweig reported to Rolland, were spoken of only unwillingly.

As time passed, Zweig's frustration with Great Britain became more pronounced. He was certainly bothered by the various restrictions placed upon exiles. In a letter to Rolland dated May 4, 1936, he connected his status as a guest in exile with his reluctance to speak out in public. At the same time, he explained that the present circumstances made it exceptionally difficult for him to remain silent "angesichts der politischen Dummheit und der abscheulichen Heuchelei" (in face of the political stupidity and horrifying hypocrisy). Zweig lamented the fact that the British did not want to see or speak the truth: "Es quält einen hier, daß man schweigen muß, und erst nach Jahren—denn man braucht Jahre, um tiefer zu blicken—merkt man, wie die unabhängigen unter den

Zeitungen im freien England mundtot gemacht sind durch unsichtbare Zäume" (*RR/SZ*, 2:628; It is tormenting to have to remain silent, and only after years—for one needs years to see more deeply—does one notice how in free England the independent newspapers have been silenced by invisible constraints).

Zweig appears here desirous to speak out and to express his opinion, but he believes it would be wrong to do so, since he was a guest in the country. In an undated letter to Rolland, written perhaps on May 1, 1937, Zweig assessed British behavior, concluding that although the British did not seem to acknowledge the great danger which Europe faced, at least they finally were beginning to realize the possibility of their eventually losing Gibraltar or the Suez Canal. According to Zweig, political egotism and power relations, but not moral sensitivity, dictated British responses: "Es ist die Gewalt, die zur Zeit die Völker berauscht. Sie sind verseucht von diesem Gift, und wir mit unseren humanistischen und humanitären Ideen erscheinen als Überbleibsel einer überholten Epoche" (*RR/SZ*, 2:652; It is power which intoxicates the nations today. They are infected with this poison, and we with our humanistic and humanitarian ideas seem like remnants of an outdated epoch).

Zweig's sense of liberty continued to become ever more frustrated by legal restrictions already in place for aliens. Even though most of these restrictions were reasonable in general, they still worked to prevent him from voicing a political opinion.[43] For example, Zweig wrote in an undated letter to Leftwich: "Here [in Great Britain] I considered myself a guest [. . .] if I were to point out the world danger which Hitler represented, it would be considered a personal, prejudiced opinion."[44] While Zweig felt that his specific exilic circumstances necessitated that he withdraw from discussions and restrict public utterances, Leftwich explained nevertheless that "[Zweig] wanted to help towards the destruction of Hitler. But he felt that his help was not wanted. He saw himself inactive and useless. Worse than that, he feared that he was regarded in spite of everything as a fellow-countryman of Hitler's, and in a way suspect because of it. This is how he interpreted the alien regulations which restricted his movements. He felt humiliated and insulted by them."[45]

However, the question remains: if, as Leftwich stated, Zweig wanted to assist in Hitler's downfall, how did his decision not to present his opinion in an essayistic form contribute toward that goal?

XI.

A complicating factor in this discussion is the collaboration between Zweig and Richard Strauss on *Die schweigsame Frau*. After the death of Hugo von Hofmannsthal, Strauss invited Zweig to be his librettist. When Zweig accepted, he ran the risk of being labeled a collaborator, since Strauss had been recently named president of the Nazi "Reichsmusikkammer." He maintained personal contacts with figures in the uppermost echelons of the Nazi regime, including Hitler and Goebbels. While Zweig may have felt that his artistic cooperation with Strauss was above politics and contemporary concerns, his critics considered the *Schweigsame Frau* (Silent Woman) project with Strauss collaboration with the enemy, and as such, another example of Zweig's abandonment of the fight against Nazism.

Despite Zweig's material situation with its many comforts, escape from the oppression in Europe was not possible for him. He wrote to Joseph Roth: "Mein politischer Pessimismus ist maßlos. Ich glaube an den nahen Krieg wie andere an Gott." (My political pessimism is beyond measuring. I believe in the coming war as others believe in God.)[46] Often melancholia discouraged him, though. As he also wrote to Joseph Roth, solace was found in supporting the less fortunate: "Think how happy I am, that in such a time of madness, I feel myself strong enough to lend moral strength to others."

By 1937, Zweig was beginning to see himself and his position as fading into the past. He was taken aback by George Bernard Shaw's critique of democracy in a play he saw in England: *On the Rocks*. This play was rather well received in England, although Zweig expressed serious doubts about it privately. (William L. Shirer has pointed out that as Zweig must have known, "some of Shaw's plays were [. . .] performed in Nazi Germany—perhaps because he poked fun at Englishmen and lampooned democracy and perhaps too because his wit and left-wing political views escaped the Nazi mind."[47]) On December 3, 1933, Zweig's decidedly enthusiastic review of this play appeared in the *Neue Freie Presse* under the title "Die neue Komödie Bernhard Shaws: *On the Rocks—A Political Fantasy in Two Acts*, Winter Garden Theatre." The play portrays the crumbling foundations of a capitalist society; however, the situation in Britain, as it is presented in *On the Rocks*, appears to be dire, given the prospect of revolution which is more threatening than ever. While Shaw attacked the political system, focusing on cabinet meetings and confrontations between the working people and the prime minister, his drama concluded almost with a warning. In the end, Zweig found the theme troublesome, especially the implications of the final line: "Suppose England really did arise!"

XII.

One of the earliest lectures that Zweig presented in Great Britain was entitled "The Jewish Children in Germany." Delivered on November 30, 1933, at the London home of Mrs. Anthony de Rothschild and again on December 20, 1933, at the Savoy Hotel in London, his remarks emphasized that "the children [. . .] must have all our care [. . .] Our [. . .] duty [is to make sure] that the new Jewish generation rises superior to the present in strength and ethical feeling [and that it does] not grow up hating people of vengeance, but rather be [. . .] a people of understanding, carrying out further our historic mission [as] the mediator between all nations, the warrior against all war and all hatred." Zweig was speaking directly to the future of Judaism here. In this context, it is interesting to note that the topics of his South American and United States lecture tours in 1936 and 1938 focused almost exclusively on literary matters. Yet, in Great Britain he hardly ever addressed literary topics and frequently discussed topics concerning the persecuted Jews. For example, in 1934 when the Vilna Yiddish Theatre performed in London, Zweig was one of the keynote speakers at the reception for theater members (held at the Whitechapel Art Gallery). He spoke about the manner in which he believed Jews should respond to opposition: "If [. . .] Jewry has been able through thousands of years to resist oppression and attack, it is because even in time of danger Jews gave the best they could. Nothing would be gained by returning hatred for hate. The Jewish way must be to go on creating positive Jewish values to enrich Jewish life and the world."[48]

A few months later, Zweig had a talk of his read at a symposium supported by the London Yiddish periodical *Dos Yiddishe Vort*. Its title was "Whither Jewry?" Even though Zweig had willingly spoken at similar gatherings, on this occasion he did not wish to appear on the platform, and Joseph Leftwich delivered his talk for him. Writing in the first-person plural, as a Jew himself together with other Jews, Zweig noted that at the present time Jews were confronted with a serious crisis that "has shaken us to our depths, and especially because the Jews never have been so weak as now. We no longer have the great spiritual strength of our ancestors [who] [. . .] were prepared to live and die [. . .] We went to the stake to bear witness to the One God. The only way of fighting the new hatred is from within. Not by external measures, not by trying to find a way of escape [. . .] but by finding the road back to ourselves. No one will find this road who seeks comfort and convenience [. . .] We must drive ourselves beyond ourselves by trial and ordeal."[49] Zweig's lecture advanced a positive, proactive attitude, which suggests significant ideological evolution on his part. In earlier days, flight—whether to another country or into the act of creative writing—almost always had functioned as his defense mechanism whenever he desired avoiding difficult circumstances. While "Whither Jewry?" preaches that escape is not the proper road to take, Zweig's opponents argued all too often that he retreated to his old habits and fled from undesirable situations. In fact, there is some truth in their criticisms because Zweig did tend to avoid difficult situations, particularly ugly political ones.

Zweig was acutely aware of the political situation and the struggles of his fellow Jews, but he fervently held to his humanist ideals. This is shown well in his "Eine Anrede" (An Address, 1936) which stated that Jews should not respond violently to the persecution they faced.[50] Also, in a thirty-six line typewritten and still unpublished commentary found among Zweig's London archival papers and entitled "Aufruf für die österreichischen Juden" (Appeal for the Austrian Jews), he wrote in the wake of the "Anschluss" in 1938 that if the Jews wished to save their honor, they must show solidarity with the refugees, which meant self-sacrificing help and active preparedness: "The enormous problem which we face is how to transport to another country the hundred thousand people whose lives have been disrupted. Reflection must now take the form of action. Money must be collected to support the transfer of these Austrians. It remains our responsibility to call upon everyone to make sacrifices."[51] Whereas Zweig discouraged Jews from being the primary speakers on this issue, he urged them to make sacrifices and to take action to support this vital cause.

Zweig reformulated this position in an essay written in 1938, "Keep Out of Politics." Written in English, the essay begins by acknowledging that at this point in time, Jews were finding themselves "in one of the most difficult periods of history."[52] Zweig appealed for "the exertion of all our powers (that of the Jewish people) to overcome this difficult phase of existence by moral means." He argued that in various countries Jews have too often been at the forefront of political debates. Such situations, Zweig claimed, make "the Jewish leader of a party [. . .] an irresistible target," which, in turn, "imperils the cause they desire to promote." Accordingly, Jewish leaders become "a danger to that party in the state to which they belong, and [additionally] [. . .] are a danger to the Jews, on whom they impose a burden of responsibility for their actions which they have no wish to bear."

XIII.

There are conflicting reports regarding the extent to which Zweig was integrated into British society. For example, the British translator and literary critic William Rose (pseudonym of Moray Firth, 1894–1961), who shared many good times with Zweig in Britain, and who also prepared some translations for him, observed:

> Stefan Zweig always found time in a busy life to help others, and whether one met him at a gathering in honour of the birthday of a German poet, where he was taking the chair, at an anti-Fascist meeting in the East End where all the other speeches were in Yiddish and he alone spoke in German, or strolling back to his flat through Upper Regent Street after attending the rehearsal of a concert at the Queen's Hall conducted by his friend Toscanini, he seemed to have become an integral part of the life of London.[53]

These remarks contradict Zweig's own statements regarding his isolation, about how he often remained at home in the evenings during his stay in London. Contrarily, Rose also noted that "at his [Zweig's] flat in Hallam Street one could meet writers from many countries of Europe, Jules Romains, Alexis Tolstoy and Don Luigi Sturzo [and numerous others, too]."[54]

One of the most important talks Zweig gave in Britain was his 1937 lecture entitled "The House of a Thousand Destinies." It was delivered in the Shelter located in Mansell Street, Whitechapel, where, as Zweig explained, individuals who escaped from Germany in 1933 and were without British friends or relations usually first found refuge. Zweig's remarks remain historically significant because they describe the dire refugee situation of the 1930s, as well as the specific purpose of the shelter.

XIV.

Zweig was opposed to National Socialism. Yet, to the dismay of a number of his contemporaries, he was not willing to call for a specific battle against Nazism, but rather for a general struggle "against all war and all hatred." Klaus Mann's reaction to this view follows:

Zweig's approach to the human drama is akin to the attitude and tactic of the "mental healer" [. . .] [His] methods and aspirations [are] the odd blend of detachment and sympathy. Zweig does not hope nor pretend to change the world by his writing; his sole ambition is to mitigate the bitterness of human suffering by amplifying our awareness of its roots and causes. [He] [. . .] is neither idealistic nor materialistic, in the Marxian sense [. . .] The only principle Zweig accepts is that of civilization, which exists for the sake of man. But if man, in devastating frenzy, turns against the very civilization which was conceived and built to protect and improve his life, what will be the reaction of the lover and analyst in such a sinister case? [. . .] How can he fail to see that those ferocious hordes threaten our civilization? Civilization implies and guarantees liberty which—as Zweig [stated] in his last, tragic letter—remains "the greatest wealth in the world." Why, then, does he not lift his hand to defend what is so dear, indeed, indispensable to him? Why does he not protest? Why does he not resist? [. . .] [How] could you understand and how forgive the crime [. . .]? He is your enemy, he will kill you—yet you understand, forgive, and pity him [. . .] "I don't want to fight," says the humanist. "All I want is to understand. [. . .] No tyrant will ever touch me. I am free." He is free to die. Nothing else remains to be done.[55]

Other critics also argued that Zweig's concept of fighting the battle against Nazism spiritually and morally and from within was insufficient. For example, Hans-Albert Walter, a major contemporary scholar writing well after the war and Zweig's death, was sharply critical of him, stating that "er blieb in Fiktionen verhaftet und werde zu einem Menschen von bestern in der Welt von heute, [. . .]" (he remained imprisoned in a fictional world, becoming an individual of yesterday in a world of today).[56] Similarly, Hannah Arendt asserted that Zweig was "concerned only with his personal dignity, [and] had kept himself [. . .] completely aloof from politics. In the midst of this disaster, he tried to safeguard his dignity and bearing as well and as long as he could."[57] Arendt felt that even though "the events of 1933 had changed his personal existence, they had no effect on his basic attitude with respect to the world and to his own life. He continued to boast of his apolitical point of view; it never occurred to him, that politically speaking it might be an honor for him to stand outside the law when all men were no longer equal before it." According to Arendt, "Not one of his reactions during all this period was the result of political convictions; they were all dictated by his hypersensitivity to social humiliation. Instead of hating the Nazis, [Zweig] just wanted to annoy them [. . .] Instead of fighting, he kept silent, happy that his books had not been immediately banned."

The criticisms advanced by Klaus Mann, Hans-Albert Walter, and Hannah Arendt may have some merit, but they do not succeed ultimately in negating the fact that Zweig never wavered in his commitment to peace and international understanding. Furthermore, he was not always silent. On the contrary, Zweig's remarks addressing National Socialism were presented from the position he always had advocated: the striving for understanding between individuals and nations by means of non-violence. Active confrontation was against Zweig's principles, and in every possible way he remained a non-confrontational person.

XV.

As late as 1937 and early 1938, Stefan Zweig believed his ideas of cooperation and a Joint Manifesto could still have a positive impact. In a letter to Arnold Zweig dated December 30, 1937, Stefan Zweig wrote: "More and more I feel the need for an organization of the kind we discussed [when they had earlier met in London]: it is fatal that we all live so far apart and are all too busy. How important it would be if we could meet one another each summer, a small circle to maintain contact and plan together some common action."[58] It is clear that he was still hoping to unify his compatriots in order to draft a powerful statement. Perhaps the major problem at this stage was that Stefan Zweig's concept of what that statement should be was very different from what others had in mind.

One thing that remains indisputable, however, was that Zweig took action to support his fellow Jews. This was one of his highest priorities, and he understood it in terms of individual responsibility. He attempted to rally Arnold Zweig, who was living in Palestine at this time, to this cause. On March 16, 1938, Stefan Zweig wrote to him: "Wir stehen vor dem größten Katastrofe und jetzt oder nie ist *meiner Meinung* nach es Pflicht, beizustehen [...] Gerade jetzt brauchen wir *jeden*—Rumänien, Österreich, Ungarn, nur die Juden allein aus diesen Ländern und dann Spanien und Polen—Sie ahnen nichts in Haifa von der Massenflucht ins Weglose, die seit einigen Wochen eingesetzt hat."[59] (We are facing the greatest catastrophe of all, and now or never it is *in my view* a duty to stand ready [...] Right now we need *each and everyone*—Romania, Austria, Hungary, just the Jews alone from those countries, and then Spain and Poland—in Haifa you have no idea of the mass flight along a pathless route which has started these past few weeks.) Still, even at this late date, he reiterated in this same letter to Arnold Zweig his philosophy that the only way to fight fascism was by means of culture: "wie [Benedetto] Croce [1866–1952, Italian critic and idealist philosopher] sagte (immer mein Standpunkt): nur mit cultureller Leistung können und wollen wir den Fascismus bekämpfen" (As Croce said [my point of view always]: it is only with cultural achievement that we can and should fight fascism).

Sometimes Zweig questioned his own stance in correspondence with his friends, and the question of his possibly supporting armed resistance against Nazism was raised. For example, in a letter to Leftwich dated November 18, 1939, he wrote:

> Sie kennen meinen Pacifismus—aber es gibt keinen andern Weg als Hitler zu vernichten—nicht nur des Judentums willen sondern zur Rettung der Civilization. Ich beklage es, 58 Jahre alt zu sein. Wenn ich mich meldete, würde jeder es für eine billige Pose nehmen, eine höchst ungefährliche. Aber ich kann die jungen Jüden in America und neutralen Ländern nicht verstehen, dass sie nicht mit Frankreich zur Verfügung stellen. Jetzt oder nie ist der Augenblick, denn wie sollen wir leben, wozu, wenn Hilter bleibt oder gar mit Ehren aus diser Katastrophe heraus kommt? [...] Sie werden verstehen, Sie allein, dass es nie sogar im moralischen Sinne angenehm war, nicht eine Vorzugsstellung gegenüber den andern Refugees zu haben. Was mich mehr stört ist die Hemmung—ich kann hier nichts wirken als enemy alien, nichts schreiben, nichts helfen, während die nordamerikanischen, südamerikanischen Staaten mich mit Äusserungen, Anfrage, Vorträge bedrängen und ich kann kein postalisch Manuscripte in deutscher Sprache von hier nicht absenden. Wie viel hätte ich für die gute Sache tun können ohne die Vertuscherung des Betriebs hier! Sie verstehen mich, Sie kennen mich, dass ich nicht eitel bin, aber immerhin bin ich mit Thomas Mann der gelesenste Schriftsteller deutscher Sprache. Nur kann durch die Uninformiertheit nichts in einer so entscheidenden Stunde tun! Hätte man wenigstens die Überzeugung dass die andern es besser oder zu mindest richtig machen! Aber wie monoton ist diese Propaganda, wie unaufmerksam.[60]

[You know my pacifist outlook—but there is no other road to take to the destruction of Hitler—not for the sake of Jewry, but to save civilization. I regret being fifty-eight years old. If I were to enlist in the military service, it would be taken as cheap posing from a position of safety. But I cannot understand the young Jews in America and the neutral countries not rallying to the support of France. Now or never is the moment, for how are we to live if Hitler remains or even emerges with honor from this catastrophe? [. . .] You will understand, you alone, that even in the moral sense it could never be comfortable not to assume a favored position in relation to the other refugees. What disturbs me more is the inhibition imposed upon me—here as an enemy alien I can affect nothing, write nothing, lend no aid, I am constantly pressed from the North American and South American countries for statements, appeals, lectures, yet I cannot send my mail or any manuscripts in German. How much I could have done for the good cause were it not for the hushing-up attitude here. You understand me, know that I am not vain, still alongside Thomas Mann I am the most read writer in German. And yet, because of lack of information, I can do nothing in such a decisive hour! If one at least had the conviction that the others are doing it better, or anyway doing it right! But how monotonous, how quietly this propaganda is being pursued.]

In a letter to Leftwich dated December 23, 1939, Zweig revealed how daily events continued to demoralize and destabilize him:

Leider werde ich Sie [. . .] jetzt noch nicht sehen können. Ich habe mich vollkommen hierher zurückgezogen, und die Lust, wieder nach London zu kommen, ist mir benommen durch den Umstand, dass ich mich dort vollkommen unnütz fühle. Ich hätte gern im Anfang meinen doch immerhin beträchtlichen Einfluss in den kontinentalen Ländern und in Amerika der guten Sache zur Verfügung gestellt, aber da man von diesem Angebot keinen Gebrauch machte, bleibe ich lieber in meinem kleinen Haus und trachte die eigene Arbeit vorwärtszubringen.[61]

[I will not be able to see you [. . .] I have withdrawn myself completely here, and any desire to return to London has been removed by the fact that I feel myself absolutely useless there. At the start I would have liked to put my still considerable influences in the continental countries and in America at the disposal of the good cause, but since no use was made of my offer, I prefer to stay in my little house and am trying to advance my own work.]

At the outbreak of the World War and by 1940, Zweig reflected more often about what the nature of his work should be and how he might support other émigrés. At this late stage and in this specific context Zweig was on the verge of becoming overtly political, a fact that is illustrated well by his heartrending Radio de Paris talk (1940), entitled "Das große Schweigen" ("The Great Silence"), which appeared in print on May 4, 1940, in the *Das Neue Tage-Buch* (Paris/Amsterdam). In "Das große Schweigen" Zweig emphasizes that it remains the duty of all individuals who presently have the freedom to speak out to do so, explaining that an untold number of individuals no longer are in a position to express their view. A similar argument was expressed to H. G. Wells, remarking that "everybody's service is a moral duty."[62]

In another commentary entitled "The Mission of the Intellectuals" (1941), Zweig stated that "the only possible means left to us to maintain the intense and strong unity among the spiritual leaders of Europe is to have a clear idea of our mission and our possibilities. Our word should become, in spite of all the odds, stronger and stronger. The louder the shoutings of fanaticism, the stronger should be our word, the voice of reason."[63] This call to speak out is very much the opposite of what one had come to expect from Zweig. Yet, during the last year or two of his life, Zweig's longstanding position regarding politics and public statements was undergoing a process of change, even if not at the pace his critics would have preferred.

XVI.

Zweig was a man of peace who during his lifetime was enmeshed in the most horrific of wars. He felt tormented by remaining silent, but would only rarely—due to his own nature and the regulations imposed on an émigré by British law—allow himself to speak out. He prized individual freedom, yet did not actively join the intellectual battle against Fascism. He considered himself apolitical, yet was troubled by the way the British avoided involvement in world politics. On the whole, Zweig held staunchly to his humanist beliefs, even when he was denigrated for not publicly protesting against the inhumanity of Nazi Germany. Yet, he believed that by remaining steadfast to his ideal of a more civilized world, he was protesting in his own way.

Zweig's work to support Jews in exile was his contribution to assuring a future for Jewish and world culture. His refusal to give up on helping modestly to create a world in which all individuals are brothers was his way of working to bring about the downfall of the National Socialist regime. Eventually, even Stefan Zweig recognized that his lifelong view was tied to a vanishing age—almost like a mirage—suggestive of, or quite soon to become but a bygone time. As he wrote to Siegfried Trebitsch in July of 1941: "Sicherheit gibt es nicht mehr; nirgends und nirgendwo. Streichen wir diese Worte aus unserem Vokabularium. Unsere Welt ist vorbei, unsere Wirkung, unser Glück [. . .] Ich fühle mich grenzlos fremd. Die Politik widert mich."[64] (There is no longer any security anywhere, anywhere at all. Let us strike the word out of our vocabulary. Our world is past and gone, and with it our influence on things, and our happiness [. . .] I feel myself boundlessly a stranger. Politics nauseates me.)

In conclusion, Zweig had always fervently avowed his convictions, which demonstrated their zealous intensity and deep-rooted nature. Sometimes, however, he changed positions that he had earlier promoted passionately. Most often, he did this out of a genuine change of heart and mind, not simply owing to criticism or opposition from colleagues. He was repeatedly frustrated by the lack of support from those who tended to agree with him. For one reason or another, too many colleagues would not commit to participating in projects like his "Jewish Manifesto" or the Jewish periodical, both of which might have signalized more clearly a change in his priorities. As time passed after his relocation to Britain and following the outbreak of war, Zweig's understanding of the dire threat of Nazism changed. Eventually, he came to understand that writers had a duty to express their views in public and to comment critically about Nazism. Zweig had come to realize in the end that symbolic language, characteristic of his *Erasmus* biography, for example, could not function as adequate criticism of or protection against Hitler. But, by the time he arrived at this conclusion, there was preciously little time left before he put an end to his life.

Notes

I would like to thank the following for various kinds of assistance provided me during preparation of this essay: the Stefan Zweig Estate (London) and its managing executors, Sonja Dobbins (London) and Lindi Preuss (Zürich); the Archives Division of the University of Illinois library (Urbana, Illinois), Marlen Eckl, Ian Huebsch, Randolph A. Klawiter, Rachel Moir, Arthur N. Levy, Mark H. Gelber, Alana Sobelman, Rainer-Joachim Siegel, Ian Wallace, Matthew Werley, the anonymous peer-reviewers of my manuscript, and the editorial staff at Camden House.

[1] Epigraph: Stefan Zweig, "Unpublished letter of 23 June 1933 to Emil Jannings," in *J. A. Stargardt, Berlin: Katalog 659: Autographen Auktion aus 16. und 17. März 1995* (Berlin: Stargardt, 1995), 120.

[2] In *Die Welt von Gestern: Erinnerungen eines Europäers*, Zweig stated that he considered himself "als Österreicher, als Jude, als Schriftsteller, als Humanist und Pazifist" (as Austrian, as Jew, as writer, as humanist and as pacifist). Stefan Zweig, *Die Welt von Gestern: Erinnerungen eines Europäers* (Frankfurt am Main: Fischer, 1970), 7 (hereafter cited in text as *WvG*). English-language citations from Stefan Zweig, *The World of Yesterday*, trans. Anthea Bell (London: Pushkin Press, 2009) (hereafter cited in text as *WoY*).

[3] While much study has been devoted to the essence of this expression and its many implications, the following two exemplary studies should be considered indispensable for comprehending the myriad historical perspectives and especially

the changes that soon altered Zweig's views: Richard R. Lawrence, "Viennese Literary Intellectuals and the Problem of War and Peace, 1889–1914," in *Focus on Vienna 1900: Change and Continuity in Literature, Music, Art and Intellectual History*, ed. Erika Nielsen (Munich: Wilhelm Fink, 1982), 12–22. Lawrence's study concludes by quoting Zweig's judgment proferred in his autobiography: namely, that "we young people [. . .] completely wrapped up in our literary ambitions, noticed little enough of dangerous changes in our homeland: we had eyes only for books and pictures. We did not have the slightest interest in politics and social problems" (Lawrence, 19). See also Steven Beller: "The Jewish Intellectual and Vienna in the 1930s," in *Austria in the Thirties: Culture and Politics*, ed. Kenneth Segar and John Warren (Riverside, CA: Ariadne Press, 1991), 309–27.

[4] Zweig frequently took short-term excursions lasting from four days to four weeks to an astonishing array of different areas around the world—from Argentina to Portugal, from the United States to Uruguay. Excluding these voyages, his residence in Britain lasted for almost seven full years, even though Zweig regarded the move at first as temporary.

[5] Almost all of these offer unique, insightful, and significant ideas about Zweig and this period. Importantly, none explore our central topic with the same rigor as that pursued in the present investigation.

[6] With few exceptions Zweig's epistolary documents illustrate his insightful and extraordinary aptitude to form a picture of what he experienced. Aside from the beauty of his artistic expression, his letters are of critical importance because they represent "ein Kulturdokument besonderer Art" (a unique document of the age and its culture), as Friderike Zweig claimed. See Friderike Zweig, *Stefan Zweig*, trans. Erna McArthur (New York: Thomas Y. Crowell, 1946), 218.

[7] Zweig's literary accomplishments are not the focal point of this essay. By focusing on his biographical studies, I draw attention to the manner in which each one symbolically articulated Zweig's position or opposition regarding contemporary political issues. In this essay, these biographical works are examined as a unified group, not as individual compositions.

[8] Otto Zarek, "Stefan Zweig—A Jewish Tragedy," in *Stefan Zweig: A Tribute to His Life and Work*, ed. Hanns Arens, trans. Christobel Fowler (London: W. H. Allen, 1951), 180 (hereafter cited in text by page number).

[9] *Romain Rolland/Stefan Zweig: Briefwechsel 1910–1940*, ed. Waltraud Schwarze et al., vol. 2, *Briefwechsel 1924–1940* (Berlin: Rütten & Loening, 1987), 522. Unless otherwise noted, all subsequent references to the Zweig/Rolland letters refer to this edition. The four-volume edition I co-edited with Knut Beck for Fischer Verlag contains many Zweig/Rolland letters, including the original French version of Zweig's letters and extensive annotations. However, to avoid complications, in this essay all references to the Zweig/Rolland correspondence are to the volume edited by Waltraud Schwarze et al.

[10] Stefan Zweig and Friderike Zweig, *"Wenn einen Augenblick die Wolken weichen": Briefwechsel 1912–1942*, ed. Jeffrey B. Berlin and Gert Kerschbaumer (Frankfurt am Main: Fischer, 2006), 268.

[11] During the First World War, while on assignment at the "Kriegsarchiv," Zweig was sent to Galicia in the spring of 1915 to collect certain materials for the Vienna

archives. As explained in his autobiography and letters, he witnessed the destructive effects of war, which resulted in his decision never again to support war activities. From this time onward he assumed the role of a pacifist. See Bettina Hey'l, "Stefan Zweig im Ersten Weltkrieg" in *Krieg der Geister: Erster Weltkrieg und literarische Moderne*, ed. Uwe Schneider and Andreas Schumann (Würzburg: Königshausen & Neumann, 2000), 263–91.

[12] *Richard Strauss/Stefan Zweig, Briefwechsel*, ed. Willi Schuh (Frankfurt am Main: Fischer, 1957), 37. Hereafter cited in the text as *RS/SZ*. English translations are cited from Max Knight, *A Confidential Matter: The Letters of Richard Strauss and Stefan Zweig, 1931–1935*, ed. Willi Schuh, trans. Max Knight (Berkeley: University of California Press, 1977), 44. Hereafter cited in the text as *RS/SZ* Knight.

[13] *Briefe 1932–1942*, vol. 4, ed. Knut Beck and Jeffrey B. Berlin (Frankfurt am Main: Fischer, 2005), 112 (hereafter cited in text as *Briefe*).

[14] *Briefe 1932–1942*, 198. This translation is not identical to Friderike Zweig's original German text.

[15] Quoted in Jeffrey B. Berlin, "Exile Experiences in Great Britain: Unpublished Correspondence between Stefan Zweig and Sir Siegmund Warburg," in *Keine Klage über England? Deutsche und österreichische Exilerfahrungen in Großbritannien 1933–1945*, ed. Charmian Brinson et al. (Munich: Iudicium, 1998), 286–301. I sincerely thank the late Harry Zohn (1923–2001) for his assistance as I was preparing this translation.

[16] Lionel Trilling, review of *The World of Yesterday*, by Stefan Zweig, trans. Ben Huebsch and Helmut Ripperger, *Contemporary Jewish Record* (August 1943): 427.

[17] Cf. Hey'l Bettina, "Stefan Zweig im Ersten Weltkrieg," 278; especially the following statement: "Die Rede vom Schweigen in der Öffentlichkeit und vom Bekenntnis im Privaten hätte vielleicht Bestand, wenn Zweig sich von nun an jeder öffentlichen Äußerung enthalten hätte, aber eben dies ist nicht der Fall. Er bleibt regelmäßiger Mitarbeiter der *Neuen Freien Presse*."

[18] Here Zweig presents an uplifting spiritual message of hope to downtrodden people. As Zweig has expressed in letters, in *Jeremias* he identified with individuals who, like himself, espoused humanistic values and principles of humanitarianism, those who were exponents of or guarded convictions of righteousness and dignity—in short, those who defended the human spirit and opposed barbarism and tyranny.

[19] Klaus Mann, *Briefe und Antworten, 1922–1949*, ed. Martin Gregor-Dellin (Munich: Ellermann, 1987), 93–94. Hereafter cited in text as KM/SZ.

[20] The complete text of both these letters remains unpublished. See Jeffrey B. Berlin, "The Unpublished Correspondence between Albert Einstein and Stefan Zweig (with an Unpublished Zweig Manifesto of 1933 and Letters to Max Brod, Ben Huebsch, and Felix Salten)," in *Brücken über dem Abgrund: Auseinandersetzungen mit jüdischer Leidenserfahrung, Antisemitismus und Exil; Festschrift für Harry Zohn*, ed. Amy Colin and Elisabeth Strenger (Munich: Wilhelm Fink, 1994), 356.

[21] An identical observation is also found in the last line of his *Castellio gegen Calvin oder Ein Gewissen gegen die Gewalt* (Castellio against Calvin, or a Conscience against Violence, 1936): "Mit jedem neuen Menschen wird ein neues Gewissen geboren und immer wird eines sich besinnen seiner geistigen Pflicht, den alten Kampf aufzunehmen um die unveräußerlichen Rechte der Menschheit und der Menschlichkeit" (With every new human being a new conscience is born, and one of these will always reflect on his spiritual obligation to take up the old fight for the inalienable rights of mankind and humaneness). Stefan Zweig, *Castellio gegen Calvin oder Ein Gewissen gegen die Gewalt*, ed. Knut Beck (Frankfurt am Main: Fischer, 1987), 227.

[22] Cited in Erich Fitzbauer, *Stefan Zweig. Spiegelungen einer schöpferischen Persönlichkeit* (Vienna: Bergland, 1959), 75.

[23] Joseph Leftwich, "Stefan Zweig and the World of Yesterday," in *Yearbook of the Leo Baeck Institute* 3 (1958): 97.

[24] Berthold Viertel, "Abschied von Stefan Zweig," *Literatur und Kritik* 261/262 (1992): 62.

[25] Klemens Renoldner, "Stefan Zweig and Austria," in *The Cultural Exodus from Austria: Vertreibung der Vernunft*, ed. Peter Weibel and Friedrich Stadler (Vienna: Löcker, 1993), 241.

[26] Vivian Liska, "A Spectral Mirror Image: Stefan Zweig and his Critics," in *Stefan Zweig Reconsidered: New Perspectives on his Literary and Biographical Writings*, ed. Mark H. Gelber (Tübingen: Niemeyer, 2007), 210–11.

[27] Ibid., 211.

[28] *Sigmund Freud/Arnold Zweig Briefwechsel*, ed. Ernst L. Freud (Frankfurt am Main: Fischer, 1984), 100.

[29] Stefan Zweig, "Die moralische Entgiftung Europas," in Stefan Zweig, *Zeiten und Schicksale: Aufsätze und Vorträge aus den Jahren 1920–1942*, ed. Knut Beck (Frankfurt am Main: Fischer, 1990), 40–56.

[30] Stefan Zweig, *Briefe an Freunde*, ed. Richard Friedenthal (Frankfurt am Main: Fischer, 1984), 227. Zweig's mother still lived in Vienna at this time. Her death shortly before the German annexation of Austria in March of 1938 provided Zweig tremendous relief, despite the immense sadness of the situation. Zweig's letter to Rolland, dated April 10, 1933, and written on the day of the book-burnings, is a remarkable composition. It is as if Zweig were debating with himself whether he should he remain in Austria or leave? Regardless of the answer, as Zweig wrote: "Ich übergehe mit Schweigen, was wir alle moralisch gelitten haben, denn selbst in diesem Augenblick will ich, mir selber getreu, nicht ein ganzes Land hassen, und ich weiß, daß die Sprache, in der man schreibt, es einem nicht erlaubt, von einem Volk sogar in seinem Wahn sich loszusagen und es zu verfluchen." (*RR/SZ*, 2:506; I consider in silence what we all have suffered in a moral sense because even at this moment I prefer, in accordance with myself, to not hate an entire country. I know that the language in which one writes does not allow one to cut oneself off from one's people and to curse them.) Yet Zweig wonders if there are periods when silence is better than speech. Even so, a decision about leaving or staying must be made.

[31] Zweig to Rolland, June 26, 1933, *RR/SZ*, 2:522.

[32] "Stefan Zweig und Thomas Mann: Versuch einer Dokumentation," ed. Klaus W. Jonas, *Modern Austrian Literature*, 14, no. 3/4 (1981): 111. In this edition the letter is incorrectly dated and should read April 18, 1934.

[33] On November 20, 1940, Zweig finally received British citizenship, which he had applied for shortly after his arrival in Britain.

[34] Unpublished letter, Leftwich Collection, Central Zionist Archives, Jerusalem. The "'verbrannten' Schriftsteller" refers to the midnight events of May 10, 1933, when, at the square on *Unter den Linden* opposite the University of Berlin, some forty thousand individuals watched the burning of Zweig's books along with those of numerous other "subversive" Jewish and foreign authors. Similar events also occurred in other German cities.

[35] Stefan Zweig, unpublished letter to Franz Servaes, Archives of the Wiener Stadt- und Landesbibliothek.

[36] Leftwich, "Stefan Zweig and the World of Yesterday, 92–93.

[37] Robert van Geldern, "The Future of Writing in a World at War—Stefan Zweig talks on the Plight of the European Artist and the Probable Form of the Literature of the Coming Years," *New York Times Book Review*, July 28, 1940, sec. 6, 2.

[38] Stefan Zweig, unpublished letter to Joseph Leftwich, June 12, 1933, Central Zionist Archives, Jerusalem.

[39] See David Cesarani, *The "Jewish Chronicle" and Anglo-Jewry, 1841–1991* (Cambridge: Cambridge University Press, 1994), 145. Cesarani presents in a model-like format an extraordinarily informative elucidation of the zeitgeist in England at this time.

[40] Leftwich, "Stefan Zweig and the World of Yesterday," 95.

[41] Stefan Zweig to Albert Einstein, June 7, 1933, in Jeffrey B. Berlin, "The Unpublished Correspondence between Albert Einstein and Stefan Zweig," 337–63.

[42] Ibid.

[43] Leftwich, "Stefan Zweig and the World of Yesterday," 419–20.

[44] Stefan Zweig to Joseph Leftwich, undated letter, Central Zionist Archives, Jerusalem.

[45] Leftwich, "Stefan Zweig and the World of Yesterday," 86–87.

[46] Stefan Zweig to Joseph Roth, undated letter but attributed to May 1934, in Stefan Zweig, *Briefe an Freunde*, 247.

[47] William L. Shirer, *The Rise and Fall of the Third Reich: A History of Nazi Germany* (New York: Simon & Schuster, 1960), 243.

[48] Leftwich, "Stefan Zweig and the World of Yesterday," 93.

[49] Stefan Zweig, "Whither Jewry?" in *World Jewry*, July 6, 1935, 211.

[50] Stefan Zweig, "Eine Anrede," Posthumous Papers, London.

[51] Stefan Zweig, "Aufruf an die österreichische Juden," unpublished commentary, Posthumous Papers, London.

52 Stefan Zweig, "Keep out of Politics." In *The Jews*, Query Publications no. 2 (London: Query, 1938), 77.

53 William Rose, "German Literary Exiles in England," in *German Life & Letters* 1 (1948): 183.

54 Ibid., 182.

55 Klaus Mann, "Victims of Fascism: Stefan Zweig," *Free World* 2 (April 1942): 276.

56 Hans-Albert Walter, "Von Liberalismus zum Eskapismus: Stefan Zweig im Exil," *Frankfurter Hefte* 25 (June 1970): 428.

57 Hannah Arendt, review of Stefan Zweig, *The World of Yesterday* (trans. Benjamin W. Huebsch and Helmut Ripperger). Arendt's review first appeared in English in *The Menorah Journal* (New York), vol. 31, no. 3 (October 1943), 307–14. The quotations cited here are from Arendt's study "Stefan Zweig: Jews in the World of Yesterday," which appeared in her influential and still well-received volume *The Jew as Pariah: Jewish Identity and Politics in the Modern Age*, ed. Ron H. Feldman (New York: Grove, 1978), 112–21, here 114.

58 For further commentary, see Jeffrey B. Berlin, "The Austrian Catastrophe: Political Reflections in the Unpublished Correspondence of Stefan Zweig and Arnold Zweig," in *Austrian Exodus: The Creative Achievement of Refugees from National Socialism*, ed. Edward Timms and Ritchie Robertson (Edinburgh: Edinburgh University Press, 1995), 3–21.

59 Stefan Zweig, unpublished letter to Arnold Zweig, March 16, 1938. Arnold Zweig Archive, Akademie der Künste, Berlin.

60 Stefan Zweig, unpublished letter to Joseph Leftwich, November 18, 1939, Central Zionist Archives, Jerusalem.

61 Stefan Zweig, unpublished letter to Joseph Leftwich, December 23, 1939, Central Zionist Archives, Jerusalem.

62 Stefan Zweig, unpublished and undated letter, attributable to September 1939, to H. G. Wells. Zweig's letter to Wells, which he wrote in English, is housed in the Archives Division of the University of Illinois library (Urbana, Illinois), along with nine additional Zweig letters to Wells, all of which were written between 1933 to 1939. Six letters and one note from Wells to Zweig, dating from 1931 to 1940, are housed at the SZ Archives at State University College at Fredonia (New York).

63 Stefan Zweig, "The Mission of the Intellectuals," *Adam International Review* 13, no. 152 (September 1941): 2.

64 Stefan Zweig, letter to Siegfried Trebitsch, July 1941, in Siegfried Trebitsch, *Chronik eines Lebens* (Zurich: Artemis Verlag, 1951), 468.

Contributors

RICHARD V. BENSON is an independent scholar residing in the United States. His present research investigates auto-ethnography and images of Eastern Europe in nineteenth- and early twentieth-century German-Jewish writing.

JEFFREY B. BERLIN is distinguished professor emeritus of comparative literature and university academic dean at Holy Family University. He has edited or coedited the correspondence of numerous German-language writers including: (with Knut Beck) the four-volume edition of Stefan Zweig's letters; (with Gert Kerschbaumer) the Stefan/Friderike Zweig correspondence; (with Donald Prater) Zweig's correspondence with Freud, Bahr, Rilke, and Schnitzler. He has also edited Thomas Mann's correspondence with his American publisher.

DARIÉN J. DAVIS is professor of history at Middlebury College in Middlebury, Vermont. His research revolves around the themes of diaspora, nationhood, immigration, and transnationalism. He is the author of three books, three edited volumes, and a number of articles on the themes of diaspora, nationhood, immigration, and transnationalism. He is the coauthor and coeditor of *Stefan and Lotte Zweig's South American Letters, New York, Argentina, and Brazil 1940–42* (Continuum Press, 2010).

MARLEN ECKL is a senior researcher at the Laboratório de Estudos sobre Etnicidade, Racismo e Discriminação (LEER) at the University of São Paulo. She holds a PhD in history from the University of Vienna and an MA in comparative literature, Jewish studies, and law from the Johannes Gutenberg-University in Mainz. Her research interests are German-speaking exiles in Brazil, Brazilian history (1930–45), and Brazilian-Jewish literature.

MARK H. GELBER is senior professor of comparative literature and German-Jewish studies at Ben-Gurion University (BGU) of the Negev, in Beer Sheva, Israel. He has directed the Center for Austrian and German Studies at BGU since 2008 and has served as visiting professor at the University of Pennsylvania, the University of Graz, the University of Maribor, Yale University, the University of Auckland, the University of

Antwerp, the Rheinisch-Westfälische Technische Hochschule Aachen, and New York University.

ROBERT KELZ is assistant professor of German at the University of Memphis. His research explores the cultural production of German-speaking emigrants in the Southern Cone of South America.

KLEMENS RENOLDNER has been the head of the Stefan Zweig Centre at the University of Salzburg since 2008. He has also been a visiting professor at the Universities of Salzburg, Bern, Freiburg im Breisgau, Innsbruck, and Verona. He has edited various books on Stefan Zweig including, most recently, *Stefan Zweig: Abschied von Europa* (Brandstätter, 2014).

BIRGER VANWESENBEECK is associate professor of English at the State University of New York at Fredonia. He is the coeditor of *William Gaddis: "The Last of Something"* (McFarland, 2010) and the author of several essays on Thomas Pynchon. His current research focuses on the integration of *ekphrasis* and mourning within late modernism.

JOHN WARREN was head of German and Austrian studies at what is now the Oxford Brookes University from 1967 until retirement. He has co-organized eight conferences on Austro-German topics, coedited a number of sets of conference papers and published several articles on various aspects of theatrical and cultural life in Austria and Germany.

KLAUS WEISSENBERGER is professor of German at Rice University in Houston, Texas, where he has taught since 1971. He is the author of three books on German poetry from Goethe to Celan, has edited a volume on German poetry between 1945 and 1975, and a volume on the genre of nonfictional artistic prose. In his articles of the last three decades he has concentrated on nonfictional prose works by modern German authors, mainly during their exile from Nazi Germany.

ROBERT WELDON WHALEN is the Carolyn G. and Sam H. McMahon Jr. Professor of History at Queens University of Charlotte, in North Carolina, where he teaches modern European and American cultural, religious, and intellectual history. His publications include *Sacred Spring: God and Modernism in Fin de Siècle Vienna* (Eerdmans, 2007).

GEOFFREY WINTHROP-YOUNG is professor of German and teaches in the German and Scandinavian programs at the University of British Columbia in Vancouver, Canada.

Index

Aitá, Antono, 158
Aleman, Ernesto, 158, 165
Alighieri, Dante, 100, 104
Altenberg, Peter, 104
alterity, 75–80, 82–83, 87
Altmann, Charlotte, 9, 21, 141, 147, 154, 173–76, 179–81, 184, 186–87, 192, 199, 209, 213–15; letters to Hannah and Manfred Altmann, 177–78, 185
Altmann, Hannah, 213; letters to, 178, 180–81, 183
Altmann, Manfred, 213; letters to, 178, 180–81, 183
Amado, Jorge, 176
American culture, 86, 100
Anderson, Wes, 3, 7
Andrade, Mário de, 175
Anschluss, 134–36, 140, 192, 194, 244
Antoinette, Marie, 17, 95, 125
Applegate, Celia, 112
Arendt, Hannah, 1, 10, 25, 72, 74, 87, 200, 209, 224, 246, 255
Argentina, 155; and anti-fascism, 156–57, 168–69; and Nazism, 165; newspapers in (*see* newspapers in Argentina); Zweig in, 158–64, 166–67
Aristotle, 77
Asch, Sholem, 104
Aslan, Raoul, 35–36
Assmann, Jan, 126–27, 131
Auernheimer, Raoul, 35, 43, 49, 51
Austrian War Archive, 37–38
authorship, 105

Bab, Julius, 39
Back, Sylvio, 20–21, 30
Bacon, Frances, 123–24

Bahr, Hermann, 38, 53, 104; letters to, 39, 71
Balser, Ewald, 36
Balzac, Honoré de, 3, 83, 95, 101
Barbusse, Henri, 40, 51, 104
Barkan, Leonard, 5–7, 10, 11
Barth, Karl, 81
Barthes, Roland, 105, 107
Baudelaire, Charles, 95, 99–100
Bauer, Alfredo, 155, 167–68
Baum, Oskar, 104
Beck, Knut, 53, 151, 253; and Jeffrey B. Berlin, 190, 209, 231, 242, 243, 252
Beckett, Samuel, 6, 29, 76
Bell, Anthea, 2, 75–76, 84–85
Beller, Stephen, 41, 50
Benário, Olga, 175
Benitez, Juan, 202
Benjamin, Walter, 62, 66, 185
Benn, Gottfried, 94
Berger, Alfred, 36
Berger, James, 81
Berlin, Jeffrey B.: and Knut Beck, 190, 209, 231, 242, 243, 251; and Gert Kerschbaumer, 151, 230, 252; and Hans-Ulrich Lindken and Donald A. Prater, 71
Berliner Tageblatt, 38
Bernanos, Georges, 84, 184
Bernau, Alfred, 51
Bernet, Rudolf, 87
biography, 122–24; and autobiography, 138–39; on E. M. Lilien, 104, 108–20; written by Zweig, 95–96, 98, 125
Blake, William, 104
Boas, Franz, 175
Böhm, Karl, 36
Bonaparte, Napoleon, 18, 36, 95

Botstein, Leon, 74–75, 87
Braun, Felix, 4, 104; letters to, 203
Brazil, 23–24, 141–44, 155, 173–75, 176–80, 184–88, 191, 206; newspapers in, 201–2; Petrópolis, 176, 181–83, 208; race in, 195, 203–4, 217; Rio de Janeiro, 192–93, 220; São Paulo, 219
Brecht, Bertolt, 94
Brentano, Franz, 78
Broch, Hermann, 125, 150
Brod, Max, 104
Buber, Martin, 78–79, 88, 108–9, 111, 121; letters to, 39–40, 44
Burschell, Friedrich, 17–20, 23, 31
Byron, Lord, 8, 99–103

Cage, John, 6, 29
Cahn, Alfredo, 155, 160, 207
Canetti, Elias, 104
Carey, Leo, 15
Castellio, Sebastian, 161
Catá, Hernández, 180, 186
Cato the Elder, 2
Cendrars, Blaise, 184
censorship, 46; by Germans in World War II, 47
Chateaubriand, François-René de, 95
Cicero, 1–2, 9, 10; Ciceronian, 124
Claudel, Paul, 184
Colonialism, 57, 70; in *Amok*, 60–61, 67, 69
communication. *See* sound recording
Confino, Alon, 112–13
Conrad, Joseph, 7, 56, 61–63, 69–70
Coronel, Jorge Icaza, 162
Critchley, Simon, 77, 82, 88
Croce, Benedetto, 247
culture, 125; and Habsburg myth, 132; and myth, 126–27

Damrosch, David, 8, 10, 22–23, 31, 96–97, 103, 106
Dang, Alfred, 166
Dantas, Luiz Martins de Souza, 201
Darién, Davis J.; and Oliver Marshall, 169, 170, 171, 188, 189
Daviau, Donald, 161

David, Jakob Julius, 104
Delacroix, Egène, 100
Deren, Maya, 182
Derrida, Jacques, 77, 88
Desbordes-Valmore, Marceline, 161
Descartes, René, 79
Dickens, Charles, 8, 100–104
Diderot, Denis, 134
Diebold, Bernhard, 35, 43
Dimock, Wai-chee, 22, 31
Dines, Alberto, 178, 182, 188, 190, 210
Döblin, Alfred, 94
Dostoyevsky, Fyodor, 101
Doyle, Arthur Conan, 56
Duhamel, Georges, 157
Dumont, Robert, 35
drama, 35; German censorship of, 47; and German Expressionism, 41, 44–50; in Vienna, 36–37

Eckermann, Johann Peter, 38, 54, 96
Eddy, Mary Baker, 3
Edison, Thomas, 63
Einstein, Albert, 237, 252, 254; letters to, 238
Eisemann, Heinrich, 213
ekphrasis, 5–7, 23
Eliot, T. S., 25, 84
English culture, 100, 102
Erasmus, 8, 128–31, 133–35, 161
Ernst, Wolfgang, 69
ethics, 77–79
Euripides, 18
evolution, 61
exile, 8–9, 21–22, 25–26; and identity, 216; and literature, 123–24, 128, 161, 192; and trauma, 200, 204–5
exile of Zweig, 93, 97–98, 122, 131, 215, 218, 222, 224, 233–35; in Brazil, 141–44, 146–47, 155, 173–88, 191–92, 195, 199, 201, 203, 206–8, 210, 217, 219–21; in Britain, 137–38, 140, 213–14, 235–36, 240–45, 247–49; in Switzerland, 40
existentialism, 86–87

fascism, 159–60
Feder, Ernst, 192, 196, 199, 201–3, 209
Feiwel, Berthold, 117
Ferdinand, Franz; assassination of, 76
Feuchtwanger, Lion, 51
Fielding, Henry, 102
Firmat, Gustavo Pérez, 176
Fischer, Gottfried Bermann, 155
Flaubert, Gustave, 29
formalism, 65–66
Fouché, Joseph, 95, 125, 161, 225
France: continuing popularity of Zweig in, 17, 20, 22, 96, 97, 98, 100; French culture, 95, 100
Franzos, Karl Emil, 104, 111–12
Freud, Sigmund, 30, 64, 67–69, 76, 81, 104, 139, 232; Freudian psychoanalysis, 58, 65–67; iceberg metaphor, 16–17; talking cure, 65–66
Freyre, Gilberto, 175

Galicia, 110–18
Gandhi, Mahatma, 134
Gartenberg, Alfredo, 192, 194–95
Gay, Peter, 85, 88
Gelber, Mark H., 9, 109, 120, 121, 122, 149, 150
Geldner, Robert van, 236
gender, 28, 67; in mass culture, 29–30
George, Stefan, 94
German Expressionism, 41, 44–50
Germany, 133; censorship in World War II, 47; occupation of France, 138, 140; persecution of Jews in, 214; unification, 112–13; Weimar Republic, 94
Ginzburg, Carlo, 64
Goebbels, Joseph, 230, 242
Goering, Reinhold, 43–48, 50–51
Goethe, Johann Wolfgang von, 4, 6, 51, 100, 125, 161–62, 203; and world literature, 22–23, 96, 99
Goldmann, Paul, 47
Gonçalves, Antonio Dias, 182
Goncharov, Ivan, 104
Görner, Rüdiger, 9, 11

Gorki, Maxim, 104
Guibourg, Edmundo, 157

Habsburg empire, 125, 127, 131, 136–37; "golden age of security," 139
Hardt, Ernst, 49
Hasenclever, Walter, 46–51
Hauptmann, Gerhart, 44, 104, 238
Heidegger, Martin, 77, 86
heimat, 110–11, 136, 140; in German culture, 112–13; in Jewish culture, 114–20
Heller, Fred, 156
Herzl, Theodor, 104
Hesse, Hermann, 94; letters to, 129–30
Heyer, Astrid, 81, 84–85
Heym, Georg, 43
Hilfsverein deutschsprechender Juden (Relief Organization for German-speaking Jews), 162–63
Hitler, 23, 127, 129–30, 138–39, 218, 224, 226, 228, 232–35, 242, 247–48, 250; and anti-semitism, 236–37; opposition to, 230–31
Hobsbawm, Eric, 113
Hoffmann, E. T. A., 104
Hofmann, Michael, 1–3, 7, 17, 19–20, 23, 25–26, 58
Hofmannsthal, Hugo von, 29, 40, 51, 76, 94, 104, 139, 215, 241
Hölderlin, Friedrich, 100
Holl, Hildemar, 9
homosexuality, 57–59
Horwath, Ödon von, 94
Huebsch, Ben, 155, 222, 229, 252
humanism, 145, 147, 233; and Erasmus, 130–31, 133; and Zweig, 134–35
Husserl, Edmund, 77–78, 86
Huyssen, Andreas, 29, 32

identity, 182, 184–85
Iggers, Wilma, 76
Ionesco, Eugène, 6

Jacob, Paul Walter, 156–57

Jacobsen, Jens Peter, 104
Jameson, Fredric, 27
Jannings, Emil, 224
Jinglei, Xu, 3, 10, 20, 31
Jonson, Ben, 35–36, 104
Jones, Ernest, 16
Joseph, Franz, 49
Joyce, James, 15, 26, 76, 92, 104
Judaism, 41; in Argentina, 162–63; in Eastern Europe, 110–16; and emigration to Argentina, 156; and emigration to Brazil, 173, 175, 198–201; Fifth Zionist Congress in Basel, 109, 119; in *Jeremias*, 42–44; Jewish Renaissance, 108–10, 116–18; Zionism, 108–10, 118–20; and Zweig, 163–64, 181, 236–40, 242–44, 246–47

Kaemmerer, Ami, 40
Kafka, Franz, 7, 29–30, 56, 76, 94
Kaiser, Georg, 46–48, 50
Kālidāsa, 96
Kant, Immanuel, 78, 134
Kasch, Georg, 52
Katz, Richard, 192, 203–6
Kayser, Rudolf, 229
Keats, John, 99–100
Kesten, Herman, 213
King, Lydia, 77
Kippenberg, Anton, 99–100
Kittler, Friedrich, 65, 69
Kleist, Heinrich von, 104
Klopstock, Friedrich Gottlieb, 100
König, Otto, 43, 51
Koogan, Abrahão, 174, 181, 184, 186; letters to, 179, 198
Kraepelin, Emil, 61
Kraus, Karl, 49, 76
Kreilkamp, Ivan, 61–63, 69–70
Kunstprosa, 8, 122–23; in Zweig, 124, 138

Lacan, Jacques, 87; Lacanian psychoanalysis, 68–69
Lacarti, Arturo, 9
Lammasch, Heinrich, 50
language, 59, 63–4, 68–69

Leftwich, Joseph, 231, 243; letters to, 213, 235–37, 241, 247–48, 253, 254, 255
Lehnhart, Markus Helmut, 109
Lernet-Holenia, Alexander, 36
Lessing, Gotthold Ephraim, 134
Lester, Charles Edwards, 191
Levinas, Emmanuel, 7, 75, 84–87; and ethics, 77–80; and trauma, 82–83
Lilien, Ephraim Moses, 8, 104, 108–20
Liska, Vivian, 27, 32, 71, 231, 253
literary canon, 102–5
Lorca, Federico García, 159
Ludwig, Emil, 8, 36, 157–61, 166
Lunt, Alfred, 36
Luther, Martin, 130–31, 134

Magellan, Ferdinand, 3, 215
Mahler, Gustav, 104, 139
Malamud, Samuel, 180
Malevich, Kazimir, 6
Mann, Klaus, 104, 122, 224, 245–46; letters to, 127–29, 228, 230, 232, 252, 255
Mann, Klaus, works by: *Die Sammlung*, 230–31
Mann, Thomas, 25–26, 56–57, 94, 104, 224, 240; letters to, 234–35, 251, 254
Marinetti, Filippo Tomasso, 160, 184
Márquez, Gabriel García, 29
Martius, Carl Friedrich Philipp von, 203
Marxism, 18–20; in Central Europe, 99; in German drama, 48–49; and Jewish culture, 111–12, 117; in Zweig, 58, 103–4
Masereel, Frans, 233
Maugham, William Somerset, 60
Medici, Lorenzo de, 191
Melville, Herman, 24
metaphysics, 80
Michaux, Henri, 184
Milhaud, Darius, 184
Milton, John, 100
Minot, Stephen, 122
Mistral, Gabriela, 180, 186

modernism, 6–7, 25–26, 28–30, 56, 62, 66; in Brazil, 174–75; in German Expressionism, 45, 47–48; high modernism, 27
Moissi, Alexander, 104
Montaigne, Michel de, 8, 21, 104, 123–24, 134, 144–48
Moreau, Clément, 157
Müller, Hans, 38, 40
Münchhausen, Börries Von, 109, 115–16
Munich Conference, 134–35
Musil, Robert, 94
Mussolini, Benito, 160

nationalism, 38
Neue Freie Presse, 35–40, 43, 49, 51, 242
newspapers in Argentina, 157; *Argentinisches Tageblatt*, 156, 158–60; *Crítica*, 158–59; *La Nación*, 161–62
newspapers in Brazil, 201–2
Nietzsche, Friedrich, 100
Norz, Martin, 51

Ocampo, Victoria, 157
Olden, Balder, 156
Ophüls, Max, 7, 15, 20, 30
Otto, Rudolf, 81

pacifism, 46–47, 51, 122, 226, 229
Patsch, Sylvia, 74
Paul, Jean, 104
pedagogy, 164; and humanism, 165
PEN Conference, 14th International, 156, 159, 161, 165
Peret, Benjamin, 184
Pestalozzi School, 165–68
Petrópolis, 176, 181–83, 208
Petzold, Alfons, 38; letters to, 39
Pirandello, Luigi, 36
Plato, 65, 80
Polgar, Alfred, 42, 46, 50
Prater, Donald, 37, 52, 53, 71, 171, 216, 222, 223
Prochnik, George, 3, 10, 30, 32
Proust, Marcel, 95

psychoanalysis, 16–17, 58, 79–80; Freudian, 58, 65–67; Lacanian, 68–69; in Zweig, 58, 60. *See also* Freud, Sigmund; Lacan, Jacques
Putnam, Hilary, 78

Rathenau, Walter, 104
Reich-Ranicki, Marcel, 94, 106
Reinhardt, Max, 42, 215
Reitler, Joseph, 36
Relgis, Eugen, 104
Renaissance, the, 123–24
Renan, Joseph Ernest, 41, 95
Renoldner, Klemens, 9, 11, 231, 253
Rio de Janeiro, 192–93, 220
Rilke, Rainer Maria, 26, 71, 76, 94, 104, 139
Rimbaud, Arthur. 95
Rolland, Romain, 2, 4, 35, 38–40, 43–44, 46–47, 50, 95, 134, 193; letters to, 218–19, 226, 229–30, 233–35, 237–38, 240–41, 251, 253, 254
Roller, Alfred, 42
Romains, Jules, 36, 245
Romanticism, 58–59; in English literature, 100–102; Victorian novel, 62–63, 102
Rose, William, 244–45, 255
Rosenfeld, Morris, 109, 117–18
Ross, Alex, 75
Rotenberg, Joel, 85
Roth, Joseph, 3, 94, 104, 150, 224; letters to, 242
Rothschild, Anthony de, 242
Rousseau, Jean-Jacques, 95
Rushdie, Salman, 15

Salgado, Plínio, 176
Sainte-Beuve, Charles Augustin, 95
Salten, Felix, 40, 224
São Paulo, 219
Schelling, Friedrich Wilhelm Joseph, 17
Schickele, René, 46–47, 49
Schiller, Friedrich, 134
Schnitzler, Arthur, 94, 104, 139; letters to, 39

Schukal, Richard, 40
Schwadron, Abraham, 44
Scott, Walter, 102
Segall, Lasar, 208; death of, 209; letters to, 195–97
Seipel, Ignaz, 50
Seksik, Laurent, 21, 30, 31, 106
Servaes, Franz, 235; letters to, 236
Shafer, R. Murray, 62
Shakespeare, William, 100, 102
Shaw, George Bernard, 51, 242
Shelley, Mary, 102
Shelley, Percy Bysshe, 100
Shirer, William L., 242
Simon, Hugo, 192, 199–201
Smollett, Tobias, 102
Sophocles, 18
Sorel, Guillaume, 21
sound recording, 166–67; disembodiment caused by, 57, 59, 60, 63, 70; gramophone, 56; phonograph, 56–58, 60, 62, 65–66, 69–70
Spinoza, Baruch, 134
Spitzer, Leo, 180, 189
Staal, D. L., 238–40
Stanislawski, Michael, 10, 110, 120, 121
Steinberg, Michael, 74
Stendhal, 95, 99
Stoker, Bram, 56, 69
Stone, Will, 3, 10
Strauss, Richard, 36, 41, 52, 241–42; letters to, 226–27, 229, 238, 252
Strelka, Joseph, 66–67, 73
Struzo, Don Luigi, 245
Stückl, Christian, 51–52
suicide, 21, 26–27; of Crown Prince Rudolf, 76; Lotte's suicide note, 187; of Zweig, 20–21, 23–27, 81, 138, 186–87, 194–95, 203, 206, 208–9; Zweig's suicide note, 23–25, 186
Suttner, Bertha von, 40, 104
Swift, Jonathan, 10

Taine, Hippolyte, 35, 95, 102–3, 105, 107, 109

Tennyson, Alfred, 36
Thackeray, William Makepeace, 102
Thermann, Edmund von, 166
time in narrative, 69
Timms, Edward, 37
Tocqueville, Alexis de, 24
Toller, Ernst, 104, 224
Tolstoy, Alexis, 245
Tolstoy, Leo, 104, 134
trauma, 18–19, 83–84, 87, 139, 226; and exile, 138, 200, 204–5, 221–22; and mourning, 81–82; and World War II, 77
Trebitsch, Siegfried, 249
Trilling, Lionel, 228, 252
Tucholsky, Kurt, 94
Turner, Victor, 174, 179

Uchida, Mitsuko, 75
Ungaretti, Giuseppe, 184
Unruh, Fritz von, 46–47, 50–51

Vargas, Getúlio, 174, 176, 187, 192–93, 199, 201, 203, 206
Verhaeren, Emile, 3–4, 35, 45, 104
Verlag, Insel, 4, 40
Verlaine, Paul, 95, 124
Verne, Jules, 56, 69
Vespucci, Amerigo, 191
Vienna, 47–49, 51, 76–77; culture in, 76, 132, 137, 139; Jewish culture in, 127
Viertel, Berthold, 231
Voltaire, 134

Wagner, Hilde, 36
Walter, Hans-Albert, 245–46, 255
Warburg, Siegmund, 227, 252
Warren, John, 7
Wassermann, Jakob, 104
Weimar Era, 22; literature in, 94
Weinzierl, Ulrich, 10, 19, 20, 31, 32, 171
Weiss, Ernst, 104, 224
Wells, H. G., 249, 255
Werfel, Franz, 41, 43, 51
Weschenbach, Natascha, 103, 107
Wessely, Paula, 36

Whitman, Walt, 3, 24, 59, 104
Wilde, Oscar, 102
Williams, C. E., 37
Williams, Daryl, 174, 188
Winternitz, Friderike Maria von, 37, 192, 214–15, 226–27, 251, 252; letters to, 142, 173
Wittgenstein, Ludwig, 29
Wolf, Alfred, 163
Wolfenstein, Alfred, 134; letters to, 135
Woodward, C. Vann, 74, 87
World Literature, 3–5, 19–24, 74–75, 93–105
World War I, 37–38; censorship during, 46–47; in *Jeremias*, 43; pacifism during, 39–40, 51
World War II, 77

Xu, Jinglei, 3, 10, 20–21, 31

Zarek, Otto, 225, 251
Zech, Paul, 45, 157, 161–62; letters to, 40, 216
Zelewitz, Klaus, 60
Zweig, Arnold, 224, 232; letters to, 246–47
Zweig, Lotte. *See* Altmann, Charlotte
Zweig, Stefan: as biographer, 124–25, 127–38; as cultural mediator, 3, 8, 24, 98–104, 111, 129, 131, 243; as dramatist, 35–55; in exile (*see* exile of Zweig); in fiction and film, 20–21, 30, 106; as historian, 17, 125–27; international success of, 20, 22, 30, 95, 106; and nested narrative, 6, 22, 29, 58–68, 75–76; politics of, 224–55; popularity of, 3, 17–19, 77, 93–97, 123; on translation, 21, 228; as translator, 4, 8, 36, 46, 204–5, 228
Zweig, Stefan, works by:
Der Amokläufer, 7, 21, 24, 56–57, 60–61, 63–64, 66–70, 79, 84
"Eine Anrede," 244
"Aufruf für die österreichischen Juden," 244
Baumeister der Welt, 101

Der begrabene Leuchter, 163
Brasilien: Ein Land der Zukunft, 8–9, 141–45, 176, 181, 184–85, 191, 194, 198, 201, 206–7, 219
Brief einer Unbekannten, 27–30, 82
Brennendes Geheimnis, 58
Castellio gegen Calvin, 225
E. M. Lilien: Sein Werk, 108, 110, 113–19
Episode am Genfer See, 84
"Das Geheimnis des künstlerischen Schaffens," 141, 148
"Die Geschichte als Dichterin," 124–25, 132, 148–49
Geschichte eines Unterganges, 7, 75–80
"Geschichtsschreibung von morgen," 128–29
"Das große Schweigen," 249
Das Haus am Meer, 36
Die Heilung durch den Geist, 16
"Ist die Geschichte gerecht?," 128
Jeremias, 7, 35, 37–52, 163, 228
"The Jewish Children in Germany," 242–43
"Jewish Manifesto," 250
Joseph Fouché, 95, 125, 161, 225
"Keep Out of Politics," 244
"Kleine Reise nach Brasilien," 216–17, 219–21
Das Lamm des Armen, 36, 157
"Leporella," 84
Marie Antoinette, 17, 95, 125
"The Mission of the Intellectuals," 249
Die Mondscheingasse, 7, 75
"Die Monotonisierung der Welt," 86
"Die moralische Entgiftung Europas," 232
Phantastische Nacht, 75, 85
Schachnovelle, 9, 21, 23–24, 67–68, 75–77, 85–87, 155, 188, 208
Die schweigsame Frau, 241–42
Sommernovellette, 83–84
Der Stern über dem Walde, 79, 80, 84

Zweig, Stefan, works by—*(cont'd)*
   Sternstunden der Menschheit, 8, 10, 11, 24, 32, 124, 125
   Tagebücher, 53, 54, 138, 151
   Tersites, 35, 41
   Triumph und Tragik des Erasmus von Rotterdam, 123, 127–34, 158, 225, 228–29, 250
   "La unidad en el espíritu," 159
   "Die unsichtbare Sammlung," 5–6, 22–24
   Verwirrung der Gefühle, 2, 56–60
   Die Welt von Gestern, 2–3, 8, 18, 21, 24, 37, 39–40, 51, 74, 98–99, 138–41, 177, 187, 198, 208, 218, 220, 222, 233–34
   "Whither Jewry," 243
   "Das Wien von gestern," 135–37, 217–18
   "Ein Wort von Deutschland," 38

Zwink, Markus, 51

www.ingramcontent.com/pod-product-compliance
Lightning Source LLC
Chambersburg PA
CBHW021658230426
43668CB00008B/662